'"I really haven't a clue how to set about the job." Harold Macmillan committed those words to his diary in 1951, shortly after Winston Churchill asked him to sort out Britain's housing crisis. Macmillan lacked the counsel of Vicky Spratt' *The Times*

'A major book on the history and politics of renting' *Evening Standard*

'Vicky Spratt's shocking and incisive indictment of private renting in Britain describes how functional and productive lives unravel as people lose their homes, sense of self and feeling of belonging in the world. Packed with powerful narratives but also a number of policy alternatives, [*Tenants*] is based on myriad human stories showing home as a central aspect of people's lives and cornerstone of trust in society and its institutions. The case studies are shocking and sobering … [but] the shifting nature of the discourse around the housing crisis is significant as they herald a real possibility of change' Anna Minton, *Financial Times*

'It is impossible to read this book without becoming almost incapacitated with rage. This astute analysis examines the toxic lottery of Britain's housing crisis, laying bare our state's lack of fitness for purpose and the devastating outcomes of having no fixed abode' Lynsey Hanley, *Guardian*

'The national need for living space is desperate – as illustrated in *Tenants* by journalist Vicky Spratt. Show[ing how] the country is blighted by landlordism, homelessness and Thatcher's legacy, [*Tenants* reveals] the human cost of a genuinely Kafkaesque bureaucratic system' *New Statesman*

'Vicky Spratt's ferocious debut *Tenants* is a comprehensive account of a dysfunctional system, in which constant precarity has become the norm for millions across Britain … [It is] relentlessly clear-sighted … rigorous as well as deeply empathetic' Francisco Garcia, *i Paper*

'Vicky Spratt's excoriating *Tenants* shows how Generation Rent is being let down, and reminds us that the power dynamic between renters and their landlords was not always so skewed. Open-minded and formidably informed, Spratt is a compelling narrator, charting the way that governments since the 1980s absolved themselves of responsibility for housing and stripped back protections for renters. The case studies of renters in the private sector whose lives are derailed after losing a secure home are heart-breaking and shocking. Whether you are a tenant or a landlord, or indeed a government minister, this is a vital read – an experience so bracing it forces you to step back, look at the whole wretched system and think: "Why do we put up with this?" That should have politicians feeling rather scared' *The Times* Best Books of 2022

'An important book by a journalist who has done so much to shine a light on, and change, Britain's broken housing sector' Lewis Goodall

'Fascinating, incendiary, rigorously well researched. *Tenants* should be compulsory reading for every politician' Pandora Sykes

'Leading journalist Vicky Spratt's important book powerfully blends an overview of political failure with the personal experiences of those going through eviction' Shelter

'A thorough and devastating analysis of Britain's current housing crisis … Vicky Spratt is one of the best-equipped people to wade into this country's housing crisis … [Her book's] radical plan for rectifying a broken system will leave you feeling hopeful for the future' *Refinery29*

'Densely researched and makes plain how paper-thin is the divide between the cheaper end of renting and being thrown out onto the street … Argues convincingly that investing in more social housing would benefit everyone, not just those who live in it' *Times Literary Supplement*

'Vicky Spratt reveals how our dysfunctional housing system is causing dire consequences for people, drawing on personal experiences from across the country, [and] calls for a radical re-imagination of the housing system' *Dazed & Confused*

**Vicky Spratt** is an award-winning journalist whose work regularly shapes public policy. Her 2016 campaign 'Make Renting Fair' led to letting fees in England and Wales being banned, and she has spoken at political conferences, all-party parliamentary groups, and panels across the country on the issue of housing. Currently the *i Paper*'s Housing Correspondent, she has appeared on BBC News, *Newsnight*, *Woman's Hour* and NTS Radio. In 2020, she was nominated as Journalist of the Year at the Drum Awards for Online Media, and in 2021 her reporting on Britain's housing emergency saw her shortlisted for a British Journalism Award.

# Tenants

The People on the Frontline of
Britain's Housing Emergency

## VICKY SPRATT

PROFILE BOOKS

This paperback edition published in 2023

First published in Great Britain in 2022 by
PROFILE BOOKS LTD
29 Cloth Fair
London EC1A 7JQ
*www.profilebooks.com*

Copyright © Vicky Spratt, 2022

1 3 5 7 9 10 8 6 4 2

Typeset in Granjon by MacGuru Ltd
Printed and bound in Great Britain by CPI Group (UK) Ltd, Croydon CR0 4YY

The moral right of the author has been asserted.

A CIP catalogue record for this book is available from the British Library.

ISBN 978 1 78816 128 2
eISBN 978 1 78283 479 3
Audio ISBN 978 1 78283 999 6

I'd like to moon around a garden
                barefoot
        And rosy, instead I wake with
              night sweats I dedicate to my
              landlord

**Helen Charman,** 'The Tenancy'

# CONTENTS

*Author's Note*     xiii

Prologue: A Crisis Foretold     1

**Part One – The Problem of Rent**     19
   1. Sheltered Dreamers     21
   2. Life for Rent     40
   3. The Problem with Generation Rent     61
   4. Root Shock     79
   5. Priced Out     94
   6. The Rent Trap     110

**Part Two – Squalor**     125
   7. No Nails     127
   8. Modern Slums     145
   9. The Shadow Private Renting Sector     161
  10. Nearly Legal     181

**Part Three – Utopian Thinking: The Problem of Change**     199
  11. Fallout     201
  12. The Utopian Realism of Housing First     218
  13. Out of Options     238

Epilogue: Dwelling in Possibility     253

*Glossary of the Housing Crisis*                265
*Notes*                                         269
*Further Reading*                               313
*Acknowledgements*                              315
*Index*                                         319

# AUTHOR'S NOTE

This is a work of non-fiction written between 2017 and early 2022, drawn from five years of research. When I began, Britain had just voted to leave the European Union and was embarking on the process of Brexit. As I finished, a global pandemic spread, making people's homes into a frontline defence amid a major public health crisis and, in doing so, revealed that home was not a very safe place for some people. During that period, it felt at times as though the country was, at once, imploding and exploding. While some British people saw their dream – independence from Eurocracy – realised, others felt that just over half of the country had voted for something they did not want but would have to live with. The Labour Party, beleaguered and led by Jeremy Corbyn (and subsequently Keir Starmer), struggled. The Conservatives, led by David Cameron, then Theresa May, then Boris Johnson, fought among themselves and yet continued not only to win elections, but win big. In the early hours of 13 December 2019, Johnson declared victory in an election which delivered the Conservatives their biggest majority since Margaret Thatcher's 1987 win and the largest overall majority since Tony Blair's landslide in 2001. This provides important context for *Tenants*, which assesses Britain's housing crisis within the framework of our country's polarised and polarising party politics.

Dates and figures were accurate at the time of writing. Unless specified otherwise, real names have been used. Where a pseudonym is used to protect a person's privacy, it has been marked with an asterisk. Most of the events described in the book were witnessed first-hand or recounted to me over the phone when that was not possible due to coronavirus restrictions. Some descriptions are pieced together from interviews with those who were there – tenants' union members, politicians, staffers of politicians or charity support workers.

The housing crisis is inextricable from wealth inequality. And to talk about wealth is to discuss the inequalities of class (as well as gender, sexuality and race, which I will get to later). It is vital that we unpack class, but throughout this book you will see that I regularly refer to 'low-income' people as opposed to 'working-class' people. Why? Nobody is an entirely reliable narrator of their own story, and the subjectivity of class obfuscates productive conversations about inequality. In 2015, the British Social Attitudes Survey (BSAS) found that 60 per cent of people in Britain identify as working class, suggesting that broad class divisions hold meaning for people. The 2021 edition of the BSAS revealed that 47 per cent of Britons in what sociologists would consider to be 'middle-class professional and managerial jobs' identify as 'working class'. Curiously, a quarter of people in such jobs who come from middle-class backgrounds (in the sense that their parents did professional work) also identify as working class. As Professor Sam Friedman of the London School of Economics (LSE) notes in his own research and analysis of this phenomenon, 'people find stories of the past – of working-class struggle, of upward social mobility, of meritocratic striving – that provide powerful frames for understanding their own experiences and identity'. A person's class can change throughout their life and they may also feel that they belong to a different class to the one that their socio-economic status puts them in. Class is an identity. Income and wealth are a reality. In their 2009 book *The Spirit Level*, Kate Pickett and Richard Wilkinson make a similar point, arguing that social class is subjective as it is classified differently in various studies and pieces of research, but income differences are more objective.

Any discussion of wealth and class in Britain necessarily intersects with race and ethnicity. The acronym BAME stands for Black, Asian and Minority Ethnic. Its usefulness is limited in terms of quantitative data and qualitative analysis because it collapses the myriad experiences of distinctive ethnic groups under one baggy umbrella. However, frustratingly, many data on the diversity of experience of housing and economic inequality in the UK have used this term, collating varied experiences as one. So, where I use the acronym, it is because the research I refer to has limited itself to it.

Speaking of acronyms, this subject is full of them. Such shorthand serves a purpose, but it has taken me years to learn the language of housing. I have tried to use technical terminology sparingly because I fear it both alienates people, preventing an understanding of the structural forces at play in the housing crisis, and dehumanises those most affected by the housing crisis. At the back of this book you will find a glossary of terms which I hope is helpful where the use of acronyms is unavoidable.

Housing policy in the UK is complex. It is devolved, so while the symptoms and causes of housing stress and inequality overlap there are some differences in legislation between England, Wales, Scotland and Northern Ireland. This book focuses on the worst-hit areas in England and Wales, meaning that London and the south-east feature prominently, but Scotland and Northern Ireland also have their own unique housing emergencies which are referred to throughout. Indeed, the Republic of Ireland also faces a huge housing crisis. I spent the start of 2020 travelling the length of the country and speaking to young people who couldn't afford homes. However, Ireland is not discussed here because it would be wrong to conflate the country's struggles, distinct and distinctive as they are, with those of the UK – though, of course, there are parallels (house price inflation, for instance).

On the subject of housing policy: homelessness is generally distinguished between street homelessness and what's known as 'hidden homelessness', that is, people living in temporary accommodation. These 'hidden' homeless have no place to call home but can be hidden from official statistics and aren't always receiving support. They may be sofasurfing, squatting or sleeping on public transport. They may also not be recorded in temporary accommodation statistics. I don't like the term 'hidden homeless' because these people are anything but invisible and the type of homelessness they face is just as dangerous as rough sleeping, albeit distinctively different. If this term is used in this book, it is because an expert, charity or researcher has used it.

Throughout you will notice that I sometimes refer to people who are 'vulnerable' to poverty or to homelessness. This is the language of the housing and homelessness charity sector, but I should be clear: I think it's important to acknowledge that these people are not 'inherently' vulnerable, they are often made so – oppressed by the structural forces of a broken social and economic system.

Finally, *Tenants* began as an investigation into Britain's precarious private rented sector. It turned out to be about what it means to have a safe and stable home in an unstable world, whether that's amid political and economic turmoil or, as it happened, during a once-in-a-generation public health crisis. But above all this book is an investigation into how housing inequality is shaping our country politically, socially and economically. I am a journalist. I am not an economist. However, there will be discussion of economics in this book and, when there is, my intention is that these discussions of the economy and the financial instruments which have shaped our collective experience of housing are accessible. I have included Further Reading for anyone who wants to go deeper into any of the ideas discussed.

It feels important to state from the outset that this book is not a memoir. But there is a difference between impartiality and objectivity. I can relay events fairly but, of course, I am not an impartial observer. I cannot absent myself entirely from the narrative. I am here, I was there when these stories were told. As a human being who needs shelter, who is hardwired to make a home wherever I go, and as a witness who has been invited into people's lives as they experience the sort of housing stress nobody should ever have imposed upon them, I am invested in change.

As a journalist, in 2016 I fronted a successful campaign which amplified the work of organisations like the housing charity Shelter, tenants' unions and Generation Rent (an independent lobby group who work to make sure that the voices of private renters are heard – by landlords, by policymakers and by politicians). It got letting fees banned and deposits capped via the Tenant Fees Act 2019. However, as I hear regularly, agencies and landlords exploit this piece of legislation and, during the pandemic, used loopholes to demand thousands of pounds of 'rent up front' from prospective tenants – which just goes to show how dynamic politicians need to be in responding to housing problems as they evolve. In 2019, I became the *i Paper*'s housing correspondent, a role dedicated not, as is the case with many newspapers, to reporting on the property market and writing about 'investment hotspots' but solely to looking at how the housing crisis is impacting people across the country. I should also declare for transparency that since beginning this book I have also joined the board of Generation Rent.

This book may have my name on the cover, but it was a collaborative project. Writing *Tenants* was possible because the individuals behind the stories in it invited me into their homes and lives over the course of several years, allowing me to shadow them during painful and challenging times. I have conducted hundreds of interviews since 2017. I couldn't give every one of them space here, but, without each of them, this book could not exist. They have all informed it in some way. I am also indebted to the work of grassroots activists, scholars of housing law, charity sector workers, special advisors, civil servants and academics, all of whom shared their wisdom on and off the record, laying the foundations for my own work. As a journalist I am constantly aware that I am a conduit for the stories and work of others. I stand on the shoulders of giants every day. It is my hope that this book will bring their knowledge, experiences, expertise and determination for change to a wider audience because, as much as the coronavirus crisis was a once-in-a-generation disaster, it presents a once-in-a-generation opportunity for change and innovation. And so, I hope *Tenants* can encourage everyone to expect and ask for more from Britain's politicians and lawmakers.

# A CRISIS FORETOLD

### Brighton

*Council:* Brighton & Hove City Council
*Average House Price:* In the year 2020/21 the majority of sales in Brighton were terraced properties, selling for an average of £520,111. Flats sold for an average of £306,081, with semi-detached properties fetching £489,681. Overall, sold prices in Brighton over the year were 15 per cent up on the previous year.
*Average Private Rent:* In 2021 the average rent for a one-bedroom home was £1,265, for a two-bed it was £1,750, and for a three-bed it was £2,087.

—

It was 4 November 2020. One day before England would be placed into its second coronavirus lockdown. The sky was clear, the autumn air crisp. Forty-seven-year-old Anthony Howell, a labourer and part-time care worker, was being evicted by his private landlord. He had been dreading this moment; oscillating between resistance and denial. For months, cortisol had coursed through his veins as he fought it – by email, over the phone – causing his muscles to tense up, the instinctive response that is supposed to guard the human body against injury. He didn't want to leave the terraced Victorian redbrick house with its white-framed bay windows that had been his home for nine years.

The house had once been full. Anthony had shared it with several other adults, but as the fight against eviction became as intense as it was futile, one by one they had left. Anthony usually describes himself as a 'glass-half-full person' but his characteristic optimism and sense that anything is possible was being tested. He had never, ever been homeless. Now he didn't know where he would sleep that night. Sitting in the bedroom at the front of his home, Anthony looked around. He was humming with adrenaline. He had tried and failed to challenge his eviction through legal avenues. The court had sided with his landlord; there were no more official paths of resistance.

It didn't matter that Anthony was not behind on his rent when the eviction notice was served at the start of 2020. This was a Section 21 'no-fault' eviction, which allows a landlord to get rid of tenants, regardless of how long they have lived in their home, without having to give them a reason why. Anthony was still not sure why his landlord, who as far as he was aware owned about twenty properties in Brighton, had made the decision. 'Is it because I made a fuss about repairs and the fact that he didn't have a valid gas safety certificate? Could it be because they got a letting agent involved who realised it was worth more money – I was only paying £450 a month? Or was it because I told him that he needed to get a proper licence for the property because it was a house share and technically a house in multiple occupation?'

A house in multiple occupation (HMO) is a property rented out by at least three people who are not from the same family but share facilities like the bathroom and kitchen. It's also known as a 'house share'. Such properties are supposed to be licensed but, as was the case with Anthony and his housemates, some landlords don't bother to do this.

In England, as Anthony learned when his life was upturned, renting a property from a private landlord for a long period of time gives you no more right to stay in it than renting it short-term. You can be a good tenant who carries out repairs, pays bills on time and never disturbs the peace, but that still won't protect you. There is a long-held maxim, attributed to both Mark Twain and the American folk humourist Will Rogers: 'Buy land – they're not making any more of it.' If you have a mortgage and pay it off, over time you accrue equity and increase your ownership over your home. Each monthly payment is an investment in your future prosperity and security. We have accepted that property is a good investment, because paying rent only pays off someone else's mortgage. This is known, in left-leaning housing policy circles, as 'landlordism': an economy where a few individuals own property and rent it out for profit.

'It can't be right,' Anthony thought, bewildered and infuriated that he had no rights over the home he had lived in for the best part of a decade. How could he be so easily turfed out when he had paid so much: £450 a month in rent for nine years comes to £48,600. If he had been able to save that instead, it would have been more than enough for a deposit on a place of his own.

His landlord had served the eviction notice prior to the pandemic, so Anthony was not protected by the government's guidance to courts, brought in in March 2020, that they should consider the impact of the coronavirus economic crisis on a tenant's income. But, in any case the guidance was just that – a recommendation, not a legal requirement. Anthony's work had completely dried up during the first lockdown. He had been furloughed from his job as a carer, which involved working with children, and all his labouring work had disappeared. Before the pandemic, he earned between £1,200 and £1,300 a month; on the day of his eviction in November 2020, it was more like £700. In a study released in early 2021, which compared average rents, salaries and the cost of living, Brighton was ranked as the worst UK city for renters who were single. Anthony knew he wouldn't be able to rent anything there by himself and that he would struggle in many other places nearby. He might be able to access Housing Benefit through Universal Credit, but, because it is capped at the lowest third of market rents, it might still leave him short. According to the council's own analysis, just 6 per cent of homes available for private rental in the area would fall within Anthony's benefit limit because there is a cap on the amount adults who are over sixteen but under the state pension age can receive.

Anthony had exhausted all legal avenues. Faced with his own fight-or-flight reflexes, he dug in, pushing back the only way he could by vowing not to leave his home. He decided to stay until he was forcibly removed. Aware that it was in vain – a death rattle – this was his final attempt to get the institutions he felt had already forgotten about his case (the local council, the court system) to acknowledge the rights he did not but believed he should have. He had always considered himself forth-right and more than capable of advocating for his best interests, but this encounter with the complex and opaque labyrinth that is UK housing law had left him feeling frustrated, disempowered and disoriented. Even trying to get the council to organise a bed for the night, or applying to the council for homelessness support, he had discovered that neither could be done until he was officially kicked out of his home.

Before his eviction Anthony had joined the community union ACORN, which he found while researching his rights, or rather lack of, online, because he realised that he might, as he put it, 'have a problem'. Just as trade unions bring workers together to fight for and enforce their rights, ACORN aims to do the same on the social issues impacting local communities. Expensive and poor-quality housing is high on its priority list in every single region of Britain. The organisation is international and not uncontroversial; it was started in 1970 in Arkansas in the US as the Association of Community Organizations for Reform Now – though it is now largely defunct there. In the UK, ACORN was founded in 2014 in Bristol, and by 2020 it had become a nationwide network of communities, with 5,000 members across the country and branches in twenty-two cities. The people at ACORN – community as opposed to party political activists, whose thinking is often rigid – had long grasped a reality which had eluded most career politicians and, indeed, journalists: something important was happening. Desperate people with nowhere else to turn were being hung out to dry and crying out for community, even if that alone couldn't help them materially. ACORN told me that during the pandemic they heard from more renters than ever before because people were turning to them for help in plugging the gaps in support which the state was failing to fill. Anthony contacted the Brighton branch and paid his £5 a month member-ship fee. For that sum, he got support. ACORN does many things but its main focus is on Section 21 evictions. They told me that in October 2020 alone they resisted twenty evictions in Brighton. They also held 'eviction resistance bootcamps' across the country, where participants were taught about renters' rights. Anthony, who had never been in a union before, was learning as he went along that 'if you go through the normal channels there is no legal aid and you've already been evicted before you get anywhere'.

Sitting by the bay window in his bedroom, Anthony looked down on to the street as other ACORN members, twenty-seven of them in total, assembled outside his house, socially distanced and wearing masks, in a peaceful resistance not only of the eviction itself but of what ACORN condemns as the 'hoarding of property' by private landlords. He wasn't due to be evicted until 12 p.m. and it was still only 11.15 a.m. The sun was shining, but not on his side of the road, and everyone was cold and nervous. The ACORN members took a fridge which had been discarded in the garden and put it in front of Anthony's door as a barrier. They reminded him to make sure all of the doors and windows were locked. Cars went up and down; with each one, the group collectively held its breath in case it was the bailiffs. When they did arrive, they stood on the opposite side of the road and observed the group. As you might expect, bailiffs just want to do the job they are paid to do. Evicting people is their work; they have bills to pay, too. The men employed to evict Anthony wanted to get on with it. They called the police.

Hours passed; the police did not arrive. Legal evictions are civil not criminal matters, so the police don't usually get involved, but that doesn't stop people calling them. Inside, Anthony barricaded the front door with more furniture. He had to stay indoors, which felt strange to him. He is someone who likes to defend himself and get stuck in, but, on this occasion, his task was to be quiet and stay put. The ACORN members, facing down the bailiffs outside, were also becoming more anxious by the minute. Anthony began to feel guilty. By this point, the prospect of staying felt as terrifying as leaving, but so many people had gathered on his behalf that he felt he couldn't just throw in the towel, and anyway he was, by nature, 'stubborn'.

From his eyrie inside, Anthony could see each mini drama unfolding: someone talking to the bailiffs; another liaising with the police; someone else filling in his neighbours on what was happening; all moving back and forth across the road. He could feel the tensions that everyone was experiencing though he couldn't hear their conversations. Periodically, someone would phone him to tell him the latest. A feeling of dread descended on him.

The police told the nervous crowd that they couldn't intervene, they could only observe. The bailiffs were becoming increasingly agitated and made it clear that they wanted to crack on. The locksmith they had called arrived and Anthony, accepting the end, agreed to leave the property willingly. It was just after 3 p.m. His twenty-seven supporters were sad but relieved; some cried. One of them, 34-year-old carer and mother of three Leila, felt particularly emotional. She lives in social housing in the nearby town of Worthing and had felt she had a duty to show solidarity with someone who did not have a secure home. She had joined ACORN in 2019 when she decided that no meaningful change was going to happen through the traditional political system. Her role in Brighton had been as the negotiator with the police. On her way home, she couldn't stop thinking about Anthony. He had seemed OK at the start of the day. The support of the group had buoyed him up and everyone was hopeful that they might be able to stop the eviction. But, at the end, he was distressed, in shock. The eviction, after months of fighting, was very final.

As temperatures dropped and new coronavirus lockdown regulations came into force pausing evictions, Anthony camped out in his work van. He did not sleep a wink. Such was the arbitrary stop/start nature of the government's support for renters during the pandemic that the second lockdown saw the reintroduction of a rule which had been in place earlier that year: bailiffs could not attend evictions personally because it could increase the transmission of Covid-19. Had Anthony's eviction come twenty-four hours later, although it might still not have been stopped entirely, no bailiffs, symbolic as they are of a landlord's power and control, would have been able to attend. That night, it was freezing. Awake, Anthony wondered where home would be now? He grew up in a council house with his brothers; he had no Bank of Mum and Dad to bail him out. 'If it was this easy for landlords to make people homeless, it should be easier to get help,' he thought as he lay there.

Anthony had lived in Brighton for twenty years. He felt that every-thing he had worked for 'meant nothing', the eviction was 'a real kick in the teeth'. 'You do a lot for the place, and it can just be taken away,' he told me a few days later, still homeless. He wanted to leave the town he called home and 'run for the hills' because he felt so rejected by it. The days and weeks that followed were lonely. He had – he has – a lot of friends but a sense of pride kicked in. He couldn't call them. It would take him two weeks to pick up the phone and tell anyone what had happened. He felt 'worthless' but 'bloody grateful' that he had his van.

## To Be a Tenant

Private renters are tenants. A tenant is someone who has temporary possession of land or property which they rent from a landlord. The word has its roots in Old French and feudalism; it is related to the verb *tenir*, which means 'to hold' and is derived from the Latin *tenere*, which means 'to keep' or 'to grasp'. To be a tenant in Britain today is to try everything in your power to hold on to your sense of security, often clutching at straws.

The business of private renting is simple: private renters add to their landlord's wealth while (usually) diminishing their own; but private renters like Anthony are generally poorer than owner-occupiers to begin with. Over the past twenty years, the number of people in England's private rented sector has doubled. There are now some 11 million people living in precarious rented homes which could be taken away from them at any time. From 2011 to 2018, rents in England rose by 16 per cent, outpacing wages, which only increased by 10 per cent on average during the same period, according to the housing charity Shelter.

In the year May 2020 to May 2021, the cost of rent to household income ratio (the amount of rent you pay compared with the amount of money you earn) increased in most regions in the United Kingdom. On average, private renters spend a third of their pre-tax earnings on rent (London 34 per cent, south-west 32 per cent, south-east 31.8 per cent, east England 31.3 per cent, north-west 29.4 per cent, Wales 29.1 per cent, East Midlands 29 per cent, West Midlands 29 per cent, Northern Ireland 27.6 per cent, Yorkshire and Humber 26.8 per cent, Scotland 25.2 per cent, north-east 24 per cent). This means that most renters (63 per cent) struggle to save. Unlike homeowners, their place in the world becomes neither legally nor financially more stable over time.

Across the UK there are currently 17.5 million adults without a safe, secure or stable home (if children are included, this rises to 22 million people). That's one in three. Maybe that's you or someone you love. Women and people who are not White British are disproportionately impacted by this. But not only has rent skyrocketed in the past ten years, house prices are now more than 65 times that of the average home in 1970. Meanwhile, average weekly wages are only 35.8 times higher. Now there is not, according to the independent not-for-profit organisation the Women's Budget Group, a single place in the UK where a single woman on an average income can afford to buy or rent a home on her own. A third of all young people will be renting privately from cradle to grave. The number of older people who rely on a private landlord has also grown.

Private renting is now so unaffordable and unstable, it has fuelled homelessness (particularly in London, but increasingly elsewhere, too). The number of families who became homeless because they were evicted or could not afford their rent despite being in work, went up by 73 per cent between 2013 and 2018. In the most basic – financial – terms, this has cost the state greatly. Figures from the Local Government Association (LGA) show that councils in England spent £142 million placing homeless households in bed and breakfasts (most of which are privately owned, and, as I have reported, sometimes funded by offshore investments) in 2019/20, compared with £26.7 million in 2010/11 – that's a 430 per cent increase over the course of a decade. At the start of 2021, 253,000 people in England, 130,000 of whom were children, were homeless and living in temporary accommodation – hostels, bed and breakfasts and even converted office blocks where you might find an entire family living in one room, sharing a bathroom and kitchen with total strangers.

And so this book is about those people – like Anthony – who don't own their homes. It's also about those who help them. And it's about the landlords, letting agents and investors who make money from this crisis while politicians look the other way. It unpacks a complex truth: that we aren't facing one homogeneous housing crisis in Britain right now. Hardest hit, as ever, are those on no and low incomes, who would previously have lived in social housing. But so, too, are those on average and middle incomes who would once have been able to buy a home relatively easily. This is the story of a series of localised crises which are distinct and distinctive. Reporting from HMOs in Bradford, modern slums in Weston-super-Mare, social housing in south London and the offices of Members of Parliament in Westminster, this book assesses the human impact of bad housing policy. It looks at how we got here, and how we can make things better in both the long and the short term. It asks a vital question: in an ideal world, what would we do with housing policy? And, ultimately, as the stories in this book show, the housing crisis underpins a range of social evils, from inequality to energy inefficiency, from mental health to regional inequity, and from the cost of living to social mobility. And so, this book asks whether fixing housing could fix everything else, too. Could a more compassionate and loving social, political and economic model, one that brings more humanity to housing, be within reach?

These are not sentimental questions. The consequences of the housing crisis reach beyond the fact that houses are more expensive to buy, that people spend more of their income on rent and that homelessness is rising. Where we live dictates every aspect of our lives. Like a virus, the housing crisis is just a piece of information, but it infects its hosts and multiplies to make everything more difficult for them, impacting everyone they interact with – their children, their families, their colleagues, their neighbours, their doctors, their Universal Credit assessors, their housing officers. Like access to clean water, the right to adequate housing is a human right acknowledged by the United Nations (UN). Yet having a secure home for life is still seen as a luxury and housing is still seen as a commodity. Rather than being protected, it is framed as something that you should work towards and achieve. As this book shows, this is partly the work of party politics, which has used the twin aspirational ideas of homeownership and housing wealth to win elections, exploiting voters' desire for stability, but equally to get rich without having to do much (and let's be real, who doesn't want that?).

While my focus in this book is on the precarity of the private rented sector and those at the sharp end of it, it is impossible to talk about that without addressing the parallel problems of homelessness, homeownership and social housing. Homeowners are regularly defined as a wealthy class of people and have become the target of much abuse, but the simple fact is that not all homeowners are rich. One third of all households in poverty after housing costs own their own homes and they experience the same sort of housing stress as the least well off private renters. Take one example, the building safety scandal which has unfurled in the wake of the Grenfell Tower disaster. This has revealed that thousands of people (many of whom bought their homes on a part-rent–part-buy basis via Shared Ownership or via the affordability scheme Help to Buy) are living in tower blocks covered in Grenfell-style cladding, or with safety defects such as missing fire breaks and inadequate and flammable insulation. Think, then, of the hundreds of thousands of social renters stuck in homes owned by local authorities and housing associations which don't meet basic health and safety standards – they also experience the housing stress that private renters do. These examples of insecurity and instability are no less important issues, and they are related to the state of private renting, but I could not and do not attempt to cover everything here. (I have included suggestions for related topics which can only be addressed briefly in this book in the section on Further Reading.)

## 'Evil' Landlords?

Drawing attention to the precarious status quo in housing is contentious; whether they are hedge fund investors, cryptocurrency speculators or landlords, those who speculate to make something out of nothing the world over don't like to be challenged on the mechanisms which facilitate it. 'As soon as the land of any country has all become private property, the landlords, like all other men, love to reap where they never sowed,' the economist Adam Smith wrote in 1776 in his book *The Wealth of Nations*, 'and demand a rent even for its natural produce.'

However, it is important to get something straight: the problem with the private rented sector is not that it is entirely a scam in which landlords are de facto screwing over tenants (although, as this book will expose in later chapters, there are rogue landlords who do exactly this). It is that the reality in which we in Britain now find ourselves is that we rely on private landlords because we don't have enough social housing and because homeownership has become increasingly unaffordable. Our politicians have consciously outsourced a vital service – the provision of housing – to unqualified individuals – private landlords – who do not always have the financial or emotional resources to carry out this service properly. Private landlords are not professional housing providers, they are not social workers and, if they don't have huge pots of cash themselves, their ability to carry out the necessary repairs to their properties may not always be straightforward. This does not excuse poor (and sometimes unlawful) behaviour, but it does reinforce the fact that all roads and, crucially, responsibility, here lead back to the state which, as it exists today in our democracy, ought to legislate to protect its citizens and enable them to live well. As the Genevan Enlightenment philosopher Jean-Jacques Rousseau noted in the second half of the eighteenth century, the unconditional and unqualified ownership of property resulted in inequality. As he saw it, powerful and wealthy people had stolen land belonging to everyone and fooled ordinary people into accepting them as rulers. This, in Rousseau's eyes, meant that the social contract – the implicit agreement between citizens and their representatives which must exist – was not a willing agreement.

Blaming landlords alone, even when justified, lets the state off the hook. Ditto blaming estate agents and letting agents. I have been vocal and public in my criticism of that industry which drove the Tenant Fees Act 2019 but, at the same time, I think caution is needed to avoid myopia.

Landlords and letting agents make convenient villains, but a focus on them obstructs real change. My sister was an estate agent for several years. I know that, like her, not everyone who goes into that industry does so with malicious intent. It is a reasonably well-paid professional job for which you need few qualifications, and not everyone can afford to go to university or, indeed, find a similarly paid job afterwards if they do. Unlike being a landlord, you don't need capital to become an estate agent. But I also know from her and from the messages from letting agents that flood my inboxes that practices that are openly encouraged by some large estate agencies (including playing buyers off against one another to inflate prices, and dirty tricks to subvert the ban on letting fees that was brought in with the Tenant Fees Act) require scrutiny and more regulation. None the less, creating bogeymen out of estate agents and landlords takes the heat off politicians and ultimately flattens the conversation about what really needs to change: policy, legislation and enforcement.

## The State of Housing

Having spent the past decade working as a journalist specialising in housing inequality, I have watched and listened as the term 'housing crisis' has been repeatedly used. I have used it myself hundreds of times; it is a convenient shorthand for an inchoate feeling of unfairness, a series of specific social and economic problems and myriad political failings. The very term housing crisis is problematic, though. It implies a sudden catastrophe. By their nature, catastrophes tend to blindside us, cannot be easily prevented and are usually temporary: a tsunami or an earthquake. That is not what this is. This was as predictable as it was avoidable.

The housing crisis is made up of a series of distinct but related emergencies: the instability of the private rented sector; rising street and hidden homelessness; unaffordable housing enabled by our country's economic reliance on the housing market; the hoarding of property wealth; and a lack of social housing. All of these are symptoms of the slow and deliberate undoing of our welfare safety net and the intentional but artificial inflation of our housing market in the past thirty years. All of these have resulted in the endemic inequality that has become the status quo in Britain.

There are myriad reasons for the emergency we now face and it's certainly not the case that all economists agree on the causes of the housing crisis. Economics is the subjective art of explaining the production, consumption and transfer of goods and services. One of its most important concepts is that of the 'free market', which is a system wherein the prices of goods and services are self-regulated by buyers and sellers negotiating in an open market rather than by government intervention. When it comes to housing, this is, of course, nonsense because the idea that everyone who needs housing has the necessary power to negotiate is pure fiction. There is nothing 'free' about the housing market, which, far from regulating itself, is controlled by politicians, banks and those with wealth and, therefore, power.

Broadly, since the 1980s, four key factors have caused the situation we find ourselves in today. Identifying these provides a framework for understanding how we get out of the mess they have created.

## 1. Diminishing Returns: The Social Housing Shortage

This has driven low-income people into the insecure private rented sector and caused it to expand. This sector has expanded because social housing has been sold off through Right to Buy and has not been replaced. To date, 2 million homes have been sold – and therefore lost to social housing – through the scheme in England alone. Margaret Thatcher's government introduced Right to Buy in 1980, but it was originally a Labour policy (albeit a tamer version). Successive governments on both the left and the right have not reined in the scheme, despite the obvious problems it has created. At the end of 2021, there were 1,187,641 households on social housing waiting lists. In the same year, 6,850 social homes were sold off through Right to Buy. In 2020 we lost 17,453. The state did not replace the homes it sold off. The number of new homes built for social rent fell by almost four-fifths in the decade 2007/8 to 2017/18. However, Right to Buy is only part of the picture.

## 2. Crash Course: Inflated House Prices

Attention must be given to one of the biggest shifts to take place in British society in the past thirty to forty years: house price inflation. Between the 1980s and the 2020s, though there have been two periods where house prices have dipped, the overwhelming story of the housing market has been one of house price inflation. And house prices have far outpaced wages. In 2007, they reached record highs before dipping during the global financial crisis (when investors pounced) and then rising again. As 2021 drew to a close, figures from the Office for National Statistics (ONS) showed British households' net worth grew to £11.2 trillion in the year 2020/21. This is an increase of 8.4 per cent on 2019 and the highest rate of growth since before the global financial crisis of 2008. What drove this rise in household wealth? Next to pension schemes, land was the largest contributor. The rapidly rising value of property, fuelled by low interest rates and tax breaks for home-owners via the coronavirus Stamp Duty cut, accounted for 40 per cent of this rise. Research by the think tank the Resolution Foundation highlighted that this inflation was merely the confirmation of a longer-term trend. It found that over the past thirty years house prices have added about £3-trillion-worth of housing wealth from main residences alone. Houses made more money than workers. It is important to note that the financial crisis had a role to play here, too. Banks became more risk averse in its wake and in 2008 banking regulations (known as Basel II) were tightened, which meant that high loan-to-value lending became more costly for them. These two factors were crucial in the collapse of homeowner-ship: rising house prices, combined with the fact that banks wanted larger deposits and tightened affordability checks made it harder for first-time buyers to get on to the property ladder, meaning that middle-income young people and those without family wealth were pushed into the expanding private rented sector. Later, inter-ventions such as George Osborne and David Cameron's Help to Buy scheme, ostensibly designed to help this group by getting credit to first-time buyers, appear to have inflated house prices further.

3. **Increased Availability of Credit, Particularly for Landlords**
While social housing was diminishing, in 1986 our financial services sector was experiencing large-scale deregulation known as the 'Big Bang'. Throughout the 1980s, mortgages became more accessible and interest rates were high (reaching 18.63 per cent in the week of 9 October 1981), making lending to people so they could buy homes a lucrative business for banks. People's wages were rising at the same time as regulations were relaxed: buyers

didn't need big deposits (the average loan-to-value ratio was about 94 per cent), and you no longer had to prove you could save before you could borrow. House prices were going up and banks were willing to lend because the yield on housing justified it. There was then a recession and, in the early 1990s, many homebuyers went into negative equity (that is, their mortgages were bigger than the value of the homes they were secured against). Repossessions rose, peaking at 75,500 in 1991. Those homes went back on the market at low prices. The housing market bounced back in 1993 and house prices began rising again. Homeownership carried on increasing until 2003, with the number of first-time buyers remaining high until 2007. But something else was going on in the background. In 1996, the Association of Residential Letting Agents (ARLA) and several lenders launched the 'buy-to-let' mortgage, making it easier for individual landlords to invest in property by offering specialist mortgages that factored in rental incomes. Over the next two decades, falling interest rates and rising house prices persuaded more and more people that the property market was a good place to invest. This fuelled price rises further and caused a fundamental shift in who owned Britain's homes – banks chose to lend to landlords in greater numbers which led to the growth of private renting. The idea that houses were assets not homes was normalised. The private rented sector grew. After the financial crisis of 2008, buy-to-let mortgages became a vehicle for redirecting lending away from first-time buyers and towards investors who were considered safer bets. By 2014, the number of loans granted to landlords outstripped the number given to first-time buyers – almost 200,000 buy-to-let mortgages were approved in one year alone.

### 4. The Rise of the Renter: Unaffordable Private Rents

The social housing shortage and difficulty in getting a mortgage (high house prices and lower mortgage availability for first-time buyers) put pressure on the private rented sector by driving up demand as more people needed to rent from a private landlord. As a result, the landlord class expanded. And those who would once have qualified for social housing were forced to rent privately. The sector became a substitute for social housing, with the state paying private landlords to house people, in some cases in properties that were once owned by local authorities. It is believed that just over 40 per cent of former council homes sold through the Right to Buy scheme have been bought by private landlords, who charge as much as twice the rent that a local authority would. In some places, such as Milton Keynes, the figure is higher – at 70.9 per cent. The government now spends an astonishing £22 billion a year on Housing Benefit. About half of that is thought to go directly to private landlords, meaning we – the taxpayers – give them some £10 billion a year via benefit payments. (As we shall see later in the book, ill-conceived attempts to do something about this in recent years by cutting Housing Benefit have been brutal, leaving many private renters on the breadline.)

Like financial services, the private rented sector was deregulated in favour of landlords by the Housing Act 1988 (more on this later), which left renters with very few rights but gave landlords a captive and subdued market as rents and house prices rose alike. Younger people were renting privately for longer, also increasing demand. Landlords put up rents because a) they could and b) people needed somewhere to live and had no choice but to pay these higher rents. In the run-up to the 2008 financial crash private rents rose; they then stabilised slightly, but in recent years they have been rising again – beyond earnings in many parts of the country – to reach new record highs in 2021. Housing Benefit (now accessed via Universal Credit) had also been slashed, and certainly had not kept up with rent rises, meaning that many renters receiving state support couldn't afford the market rates they were facing, while private renters without state support stretched themselves, sometimes even getting into debt to make rent. According to the ONS, the number of households living in the private rented sector in the UK grew from 2.8 million in 2007 to 4.5 million in 2017. This was an increase of 61 per cent. In the twenty-five years since buy-to-let mortgages became available, Britain began to turn back from a country where there was social housing and homeowner-ship (which peaked in 2003 at 71 per cent) into an almost feudal nation of tenants living at the behest of landlords, paying unafford-able rents and living in substandard, mouldy, overcrowded, cold or vermin-infested homes.

Many of us, I am sure, have long sensed an unravelling, felt that something is wrong. But now there is a palpable feeling that we are on the verge of *something*, that change is possible. The pandemic exposed ethical and socio-economic fault lines that already existed and has widened them. A grassroots resistance to housing inequality is already underway because of the work of many dedicated individuals – like those ACORN volunteers – who plug gaps in state housing support. A new approach may yet be conceivable. We are seeking answers about the future, so it's time to start asking the right questions about how the housing crisis was created and how it might be resolved, about how someone like Anthony could find himself homeless and struggling to access support. To do that, let's scroll back two generations.

# PART ONE

# THE PROBLEM OF RENT

*In his landmark 1942 report on Social Insurance and Allied Services, Sir William Beveridge set out to slay 'five giants on the road to reconstruction': want, disease, ignorance, squalor and idleness. There was one problem he struggled to solve. He called it 'the problem of rent' and he devoted nine pages of the report to it. The issue he identified with private rent still rings true today. He wrote: 'The attempt to fix rates of insurance benefit and pension on a scientific basis with regard to subsistence needs has brought to notice a serious difficulty in doing so in the conditions of modern Britain. This is the problem of rent. In this, as in other respects, the framing of a satisfactory scheme of social security depends on the solution of other problems of economic and social organisation.' The problem of rent was that it varied across the country and changed according to what landlords felt they could charge. So, a flat rate benefit with an average allowance for private rent would leave people in more expensive homes below subsistence level, once they had paid their rent, and people in cheaper homes with a surplus. Today we have the Local Housing Allowance to help calculate Housing Benefit, which is administered via Universal Credit. But, for many, it just doesn't stretch far enough.*

# 1

# SHELTERED DREAMERS

'I should say: the house shelters day-dreaming, the house protects the dreamer, the house allows one to dream in peace.'

Gaston Bachelard, *The Poetics of Space* (1958)

### Addington Road, South Croydon

*Council:* Croydon London Borough Council
*Average House Price:* In the year 2020/21 most sales in Croydon were terraced houses which sold for an average of £421,298. Flats sold for an average of £306,857, and semi-detached homes fetched £521,585. During that year, sold prices in Croydon were 7 per cent up on the previous year.
*Average Private Rent:* In 2021 the average rent for a one-bedroom home was £1,046, for a two-bed it was £1,403, and for a three-bed it was £1,693.

—

There were two periods in the twentieth century when the political will to deliver truly affordable housing matched the need for it. The first was immediately after the First World War, when Prime Minister David Lloyd George's 'fit country for heroes' pledge made housing a priority. Assisted by government incentives, developers built affordable homes for people on middle and low incomes. The second was in the decades after the Second World War, when publicly funded housing made up about half of all homes built. This is what my own grandparents benefited from – council housing, or what we now know as social housing. But tempting as it is, it's vital not to romanticise this, because hundreds of thousands of people still lived in slums and languished on housing waiting lists. None the less it's the intention – so lacking today – that deserves acknowledgement and ought not to be brushed over.

Croydon, where my family is from, is an edge city; a town that yearns for its own city status. It is only a fifteen-minute train ride from London Bridge, but it is in some ways unlike the capital's other satellite towns. It receives bad press for its poor urban planning and being an architectural hotchpotch; a jumble of substandard rabbit hutch flats in office-to-residential ('permitted development rights') conversions, new build tower blocks and mid-century buildings, including the octagonal 'No 1 Croydon' or '50p building', designed by Richard Seifert. Seifert headed up the firm of architects who built Centre Point – the brutalist building that rises up as you exit Tottenham Court Road tube station. The one which was occupied by homelessness campaigners when it stood empty, which led to the homelessness charity of the same name being formed. The one where flats are now on the market for more than £7 million.

Croydon lies between central London and the suburbs which fan out into the green belt home counties of Surrey and Kent. Haunted by bombing during the Second World War and damaged by an ongoing social housing conditions scandal, it became home to good-quality municipal housing.

My grandad loved to drive. As he got older, he suffered with progressive emphysema and he would have been completely housebound in the semi-detached home he shared with my grandmother on Addington Road in south Croydon were it not for his car. When I was a teenager, we would drive all around south London, sometimes for hours. I didn't live with my grandparents but, if I was going to meet friends in Peckham, Brixton or Camberwell, Grandad would insist on taking me. It was always quicker to get the train. That didn't matter. And there was one spot we would always visit whether it was on the way or not: South Norwood Hill.

It was here that in 1956 my grandparents were given a ground-floor maisonette in one of three new blocks of flats there by Croydon Council.

Constructed from red brick, punctuated with rectangular, white-framed windows, held together by dark, quasi-Scandinavian wood panels which appear, from afar, to hold the buildings together, 190 South Norwood Hill still stands, perched on a landscaped grassy patch opposite mock-Tudor semi-detached properties.

Addiscombe Road is at the bottom of the hill. There's a particularly good independent record shop there, called DnR Vinyl, that specialises in grime, dubstep and UK garage classics, and to which people make pilgrimage. If you drive to the top of the road, you'll find Crystal Palace on one side and Thornton Heath on the other. The road is lined with a mixture of mid-century and Victorian terraced houses but, intermittently, there are 1950s, 1960s and 1970s maisonettes. Neatly stacked on top of each other, they epitomise the functional brutalist sort of social housing that was built all over the country in the second half of the twentieth century. There's nothing special about them. In fact, it's unremarkable. But for my grandad and me it became a symbol, a stop on every journey we took, because, particularly at the end of his life by which time he was a homeowner, he felt that he, and by extension I, owed everything to that flat.

My family's origin story is not unique. It will be mirrored in the narratives told by thousands of parents and grandparents to their children and grandchildren, for it is representative of the sort of rapid social and economic progress that was possible in the second half of the twentieth century, entirely because of social housing and the expansion of mortgages. When my grandparents met in 1954, my grandad had moved to London from Brighton and was living in a Croydon bedsit, while my nan was living in her parents' privately rented home in Nicholson Road, at the Croydon end of Addiscombe Road, with her eight siblings as well as her parents, making them a family of eleven. In 2018, I sat down with my nan to interview her about my grandad's and her housing story – spanning the post-war years of social housing and the epic house price rises of the 1980s, 1990s and 2000s. I asked her if her parents had owned that house. 'No!' she said, and laughed. 'We rented it from a landlord. Not many people owned their own homes in those days, love. Most houses were rented unless you were very well off. I don't think we knew anyone who owned a house.' The property in Nicholson Road wasn't big, certainly not for a family of that size. As my nan remembered, 'It had three bedrooms, gas lighting and an outside toilet.' It was the best they could do. 'My mother had trouble finding a house,' my nan said matter-of-factly, sitting in the kitchen in Addington Road shortly before my grandfather died in May 2019. 'I remember her pushing around her pram in Croydon and worrying where we would live. It wasn't easy to get houses then, especially if you had lots of children like we did, and you didn't have a big income. Landlords didn't like that.'

After my grandparents married, my grandad moved into Nicholson Road, living alongside some of Nan's siblings. They paid my great-grandparents £2 a week in rent for their small room. My nan became pregnant with my eldest uncle in 1956, and at the same time my great-grandfather contracted tuberculosis. That was when the council stepped in, offering my grandparents a brand new maisonette. 'I was still in hospital when we got the keys,' my nan remembered. She has since told me that she never talked about her father's TB – not even with my mother – as TB carried huge stigma and shame because it 'suggested that you were poor and dirty'. At the time, there was rightly great concern, not only in Britain but across Europe, about young children living in close proximity to anyone with the disease; and my grandparents' experience weaves into a wider story about the genesis of social housing as we conceive of it today. By the nineteenth century, one in four deaths was caused by TB and there was a huge focus on stalling its spread. The provision of decent homes thus became a crucial part of conversations about public health in the early twentieth century. Charitable housing organisations such as the Guinness Partnership (formerly Guinness Trust) and Peabody (formerly the Peabody Trust) were first set up in the late Victorian period as a direct response to TB and cholera, both diseases which were spread by poor sanitation, overcrowding and bad-quality housing, and which were rampant across the country but particularly in urban areas.

Though state-sponsored housebuilding began at scale at a later date, the concept of social housing and recognition of the need for it (which would be supercharged by the First World War) came out of the Industrial

Revolution. Britain had transitioned from mostly rural communities to a country in which people increasingly lived in urban areas which had grown to accommodate them. The provision of decent homes became the cornerstone of conversations about public health, because it had become clear that poor living conditions were enabling the transmission of infectious diseases. Britain's first attempt at social housing was built in north Liverpool in 1869, on the advice of Britain's first Medical Officer of Health, William Duncan (a role similar to that held by Sir Chris Whitty during the pandemic), who was one of the first people to establish a link between unsanitary housing and poor health. At the time, a third of the area's working-age population – 86,000 people – was squashed into just over 2,000 crowded and poorly ventilated tenements, with 38,000 more crammed in cellars in crowded courts where there were open drains.

It was believed that disease spread by miasma – noxious smells in the air – and not in unclean water or via rats and mice, but, thanks to the work of reformers such as Duncan and Edwin Chadwick, the middle classes became convinced of the need to make the places lived in by the country's poorest more sanitary.

Unilateral concern about public health – and, more cynically, the fact that those in charge were worried about themselves – eventually won out over party politics, putting housing at the centre of the welfare state. In 1848, across Europe, there had been riots and revolutions: though the causes of these uprisings were specific (food shortages, mainly), it was feared that the discontent might spread, meaning the same could happen here. Chartism – the first mass movement driven by the working classes – was rising in popularity following the failure of the Reform Act 1832 to extend the vote beyond property owners. In 1838 the founding document of the movement, the People's Charter, was drawn up. It had six demands which, crucially, focused on giving those who did not own property or have inherited wealth a say in politics by calling for (among other things) the vote to be extended beyond the property-owning classes and for the abolition of the edict that only those who owned property could become Members of Parliament. This collection of radical demands caused nerves to fray among the landed elite. Could it, they wondered, be a precursor to some sort of lower-class revolt?

At around the same time, the communist German philosopher Friedrich Engels visited Manchester and Salford to research the conditions of industrial Britain's workers. He found them wanting and, like British reformers, lasered in on housing. This was before Engels authored *The Communist Manifesto* with Karl Marx; this visit inspired his book *The Condition of the Working Class in England*, which was published in Germany in 1845 but in London not until 1891. In it, he wrote that 'the social order makes family life almost impossible for the worker' because normal working people were being housed in 'comfortless, filthy' overcrowded slum homes which were 'hardly good enough for mere nightly shelter, ill-furnished, often neither rain-tight nor warm'. 'What family life is possible under such conditions?' Engels asked, in a question one might reasonably ask of much privately rented accommodation today.

What all of these social reformers did was challenge the generally accepted idea that it was the fault of the poor if they became sick; the reformers viewed social poverty as the cause of disease and pushed the then radical and contentious idea that getting the state to intervene to improve sanitation and housing would give working people a fair chance in life but moreover would benefit society as a whole.

Despite much laissez-faire opposition to change, several key pieces of transformative legislation came into force in the nineteenth century: the Reform Act 1832, which gave a vote to the middle classes; the Slavery Abolition Act 1833, which immediately abolished slavery in most parts of the British Empire; the Labouring Classes Dwelling Houses Act 1866, which allowed local authorities to buy land; the Reform Act 1867, which gave the vote to every male adult householder living in a town; the Education Act 1870 and the reforms that followed it, which made school free and attendance compulsory; the legalisation of trade unions in 1871 and ratification of their right to strike, which came in 1875; the Public Health Act 1875, which established local health authorities across England and made it compulsory for them to oversee decent sanitation; the Artisans' and Labourers' Dwellings Improvement Act 1875, which saw large slum clearance in England; and the Reform Act 1884, which gave poor farmers and labourers in the countryside a vote. By 1900, the Chartist movement had burned out, but its legacy was strong, and by

1918 five of its six demands had been achieved – only the demand that parliamentary elections be held every year was not implemented.

Unlike other European countries, Britain never saw the widespread rebellion of ordinary working people. When you consider that in France, for example, tenants can never be evicted during winter, perhaps things would look different if it had. However, the fear of a Bolshevik-style revolution in the UK itself is thought, by historians such as John Boughton, to have been a key motivator for the post-war drive to build council housing and thus stave off the sort of unrest seen in mainland Europe.

Did the ruling classes' reform of old laws go far enough? No. The point of revisiting these changes here, really, is that this is a story of change. It is a story which demonstrates that change is slow and seldom top-down, that change may be imperfect but that it is possible to push things forward when there is enough impetus and appetite to do things differently. The story of the housing crisis is a continuation of our post-industrial relationship to labour, to capital, to property, to wealth and to power.

Historically, radical change has resulted from major crises such as wars, civil unrest, famine and epidemics. The First World War was a catalyst which sped up change after the Industrial Revolution. All of the piecemeal reforms above paved the way for further legislation in the 1900s that became a confected foundation in the late 1940s for what we know today as 'the welfare state'. Enough people spoke out, campaigned, and, in the end, society was changed by the number of voices in favour of reform reaching critical mass at the same time as global events revealed the need for change. For a new way of doing things to become reality, we must take responsibility for the fact that the current systems are not working.

The world-changing nature – and world-making potential – of 2020's coronavirus pandemic was, in fact, not quite so 'unprecedented'. In 1918 and 1919, another pandemic killed at least 50 million people worldwide. In the United Kingdom, the so-called 'Spanish Flu' killed an estimated 228,000 people. This made 1918 the first year on record in which the number of deaths exceeded the number of births. Globally, about a third of the world's population contracted the virus. It was the acknowledgement that many of these deaths were due to the conditions in which people lived and the pursuit of new, affordable, safe and secure homes for the many that was a defining feature of the nascent social democracy that emerged in Britain. The Housing, Town Planning, &c. Act 1919 (also known as the Addison Act because it was overseen by Dr Christopher Addison, then Minister of Health, who understood the need to improve the health and living conditions of working people) ushered in a new way of doing things. For the first time, it tasked local authorities with building housing for ordinary working people, and facilitated this with a system of open-ended Treasury grants to cover any losses. The principle of state-subsidised housing was established and, following the recommendations of the 1918 Tudor Walters Report (authored by Sir John Tudor Walters, an idealistic architect-turned-Liberal MP), these homes were not to be terraces of houses packed into narrow plots but instead garden suburbs where properly proportioned cottage homes with large gardens were to be built 'no more than twelve to the acre'. The report also recommended environmentally friendly policies which used waste from power stations to promote district heating schemes and noted that these new homes would need to be integrated with local public transport.

The Addison Act resulted in the UK's first national programme of social housebuilding; it was thoughtful, comprehensive and treated housing as a public health issue and a social good. It made housing a national responsibility and implicitly acknowledged that private landlords and landowners would never be able to provide the quantity or quality of homes needed by ordinary people.

Over time, though high standards were not always upheld as Britain experienced economic pressure and depression through the 1920s and 1930s, the state continued to step up. Nationwide, slums were cleared and mass housing schemes were commissioned to meet the needs of growing cities. Depending on the leanings of the government at the time, the quality of these housing schemes varied. Between 1924 and 1929 there was a revolving door of Labour and Conservative prime ministers at Number 10. However, this period still saw minimum standards for council-owned homes introduced before being reversed by the post-crash 1930s interwar National Government. It was then brought back in a new and improved version by Aneurin 'Nye' Bevan, appointed by Clement

Attlee as Minister of Health in 1945, who, famously, introduced perhaps the most luxurious minimum standards, with council homes averaging 98 square metres (1,055 square feet) for a three-bedroom house. To put this in context, the Royal Institute of British Architects (RIBA) estimates that the floor area of the average new three-bedroom home in the UK is 88 square metres (947 square feet) – some 8 square metres (86 square feet) short of their recommended space guidelines.

It sounds almost far-fetched.

The world soon experienced another global conflict. National debate revolved around what should happen next, and in 1942 a consensus was reached, following the Beveridge Report which set out the blueprint for a welfare state to counter the 'giant evils' he saw in society: want, disease, ignorance, squalor and idleness. The idea was that National Insurance (introduced in 1911 but expanded in 1948) would indemnify us all – collectively and individually – against future economic, social and public health disasters. The report caught the public's imagination; people queued up to buy it and between November 1942 and February 1943 thousands of copies were sold each day. The Labour Party won the 1945 general election on a platform that promised to address these 'evils'.

It was also Bevan who brought in the Housing Act 1949. He had a pastoral vision of 'a living tapestry of mixed communities' where 'the doctor, the grocer, the butcher and the farm labourer all lived in the same street' and so he removed a restriction which had, until that point, stipulated that social housing could only be for 'working-class' people. From then, there was a clear focus from parties of all political persuasions on state-funded housebuilding during the post-war 'golden age'. Between 1939 and 1953, 1.3 million council homes were built. By 1961, another 1 million had been added. Social housing was a national asset, literally, because it was state-owned, and metaphorically, because it benefited society, empowering those who had previously been disempowered by giving them secure, healthy and habitable homes. There is nothing more radical. Instability begets instability. When a person lives in chaos they are usually oppressed by forces beyond their control – unstable work, homelessness, financial stress. Social housing provides stability, enabling people not merely to survive but to build their lives.

Built in the 1950s, the 190 South Norwood Hill flat was exemplary of the standards of its time. It had two bedrooms, a neat and compact kitchen-diner, a small living room and even, to my nan's astonishment, 'a bathroom with an inside toilet!' For a young, newly-wed woman who had grown up sharing a room with three or four siblings, this small flat was more than housing. It was a foundation, a chance at the sort of security a family needs in order to build a future. 'We absolutely loved it,' she said, excited by even the memory of it. 'We couldn't afford any furniture, but we didn't care.' For my grandparents the flat was just about affordable. Grandad had put himself through night school to become a junior engineer at Mullard, the company known today as Philips, and was earning around £9 a week. My nan didn't work, but remembers that their rent was about £3 a week. To give you some context, £9 then is the equivalent of about £220 today, so £3 works out at £73.33. Council rent in Croydon is higher in real terms now, at £84 a week for a one-bed home, £102 for a two-bed and £124 for a three-bed. When Margaret Thatcher's government came to power in 1979, the average council house rent stood at £6.40 a week. Two years later, by April 1981, that rent had risen to £11.39 – an increase of 78 per cent. Today both of my grandparents might be working or in receipt of tax credits, so perhaps they would still make rent. But they might find themselves – as many families do right now – living in the dilapidated and run-down social housing which has become a huge issue in Croydon.

'We were so, so proud of it,' my nan told me when I asked her how she felt about moving into our maisonette flat. 'We just couldn't believe we'd been given this amazing new home. Of course, we had to pay rent, but it was ours. I remember it so clearly – it was a pivotal moment.'

Neither well off nor on the breadline, my grandparents were exactly the sort of people that the government wanted to give homes to. Council homes were not only for those facing destitution, they were for working people, and even for those doing a bit better than OK. Council housing was deliberately aspirational. And while my family were bumped up the list because a newborn baby couldn't live in a house where someone had TB, it is a sad fact that council homes were just not as scarce then as they are today. My grandparents' enduring excitement at that brand-new, shiny, modern maisonette speaks to something that has been eroded today – the notion that getting a council home was desirable rather than something to be ashamed of. Why am I telling you their story? Because having access to council housing provided my family with a springboard from which they could change the course of their lives, and even their socio-economic class. I tell it because everything my family has now was made possible by the welfare state, by the stability that that flat afforded them, and by the money it allowed them to save. To understand the crisis in private renting today we must first understand the impact of the political decision to systematically dismantle municipal housing by selling off social homes, by failing to see them as a national asset. 'Those who cannot remember the past are condemned to repeat it' and, across the country, that is exactly what is happening.

At the start of the twentieth century the private rented sector was home to most people, with 90 per cent of the population renting from and relying on a private landlord. By 1981, 5.5 million homes had been built by or on behalf of local authorities. This housebuilding drive meant that, by the end of the 1970s, almost a third of all households – that is, more than 40 per cent of the population – lived in stable social housing. But then something changed. And by the period 2016–18, according to the government's own data, just 17 per cent of households in England rented their homes from a local authority or housing association. Many of those who would once have lived in affordable social housing were instead renting from a private landlord – which put us back to 1950 levels.

## Dismantling the Safety Net

How did that happen? Consider Margaret Thatcher's premiership as ground zero for the mess we are in now. Broadly, the answer lies in two of her government's policies. They were: Right to Buy, which formed part of the Housing Act 1980; and the deregulation of the private rented sector in favour of landlords through the Housing Act 1988. When Thatcher was elected, there were more people in social housing than were renting privately from a landlord, and those who did were protected by rent regulations. The introduction of Right to Buy and the Housing Act 1988 changed all that. Among other things, the act (see chapter 2) introduced Section 21 evictions – like the one Anthony was served with. In the years leading up to the pandemic, this sort of eviction had become a leading cause of homelessness. In 2021, in the first full months after the Coronavirus eviction ban ended in England, an average of 400 households became homeless every day.

Those who came after Thatcher (with, perhaps, the exception of Theresa May, who, though she was not around long enough to see change through, hired housing policy experts from the charity Shelter, instigated a review of social housebuilding and promised to regulate private renting) did nothing to roll back these measures or to build more social housing. New Labour's leadership bopped victoriously as they sang along to D:Ream's dance anthem 'Things Can Only Get Better' as they celebrated their 1997 landslide. The song had soundtracked their election campaign videos, which featured smiling young people walking down neat and welcoming streets of terraced homes. But during their thirteen-year stint in power things did not quite get better in housing. During the Blair and Brown years, while it's true that huge numbers of new homes were built for private sale before the financial crash, between 1998 and 2010 New Labour actually managed to build fewer council homes (6,330) than Thatcher did in 1990 alone, the last year of her premiership, when 17,710 were built. David Cameron and his Chancellor George Osborne actively made things worse when they ignored the burgeoning demographic of private renters all together, turned a blind eye to the growing social housing shortage and introduced the Help to Buy scheme in the 2013 budget, further inflating house prices. From the Second World War until 1980, this country built an average of 126,000 social homes every year. In 2020, we only managed to build 6,463 social homes; but in the same period, more homes were lost through Right to Buy.

Right to Buy allowed council tenants to buy their home from the state with a discount of 60 or 70 per cent on its full market value (depending on the length of their tenancy). This was politically useful for the right. However, it is often, perhaps wilfully, forgotten that the enthusiasm for Right to Buy was shared by politicians on both the right and the left.

A less heavily discounted version of this policy appeared in the Labour Party's manifesto in 1959. 'Every tenant ... will have a chance first to buy from the Council the house he lives in,' it read. Labour knew as well as the Tories that homeownership was, however irrationally, a signifier of independence, success and aspiration.

In 1977, James Callaghan's Labour government conducted a housing study and found that 'for most people, owning one's house is a basic and natural desire'. By the end of the 1970s it was less a question of whether some form of Right to Buy would be implemented but which party would be in power to do it. In the 1979 Conservative manifesto, the Right to Buy council home was given a huge amount of space and explained in granular detail. The discounts offered to tenants were to start at 33 per cent off their home's market value and rise to a maximum of 50 per cent for tenants of twenty years' standing or longer. 'We shall also ensure that 100 per cent mortgages are available,' the manifesto declared.

Right to Buy was a wildly successful political manoeuvre. It created Conservative voters, a new type of homeowner who was able to traverse conventional class boundaries and confound traditional social hierarchies. As a result, while inequality has grown in recent years, it is now harder to identify and organise along traditional left/right lines.

This was no mistake. Right to Buy was underpinned by the idea that housing security could be good for democracy. In 1923 Noel Skelton, a Scottish Unionist politician and Conservative thinker, wrote that 'to make democracy stable' the government needed to promote and engender 'a property-owning democracy'. He believed that the political right in Britain needed to meet the rise of socialism with what he called 'constructive conservatism', and his thinking informed the policymaking of Conservative prime ministers from Harold Macmillan, Anthony Eden and Alec Douglas-Home to Margaret Thatcher and beyond. Skelton's principal idea was that if most people owned their homes, they would be less likely to back taxes on property or wealth, and would therefore maintain the status quo and, ultimately, protect the wealthy because it was in their own interests.

Whether you consider Right to Buy a success depends on your perspective. It did help some people who would never otherwise have bought homes to access the most secure tenure: homeownership. However, it was not a catalyst for increased homeownership across the board, which has remained broadly steady (56.6 per cent in 1980; 64.6 per cent in 2019–20). Above all, it has enabled the transfer of social housing – and the rental income it generates – from local authorities to private landlords, who can charge renters as much as they like. This, as Jim Strang, the then president of the Chartered Institute of Housing, wrote in a 2019 opinion piece for the magazine *Inside Housing*, made 'Right to Buy ... the biggest act of economic and social self-harm ever inflicted on this nation'. Probably the largest exercise in state asset-stripping in British history, Right to Buy was, as the historians Colin Jones and Alan Murie put it in their 2006 book on the subject, 'the most significant and lucrative act of privatisation' associated with any UK government. Between 1980 and 2015 it resulted in the sale of more than 2.8 million dwellings. In the same period, the number of newly built social homes fell far short of the volume of sales; we did not replace the affordable homes that were sold into the private market.

By the 1990s, it was clear that we were staring down a serious problem. Rents in both the social housing sector and the private rented sector were rising. There was not enough social housing. House prices were creeping up. And the Housing Benefit bill was also racking up – faster than any other welfare spending. Who was benefiting? Right to Buy homeowners turned private landlords, and investors who had bought up former social homes initially sold through the scheme to rent out. Right to Buy had become Right to Buy-to-let. In 2017, an investigation by *Inside Housing* revealed findings as inevitable as they were shocking. In Milton Keynes 70.9 per cent of Right to Buy properties had ended up in the hands of private landlords. In Brighton and Hove, Bolsover, Canterbury, Cheshire West and Chester, Stevenage and Nuneaton and Bedworth more than half of council properties sold through the scheme had fallen into private hands. And in London, more than 40 per cent of council homes sold under Right to Buy were being privately rented from landlords. Hundreds of private landlords now own five or more Right to Buy properties; they are hoarding them. It's good business.

This meant that the government was (and still is) paying significantly more in Housing Benefit that went straight into the pockets of private landlords than they would have if they had kept council properties in state ownership. This – the privatisation of renting – is costing us dear via the bill for Housing Benefit. The fact that spending on this one benefit has doubled since the early 2000s because of the social housing shortage and rising private rents ought to have been a 'very expensive canary in the coal mine' warning us about the extent of the housing crisis, as Paul Johnson of the Institute for Fiscal Studies put it in 2019.

Initially considered as beneficial to lower social classes because it helped them to move from renting to homeownership at a relatively low cost, gaining assets and increasing their wealth in the process, Right to Buy ended up enabling housing speculation because no safeguards were put in place to stop those homes becoming buy-to-lets. This could have been an easy fix. Instead, we now have a social housing shortage and people who would once have rented social housing live in the private rented sector where it's possible that their landlord is letting out an ex-local authority home. While social housing had been a national asset which generated income for the state, Housing Benefit is now a state subsidy to private landlords.

Local Housing Allowance (LHA) is the mechanism through which Housing Benefit (as delivered through Universal Credit) is calculated. In his 2010 austerity budget, the Chancellor of the Exchequer George Osborne announced that he would cut LHA from covering the lowest half of market rents in any given area to the lowest third. He also made it impossible for single people under thirty-five to get Housing Benefit for a place of their own. His reasoning was that this would encourage people to look for cheaper properties. The cut came into force in April 2011 and then, in April 2016, the government announced a four-year freeze in LHA. There was a fly in the ointment of Osborne's plan: rents kept rising, which, as we will see in the coming chapters, collided with social housing shortages harming mainly low-income renters and causing them to choose between eating and paying their rent or forcing them out of the places they knew as home. Osborne's thinking was back to front: none of these cuts reduced the amount that private renters had to pay their landlords, so what they did was take cash out of the pockets of renters.

If we follow the canary in the coal mine theory of Housing Benefit, this was its logical conclusion. The Scottish physiologist John Scott Haldane introduced the use of 'sentinel animals' – caged canaries and white mice – to test for gas leaks in coal mines in the late 1890s. An ailing or dead canary signalled the presence of dangerous levels of carbon monoxide or other gases meaning that workers needed to be evacuated. That state spending on Housing Benefit – because people couldn't afford their rent – had expanded so much by the late 2010s was an early warning sign that the private rental market was out of control and that both rising house prices and the social housing shortage were enabling it. Nobody understood this message, which was not that the state was spending too much on Housing Benefit, but rather that private rents were too expensive. If the benefits bill was the canary, coronavirus was the explosion it foretold. When the pandemic hit, a public health crisis exposed the fault lines of another: the housing crisis.

On 26 March 2020, the housing market was frozen by the government; buyers and sellers were urged not to move home or to hold viewings, and mortgage offers were extended in a bid to insulate house prices from incoming economic shocks. Homeowners and landlords were offered mortgage holidays. 'Nobody' would lose their home because of the pandemic, Robert Jenrick, the then Secretary of State for Housing, said. But private renters, a demographic who are less likely to have savings and more likely to be in unstable work than homeowners, were not cut so much slack. Their offering? The stop-start suspension of evictions (which initially ended in September 2020 and was brought back in the November when Anthony was evicted) and inadequate financial support.

George Osborne's cuts came back to bite us. In 2020 record numbers of people applied for Universal Credit – some of them probably considered themselves 'middle class' and did so for the first time – and too many found out just how paltry the available support really was. As part of its coronavirus support package, Boris Johnson's government unfroze LHA; it had to do this because it knew it didn't fully cover rents, but in many parts of the country this slight rise still didn't stretch far enough – and it certainly didn't restore the benefit to its pre-austerity levels, even though rents had risen since then. This mattered. In areas where there were high numbers of coronavirus cases, there were also high levels of unaffordable housing. At the time, the Joseph Rowntree Foundation (JRF), an independent charity which works to end poverty, found that private renters in these places – large areas of London such as Lambeth, Wandsworth, Westminster, Tower Hamlets, Hackney, the City of London, Kensington and Chelsea, Hammersmith and Fulham, Islington, Haringey and Camden, for example – faced significantly higher than average rents as well as higher than average rates of child poverty and temporary accommodation. The cap on LHA meant that renters in those areas who had, until then, just about managed their expensive rents would not be adequately protected if their self-employed or zero-hours income dropped due to sickness or they lost their job because of the economic turbulence – LHA, even with the pandemic increase, would still not cover even the cheapest rents in those areas. The extent to which successive governments had undone the welfare safety net was exposed as our society was tested by the exact type of event it was put in place to protect us against.

As an advisor who was at the Treasury when this decision was being made wrote to me, prefacing a WhatsApp message with the zipped-lips emoji: 'It could always have been better.' The Chancellor's support package made no mention of financial assistance for anyone who lost their job and fell into rent debt to their landlord as a result, but instead a flimsy suggestion that landlords – who could access mortgage holidays – should be 'flexible' and 'negotiate' with renters whose finances were damaged. That is how Anthony – like many others – found himself caught in the crosshairs of two social and economic disasters: a global pandemic and a housing emergency. If you do not own your own home in Britain, precarity is a fact of life. It comes in the form of rent rises, eviction notices and knowing that, ultimately, your landlord has control over the one place in the world you should feel safe.

## Banking on Housing

My grandparents, though they had the chance to, didn't buy their flat in South Norwood Hill through Right to Buy. This is partly because my grandad was then still a self-described communist who was ideologically opposed to the idea, and partly because my nan, a Conservative since she was young, wanted to buy a house the 'proper' way. Bluntly, it was probably the worst financial decision they ever made. The flat would have increased rapidly in value and, had they remortgaged it and become landlords, they probably wouldn't have had to work so hard throughout their lives. Today, you can buy a similar flat on South Norwood Hill on the open market for almost £300,000 or rent one privately for £1,300 a month. Mid-century former council flats like my grandparents' are now coveted because of their scarcity and, ironically, fetishised because of their municipal, utopian origins.

I am not immune to the appeal of all that. During the first lockdown, I scrolled the Instagram of a particularly trendy estate agent and clicked on a link to a brutalist building. It showed the details of a four-bedroom maisonette in the Dawson's Heights estate in East Dulwich, priced at just shy of half a million pounds – £499,000. This luxury, much sought-after flat was once social housing, part of a 300-apartment estate that sits on a hilltop in south London. It was designed by the Scottish architect Kate Macintosh when she was just twenty-eight years old and built between 1964 and 1972. The complex, which rises to twelve stories at its apex, is mesmerising; at first glance it looks like a self-contained concrete cliffside town, from another angle like an Italian hillside village and through squinted eyes a ziggurat. Macintosh designed bold buildings, but always with human benefit in mind. From afar, Dawson's Heights' soft silhouette signifies the inventive and revolutionary social housebuilding of a bygone era. Up close, it is intimate and intricated.

Macintosh's work, her vision, like my grandparents' flat, was once available to those not only on low but also on middle incomes. Now, commodified, it was being sold on the private market at a sum few could afford to mortgage themselves to pay. As I moved my thumb across the screen, I noticed that the estate agent in question had borrowed a quote from a philosopher I return to regularly for his human and poetic descriptions of home, Gaston Bachelard:

The house shelters day-dreaming, the house protects the dreamer, the house allows one to dream in peace.

But if they are unaffordable, houses are not places where people can dream, let alone live in peace.

We all need somewhere affordable to live, but it is our collective home – the state – which should provide for all eventualities. It took a global pandemic to remind us that human society is a delicate ecosystem: overcrowding spreads disease, bad housing makes people sick. Similarly, the slightest temperature rise in one corner of the housing market risks infecting other parts of the economy – how much we spend on housing dictates how much disposable income we have, how much we can save, how much we can borrow and how well we fare if we fall on hard times. In *The Road to Wigan Pier*, his 1937 examination of the living conditions of the working classes in Lancashire and Yorkshire, George Orwell warned that expensive, poor-quality, privately rented housing and low-paid, zero-hours work meant that we were 'living in a world in which nobody is free, in which hardly anybody is secure'. That could just as well have been written in 2020.

As the virus spread across the globe, Britain, like other capitalist economies, was turned inside out. Home ceased to be the centre of private life and became the locus of public policy, the frontline defence against the virus because 'stay at home' was the only way of preventing deaths. But home was not a safe place for everyone to be. We now know that poor housing likely led to deaths which could have been avoided (more on that in chapter 9). Historically, ruptures – pandemics, wars, revolutions – have encouraged humans to break with the past and reimagine their society. The coronavirus pandemic, wrote the Indian novelist and political campaigner Arundhati Roy, 'is no different. It is a portal, a gateway between one world and the next.' As lockdowns were imposed, all of us occupied a unique position. Janus-like, we were able to see forwards and backwards, assessing life before and after the rupture happened. In disaster, there is opportunity. In the pandemic, British politicians were given a historic once-in-a-generation chance to overhaul housing and homelessness. Would they take it?

# 2

# LIFE FOR RENT

### Peckham, London

*Council:* Southwark Council
*Average House Price:* In the year 2020/21 most property sales in Peckham were flats, selling for an average of £450,865. Terraced houses sold for an average of £828,957, with semi-detached homes fetching £1,097,110. Overall, sold prices in Peckham over the last year were 10 per cent up on the previous year.
*Average Private Rent:* In 2021 the average rent for a one-bedroom home was £1,394, for a two-bed it was £1,925, and for a three-bed it was £2,360.

—

It was the summer of 2017. Twenty-five-year-old Limarra's iPhone alarm went off at 4 a.m. She snoozed it for fifteen minutes, cocooning the covers around her body and savouring the womb-like safety of bed for just a little longer. At 4.30 the grace period was up. It was time to drop her 7-year-old daughter, Nevaeh, off at her grandma's (Limarra's mother still lived in the family home, just a few streets away in Peckham) so that she could take her to school later that morning. Limarra set off on the Overground train towards the City to start her job as a manager in a busy Starbucks where a revolving door of office workers and tourists kept staff making hot drinks all day long. She had big ambitions – your twenties are a becoming decade, for plotting your path for the rest of your life. Having a career was important; she had not one but two degrees, including a master's in business management and human resources (HR). Wanting to progress from management into HR, she was looking to move to a company where she could progress.

The day Limarra got the letter started like any other. She made her way towards London Bridge, looking out through the window at the glass and steel of the City rising above the clamouring morning commuters and thought about the future as the sun came up. Money was tight. After tax, she earned about £230 a week. She was renting a two-bedroom flat from a private landlord for £1,000 a month before bills – more than she was earning. Each month, her earnings were topped up by Housing Benefit, which helped, and it was worth stretching herself if it meant Nevaeh had her own bedroom. She wanted that for her daughter's development, for her sense of self. It was expensive, yes. But for Peckham, she knew it was a steal. Peckham was, is, her home and she was prepared to pay to stay there.

In the near-decade Limarra had been living in that flat – the only home she and her daughter had ever known together – rental prices in the area had shot up. According to research conducted by the estate agent Savills using Land Registry data, average house sale prices in Peckham increased by 45.7 per cent in the four years to April 2018 alone; local estate agents said this had been fuelled by the government's Help to Buy scheme and first-time buyers. One of the agents – Becky Munday, the managing director of the Peckham firm Munday's – explained in an interview in the *Financial Times* that in 2018 she had 'a tattoo artist looking with £900,000 in the bank'. Was this from tattooing? the paper asked. 'No,' she said, 'from Mum and Dad', before adding, 'We haven't sold a house to a family in a long time.' Peckham has been changed by this shift – gentrification, the process whereby a place is 'improved', often when wealthier people move in or private companies or local government (sometimes both) knock down old buildings and local people are displaced, is a double-edged sword like that. In 2017 Peckham was named the best place to live in London by the *Evening Standard*, which decided to sum up the area's story as the 'swift transformation of a crime-ridden, no-go patch of south London into a hipster rival to Dalston, and latterly a middle-class hotspot'. Limarra didn't quite see it like that; Peckham was just home, where her support network was. She'd never felt unsafe there. She had also never been to the rooftop cinema at the Bussey Building dubbed a 'must-visit' by the London paper.

For Limarra, the early morning Starbucks shifts were ideal. They might mean getting up at the crack of dawn, but they also meant she finished in time to pick Nevaeh up from school. On the day that everything changed – the day Limarra's life, as she puts it, 'sped up' – she got home and picked up her post from the communal hallway as usual. Expecting bills, she tore the envelopes open quickly so she wouldn't be late for school. One letter jolted her. It was worse than a surprise payment request from the water company. She sat down, holding it hard with both hands, reading it again and again. Slowly, the words sank in. Her landlord was asking her to leave: he wanted his property back in two months' time, as was his legal right under Section 21. When you rent privately your life can change any second, in an ordinary moment. You lack control and autonomy; someone else decides basic things like where you live, how long you will live there for and how much it costs. Just like that, on the whim of another, Limarra's life had plunged into uncertainty. Her plans, so carefully laid, derailed.

'The day that I got it,' Limarra said, 'I started Googling "eviction" and the first thing I thought was, "Oh wow, to get one of these you don't need to have done anything wrong." I was so confused. I cried and cried because I didn't understand why the landlord was doing it to us.' She had never met her landlord in person. She knew via the letting agent who managed the property that he owned several other homes in her building. During the time she had rented from him, his company's name had changed three times. Like so many renters, including Anthony, she had never heard of Section 21 of the Housing Act 1988 until it took away the roof over her head.

## The Return of the Rentier Class

It wasn't always this way. Remember Margaret Thatcher, ground zero. Everything Limarra experienced can be traced directly back to a piece of legislation introduced under her leadership. Like so many members of Generation Rent, the Housing Act 1988 is a millennial.

The 1988 act, brought in by Thatcher's environment secretary, Nicholas Ridley, was intended to boost the private rented sector where housing conditions were poor and there were few incentives for landlords to improve them. This was undoubtedly a problem that needed to be addressed, but Thatcher, who supported free market economics, believed in the social good of unfettered capitalism, which, she thought, bestowed liberty on people – so her approach was to give landlords more rights. That Thatcher turned to a policy solution that shored up landlords is no great surprise, given her zealous belief in the moral good of property ownership. 'If a Tory does not believe that private property is one of the main bulwarks of individual freedom,' she wrote in the *Daily Telegraph* in 1975, when she was leader of the opposition, 'then he had better become a socialist and have done with it.' What this meant for renters was less considered because, in her world, those who were hard-working and deserving would own property.

The act did three things which rebalanced the market, taking power away from tenants and giving it to landlords through deregulation. The first was the introduction of Section 21 'no-fault' evictions (probably the greatest erosion of a renter's stability). The second was doing away with rent control, which no political party in government has attempted to bring back. The third was scrapping lifetime tenancies, which had given people the right to live in their property until death (brought back in in Scotland in 2017) and introducing the unstable short-term tenancy agreements (or Assured Shorthold Tenancies (ASTs)) that most renters sign today. The idea was to make becoming a landlord a more commercially attractive prospect by giving landlords the right to charge whatever they wanted and to evict tenants whenever they wanted. If there were more landlords, the theory went, then renters would have more options to choose from. By encouraging landlords into competition with one another, it would make the market more competitive and would, by extension, push landlords to improve the quality of the housing they offered.

In reality, all of this only dramatically reduced the power and security of renters, which is why John Bryant, a policy leader at the National Housing Federation, described it as 'year zero' in an interview he gave to *Inside Housing*. The act was a seismic event and a catalyst for much of what has happened since.

Private renters were now less protected than they had been for decades, and the stage was set for the rise of the all-powerful buy-to-let landlord when high loan-to-income mortgages were introduced in the 1990s and 2000s. Of particular significance and hot on the heels of the Big Bang in 1986, new buy-to-let mortgages assessed buyers' creditworthiness on the rental yield for the property rather than on their existing income. The buy-to-let market became a public casino in which anyone with a deposit and a buy-to-let mortgage could gamble. It wasn't all Thatcher's fault: for a long time landlords were even able to claim mortgage interest relief; this wasn't scrapped until the late 2010s.

This easy access to credit gave landlords an advantage over first-time buyers when the financial crisis hit in 2008. The dynamic is now such that whenever house prices are seen as wobbly by lenders, banks tend to give mortgages more readily to people with bigger deposits (that is, landlords and investors). Providing investors with a direct credit line in this way has engendered a wealth-based class system consisting of two types of people: those who own property and those who do not. Today, there are about 2.5 million landlords in the UK. That makes them a small minority compared to the 11 million individuals renting privately, but they hold all the power. In 2017, 20.3 per cent of households in England alone rented from a private landlord. But because the market has been loaded in the landlords' favour, they were responsible for 18 per cent of all residential property purchases in 2019, making private renting (as opposed to social housing, as was previously briefly the case) the second-largest housing tenure after owner-occupier homeownership. In the years that followed Thatcher, landlords also received tax breaks: alongside mortgage interest relief there was even a wear-and-tear allowance to repair any damage to their properties. Some of that relief has since been clawed back in an attempt to even things out. This has stalled the growth of the private rented sector, but the impact on British society and our economy is deep set. We have witnessed what the French economist Thomas Piketty describes in his 2013 book *Capital in the Twenty-First Century* as the return of rentier capitalism. This is a system in which one class monopolises access to any kind of property and resources and gains significant amounts of profit from that without properly contributing to society. It's a lot like feudalism. In Britain, it has given birth to a new wealth-based class system in which the ownership of housing is a key decider of someone's freedom: their social status, their spending power and their social mobility.

This shift has turned private landlords – many of whom are individuals with no formal qualifications in social work, safeguarding or health and safety – into key housing providers. The problem is that their interests – maintaining an income and, ideally, making a profit – do not align with the needs of renters like Anthony or Limarra: stability and security.

The situation we are in is neither accidental nor coincidental. Thatcher is famously quoted as saying that 'there's no such thing as society', but it is rarely referenced in context. 'They,' she said of people who, for whatever reason, faced hard times, 'are casting their problems at society. And, you know, there's no such thing as society. There are individual men and women and there are families. And no government can do anything except through people, and people must look after themselves first. It is our duty to look after ourselves and then, also, to look after our neighbours.' This individualistic ideology of self-reliance directly shaped her government's housing policy. Today's private rented sector is built on the foundations of Thatcher's doctrine; exploitation and inequality are baked into it because the operating logic of those capitalist 'freedoms' is not to ensure that everyone is free. Rather, it is the justification of the freedom – through material benefit – of some people (property owners) at the expense of others (their tenants). Thatcher claimed that her convictions were 'based not on some economics theory' which understood or explained the housing market but, instead, on seemingly sensible maxims which give off an air of logic such as 'an honest day's work for an honest day's pay', 'living within your means' and 'paying your bills on time'. Like motivational Instagram aphorisms, these slogans sound good. You want to like them, but, on closer inspection, they fall apart. As Limarra's case shows, you can do all these things and still struggle because our housing market doesn't behave rationally: house prices rise faster than wages; and houses earn more money than many people in work.

Since 1996, average house prices have risen by an extraordinary 281 per cent across the UK, while in London the figure is 501 per cent, according to the Nationwide house price index. In 2015, it was reported by the lender Landbay that buy-to-let landlords were earning returns of almost 1,400 per cent since 1996, leaving the returns on more traditional investments – shares and bonds, or savings accounts – looking measly compared to homes. It was called a housing 'boom', but private renters didn't benefit. In 2019, the consultancy firm PricewaterhouseCoopers found that private rents were unaffordable for workers on average wages in London, the south-east, the south-west and the east. Its report was followed by the annual English Housing Survey, which found that 29 per cent of people were finding it difficult to pay their rent. Of those who could afford their rent, 63 per cent could not afford to save at all and just 1 in 10 had more than £16,000 in the bank. Hardly freedom. Hardly choice.

It is worth noting that, despite Thatcher's insistence that her views had not come from 'some' economic theory, she actually got these ideas from the work of an Austrian-British economist who was classically liberal and vehemently opposed to socialism: Friedrich Hayek. He believed that social justice was a 'mirage', that state regulation was the enemy of competition and, therefore, of freedom of choice. There is a famous anecdote that during a Conservative Party policy meeting, Thatcher removed her copy of Hayek's *Constitution of Liberty* from her handbag, slammed it down on the table and declared, 'This is what we believe.' When people talk about neoliberalism, this is what they are referring to: the twentieth-century resurgence of the sort of nineteenth-century ideas which had originally been used to argue against implementing a welfare state, now being used to defend its deconstruction. Thatcher was convinced of her creed: 'personal freedom and economic freedom are indivisible,' she said; the market should rule, the state should recede. But her logic doesn't quite track. Capitalism is defined in the *Cambridge Dictionary* as 'an economic and political system in which property, business, and industry are controlled by private owners, rather than by the state', with the purpose of making a profit, but democratic socialism is 'a set of political beliefs and principles supporting equal opportunities for everyone, under a fairly elected parliament'. Which of these sounds like it privileges personal liberty?

Limarra's is a story in which the economic freedom of private landlords comes at the expense of the personal freedom of renters. Would freedom, for Limarra, not look like being able to choose how long she wants to stay in her home?

### 'Intentionally Homeless'

It was only when she Googled to find out what her rights were that Limarra discovered how few she had. She went to her local council, Southwark, to find out what would happen next. 'The guy at the council asked me, first off, am I in rent arrears? I said no. I never had been. I always paid my rent on time,' she remembered. 'He was, like, so why does the landlord want the property back? I was, like, well, he just said that he wants it back, I think he's selling it. Then the council told me I'm not actually homeless until the landlord gets possession from the courts so there was nothing they could do.'

Technically, as she was at risk of imminent homelessness (defined as within eight weeks), she should have been offered more help, but Limarra didn't know that. According to the housing officer she wasn't 'homeless enough', yet. He told her to call back once she had received the possession order (a court instruction which a landlord must apply for to complete an eviction).

'I went home. What else could I do?' she told me, shaking her head. 'One minute everything is fine and the next minute you feel completely powerless. I called my landlord. I wanted to know if there was anything, anything at all I could do to change his mind, because I'd been living in my house for nearly eight years since I had my daughter at seventeen. It was near her school; I couldn't even contemplate having to move her from there.' Limarra's landlord wouldn't budge. In fact, he would barely speak to her. Reading between the lines (the lines being that he was doing up other properties he owned in the same block), it seemed he was ready to cash in on Peckham's new status as 'an investment hotspot'. 'I guess it wasn't his problem,' Limarra said, her eyes flicking to the floor. 'He wants to make money ... that's why he's a landlord, right?'

As Limarra awaited her eviction, building works elsewhere in her block disturbed a nest of mice. 'Mice started coming. Mice were literally running through the property all the time, jumping out from underneath the cooker,' she said. 'My landlord didn't care. I think he must have thought, "Oh, maybe she'll leave now that there's mice there," but if I had left – which, believe me, I wanted to do – I was told by the council that I would have been making myself "intentionally homeless", which would have ruled me out of any support. So I had to stay put and wait to be evicted. I just had to put some traps down and get on with it. Nevaeh was terrified.'

You make yourself 'intentionally homeless' if the council decides it's your fault that you have nowhere to live. This may be because you have been served with an eviction notice and choose to leave before you are kicked out. Or it can happen if you refuse a housing offer which the council deems suitable, whether that's for social housing, a privately rented property or temporary accommodation. In the current climate, with a dearth of social housing, the legal position of stretched local authorities which, every day, find themselves over a barrel is 'take it or leave it'.

In the context of the instability of the private rented sector, the notion of 'intentionality' in homelessness is pernicious. In this, England differs from Wales, where the concept doesn't exist, and Scotland, where it is much fairer. Dr Kesia Reeve, an expert in motherhood and homelessness and a principal research fellow at Sheffield Hallam University, told me that it is 'a ridiculous idea' which should be done away with right away.

'The concept of intentionality is too elastic,' she explained. 'It's often used when people fall into rent arrears, too. And, as we all know, there are many reasons why people get behind on their rent. The concept of "intentionality" in homelessness legislation is problematic, full stop, particularly for women. Nobody makes themselves intentionally homeless.' As she and many other homelessness sector experts see it, the idea of making yourself intentionally homeless is outdated and dangerous. 'It is now being used to ration housing,' she added unequivocally. 'The intentionality clause just punishes people for having had some difficulties in their lives. And this is where women and mothers come in – our research shows that they are often intensely vulnerable. Domestic violence is often involved, as is other trauma.'

## Renting in Relative Poverty

Limarra was determined to stay in Peckham. How could she move away from her mum, her only affordable childcare provider? From everyone she knew? With help from the council unforthcoming, she started to look on Zoopla and Rightmove. 'In the time I'd been renting, minding my own business, the price for a two-bedroom flat in the area had gone up so much. I was looking at at least £1,300 to £1,400 a month.' Even with her Housing Benefit top-up, there was no way she could afford an extra £300 to £400 a month.

Limarra was not eligible for help until she was made legally homeless by a bailiff, so she called the courts constantly, ringing almost every day to find out how long she would be tortured like this. She had done everything right. She had done what she was supposed to do: dutifully got into debt to do a degree and then more debt to do a master's, worked to support her daughter. She paid her rent on time. Poverty has been othered by programmes such as Channel 4's *Benefits Street* (2014) and Channel 5's *The Nightmare Neighbour Next Door* (also 2014). We don't associate the word poverty with people who work, take their children to school every day and pay their bills on time. This is, in no small part, because those TV shows traded on the shock factor of implied questions such as 'Why do poor people have big TVs?!' and, in doing so, caricatured and sensationalised low-income life. Television news itself has been no better. In 2012, the BBC's flagship current affairs programme *Newsnight* was forced to issue an apology after then presenter Allegra Stratton (who went on to be Boris Johnson's press secretary) conducted a controversial interview with a young single mother which included harmful stereotypes on the show.

Stratton asked Shanene Thorpe from Tower Hamlets whether claiming Housing Benefit was a 'lifestyle choice' and said, 'Don't you think you should have possibly lived at home until the point at which you could support your own house?' The implication appeared to be that Shanene was a scrounger. These value judgements seemed not only to be embedded in the report, but Stratton and *Newsnight* also neglected to mention house prices and rent costs and failed to make it clear that Shanene was in work.

Writing in the *Guardian* after the segment aired on *Newsnight*, Shanene said, 'I am forced to claim benefits despite the fact I am in work because rent is so high in my borough, as it is across most of London.' She added that she felt 'judged and victimised'. The stigma, perpetuated by that *Newsnight* segment about those who cannot afford to buy homes of their own, or indeed pay expensive rents, was demeaning and disingenuous benefit bashing which attacked the symptoms of the housing crisis – young people unable to support themselves or their families and rising benefits bills – but failed to address its causes: unregulated rents, a shortage of social housing and house price inflation.

Shanene's situation, like Limarra's, is what poverty looks like in a world where essentials – like housing – are unstable and unaffordable.

In this country, the less you have, the more you pay for the basics. It's not only cheaper to have a mortgage than it is to rent, it's cheaper to borrow money if you own a home and easier to plan ahead, which, in the long run, saves you money on bills and food. The idea of a poverty premium, the idea that people on low incomes pay more for essential goods and services, was explored properly for the first time by researchers at Bristol University in 2016. They estimated that the average annual poverty premium per low-income household is £490.

And we know that the number of people in poverty in the UK is substantial. More than 1 in 5 (22 per cent) live in poverty in our country – 14.5 million people. Of these, 8.1 million are working-age adults, 4.3 million are children and 2.1 million are pensioners, according to the JRF. They are in what's known as 'relative poverty', meaning they struggle after paying housing costs. For this group, for people like Limarra, it doesn't take much to turn a precarious situation into a disastrous one. The JRF warns that two key drivers of poverty are housing costs and inflation. It estimates that both will worsen in years to come, which could increase the need for state support. At the end of 2011, the total number of private renting Housing Benefit claimants in England was 1.4 million. In Wales it was 82,000 and in Scotland 93,000. This decreased slightly in 2016 to 1.2 million in England, 76,000 in Wales and 84,000 in Scotland. But during the pandemic the number of private renters claiming Universal Credit soared from 749,000 in 2020 to 1,549,000 in February 2021 – that's an increase of 800,000 and more than 100 per cent, according to the Department for Work and Pensions' own data. If interest rates rise, increasing the cost of mortgages, and rents keep going up, this number could well rise, too.

But though it is neither a rare nor a remote experience, it's not only the media which is hostile to people who need state support in Britain. Landlords openly discriminate, too; they know that Housing Benefit doesn't always cover rent. 'I started ringing up estate agents to explain to them that I work full time, I just get my rent propped up by Housing Benefit,' Limarra told me. 'But I kept being told off the bat, "No DSS, no Housing Benefit." They didn't even want to hear me out. I could tell some of them weren't happy that I had a child, either. I guess they have to watch themselves if there are kids involved. I felt so desperate.' It's an old British tradition: landlords turning away single mothers and those receiving benefits. DSS stands for the Department of Social Security, which was a governmental agency from 1988 to 2001. Today we have the Department for Work and Pensions (DWP) and it is unlawful to discriminate against renters who receive state support under the Equality Act 2010, according to a landmark court case brought by Shelter at York County Court in July 2020 (too late to have an impact on Limarra's case). However, it still happens. There is one online letting agent which asks renters whether they will be 'using housing benefits/DSS to pay rent' and then calculates whether the LHA rates in that area will be enough to cover it. If not, it advises them not to submit their enquiry. Added to the stigma of being 'on benefits', other prejudices are created in our racist, classist, patriarchal society. Did these also come into play for Limarra, as a young Black woman and a single mother?

Almost definitely. Just as it does for the many mothers who are also migrant workers from eastern Europe and find themselves housed in tiny box rooms in converted office blocks when they become homeless. Women experience inequality acutely in relation to housing. There is a gender housing gap in Britain. The majority of people recorded as sleeping rough are men (86 per cent), but two-thirds (67 per cent) of all statutory homeless people – of whom Limarra was one – are lone women or women with dependent children. This, of course, intersects with domestic abuse. And as the Women's Budget Group found when it looked at data from the ONS, because women earn less on average than men, in 2019 there was absolutely nowhere in the country where it was affordable for a single woman on an average salary to buy or rent a home. The data also showed that, when it comes to buying a house with a typical mortgage, women's incomes fall more than 50 per cent short of what's needed in every part of the country apart from the north-east, the north-west and Yorkshire and Humber, where property was, at the time of their analysis, slightly cheaper.

Added to that, Britain's housing market has a long history of insidious racism. This is because the housing market is an extension of our political system and economy which have, over time, been designed to privilege some people above others. A 2016 study conducted by the Human City Institute found that the level of what experts call 'housing stress' is much higher in Black, Asian and minority ethnic communities than it is among white people. At the same time, homelessness has jumped in the past two decades within these communities in comparison to the rest of the population. According to government data, Black people are disproportionately affected by homelessness, with 1 in 23 Black households becoming homeless or threatened with homelessness, against 1 in 83 households from all other ethnicities combined. Of those homeless people applying for help, 11 per cent are Black, even though Black people make up only 3 per cent of all households in England. It is crucial to join the dots between race, class and wealth, as doing so busts wide open myths about who is 'hard-working' or 'deserving' of support.

As the clock ticked down, Limarra crumbled. It was almost Christmas. Nevaeh had turned eight. Limarra hadn't told her what was going on, as she feared the disruption would cause her anxiety. All she could do was wait and wait. Her choice, her freedom and her power had been taken away from her. Limarra loves Christmas but she didn't really celebrate that year. It came and went and nothing had changed. She was starting to feel trapped, claustrophobic; the flat she had once felt at home in had turned into purgatory. She couldn't leave because leaving would mean forfeiting the little support she would be given. She still didn't really understand the eviction process, but she knew that she had to wait to be evicted and thus made officially homeless to avoid any accusation that she had made herself intentionally homeless. At the start of 2018, Limarra went back to the council for help. 'They told me that I should sort myself out in the private sector because there's "no such thing as social housing now",' she told me, still in disbelief. In fairness, at least the council worker who told her this wasn't wrong: their latest estimate puts Southwark's social housing waiting list at over 16,500 people. Half of these are families including children. 'I was so scared,' Limarra said of that time. 'I started feeling very suicidal.'

### Not Homeless Enough

In early January Limarra was signed off work with severe anxiety and depression. She was forced to take nearly three months out from the career she loved and had worked so hard to forge because the endless 'not knowing' was affecting her mental health. 'I felt like a failure to Nevaeh,' she told me. 'I felt really embarrassed about my situation. I felt ashamed to go to the doctors because I felt like I'd done something wrong. Ashamed to tell people what I was going through. You just start thinking it's your fault, don't you? When even the council obviously doesn't want to help, you feel worthless.' Months passed, nothing changed apart from the seasons. By spring 2018, Limarra, who was about to turn twenty-six, was still in her flat, waiting to be evicted. Her new boyfriend was so concerned, he booked and paid for a holiday to Bali and arranged for Nevaeh to stay with her grandmother.

Home is the centre of your life, and when that centre cannot hold, everything falls apart. New research conducted by psychologists at the

University of Granada in Spain has, unsurprisingly, shown that people who have been evicted from their homes suffer very high levels of anxiety and depression. More than this, the research team found that there is a high incidence of post-traumatic stress disorder in individuals who have been subjected to eviction. There is further evidence to back this up: in 2016, research conducted in Sweden found that people facing eviction were more likely to attempt suicide than the rest of the population. Halfway around the world in Bali, Limarra was drowning in anxiety. 'I couldn't really enjoy myself,' she remembered. 'All I could think was, "When I come back, I might not have a home."' A few days after she got back, she took an overdose. In less than a year, her state of mind had changed so much that she now wanted to end her life – and all because her home, the one place in which she should have felt safe, was being taken away from her.

In 1960, the Scottish psychiatrist R. D. Laing established a new way of thinking about mental health. He described the experience of 'ontological security' as one in which 'the ordinary circumstances of life do not afford a perpetual threat to one's own existence'. If something is ontological, it concerns the very nature of being. Anything that is a threat to our ontological security is existential, it creates the feeling of being constantly in danger, under siege.

Ontological insecurity, then, which Laing described as a condition in which 'the ordinary circumstances of everyday life constitute a continual and deadly threat', is experienced by private renters because every aspect of their stability relies on a landlord. Home is meant to shield you, to provide you with sanctuary. If you are a homeowner, your house is a bulwark against the chaos of the world outside, but as a renter it is somewhere where you are actually *more* vulnerable to external forces than anywhere else because, ultimately, your landlord controls how much it will cost you, whether you can hang pictures on the wall, how long you can live there and, in some cases, depending on your contract, even whether you can turn the heating up – but, most fundamentally, whether you can stay there at all. It is no coincidence that today people with mental health conditions are one and a half times more likely to live in privately rented accommodation than in other forms of housing. Denying private renters autonomy and stability by shoring up the freedoms and power of landlords is having an immeasurable human cost. But what if we are only just beginning to understand the true impact of that?

The court possession order finally arrived just as Limarra was released from hospital. It was now May. June rolled around, Limarra got a new job at a nearby Nando's, which meant a later start because she wasn't sure where she would be living and was worried about commute times. Finally, she had the piece of paper she needed to access support – a signed eviction warrant. Even if it wasn't welcome, at least it provided finality and certainty and, crucially, served as a permit for accessing state support.

### Where Now?

There is a key scene in Ken Loach's 1966 film for the BBC about homelessness, *Cathy Come Home*, where Cathy and Reg (the young couple who become homeless after Reg suffers an accident and loses his well-paying job and Cathy becomes pregnant) are being evicted. On the day of their eviction, like Anthony, they barricade themselves in. Bailiffs beat the door down and throw their belongings into the street in front of a crowd. It is a relentless and rolling story of a family being demolished by housing instability, of a descent into destitution punctuated by landlords who won't rent to a woman with a young child and a system which was supposed to help them but did not. The film has, in the years that have followed, become a symbol of the treatment of homeless people all over the country. Over fifty years later, Limarra's story bore a striking resemblance to Cathy's. Limarra still didn't know when her eviction would be, she was being left hanging. You are supposed to be given help if you are within eight weeks of eviction, but Limarra was left right down to the wire because it took time for her Section 21 to be processed, which in turn delayed her access to support. An administrative error held everything up.

Limarra was evicted on Monday 18 June 2018 – her little sister's birthday. She took a day off work to be thrown out of her home. It was a warm morning; London was experiencing a heatwave. She never thought she'd be excited to see bailiffs but, like Charon, the ferryman of

Hades, they could at least move her from one unpleasant waiting room to another.

It was over in less than two minutes. Everything Limarra owned in the world was in a van that she was paying for by the hour. 'I had no idea removal services cost so much,' she joked later, aware that there's nothing funny about what happened next. Limarra got into her car and drove to the council offices. She didn't know how long she'd have to wait to be seen when she got there, and, like Anthony, she didn't know where she would be sleeping that night. Waiting, again, all she could think of was that she was grateful that at least Nevaeh was with her dad; that she couldn't see what was going on.

Her homelessness application was taken and accepted that day. 'OK – now you are homeless,' a housing officer said – words she hoped she'd never hear but which actually brought relief. She was told that the 'placement team' would house her and Nevaeh in temporary accommodation while they were on the waiting list for social housing, but there was a catch – she would have no say as to where that would be.

'I couldn't quite believe it,' Limarra said later when she revisited the experience. 'I stressed to them that Nevaeh's school was in Peckham, that my mum was in Peckham. I don't think they cared, to be honest.' Dystopian fiction is trending right now. Well, I challenge you to find a more dystopian story than this. Limarra was told to go back to the waiting room. She was there for 'somewhere between three and four hours'; her belongings still outside with the removal guys, their fee steadily going up.

Finally, news of her fate came. 'A lady placement officer came and said, "Oh, we only have two properties for you to live in that are suitable. One is in Redbridge" – which when I Googled is basically in Essex – "and the other one is in Croydon." I literally said to her, "I can't live in Croydon," because I was still seeing the community mental health team in Peckham twice a week at that point. She told me that if I didn't accept the property in Croydon – the closest one – I'd be making myself intentionally homeless and forfeit my right to support.'

There's that phrase again: intentionally homeless.

Limarra broke down in tears. She asked how she was supposed to get to work or take her daughter to school if she took the temporary accommodation rented from a private landlord in Croydon. The placement officer told her to 'get up earlier'. With nowhere else to go and backed into a corner by the consequences that would follow refusing either of the properties offered, Limarra decided to go with the Croydon flat at £175 a week. She called the social worker who had been allocated to her after she tried to end her life to let her know what was going on. The social worker called the council to explain that this was an unviable solution, that Limarra needed to be near her family, her support and the mental health team. It made no difference.

'I remember sitting there in shock. The lady from the council printed out the tenancy agreement. She asked me to sign it. I hadn't even seen the place and it was all happening so quickly, but I knew if I didn't that I'd be forfeiting.'

Kesia Reeve made an important point about the intentionality clause in homelessness legislation when we spoke. She believes that it is retraumatising people who are already experiencing trauma – because they have been evicted, lost a job or been forced to flee their home for any number of reasons. 'To me it is a social injustice,' she explained. 'This applies to all people who become homeless and have to deal with a local authority, but, when it comes to women, the system is punishing a particularly vulnerable group of people when they are at their lowest.'

'I'll never forget it,' Limarra told me, visibly shaking. When she got to Croydon, she found that her new 'home' was a small room with a dirty divan mattress where the cooker was basically the bedside table. In the corner there was what looked like a cupboard, but it was the shower.

Temporary accommodation is a racket. You could call it a lucrative cottage industry that has sprung up in place of social housing to cash in on the precarity of the private rented sector. In 2019, a Freedom of Information investigation by the *Observer* found that councils in England's top fifty homeless blackspots had paid the 156 largest private providers of temporary accommodation in those areas more than £215 million in the previous financial year alone. On average these firms received £10,000 of public money for each booking. Temporary accommodation is rarely decent. Some of the most successful business models are built on the worst types of emergency accommodation, such as B&Bs, where families might share bathrooms and cooking facilities with vulnerable adults, and self-contained studios, where whole families are sometimes housed in one room together.

Perversely, though, Limarra had been lucky: she had somewhere to stay that night. She did her best to stick it out, turning the words 'intentionally homeless' over in her mind as she tried to sleep. She lasted a week. The tears wouldn't stop coming. She called the council, who offered her an emergency hostel closer to her old home and her family, in Camberwell. It was now July. Almost a full year since her torment had begun. Once you enter this system, things can go from bad to worse. 'My life just sped up,' Limarra said. She arrived at the hostel, which had thirty-eight rooms and more than forty people living in it. It may have been closer to her family and mental health support team, but it was no move up. With no working kitchen, Limarra couldn't make food for Nevaeh or herself. The only saving grace was that she was able to bring food home from work because of her job at Nando's.

'I was told it could be years before we're moved up the waiting list to get something permanent,' Limarra said. Most of her belongings were in storage (which speaks to the fact that being evicted is costly for the person who has been turfed out), so the sparse, soulless room contained only the essentials, a few black bin bags full of clothes, standard-issue bunk beds and a mini fridge. 'I remember one of the other girls actually telling me she thought my room was nice because it was bigger than hers. I just couldn't believe we were living somewhere with a shared bathroom, which had those push-button showers that run out after a certain amount of time. You had to go down the corridor to shower and use the loo. How is that suitable for a young child?'

Limarra had shielded Nevaeh from their situation for as long as possible, but this place began to have an impact on her daughter. Nevaeh started wetting the bed. 'She didn't want to go out of the room, down the hall and use the toilet where there were so many strangers,' Limarra told me. 'And, do you know what angers me the most, to live in that hostel was costing more than some people's mortgages. My own money and my Housing Benefit were going towards the £996 a month to live somewhere totally disgusting! It's mad!'

Housing displacement shapes young children in serious ways. It's something that concerns every single one of the housing researchers I speak to regularly. Dr Kim McKee, a senior lecturer in social policy and housing at the University of Stirling, told me in no uncertain terms that 'being forced to move at every contractual break undermines people's sense of belonging and attachment to place. For families with children, the constant churning between properties is especially disruptive to schooling and family and friendship networks that often provide important informal sources of support.' There has, so far, McKee also noted, been very little large-scale exploration of the emotional fallout of this crisis in private renting. She calls it a 'research gap' and, if it is ever closed, it will surely bring shame on our country.

Work became Limarra's solace. 'It was my escape,' she said. 'But I reached breaking point when they messed up my Housing Benefit and I couldn't afford the hostel. It was so expensive, and I was having to pay for storage for all of my furniture on top.' She kept asking the council if she was eligible for more help. They told her no. Why? Because she was earning too much.

'I remember the guy telling me it wasn't his fault that I "had too much pride" to drop my hours,' she said, throwing her arms up in the air. 'I was, like, NO, sorry. It's not that I've got a lot of pride, it's just not going to happen. I didn't go and educate myself to now go and sit on benefits and share a shower.' Just as she had not been homeless enough to get help, she was now working too much to get support.

In September 2018, Limarra moved back in with her mum. It was the only thing that made any sense. Her mother doesn't have a spare room, so Limarra and Nevaeh were sleeping in the living room, like at least 68,000 other homeless sofa-surfers nationally. This is how hidden homelessness is concealed in plain sight. Waiting, dwelling in uncertainty, has become Limarra's normal state of being. Throughout our meeting, she would trail off when recalling that time, looking out of the window. She clutched a cushion to her stomach and didn't let go until she got up to show me out.

It is a journalist's job to hold space for people's stories, that means bearing witness to traumatic events and recording them. No matter how much we might want to step in and help, we are trained not to. It was only when I played the recording of our chat back to commit Limarra's story to the page for this book that I was able to process it properly. I bristled with anger. I cried. I am not, I am afraid, an unbiased conduit for her story. This cannot, just cannot be how we treat people in Britain. To have your security and sanctuary taken from you is rupturing. Then to be treated as Limarra was by the very people who were supposed to help her is nothing short of Kafkaesque, a farcical real-life 'computer says no' situation brought about by a system that is overloaded and short-circuiting.

As I was about to leave, Limarra's mother called us into the kitchen. She was cooking up a storm with about five different pots on the boil. They all smelled incredible. What did she think about all of this? I asked. 'I'm furious, to be honest,' she said, stirring a bubbling goat curry which was shortly going to be packaged up and delivered around the corner to her own mother, Limarra's grandmother, who wasn't well.

'I can't even really talk about it or get my head around it,' she added, taking her frustration out with the wooden spoon, stirring vigorously. 'It's shameful. What have we become?'

# 3

# THE PROBLEM WITH GENERATION RENT

**Coggeshall, Essex**

*Council:* Braintree District Council
*Average House Price:* In the year 2020/21 the majority of sales
in Coggeshall were detached houses, selling for an average of
£563,675. Semi-detached houses sold for an average of £437,733,
with terraced homes fetching £388,500. Overall, sold prices in
Coggeshall over that year were 21 per cent up on the previous year.
*Average Private Rent:* In 2021 the average rent for a one-bedroom
home was £790. There were no two- or three-beds listed at the
time of writing.

—

It was 6 a.m. in the spring of 2019 and Tony woke up. He wasn't sleeping much; it was usually at least 2 a.m. before his mind finally quietened enough to drift off. Tony, 66, a retired salesman, went downstairs in the listed cottage he was renting in Coggeshall. This small and picturesque town sits between Braintree and Colchester. It is full of historic mediaeval and Tudor buildings, picture-postcard pubs and period properties painted in pastel colours. Tony had lived in this area for twenty years, but didn't know how much longer he would be able to stay. He put the kettle on for his morning tea, adding first milk, then water. As he sank into the sofa, the warm cup in his hands, his 13-year-old rescue dog, Rebel, plonked herself next to him. She was arthritic, but that didn't stop her demanding a walk after she had had her breakfast. Tony would usually have some muesli for his breakfast – fry-ups were only allowed for special occasions – but that day, with his stomach in knots, he couldn't face it. His mind wandered. He would soon be made homeless; in a month's time he would be living who-knows-where – because he was being evicted, again. This would his fifth eviction in just over a decade. Each time it was because he had been evicted via Section 21 of the Housing Act 1988, his later life punctuated by the abrupt and bellicose endings of 'no-fault' evictions.

Tony has four children. His eldest daughter was then forty, his youngest was twenty-two. He also has four grandchildren, three boys and one girl – he brims with pride whenever he speaks about them, as grandads do. Tony had rented privately since his divorce more than thirty-five years ago; after he and his wife separated he could never afford to buy a property, but because he had always been earning, he never quite qualified for social housing. Then, eighteen years ago, he had a breakdown after his partner died from breast cancer. At that point, his two youngest children went to live with their maternal grandmother. It had taken him a while to get his life back on track, grief seeps into everything – life falls apart and has to be put back together again – and just when he finally felt as if he had managed to, this latest eviction notice arrived in January 2018, throwing everything into disarray once again.

Tony remembers every home he has ever rented. There was a place in Braintree. Two years. The landlord wanted it back. Then there was his first cottage in Coggeshall. Three years. The landlord decided to sell. On to another place in Coggeshall. Two years and one month. That landlord also decided to sell. Tony got lucky that time, the owner had another cottage nearby and agreed to transfer his deposit over. That place was in bad shape when he moved in: there were no kitchen units (he fitted his own); the sink in the bathroom and the bath leaked; everything was mouldy. The landlord did eventually sort some of it out, but the rest he did himself with the landlord's permission. He made so many improvements to that one it really did feel as if it was his home. Of course, it wasn't. Six years and ten months there. The landlord's company went into liquidation. Tony was evicted by the new landlord. He never got his deposit back.

Change can be good, and it can be dislocating. Disruption had become Tony's normal; he could have done without it but he coped, absorbing the shocks, getting past them. That's what people do. They think, 'It could always be worse' as they face down events that are objectively difficult to deal with. This eviction was different. Tony was older and, because rents in the area had been rising steadily beyond what his pension, savings and benefits top-up could stretch to, he was struggling to find anywhere else that he could afford. As in Peckham, there was a social housing shortage in Essex. In nearby Colchester, the average rental cost of a two-bedroom home increased by 17 per cent between 2011 and 2017 – while the growth in household income rose by just 4 per cent. He felt squeezed, and not only by his rent. It had begun to feel as if everything was more expensive. He wasn't imagining it. The same factors that had diminished Limarra's life choices in London were impacting Tony in Essex. Over the past decade, living costs for poorer households in Britain have increased faster than for those who are better off.

'Coggeshall is a lovely place,' Tony told me. 'I thought I'd hit the jackpot when I moved into this cottage. The rent was £600 a month – for a whole house. There was nothing not to like. It was idyllic.' The cottage, from which he was now being evicted, is surrounded by landscaped grounds complete with an arboretum on an estate owned by a charitable trust. He moved in in May 2015. 'This was it,' he thought. Where else would he find a home like this that he could afford? But, now, he was being turfed out – the trust needed his home as part of a wedding venue they ran on the estate – and he couldn't afford to rent privately in the surrounding area. In the forty years he'd lived in Essex, Tony had been priced out. That's why he woke in anguish.

Every night, he scrolled through Rightmove and Zoopla for properties to rent. Which only confirmed that he could afford absolutely nothing in the area he had lived in for most of his life. He wanted to stay there; it was where his children were, where his friends were.

Not only could Tony not afford any of the privately rented properties he was viewing online, he was struggling to find one that accepted dogs.

The ones that did wanted to charge extra for Rebel. Private landlords are completely within their rights to do this; they have the right to refuse renters with pets and, though they can't request a larger deposit for them, they can up the rent. But this was yet another factor that made him feel like a second-class citizen, systematically discriminated against by rules intended to favour landlords and homeowners. Rebel was his lifeline. She saved him from ruin, he believes. If it hadn't been for her, he is not sure he'd still be here. She gave him something to care for, to get up and out for when everything felt hopeless. Living without her was unfathomable.

Before bed, Tony also checked his council portal to see if any of his bids on social properties had been accepted. They hadn't. A single older male in good health, Tony was not considered a 'priority need'. Besides, the average waiting time for his band, for a one-bedroom bungalow, was 20.5 months. The length of time a person has to wait for social housing and the way housing needs are calculated varies for each local authority. The volume of housing available is a huge deciding factor, but, generally, people living in unsanitary or overcrowded housing are given priority, along with those who have to move for medical or welfare reasons and those who need to be near specialist medical or educational facilities.

It was April 2019 now. Tony had been living under the threat of eviction for over a year. Like Limarra, he had faced a long and drawn-out period of uncertainty and worry – purgatory. Although, as mentioned previously, a landlord does not need a reason to issue a Section 21 notice, Tony believed that his landlord did have one: he had complained about noise coming from the wedding venue within earshot of his cottage where celebrations continued into the night. 'Easier to get me out, isn't it,' he told me, 'but they'd better not think I'm going without a fight.' One of the reasons that Section 21 is supposed to be being abolished is because it can be – and is – used in this way to get rid of renters who make valid complaints. But even if Section 21 is overturned, organisations such as Safer Renting, which works across ten London boroughs supporting people at risk of illegal eviction, warn that rogue landlords will still find a way to pull the plug on tenancies which become 'hard work'. What is a rent hike beyond what the tenant can pay if not an eviction by proxy?

Tony's landlord was no reprobate, and nor was it one of those faceless international plutocrats who own huge blocks of flats or, in some places, entire streets that we often like to imagine are responsible for our crisis in housing. It was a local charity.

Tony felt as if he was going mad, being gaslit. After the eviction notice was served, he found piles of rubbish at the end of his garden – broken fridges, waste food and leftover cooking oil from the estate's wedding venue. He complained again, not just because it was so unsightly but because he was worried about rats. He was stonewalled, which made him feel deliberately unwelcome on the estate. The trust had even started to say that he had failed to keep the property in good repair, which was simply not true. 'I guess I made myself a nuisance,' he told me, 'by pointing out what my rights were.'

The toll all of this took on Tony was severe. He felt harried – pressured, harassed and depressed. His moods became uncontrollable. At the urging of his youngest daughter, he went to the doctor, who diagnosed him with depression, anxiety and high blood pressure. He had to take sleeping pills, anti-depressants and statins for his blood pressure. The doctor also recommended that he took an anxiety and depression management course, which he did. It helped, but there's only so much mindfulness you can apply to having your home pulled out from underneath you once again. 'The stress is terrible,' he explained. 'I don't like taking medication, but I can't do anything. I sit at home and just go over and over it. I feel emotionally exhausted.'

Some days were easier than others. As a younger man, drinking had been Tony's crutch; he began leaning on booze after his divorce but got it under control. It was times like this, though, that tested his resolve not to drink anymore. Waiting for the eviction to be made final, he needed to pull himself together and walk Rebel, so he could get on with his day. Colchester Renters – a local grassroots campaign group that he had found support and solace in – were marching through Coggeshall as part of a campaign they were running called 'Vent Your Rent'. There would be a stall in the town centre where people could drop by and find out how to get support with their housing problems. Tony was going – he wanted to talk about his situation and spread awareness, to let people know that it's not only young middle-class professionals who make up Generation

Rent. How could it be so hard for someone like him – an older man who was perfectly capable of sorting himself out in every other way – to get help? He felt he had to do something. He wanted to take back control of his life. He couldn't just sit here, stewing. Where would he live? What would his future look like? Would his health hold up? Would the council be able to find him a home before his eviction date? Would he be able to negotiate a stay of eviction with his landlord? Such questions did not throw up any answers, only more unknowns.

## Intergenerational Infighting?

Imposing narrative on chaos is the only way humans can make sense of anything, but who tells the story matters. For too long, homeowners – older people and landlords – spoke for the private rented sector. Some, like David Smith, who was the policy director of the Residential Landlords Association (before it merged with the National Landlords Association to become the NRLA in 2020), even argued before Parliament in 2016 that landlords should be given more tax breaks because they were 'increasing the overall supply' of homes. While others, such as HomeLet (a private company which sells insurance to landlords and tenants, but mostly landlords), tried to extol the 'benefits' of renting for a generation who, thanks to the likes of Spotify and Netflix, consume much and own little. These were, apparently, flexibility and being able to live with friends. Yet, according to 2017 figures, 35 per cent of all single parents with children were renting privately and almost a quarter of all privately rented households contained families with children. There are now more households with children who are renting privately than in social housing. Do they want to live flexibly with friends? The Generation Rent narrative was born to explain the housing crisis but it excludes people like Tony and Limarra who, though far apart in age, both need housing security and stability.

It is true that intergenerational inequality has become acute in recent years. Millennials like me – the group traditionally thought of as Generation Rent – are the first generation in decades to have less disposable income and are therefore worse off than their parents. This is partly because our finances were badly impacted by the 2008 financial crash. As the think tank the Resolution Foundation noted in 2019, more than ten years on, as older millennials entered their mid-thirties, we were still suffering from a 'scarring' effect on our wages which was making it even harder to cope with the income pressures that people generally face in their thirties, including raising children. But the other big factor is rising house prices. Although inherited wealth was a factor in whether some members of Generation X and even the Baby Boomers could buy property, there's no getting around the fact that it was a stroke of enormous good luck for them to be born when they were: they came of age at a time when there was more social housing and private homeownership was more affordable compared with wages.

The term Generation Rent excludes those from older generations – like Tony – who have been equally hung out to dry by the housing market in the past few decades. Young people are not the only ones struggling, and the focus on Generation Rent as a homogeneous group, when in fact it now contains people from a wide range of backgrounds – older people, low-income workers, those on middle incomes, single mothers and families – has obscured the intersection of race, class and wealth with housing stress. Tony may be nearly seventy now, but he is a fully paid-up member of Generation Rent. In fact, he is one of a growing number of older renters who find themselves at the sharp end of Britain's affordable housing shortage: the number of over fifty-fives renting has more than doubled in the past ten years, the cost of living has risen, divorce later in life has become more common and the number of pensioners living in poverty has topped 2 million (with Black and Asian older people most at risk). According to analysis of ONS data by the buy-to-let mortgage lender Paragon, in the 2010s there was a 118 per cent surge in 55- to 64-year-olds renting over the course of a decade, while the number of people aged sixty-five and over in the same boat rose by 93 per cent. This trend has broadly been seen across England, but particularly in the south-east (where Tony lives), London, the south-west, the north-west and the East Midlands, which have the highest numbers of older renters.

Yet, ask Siri to show you Generation Rent and a stock photo appears of three young white professionals gathered around IKEA Billy bookcases eating avocados. The moniker, which became synonymous with the human cost of the housing crisis, stuck. It made good headlines and fuelled Twitter rows the sentiment of which are perhaps best encapsulated by a *Guardian* article published in 2017 with the headline 'Millionaire tells millennials: if you want a house, stop buying avocado toast'. It was a precis of the 'pull yourselves up by your bootstraps' mentality of those who had benefited from relatively low house prices in the 1980s, which fails to recognise that it's impossible to pull yourself up by the bootstraps if you can't afford the boots in the first place. That article was just one of countless of a similar ilk. Some commentators, like James Delingpole in the *Spectator* in 2014, even tried to argue that 'the young have never had it so good'. He wrote, 'Yes, it's true that the current QE [quantitative easing]-fuelled asset bubble is driving house prices unsustainably high, but otherwise news on the home front is good. Mortgages have never been cheaper, which more than compensates for higher prices.' This was not only completely incorrect, it made no sense. You can't reap the benefits of cheap credit if your rent is so high that you can't save for a deposit to get on to the housing ladder in the first place. Cheap credit – low interest rates on mortgages – was not compensating for high house prices, it was fuelling them. 'Now shut up and start showing some gratitude,' Delingpole concluded, voicing the irrational contempt that had come to typify the intergenerational conflict between the young and old over housing. Who was he talking about? Limarra? Tony? Anthony? What, exactly, were they supposed to show 'gratitude' for?

Generation Rent became de facto shorthand for white, educated middle-class kids who were struggling before they inherited or were gifted the cash to buy a house. As a narrative, it appears to parse a complex problem, but in fact it glosses over both the significant inequalities between young people and the fact that the crisis in private renting affects older people too. And yet it has stuck. Why? Because it resonated with those in charge of commissioning reports and editing newspapers and news programmes – they saw their children and grandchildren in the stories about successful young university-educated people who couldn't buy homes. This shouldn't come as a surprise. It matters who makes the news and, in Britain, it is by and large still people who come from privilege. According to the education charity the Sutton Trust, only 7 per cent of the British population go to private school, but 51 per cent of the country's leading journalists and 80 per cent of its editors were privately educated. There is no official data as to how many grew up in social housing or in houses that were rented as opposed to owned by their families, but, based on these statistics, it's fair to say that anyone who did so would not be in the majority on any given desk in any given newsroom. Even the BBC has a serious class problem and, while much has been (rightly) made of the corporation's gender pay gap audit, by contrast relatively little attention has been given to its class gap. On the list of Auntie's highest-paid staff, no fewer than 45 per cent went to private schools.

Beyond the BBC, only 11 per cent of journalists are from a working-class background and, according to research from City University, 94 per cent are white. In 1996, the late French sociologist Pierre Bourdieu remarked that the fact that journalists 'have much in common in social origin and education' limits the ideas they are exposed to because it 'produces closure' which is akin to 'censorship'. Journalists, he added, 'meet one another daily in debates that always feature the same cast of characters' – too often, the news trades in clichés and stereotypes which confirm our understanding rather than challenge it, he said. 'You can only break out of the circle by breaking and entering it,' he added. If people who truly knew what it was like to be homeless, to get into debt to pay their rent or had ever had to navigate the benefits system created the news, it would look a lot different. If those with the power to commission stories they deem to be important and kill those they do not came from more diverse backgrounds, our understanding of the housing crisis would have been more nuanced. But, because living through instability impacts your life chances and, therefore, your education and career prospects, Bourdieu's 'circle' is seldom broken into by those we most need to hear from. I know this first-hand because I, as a very junior producer at BBC *Newsnight* in the early 2010s (about the same time that Allegra Stratton's segment shaming Shanene Thorpe ran), suggested that we might want to cover more housing stories. My editor – a homeowning and privately educated person – looked at me dead on and said in a dismissive tone, 'It's just not that interesting.'

When it comes to failing to acknowledge the link between housing and social inequality, the British media has form. Writing in 1870, Engels was clear-sighted about this. 'The so-called housing shortage' which he saw playing 'such a great role in the press' at the time had nothing to do with 'the fact that the working class generally lives in bad, overcrowded or unhealthy dwellings'. Instead, he argued, 'all oppressed classes in all periods suffer more or less uniformly' from improper housing because those who own it can profit from that suffering. The questions that ought to be asked today are what is this suffering doing to our society and how do we end it?

There is a direct parallel between Engels' observation over a hundred and fifty years ago and the way we have understood the shortage of good-quality affordable housing in recent years. Journalists largely focused on house prices, 'Generation Rent' and how they might struggle to buy homes of their own above other aspects of the crisis in housing, because it was what they knew, what they too feared.

Dan Wilson Craw is a man who knows all about this. From 2014 until 2020, when he handed over the reins, he was the director of the lobby group Generation Rent, which made it its mission to champion the rights of private renters long before anyone else was seriously engaged with the issue, making a virtue of the growing sympathy for young professionals and gaining significant media attention as a result. 'When I started out, the main issue the media were interested in was how difficult it was to buy a home – particularly for young professionals,' he told me in 2019. 'There just wasn't a huge amount of interest in stories that lay outside of that scenario – and we'd get a lot of requests to comment on the latest house price index. Recently, journalists have had to delve deeper and explore why renting is so inadequate. As the renters' movement has developed, our collective understanding of the landscape has improved – become more nuanced – and we've been able to help people who aren't young professionals to tell their stories, but it's taken time for the media to take the same interest in those stories.'

Politicians, often well-meaningly, also seized on the story of Generation Rent. Conservative peer and former Minister of State for Universities and Science Lord David Willetts took on young people's plight with well-intentioned zeal but inadvertently stoked intergenerational conflict by accusing the Baby Boomer generation (to which Tony belongs) of 'stealing their children's future'. Similarly, in 2011, the Intergenerational Foundation, an independent think tank, released a report which argued that the older generation were 'hoarding homes' by refusing to downsize in their old age. At the time, an estimated 16 million people lived in underoccupied homes – equivalent to 37 per cent of the total housing stock in England – meaning there were some 25 million empty bedrooms. This might technically have been true but, equally, supply – a shortage of available and affordable housing – is only part of the problem. As we know, there were other market forces inflating house prices and rents. Even if these homes were being 'hoarded' by our parents and grandparents, and even if new ones were built, there would be no guarantee that younger people could afford them. In any case, shouldn't we aspire to be a society where people can stay in their homes for as long as they wish without it coming at the expense of young people's housing security? Shouldn't we have enough social housing to go around, and shouldn't we impose limits on landlordism to create a safe and secure private rented sector? Isn't it government's responsibility to regulate the private rented sector?

Older generations became fair game when there ought to have been a growing coalition between the increasing number of low-income older people who were renting and younger people caught in the private rent trap without family wealth to bail them out. In reality, the conflict is rich versus poor, not young versus old. A more equal distribution of wealth between the generations would, of course, only be a good thing – younger people today undoubtedly find themselves in a hostile economic environment where house prices keep rising and, according to the Institute for Fiscal Studies, they are increasingly concentrated in low-paid occupations, which particularly affects young men born after 1985, for whom job progression has especially slowed down – but it would be no panacea. This tale of intergenerational unfairness, of age as 'the new political divide', has, perhaps inadvertently, become a distraction: playing generations off against one another, encouraging families and friends to fight among themselves, takes the heat away from politicians, the systemic failures of housing policy and, above all, our economic system in which the international finance market feeds on these injustices and is bailed out by us all – as taxpayers.

This narrative about intergenerational unfairness also misses a crucial point. The reason that older people – particularly those we might call middle-income who are neither mega rich nor struggling – want to hoard wealth in the form of property is so that they can pass it on to their children and grandchildren, because they are worried about them. Even as they have benefited from house price rises, strong unions, decent pensions and full employment, they can see that this is not the case any longer, and that most work does not pay properly, and they know that the social safety net has been unravelled. That was certainly the case for my own grandparents, who knew that they had benefited from social housing, state support and low house prices, and worried that my sister and I and their other grandchildren were accruing student debt and working hard to barely pay it off. The Conservatives know this, too, and they exploit it by introducing policies which promise to protect people's housing wealth from adult social care costs such as Boris Johnson's 2021 social care cap. This controversial reform – a cap on the cost of social care at £86,000 funded by raising National Insurance contributions – came almost two years after the Conservative Party made a manifesto promise that 'nobody needing care should be forced to sell their home to pay for it', which was intended to play to voters who are now wedded to the idea of making huge amounts of money through property and passing it on to their children.

Once again, the problem is that work does not pay enough. Housing wealth tops people's coffers up. Today, you may have grown up feeling middle class, gone to university and now be earning a slightly above average salary, but find yourself spending so much money on rent that you're one month's pay away from precarity, and with parents who are only just solvent themselves and cannot help. You might be a teacher, the first person in your family to go to university, truly believing that you'd be better off than your working-turned-middle-class parents and find that you're in a worse financial position now than they were when they had you. It might feel like the middle classes have expanded culturally because more people go to university today, but its members are not necessarily wealthier. As the Serbian-American economist Branko Milanović found, between 1988 and 2008 the global top 1 per cent had an income increase of almost 70 per cent. He argues that this has not led to an increase of income for the middle classes and thus a corresponding increase in class equality, rather it has deepened pre-existing inequalities. We should therefore look at how much wealth someone has because this determines how they are able to navigate housing stress. Do they have savings? Do they have capital or access to family members who do? Do they or their nuclear family own assets that they can leverage? Age and occupation are less relevant.

It is understandable that older people – many of whom know how lucky they got – want to help their families in this economy. They, particularly those who aren't hugely well off, have internalised the notion that housing is the best possible investment and, indeed, in their lifetimes they won't have seen similar returns on other assets. But the fact remains that this 'hoarding' of homes, even when it is well-meaning or is done by those who are hardly what we might call rich, is exactly what makes it so hard for younger generations to accrue wealth in any way other than through inheritance. It is making Britain's housing market less fair and less efficient, underpinning undersupply and high house prices, but it is a direct consequence of those issues, too. We are in a feedback loop. And there's another side effect: younger generations – both millennials and Generation Z – are more right-leaning than you might think. 2021 polling found that Generation Z are financially conscious and have a tendency towards self-reliance even though they have a relaxed and progressive take on social issues like sexuality and gender. They are classically liberal, committed to personal liberty but individualistic. In this economy can you blame them? They know that hard work is not always enough to get you where you want to be, let alone on the housing ladder, and that you need inheritance. As Professor Bobby Duffy, author of *Generations: Does When You're Born Shape Who You Are?*, told me: 'It shouldn't really be a surprise that Gen Z are very focused on personal responsibility, rather than looking for help from others. They are coming into adulthood at the end of a long trend towards individualisation, where their direct experience is of less support from government, despite really tough economic circumstances.'

And so, where it does exist, intergenerational inequality is a symptom of the housing policy failures that have caused the housing crisis among private renters and those on low incomes today. As a result, there is more support and solidarity between the generations than you might expect (as testified by Limarra's mother's reaction to her daughter's experience). If you actually speak to young people around the country, if you join grassroots organisations who fight for renters' rights, you will find that everyone is united in who they blame for our current situation: not their parents, not their grandparents, but this government, the one before and the ones before that for their collective failure to address house price inflation, rent inflation and the growing shortage of affordable housing people so desperately needed. We have more to lose than we have to gain from playing generations off against one another; we need connection and coalition, not conflict.

## Vent Your Rent

Tony returned from the Vent Your Rent event. Rebel was pleased to see him. People of all ages – old, young and everything in between – were there, and he felt a sense of community that, too often, he was missing in his lonely fight. It wasn't his first protest. He had recently attended an event organised by Generation Rent in London, which is where we first met over supermarket snacks – tubs of millionaire shortbread – and milky tea. He rarely went into the city anymore, but for that he made an exception. It was a 'renter spokesperson' training event where I was speaking about how renters can best get their stories across in interviews for print, online, TV and radio. Tony was there because he wanted to know more about how to tell his story. 'I want people to know,' he said that day, 'this stuff needs to be heard. I want to change the perception of renters – we are not young and lazy. This isn't our fault.' He also went because he was angry. Angry that homes have become assets. Angry about being overlooked and poorly treated, not only by his landlord but by the private housing market and the system that dictates whether he would be given social housing.

During his eviction battle, every time Tony and I spoke he would ask me if I had spoken to Colchester Renters. 'I really want their story out there,' he would say, firmly. 'I can't tell you what a support this community is to me, it makes me feel less alone, it is a weight taken off my shoulders, because a problem shared is a problem halved. I don't think most people even know that help and support is out there for them. By spreading the word, I want to help them also feel less isolated.' It wasn't easy for Tony to attend those meetings or protests. He is not a young man and, he told me, they were as exhausting as they were energising. I know how much it all took out of him.

On the ground, Generation Rent as an organisation is bringing all kinds of people together. Perhaps they should change their name to 'Generations Rent'. But, as a concept, the idea of Generation Rent obscures the causes of the housing crisis: the social housing sell-off; politically sanctioned house price inflation; the deregulation of the private rented sector in favour of landlords. It limits our attention, focusing on the young instead of looking forward; stories like Tony's, are, in more ways than one, a portent of things to come. We are, as the Chief Executive of Shelter, Polly Neate, has previously described to me, sitting on a 'ticking time bomb' of private renters who will get older with no savings and no assets while the state has nowhere affordable for them to live. The instability of tenancies in the private rented sector, caused by both evictions and rent rises, causes displacement. For an older man like Tony, this has serious health implications which, as he gets even older, will only become more serious. This 'ticking time bomb' should concern us all. In 2019, a study conducted by the Royal Institute of British Architects (RIBA) and the Centre For Towns think tank warned that the lack of suitable homes for older people was already fuelling the housing crisis. England's small towns, they said, are set to swell with increasing numbers of elderly people as they reject city living amid a hidden housing crisis caused by a lack of appropriate homes for a rapidly ageing population. Bexhill in East Sussex, Corby in Northamptonshire and Denton in Greater Manchester were forecast to see the biggest increases in populations aged fifty-five and above during the next two decades. This will likely be an even bigger problem in the wake of the coronavirus pandemic, which has caused large numbers of people to relocate to less urban areas from cities like London, Liverpool, Birmingham and Edinburgh. Concern about what happens when Generation Rent grows up is increasing. This was echoed in a report published around the same time as the RIBA report by the All-Party Parliamentary Group (APPG) for Housing and Care for Older People, chaired by Lord Richard Best. It lays out the issue: we have an ageing population which will become increasingly reliant on rented housing – both in the private and social sectors – but that housing isn't secure enough, or sufficiently adapted for ageing bodies, and those people, because they've never owned, won't have a money pot of housing equity to fall back on.

To get a sense of the scale of this problem, consider this from the APPG's report: the number of households in the private rented sector headed by someone aged over sixty-four will more than treble in the next thirty years, from 450,000 today to at least 1.5 million by 2046. Because private renting is less stable, more expensive and, generally, of less good quality than social housing or owner-occupier homes, this risks creating a perfect storm. It's a disaster for people's wellbeing which, as the charity Age UK has put it, could see older renters 'ageing in distress and squalor'.

The All-Party Parliamentary Group for Housing and Care for Older People has warned that more than 600,000 members of Generation Rent are facing an 'inevitable catastrophe' of homelessness when they retire. If rents rise at the same rate as earnings, the inquiry found that 52 per cent of pensioners in the private rented sector will be paying more than 40 per cent of their income on rent by 2038. This will mean that at least 630,000 millennials will be unable to afford their rent and will find themselves homeless or with no choice but to move into temporary accommodation, at the state's expense. Given that rents were rising faster than earnings in 2021 and, like house prices, reaching all-time record highs, stories like Tony's could become a lot more common in years to come.

The effect of this would be devastating on the mental health of private renters in old age, just as it has been on Tony's. Research which has compared the mental health of older homeowners and older renters has found that housing – 'a structural variable' – has a huge impact.

Older people who rent are more likely to experience mental health problems than those who own their homes. Alongside financial stress, the emotional and physical displacement caused when tenancies end is a huge factor in this. Tony is struggling because he is being deprived of the basic ontological security that was also taken away from Limarra. The sociologist Professor Saskia Sassen of Columbia University sees this as a direct product of contemporary neoliberalism. She calls it the 'logics of expulsion', and is the direct opposite of the post-war creation of the welfare state which was 'driven by a logic of inclusion'. She sees this shift and the normalisation of accepting a system which privileges some people's fortunes while systematically destroying others as a deep rupture not only for modern society but for humanity. An eviction, as she sees it, does not just throw someone out of their home, but out of their dignity.

Thinking about exclusion from housing security as an expulsion from a core social and economic order brings humanity back into the conversation. If we see an eviction for what it is, the end of what Sassen identifies as a 'long transaction chain' which involves politicians, investors, banks, the landlord, possibly a letting agent and, in the end, a renter who bears the brunt of their collective decision-making, then we force ourselves to remember that the pathologies of modern capitalism are not so opaque and remote but, in the end, the direct consequence of human actions. Humanising this process and its consequences is vital to making the case for change: banning Section 21 evictions and giving private renters lifetime security in England (as they have, at least theoretically, in Scotland) is one way to do this.

As his inevitable eviction approached, Tony's mental health was hanging on by a fraying thread. We spoke on the phone one evening as he sat on the sofa, the adrenaline of the day wearing off. 'I know I should cook but when you're living alone it feels like a lot of work to then eat the results alone,' he joked. I asked what he was eating. 'I get these microwave meals from Iceland on the sly from my daughter,' he confided, reminding me of my own dad. 'They're only £1.50, which isn't bad, is it?'

'I make sure to balance it out with fresh fruit throughout the day,' he added. Clearly he'd been grilled about this before!

The microwave pinged. Tony ate at the table and then returned to the sofa and put on the TV. Rebel sat down next to him, resting her head on his lap. Looking around, he thought of how much he loved his home. He thought again of his children – one newly married – and hoped he wouldn't be housed too far from them. 'The kids all want to help me,' he explained, 'they're so worried. But they can't afford to help. I don't want to keep having that conversation. It should be me helping them! I don't even have the words to talk to them right now.'

I asked him, if he could pick out his next home, what would it look like? 'I just want somewhere I can look after,' he said, excited. 'Maybe with a garden so I can invite people over? I could have the grandkids come and stay.' When would he have an idea where home would be next month? When would he be able to think about the future and, once more, get ready to start again? To move again? To turn a new house into a home again? Neither he nor I knew.

# 4

# ROOT SHOCK

### Chatham, Kent

*Council:* Medway Council
*Average House Price:* In the year 2020/21 the majority of sales
in Chatham were terraced houses, selling for an average of
£247,438. Semi-detached homes sold for an average of £292,988,
with detached homes fetching £439,472. Overall, sold prices in
Chatham over that year were 11 per cent up on the previous year.
*Average Private Rent:* In 2021 the average rent for a one-bedroom
home was £778, for a two-bed it was £1,031, and for a three-bed it
was £1,197.

—

Kelly, too, knew inconstancy. She hadn't felt at home for seven years.
'Sometimes I get frustrated,' she told me over coffee in Chatham, Kent,
in the August of 2018. 'I wish I could make people – the powers that be –
listen. I get angry with myself. I think that I don't try hard enough, that
I'm not fighting enough, that I've given up. I should be kicking down
politicians' doors, trying to make a difference. But … I am exhausted.'

Her tone was measured but desperate; angry but never shrill. Her
voice had the inflection of someone who had had to make their case so
many times that they have grown weary of their own story. In 2013 Kelly,
42, and her family were evicted by proxy from their home in Bromley,
south London. They were never served an eviction notice but, instead,
faced an unaffordable rent hike. Along with her then partner and their

seven children, she was renting a four-bedroom house through a private landlord who decided he wouldn't renew their annual contract because he could put the property back on the market at a higher value. At the time, Bromley's housing market was booming; analysis of Land Registry data by the estate agent Kinleigh Folkard & Hayward shows that house prices rose steadily between 2011 and 2017. Kelly's then partner worked full time at the local bus garage while she was working more than full time at home looking after their young family. Their income was not elastic, it could not stretch to fit their landlord's new demand.

Kelly now lives on the Kent coast and life looks very different. Inside her temporary, privately rented one-bedroom home a heart-shaped slab of slate hangs on the wall. In bright red chalk a name has been tenderly handwritten: 'Morgan Sheen xxx'. On the other side of the room, a silver-framed photograph of Morgan holds space for a memory. He is a young boy, not yet in his teens, beaming and fresh faced. He has a small gap between his front teeth and curly hair. Light catches on the frame, bouncing around the room.

Morgan was Kelly's son. He died eight years ago, shortly after they were forced from their home. 'I've never been the same since that night,' Kelly said. 'None of us have.' All around her there was a sadness so heavy that it weighed everything down. Kelly is still grieving and, wherever she moves, she keeps Morgan's memory alive. She knows that she will never get over losing her son completely but feels that she cannot even begin to let go until she knows where she herself will end up. She remains displaced, waiting for Medway Council to tell her they've got somewhere suitable to house her and her 4-year-old daughter. The rest of her children, who are now young adults, live across the south-east, although one daughter lives nearby in Gravesend. Really, Kelly wants to move back to Bromley. She wants to go home. Home is not just the physical house you live in; home is the place you know and the networks you create. Any home move involves disruption, but when the displacement is involuntary, it can cause the sort of trauma that alters a person's life course.

Reports of homeless families being 'exported' from one council borough to another began to emerge ten years ago. But, since then, it has become standard practice for councils in London to rehouse people outside of their local area. The situation intensified in the 2010s due to a combination of rising rents, a diminished social housing stock, the introduction of the cap to Local Housing Allowance, and new powers granted to councils under the Localism Act 2011. This act allows councils to offer out-of-borough housing placements and also to discharge their legal duty to help those who refuse such an offer by invoking the idea of 'intentionality' (which came up for Limarra).

In 2018, the number of homeless households moved out of London by councils rose by almost 50 per cent. Families reported being moved as far away as Glasgow, Newcastle and Cardiff. One hundred and eighty-one were sent to the West Midlands, 574 to Essex and 750 were relocated to Kent, the displacement capital of England. From Bromley alone, almost 200 homeless households were relocated about thirty miles away to the Medway area in the space of sixteen months between January 2017 and April 2018. Local councillors say that these moves not only put pressure on the area's already limited housing stock but increased the demand for local services such as education and healthcare. Still, it's not uncommon for councils, particularly in areas like London where there is high housing demand, to offer those on social housing waiting lists accommodation in other places. That's why Limarra was initially moved from Peckham to Croydon. In 2021, I was still speaking to homeless mothers with children who were being 'exported' out of their home borough by their councils. One, Nadia Zaman, a mother of three, was told she must move to Stoke-on-Trent from Waltham Forest in east London or risk making herself 'intentionally homeless'. This meant leaving her close family, including her mother and sister who helped with childcare, and her local Muslim community. Jane Williams, the founder and CEO of the Magpie Project, a grassroots charity which supports mothers living in temporary accommodation with children under five, told me she was concerned that out-of-borough placements were on the rise. This is in no small part because the number of homeless people in temporary accommodation across the country swelled during the pandemic. The 98,300 households in temporary accommodation in June 2020 included 127,240 children; 64 per cent of those households were placed there by local authorities in London.

'The reason we were living in private rented is that Bromley Council didn't have a social home for us,' Kelly recalled. 'We had to go private and it was just about "affordable", I guess. The rent was about £1,800 a month. We paid most of it and got topped up by Housing Benefit. The landlord kept putting the rent up, which stretched us a lot, but we did our best to make it work.'

Shortly before Kelly and her family were asked to leave, David Cameron and Nick Clegg's Coalition government's benefit cap, first announced at the Conservative Party conference in 2010, kicked in. The government predicted that this policy would reduce public expenditure by £225 million by 2015, which, during a 'so-called' credit crunch, they passed off as 'rebalancing the books'. Housing and poverty experts warned that the reduction to the amount of rent that state support covered would have serious implications for at least 100,000 households, predominantly in the south-east where rents were higher than in the rest of the country. Kelly was among them; her family's benefits were capped. In real terms, the average gap between private rent and Housing Benefit for families like hers was £3,750 a year. A study conducted at the time by the social policy software and analytics company Policy in Practice found that renters affected by the cap were two-thirds more likely to find themselves in rent arrears than other tenants. And, like so many others, slowly but surely, Kelly and her partner began to fall behind on their rent because of this shortfall. 'It was quite obvious that the landlord was going to chuck us out,' she said. 'We started not being able to make rent. He wasn't happy and he made that known whenever we spoke to him. He said he could get so much more for the house if he relisted it. We looked but couldn't find anything else affordable in Bromley. Leaving the area wasn't really an option because two of my boys were in specialist schools – Aidan has mild global learning difficulties and Kieran has ADHD, so he needs to be in a specialist unit – and I didn't want them disrupted.'

In all but name, Kelly's family were evicted. Bromley Council left rehousing them right up until the last minute, as Southwark had done with Limarra. Finally, and somewhat ironically given that Limarra could not be housed there, they were offered a house in Peckham which, although nearby, is not exactly close. It's roughly a forty-minute drive from Bromley, but in traffic can take much longer.

'I remember the moment the council told us we had to move to Peckham,' Kelly said, blinking slowly as she sipped her coffee. She recalled everything calmly and in photographic detail. 'You don't know what's going to happen to you. You're standing in the council offices and all you know is that you're being asked to pick up your life and move somewhere.'

Anyone – Anthony, Limarra, Tony and, now, Kelly – who is forced from their home, whether through eviction, rising rent or a natural disaster, experiences an existential, physical and psychological rupture. The consequences of that play out in real time and can define the displaced tenant for the rest of their lives. This is what Professor Mindy Fullilove, psychiatrist and professor of urban policy and health at the New School in New York, calls 'root shock'. As she sees it, the 'ecology of inequality' impacts us all. She defines 'root shock' as the 'traumatic stress response to losing all or part of one's emotional ecosystem' and notes that it has 'parallels to the physiological shock experienced by a person who, as a result of injury, suddenly loses massive amounts of fluids'. Fullilove has spent decades of her career studying how people from urban areas in the United States invest in the places they inhabit and what happens to them when they are suddenly forced to leave, through the so-called 'regeneration' programmes that so often result in social cleansing. But 'root shock' can also be seen in the psychiatric trauma experienced by people who are evicted or displaced for other reasons. When there is emotional pain, psychiatrists like Fullilove like to believe they can help. But, as she wrote in her 2004 study of the psychological impact of urban renewal policies on the people they displace, psychiatrists cannot act in the interest of those in suffering until they find 'some handle for the problem, some name to guide action'.

When a plant is moved, gardeners know it must be done carefully. If it is not, the transplanted tree or shrub can experience 'root shock'. This is a biological process that occurs when the plant is repotted or planted in conditions that are too shallow, where not enough of its root ball has been lifted with it. As a result, it endures great stress because its trimmed and disturbed roots cannot absorb enough water to keep it alive. If a plant is experiencing root shock, it might be more susceptible to other injuries and damages, too: disease, insects, the elements. With proper care and extra watering until its roots are more established in their new location, a plant can overcome root shock. If that care isn't provided, it will decline.

'I borrowed the term from gardening because it's the closest thing to what I could see in my research,' Fullilove explained to me over email. 'The experience of displacement includes lots of anxiety, depression and anger … Anything that disrupts the emotional ecosystem causes root shock, for example, climate change has caused worldwide root shock, as has the coronavirus pandemic. Look at any living creature, we need to be rooted in the world to find food, shelter, social life and meaning. This is the foundation of our attachment to home, to place.'

Our bodies contain complex systems to maintain an internal balance that keeps us alive, but we require an external balance between ourselves and the outside world in order to survive. We grow into a place, we spread out through a community of people, forming attachments. We plot our routines around particular locations – the supermarket, the post office, the doctor's surgery – and learn to understand our social, emotional and logistical ecosystem in relation to them.

'The main thing that has stuck with me is how blasé the woman behind the counter was about it all,' Kelly told me about the day, keeping one watchful eye on her daughter who, as young children do, was going up to strangers in the café to show them her toys. 'I remember her saying, "You'll be back in the borough in no time. I wouldn't even bother plumbing your washing machine in," like it wasn't even a thing for a mother of seven kids to go even a few days without a washing machine!'

Fullilove's research is complemented by the work of the American sociologist Professor Matthew Desmond (who is also the author of *Evicted*, a study of eviction in the poorest neighbourhoods of Milwaukee). Like Fullilove, Desmond has studied the implications of displacement and eviction up close in the US. In 2015, he co-authored a paper entitled 'Eviction's Fallout: Housing, Hardship, and Health' with another academic, Professor Rachel Tolbert Kimbro of Rice University. In it they wrote that debates about poverty do not 'fully appreciate how housing dynamics are deeply implicated in creating and deepening poverty'. This was Anthony's, Limarra's and Tony's experience. It was also Kelly's. In each case, the person went from having somewhere to live to being in freefall and even sleeping rough or sofa-surfing for a period. They were uprooted. Research is beginning to emerge that documents the association between housing instability and health and it confirms that the trauma of eviction and its aftermath may have significant effects on the mental health of mothers. In their research, Desmond and Kimbro found that mothers who had been evicted in the previous year experienced higher levels of material hardship and parenting stress, as compared with mothers who have not experienced eviction, leading to an increased likelihood of depression. They also found that evicted mothers are more than twice as likely to report that their children are in poor health. They cite several studies which suggest that 'the extended periods of homelessness that follow eviction can take a toll on one's physical health', as well as qualitative studies that show that people who are evicted experience psychological distress. In the United States, the research has confirmed a link between evictions, depression, higher stress levels and poorer health overall. It therefore follows that this would be true in the UK, too, as, although the legislative specifics differ, the experience of being torn from your home is universally brutalising. This is hard enough for those living alone, like Anthony and Tony, but for mothers like Kelly and Limarra, it impacts their children, too, because you cannot parent to the best of your abilities when you are under such strain. Knowing all of this, should private landlords be allowed to evict anyone, let alone children? It is such an obvious practical, moral and ethical question, why are politicians not asking it? At best, being expelled from the place you call home, your emotional ecosystem, rips out the fabric of who you are. At worst, it can have devastating, even fatal, consequences. As it would turn out, Kelly's move set off a chain of events resulting in unfathomable trauma that changed everything for her family for ever.

## Miles Away

When you buy or rent a home, you usually do some research first. You choose an area – scoping out schools, hospitals and commuting distances

– before looking at properties. For private renters on low incomes, the first thought is to find an area where the rent is vaguely affordable, even if it happens to be in the wrong location. For those waiting for social housing in England there is even less choice, because of the intentionally homeless label.

That's how Kelly ended up in Peckham. She couldn't refuse. From there, she and her partner struggled to get the kids to their schools in Bromley on time through the south London rush hour. As they straddled the distance between their lives and their new location, a new challenge presented itself. It was in November, six weeks after they moved in, and Morgan, who was playing football with the Chelsea FC Foundation Development Centre – he hoped one day to play professionally – ran out of prescription asthma inhalers.

'We'd all had the same GP in Bromley for years,' Kelly remembered, her voice flinching with anger. 'All of my kids had been under the same surgery all of their lives. I knew them so well in there. Morgan had bad asthma, and he'd had a few trips to A&E. The Bromley GP was amazing – they'd given him a special inhaler – it was a combination which worked really well for him and we hadn't had a trip to hospital for over a year.'

Despite being told by Bromley Council that she would be 'back in the borough in no time', Kelly didn't feel right not registering her children with a GP in Peckham. If the worst happened, she wanted to be safe.

'I remember Googling where the closest GP surgery was when Morgan started struggling. I told them I needed an appointment urgently to look at my son's inhaler. The doctor listened to his chest. I can see her now if I close my eyes,' Kelly said. 'She asked me what inhaler he used. I explained that it was a special combination inhaler. She nodded in acknowledgement and tapped at the keys of her keyboard. She printed off a prescription and that was that. I went straight with the slip to the local chemist.'

It was only after Kelly got home and opened up the stapled paper bag that she realised the inhaler was green and not purple. They'd been using purple inhalers for years. Purple inhalers worked. She didn't know anything about the green ones. 'I just thought, she's the GP, she must know what she's doing. I gave it to Morgan to start using.'

Initially, everything seemed to be fine. Better than fine. Morgan's condition improved. His chest loosened up. But then, a few days later, he started wheezing again. It was evening, about 8 p.m., and Kelly gave him the inhaler, but he didn't improve.

'I said to my partner, "We need to go to the hospital, I think he needs to go on the nebulising machine. His inhaler's not doing anything." Morgan had his pyjamas on, so I got his coat on because it was cold outside. My partner was going to take him to the hospital, that's how we usually did it – I stayed at home with the other children and my partner went, because he drove and I didn't. We Googled the nearest hospital. I wanted the best one. I watched them walk out of the front door and get in the car, I turned around to go back up the stairs, and the next thing I heard was my partner screaming my name. My initial thought – and I know it's quite a stereotypical one – was, "Oh my God, we're in Peckham, someone must've pulled a knife out."'

But that was not what had happened. Kelly ran back to the front door. Her partner was stooped over, holding Morgan in his arms. 'He was just limp. He wasn't responding. He looked like he'd passed out,' she remembered, gripping her cup.

Kelly didn't know exactly how bad it was, but she was sure Morgan had stopped breathing. Her motherly instincts took over. She knew he needed CPR, so she laid him out there, on the driveway.

Suddenly the Vinnie Jones 'Stayin' Alive' campaign – which taught people the resuscitation technique of administering chest compressions to the beat of the Bee Gees classic – popped into her head, and she tried to replay it over and over as she pumped her son's chest. An ambulance had been called. She kept going. Stayin' Alive. He still didn't respond.

The ambulance came. They scooped Morgan and Kelly up and sped to King's College Hospital in nearby Camberwell. The paramedics continued to work on Morgan on the journey and for about twenty minutes on arrival at the hospital, but there was nothing they could do. Morgan had died on the driveway. Kelly remained eerily calm as she recounted this, the worst night of her life, to me. Morgan's funeral wasn't until the following month, on 6 December, and then it was Christmas. She was still disoriented, in a strange place, living in a strange house and now grieving the unnatural horror of the premature loss of a child.

What is the real cost of not having enough social housing? The real cost of putting families who once would have called the state their landlord at the mercy of the private market? It's not just financial. Bromley Council's decision to move Kelly's family did not kill Morgan directly. But the family were victims of a flawed system that fails those it is intended to help. When we discuss the housing crisis, we focus on who can afford what and it has skewed our understanding. We only observe housing, the social and political conditions of acquiring property and the permanence it provides, through a lens of privilege: of who owns and who does not. But, in doing so, we overlook the outward ripple effect of that privilege. The difference between owning your home and not can be summed up like this: it is the difference between owning your circumstances and being owned by them. This is why secure and affordable social housing is so important, but also why the private rented sector needs to be regulated properly in favour of tenants. What occurred in Limarra's, Tony's and Kelly's lives was the direct result of the impermanence that comes with lacking the privilege of homeownership, of the enforced relinquishment of control it causes. Systematically, Kelly's stability had been arbitrarily stripped away from her through the bureaucracy of administering state housing support at a time when there aren't enough social homes to go around. The precarity of her housing situation had infected every aspect of her family's life. 'If we had been at home, in our home,' Kelly said, 'our GP's surgery was across the road. The hospital was down the road in the other direction. You know where all these things are when you've got kids. I know that night would never have gone the way that it did if we hadn't been moved.'

Kelly's agony was compounded in March 2014. Four months after Morgan died, an envelope dropped through her letterbox. It was from Bromley Council. It was the letter she had been waiting for, containing news that her family was to be rehoused in temporary accommodation in Orpington – no more permanent than the current place, but at least it was back in Bromley borough.

'This was just another trauma,' Kelly said, her chest heaving hopelessly. 'When they lose a child, some parents get to stay in the same family home for years after. They can grieve with their child's bedroom still there, they don't touch it … It takes many, many years to be ready to move on, if you ever are. But we didn't have that time. I remember packing up the Peckham house and having to pack the hospital bag from *that* night – when we left the hospital, when we left him, they put all his clothes into a bag – and I really wasn't ready to deal with that, it'd only been four months. But that had to be packed up, moved again, and then there we were in this other temporary home in a new place. Again.'

One of the most dumbfounding things about the housing crisis, for me, is this: temporary accommodation is often anything but temporary. A year passed, but no permanent home was found for Kelly's family. Tenancies are, by their nature, temporary. That's why, according to figures released by the ONS in 2018, 62 per cent of households in the private rented sector spend less than three years in the same accommodation, with only 4 per cent staying in the same home for twenty years or more. That might work for some people, but if you have children, three years is not even the duration of primary school. When it comes to temporary accommodation, though, depending on where you are in the country, you will find displaced people who have been stuck in limbo for years at a time because there's nowhere to move them on to. Kelly was still living in temporary accommodation when the date of the inquest into Morgan's death rolled around in 2016, which made it seem anything but temporary.

Kelly attended. It was confirmed that the GP who saw Morgan 'hadn't had a lot of experience with paediatric asthma and had actually clicked on the wrong box in the drop-down menu when she was printing out his prescription'. Nobody checked it. Not the GP and not the chemist. Kelly was right to question the green inhaler; 'it turned out the inhaler they prescribed him shouldn't be used for children under twelve and it should never be used without a steroid inhaler'. She felt vindicated but crushed. 'I think shock carries you through for the first six months, a year or so. I knew I had to get to the inquest, but that's when it hit me, and I just … I couldn't cope in this other house we'd been put in,' she said shakily. 'The amount of work that it needed … the wiring was awful, there were cables stapled to the walls even in the kids' bedrooms, there was an incessant leak in the hallway, the sink was blocked, and the washing machine waste water would fill up the sink whenever we used it and there was so much going on around me, everyone's grief. It was my family, but it'd been broken for ever, and it wasn't our home. Everything was wrong.'

'Housing instability' won't be recorded anywhere on the paperwork from Morgan's inquest, but there's no doubt that it played a role in his death. It's no secret that children's health worsens in temporary accommodation. Research conducted by Shelter found that 60 per cent of those suffering with asthma or other chest and breathing problems saw their condition deteriorate once they had been moved. This is backed up by countless medical studies which have found that psychological stress and low quality of life are asthma triggers. A longitudinal study of children in the UK found that moving is associated with poorer mental health, so it follows that children from low-income backgrounds – like Morgan, and Limarra's daughter Nevaeh – who are more likely to rent and be forced to move more frequently will be in worse health than those who grow up in stable housing. We also know that there is serious racial inequity here. Almost a quarter (24 per cent) of people making homelessness applications to local councils are from Black, Asian and minority ethnic groups, even though these individuals and families only make up just over a tenth (11 per cent) of all households in England.

I asked Mindy Fullilove why she thinks the psychological and societal impact of the global housing crisis is being ignored by lawmakers worldwide. 'Lies shelter the guilty,' she said plainly. The ramifications of displacement for private renters in Britain is an emerging field of research. A leading academic in this area is Dr Jenny Preece, a research associate at Sheffield University's Department of Urban Studies and Planning.

'Place is one of the most fundamental concepts in human geography,' she told me when we first spoke in 2019. 'You can't just plonk people anywhere. Regardless of whether they are low income or not, they need to read their environment and decide whether or not it's somewhere that they want to be.' In her work, which consists of hundreds of interviews conducted across the country, Preece has found that, over time, our lived experience of the world around us informs our sense of self, our consciousness. The experience of homelessness and what she calls the 'spoiled identity' of being labelled homeless has a profound impact on those who live through continual displacement.

This thinking – that every aspect of our environment and how we perceive it, whether through sight, taste, smell, touch, hearing or feeling, holds great psychic significance for us – has a long history and can be traced back to the philosophy of phenomenology in the early twentieth century, but researchers are only just beginning to draw on it in the context of the housing crisis. Preece notes that 'belonging' to a 'place' is not something that happens instantly, 'in the present', but over time by 'interacting with personal and place histories'. For many people, this involves 'longstanding connections to places, through childhood experiences and the presence of wider family networks'. It takes time, then, to feel at home. And that's something that renters often don't have. Kelly's dangerous disquiet, Tony's fearful frustration, Limarra's anxious dread and Anthony's desperate resistance are all testament to this, with each in their own way reacting to a loss of their community, a blow to their sense of belonging. And, above all, they are reacting to the lack of agency that the housing market imposes on those who have the least financial autonomy. Some might argue that attachment to a home or a place is trivial, but, as Kelly's, Tony's, Limarra's and Anthony's stories all demonstrate, this is also about access to education, childcare and consistent healthcare services, too.

In the aftermath of Morgan's inquest, Kelly's world disintegrated. She and her partner, the father of her children, separated. Things fell apart. After a brief period of sleeping rough on Blackheath while her children were in temporary accommodation with their father, she ended up in Kent. She was still in the shock of grief, thinking that a fresh start in a new place might help this time. But, by the end of 2015 she was diagnosed with PTSD. To this day, she needs to live somewhere that is in walking distance of a hospital and experiences overwhelming anxiety if it is not.

In spite of it all, there is something striking about Kelly. It's not what she's been through but that she is so much more than the sum of those experiences. 'Sometimes I worry that I'm not fighting enough to be heard and to help other people be heard,' she lamented to me that day in the coffee shop. 'I want to retrain. I want to work for a charity or a council, I want to make sure nobody goes through what I went through. We need more empathy in the system. People aren't just numbers in a spreadsheet or boxes to be ticked,' she said. 'I remember how the councils worked ten years ago even. All right, you had to sit there all day and go through your forms and whatever, but there was always a safe, suitable, affordable property given to you. I can't believe how quickly it's changed – the way we treat people now is almost Victorian. It's cruel and we make judgements about people who don't have enough money.'

'When you're just thrown out into an area, you don't know anything about it,' Kelly said as we left the coffee shop and started walking around the historic royal dockyard which was once, fittingly, the stomping ground of that great Victorian chronicler of injustice, Charles Dickens; his father was a pay clerk here. 'I've lived in Kent for five years now and I don't have a community like I used to because I'm always somewhere temporary. I feel like that was taken from me. Anyway, the council still hasn't found me a permanent home, so everything about my life is still, technically, temporary and, ultimately, down to a private landlord.'

Kelly wants to leave Chatham but fears she never will now. She feels she has 'adapted', even though she is waiting for a suitable home for her and her daughter, who is sharing a bedroom with her. She told me that this is, in part, because it was deemed that she made herself intentionally homeless all those years ago by leaving Bromley after Morgan's inquest. She's sure there is a mark against her name on her records because of that grief-stricken decision. More than that, she added, 'It's been such an ongoing process that I'm convinced that I'm now institutionalised to being homeless. I don't even know what it would be like to have a secure home, a secure tenancy.' Kelly is, in her own mind and in that of the state, defined not by who she is but by what she does not have, by all that she has lost. She feels that absence, wherever she goes.

As we finished our walk around the docks, we passed branches of Nando's and PureGym. Until 2016, there was a theme park there called Dickens World, which aimed to transport its visitors back to Victorian England for the tidy sum of £12.50 per person. What might Dickens have made of the callousness of the benefit cap which, ultimately, started a chain of events that led Kelly here, by the waters of the river Medway? If his acerbic ridicule of the men who sat on the Poor Law boards in *Oliver Twist* is anything to go by, he'd have been unimpressed. We need neither fiction nor theme parks to return us to overpriced, overcrowded and improper living conditions. This is modern England, where displacement and suffering are not naturally occurring conditions but have been actively caused by bad policy.

Kelly walked me back to the station. It was a warm afternoon. 'If I was Prime Minister for a day,' she said, 'building enough social housing would be my priority. I know that they're building a pitiful amount at the moment. I think ignorance has driven a lot of the decisions that politicians have made.'

The high-speed train I caught back to London, designed to reconnect parts of the neglected Kent coast with the capital, zoomed past a blur of Kent towns, including Gillingham and Rochester. Out of the window I could see countless construction sites; at least three major housing projects were being built, which would create an extra 460 homes in the area but for private sale, not as social housing. The maxim of countless housing ministers who have all blurred into one has been 'We need to build more homes'. Even if we continue to build, what is the price being paid by society at large for what Professor Loretta Lees, a geographer and the chair of the London Housing Panel, calls the 'accumulative dispossession' of renters like Anthony, Limarra, Tony and Kelly? This is a concept developed by the Marxist geographer Professor David Harvey and used to describe how the privatisation of public assets such as housing or land alienates its inhabitants. When those affected question the housing market they experience confusion and frustration. Given that, in our current era, disruption in pursuit of profit is legitimised, it makes sense that they feel estranged in their own country, in their own homes, because they are constantly faced with the loss of their autonomy. The impact of forced displacement is severe. In the US, a study published in the journal *Urban Studies* quoted an American public housing resident who said that 'moving three times is the same as having your house on fire once' – it is stressful, disruptive and traumatic. The specifics of housing policy may differ from country to country, but the impact of dislocation is universal.

# 5

# PRICED OUT

### Bristol

*Council:* Bristol City Council
*Average House Price:* In the year 2020/21 the majority of sales in Bristol were terraced houses, selling for an average of £336,329. Semi-detached homes sold for an average of £373,168, with flats fetching £270,628. Overall, sold prices in Bristol over that year were 11 per cent up on the previous year.
*Average Private Rent:* In 2021 the average rent for a one-bedroom home was £1,102, for a two-bed it was £1,592, and for a three-bed it was £1,540.

—

'I grew up in social housing in Whitehall in the north of the city,' 25-year-old Henry Palmer told me as we sat in a café serving flat whites and craft beer in an old tobacco factory in south Bristol that has been turned into an events space. Henry had deliberately chosen it because he thinks it 'epitomises gentrification' and is 'the equivalent of east London in south Bristol'. Henry had left Bristol to do a degree at the University of Kent – the first person in his family to enter higher education – and returned, in 2017, to a city ranked as 'the most desirable place to live in Britain'. This was according to the *Sunday Times* Best Places to Live in the UK guide and, he thinks, is part of what consequently made his home city unaffordable for him to move back to and rent privately in. Regional winners that year included Frome in Somerset (where house prices rose by a whopping 13 per cent between 2020 and 2021), Peckham in London (where locals like Limarra were being priced out) and Ballycastle, on the north-east coast of County Antrim (one of the most expensive places to set up home in Northern Ireland). Britain's love of such lists is deeply connected to our obsession with property. Only this country could birth them as well as producing shows such as *Escape to the Country*, *Location, Location, Location* and *Property Ladder*; they tap into our national psyche, our fetishistic fixation with homeownership.

Henry had not been evicted by a private landlord, nor housed away from his home by the state, but, like Anthony, Limarra, Tony and Kelly, he could feel that he was being pushed out of the place he knows best by invisible but tangible socio-economic and political forces. Speaking fast and, ironically, with the urgency of someone trying to make a quick sale on a home they know is overvalued, he threw around the terms 'bourgeois', 'Marxist' and 'proletariat' with such excitement that they almost sounded like new ideas. But Henry was no estate agent and nor was he a salesman. Working as a caretaker by day because it was one of the first jobs he could get, he had just finished writing a book of his own called *Voices of Bristol: Gentrification and Us*.

He talked like he writes: loud and lamenting, angry and persuasive. And, if the rhythm of Henry's speech implied urgency, it's because he felt the acute desperation of a young person being priced out of their home. 'Whitehall, which is in Easton, was still rough and ready when I grew up there,' he said, sipping his overpriced coffee through a deliberately wry smile, 'but, even so, when I got back from uni, I started hearing people say that Easton – and similarly poor areas like St Paul's and Bedminster – were "up-and-coming". It riled me up. It felt like our spaces – working-class spaces – were being taken over and turned into investment opportunities. I went to a reggae pub called the Star & Garter, which is in Montpelier, with my mates, and it was uncomfortable. You had locals, all standing around the edge of the dance floor and then middle-class students from Bristol Uni in the centre raving it up.' This incident still confounded him. 'Nobody was mixing … nobody!' Henry added, 'It was like a sort of social segregation. Beenie Man's "Girls Dem Sugar" was playing, how can you not dance to that?'

'I considered the class divide, the disparity at play in the pub that night, for a long time afterwards,' he continued. 'It sort of haunted me. I saw the dismayed looks on elderly local faces over and over again in my mind. It upset me gravely. Growing up in Easton, everyone was socio-economically the same. Of the same class, I suppose. What I saw that night in that pub was different. It was rich, privileged people dipping their toe in an area they knew nothing about, before retreating to pristine Clifton, and it just hit me differently.'

Henry had also worked as an Uber driver and in a Bristol call centre. He told of customers getting into his car and saying, 'So, that's the famous Bristol accent I've heard so much about!' and of callers who couldn't believe that it was real when he spoke. When we met, Henry was earning approximately £16,000 a year and could not afford to move out of his mum's Victorian two-bedroom house – a rare and stable long-term social tenancy which she had had since 2010 – in Speedwell, near Whitehall. 'I could afford to live in a shared house in multiple occupancy with other people and pay around £500 a month,' he explained, 'but even that would be difficult, it would literally mean living hand to mouth after bills. My friends who also come from the more "working-class" parts of the city – like Bedminster – are in a similar position. Most people I know who are actually from here and in their early thirties are, too.' Even though his income was low, Henry would not qualify for social housing. Rightly, because of the scarcity of such properties, you are considered a 'priority need' only if you are homeless, live in cramped conditions or have a medical condition made worse by your current home. And, even then, you may have to wait.

There was a clear explanation for the predicament of Henry and his peers: the city had (and still has) a housing crisis. By 2019, the average house cost £304,900, 11 times the average Bristolian's salary of £27,400. And, as we know, when the price of houses rises such that people can't afford to get a deposit together, more are forced into the insecure tenure of the private rented sector.

The coronavirus pandemic only exacerbated this. During the first year, London was actually the only place in the country where rents fell – down 6.8 per cent on average. By late 2021, rents outside of London were rising at the fastest rate on record. But even before that, an exodus of renters and buyers moving away from the capital and the south-east was in motion. A 2019 survey by the online property website Zoopla identified the rising cost of housing in Bristol, not only to buy but to rent. Although rents were stabilising and even falling in some other places – such as Aberdeen – the cost of renting a home in the year 2018/19 had risen fastest in Nottingham, Leeds and Bristol. The survey noted that tenants moving into a Nottingham home in the summer of 2019 paid 5.4 per cent more in rent than they would have done in 2018. Meanwhile, in Leeds and Bristol rents were up 4.5 per cent on 2018, faster than the average UK wage growth, which was 2.6 per cent. That year, there were also 11,000 households registered and waiting for social housing in Bristol; by 2021, it was more than 13,000. The number of people sleeping rough was also rising, and homeless people in the city were dying at more than double the national rate. Nearby Bath had recently become one of the least affordable cities in which to rent in the country – second only to Brighton, Anthony's home.

'I do worry about what happens if these trends continue. I'm being financially pushed out of my own city,' Henry told me, his sardonic defences slipping for a moment into something more sincerely sombre. He saw the problem clearly – that people who could no longer afford London were moving out. 'I've heard Bristol touted in "best places to live" guides as a mini-London for people who can't afford to live in the capital,' he said. 'It's always billed as a "greener" and "more affordable alternative". But, for Bristolians, there is a knock-on effect. The housing crisis is not limited to London and the south-east, and when London and its overflow towns push people out, it pushes prices up here. People – middle-class migrants – move to up-and-coming parts of Bristol. University students who come from other places decide to stay.'

The forces displacing Henry, it turns out, are related to the forces impacting the other people we've already met in this book: they spread out economically through Britain's housing market and politically via policies made in Westminster. There is nothing wrong with relocating, of course: migrating to another part of the country because you get a new job, you want to have more space, you fall in love with someone who lives there or need to move because you can no longer afford your current area, you want to be near a certain school or you have caring responsibilities – is a vital part of life. But without enough social housing, no rent controls and a dearth of truly affordable new homes across the country, landlords in the private rented sector have been given a licence to print money. And print money they do. The coronavirus pandemic gave people the opportunity to pause, a chance to reconsider their lives. In 2021, the resultant lifestyle changes, such as relocations, combined with the Chancellor's Stamp Duty holiday which also applied to second-home buyers, sent the housing market into overdrive. House prices rose, and so did rents. Particularly outside of London. According to Zoopla, in 2021 private rents across the UK rose at the fastest rate since 2008, with demand greatly outstripping supply. The south-west was particularly affected, with rents up by 9 per cent annually; the area registered the UK's fastest rental growth in the third quarter of 2021.

## Gentrification, Gentrification, Relocation

As Henry noted himself, there's a word for all of this – one that gets thrown around a lot: gentrification. As a form of redevelopment, gentrification is the opposite of sustainable regeneration; the former prioritises profit, the latter improves an area while protecting the community that inhabits it.

The term gentrification was coined in 1964 by the sociologist Ruth Glass to describe change in London. In the early 1960s Glass, who had left Nazi Germany and come to the UK in 1932 to study at the London School of Economics, began writing about the changes in housing she had witnessed in her home area, Islington, in north London, which had resulted in social shifts and physical displacement. She gave those changes a name and, in doing so, gave generations of those affected by them a language for the inchoate forces they felt the hand of. Glass's writing is now largely out of print, though leading academics such as Professor Loretta Lees and Professor Mindy Fullilove continue the study of gentrification and displacement.

Glass's definition of gentrification has become *the* definition of the inequity sparked by estate 'renewal' or urban 'regeneration' the world over. London was and remains a petri dish for studies of dysfunctional housing markets. Glass wrote, in the introduction to her seminal book on the subject, *London: Aspects of Change*:

> One by one, many of the working-class quarters of London have been invaded by the middle classes – upper and lower … Once this process of 'gentrification' starts in a district it goes on rapidly until all or most of the original working-class occupiers are displaced and the social character of the district is changed.

That was in 1964 and, on the surface of things, it sounds all right, doesn't it? Almost natural and inevitable. Wealthy people move into less wealthy areas, bringing money with them. But gentrification is a story of conflicting parts, where the negative impact is usually glossed over. After all, when you renovate a home it is generally with the intention of increasing its value. You make an investment, whether that's with capital or your time, expecting a return. That return might make a profit for you – the person doing the renovating – but it usually comes at a cost for others because the value of that home has increased. If rents and house prices are driven up in an area where there isn't enough social housing, people on low incomes will be priced out. The more you read Glass's writing on gentrification today, the more prescient it becomes as a portent for what an unregulated housing market can do to society. In the same book, she wrote: 'the competition for space thus produced is bound to get out of hand and lead to a spiral of land values if it is neither anticipated nor controlled'. That was almost sixty years ago. In London that's exactly the situation. 'Any district in or near London, however dingy or unfashionable before, is likely to become expensive,' she continued, 'and London may quite soon be a city which illustrates the principle of the survival of the fittest: the financially fittest who can still afford to live and work there.' And, as we have seen in Bristol, London is not the only city where this is true; it is happening in urban areas across the country.

Think of previously 'undesirable' areas – Notting Hill, Bow, Hackney,

Elephant and Castle, New Cross, Catford or Deptford (where my own family originates). The scale and speed of regeneration in those areas in the past few decades or so has been profound and, many would add, merciless. Investment – whether from local government, housing associations, private developers or offshore funds – flows in, high-rise new builds spring up with paltry numbers of genuinely affordable homes inside them, buy-to-let investors seize their chance, some homeowners (who may even have bought their formerly social homes through Right to Buy) sell up or decide to become landlords. As a result, private rents rise and many long-term residents – particularly those who rented privately – are priced out or, as was the case for social tenants and homeowners alike in the Aylesbury and Heygate estates in Elephant and Castle, the last of whom were relocated in 2013 by their local council, forcibly removed. There, south Londoners were pushed as far away as Slough and St Albans when the site their homes stood on was sold to the behemoth real estate investment group Lendlease. The development Lendlease are building – Elephant Park – will eventually consist of around 3,000 new homes, only 116 of which will be socially rented housing. Ordinary people become mere collateral damage in the pursuit of profit and a supposedly bright regenerated future.

State or investor-led gentrification is distinct from but related to the creep of relocators, second-home buyers and buy-to-let investors. Either way, while something is always gained by some, as Henry saw in the Star & Garter that night and as Limarra witnessed in Peckham, something is always lost by others. Usually because communities are disrupted. It's a story familiar to residents of Elephant and Castle, who have witnessed the destruction of their iconic shopping centre and the displacement of the Latin American community for whom it was once a hub. It's a truth that locals in Brixton acknowledge in their resistance to proposals by an offshore fund to destroy and 'rebuild' their historic local market as a shiny emporium beneath a tower housing office space and a hotel. And it's why local people in Manchester are fighting back against what they perceive as an 'Airbnb assault' on their city and the gentrifying nature of regeneration schemes put forward by the council's former leader, Richard Leese. A building can be physically replaced, rebuilt in the most literal terms, but once uprooted a community is fundamentally changed and cannot be artificially reconfigured.

There is one national housing crisis, but it is made up of locally specific issues. Too often, what happens in London and the south-east is conflated with a national reality. This is something that the housing market analyst Neal Hudson has looked at extensively. He notes that in many parts of Scotland, Northern Ireland and the north of England, the problem is less about lack of homes (supply) and more about lack of demand. In the north-east, for instance, where housing, on the face of it, looks affordable, there are huge challenges facing local young people who are often in low-paid, insecure employment, which means they can't save for a deposit to buy those homes. He calls this a 'low-price low-income market'. In such areas in the UK, which include Derry, Redcar, Pendle and East Ayrshire, there is more than enough housing, but because many residents cannot afford it or have moved away to seek employment elsewhere, many of those homes lie empty. Of course, this is not divorced from the capital, because Britain's job market is so London-centric. Meanwhile, in areas such as Ceredigion and Blackpool, Liverpool and Thanet, poor-quality housing is the issue, because a high proportion of homes are old and in disrepair, particularly in the private rented sector. But there are parallels, and even direct links, between what happens in London and what happens elsewhere, because those who leave London take their wealth with them, which then impacts regional housing markets.

As Glass wrote, 'adjacent places to any gentrified area become lodging-house districts where people who want to keep or obtain a foothold in central London are crammed together and frequently have to pay exorbitant rents for the privilege'. Traditionally, this has meant London's suburbs, but it is now also happening in other towns and cities because in the decade leading up to the pandemic 550,000 more people left London than moved to the city, with some 800,000 people commuting into London each day – more than the entire populations of cities such as Leeds and Bristol. That figure is probably higher now, as record numbers of Londoners bought homes outside the capital in 2021. People were already commuting to London from places like Margate and Milton Keynes and as far afield as Manchester and Cornwall before coronavirus. It is easy to understand why, as the national estate agency chain Jackson-Stops says in its blurb about Manchester, 'a Cheshire life is closer to London than you think' and the cost of living is lower.

Equally, in a desirable place like Bristol, which has good links to London as well as its own local economy, just as people move and buy, people move and rent and, as they do, local landlords hike up rents. Not all of these renters will be the 'young creative middle-class migrants' that unsettled Henry, but, as Glass observed in the 1960s when her neighbourhood began to change, also 'people at the end of the municipal housing queue or ineligible for municipal housing like new migrant workers'. These will be people who need to be near low-paid jobs in the city centre but cannot afford to live there, or have moved away from another place because it got too expensive. That is how the invisible but firm hand of the market moves unrelentingly to change an area. Creatives beget the professional middle classes who beget investors. Low-income workers and families stay until they can no longer afford to do so. The elegiac cries as local institutions and family-run businesses change and eventually close are drowned out by the buzz over the bougie restaurants and cafés that replace them.

## Accumulative Dispossession

Bristol has a long history of fighting for renters' rights and resisting gentrification. In the UK, the community union ACORN was founded in Bristol in 2014 and remains incredibly active; local residents also founded the Bristol Community Land Trust in 2011. Community land trusts are democratic non-profit organisations, run by ordinary people, which own and develop land for the benefit of the community. In this sense, they aim to build financially sustainable homes and create inclusive communities to provide a grassroots bulwark against gentrification. Henry, who had close relationships with other local activists, had joined a long tradition of regional defiance.

As he and I sat discussing what was happening in Bristol, we were joined by his friend Paul Smith, then Bristol Council's cabinet member for housing. In 2016 the council had been heavily criticised by the *Bristol Cable*, a community-led journalism platform, after it revealed that the council had sold off via auction almost 300 council homes – nearly 1 per cent of its total social housing stock – since 2005. There was a wider context for this. At the time, the Housing and Planning Bill was going through Parliament. It included a section proposing plans to extend Right to Buy to housing association tenants and the forced sale of any (empty) 'high-value' housing – its most desirable properties – owned by councils. The *Bristol Cable*'s digging then revealed that on 20 April 2016 a further fifteen of the council's homes – located across the city from Hotwells to Cotham to St Paul's to Easton – were about to be auctioned off. Righteously angry locals set up an online petition calling on the council to stop the sales. Why, they wanted to know, were these homes being sold on the open market where landlords and private developers could buy them? In May that year, Paul, having been recently elected to his housing role, did put a stop not just to those sales but to this practice. He used his power as a member of local government to take a stance on the state's own role in gentrification, ensuring that the council renovated the properties earmarked for sale and put them back into circulation as social housing or leased them to reputable homelessness charities for a peppercorn rent. To his mind, what the council had been doing, intentionally or not, was 'helping to accelerate the gentrification of inner-city Bristol areas' by selling off the state-owned Victorian and Georgian housing that, though in poor condition, commanded high values.

'The view I took at the time is that actually we want socially mixed communities,' Paul said. 'You could move all of the low-income people out into the suburbs and gentrify the central areas of the city, but the only thing that stops any area from becoming mainly for wealthy people, that keeps it balanced, is social housing. The housing market – for buyers and renters – is so strong and has such a life of its own that, for me, maintaining social housing in those communities, especially as people bought homes and did them up there, was really important.'

Now in his fifties, Paul, like Henry, grew up in social housing in Bristol. He understood Henry's frustrations and expanded on the problems playing out in Bristol as a symptom of the financial assault on

housing that had taken place, unregulated, for decades. 'I think gentrification is actually a consequence of a dysfunctional housing system, not
its cause,' he told me. 'It's also a consequence of the retreat of the state
because, if you look at the areas which are gentrifying, the only thing
that's holding them back a bit is the presence of social housing. But there
just isn't enough of it to truly even these communities out.' This 'evening
out' was the intention of municipal housing, as envisaged in Aneurin
Bevan's Housing Act 1949.

One particular policy has done more than any other to undo this
vision: Right to Buy. As we talked, Paul confided in me that as a young
graduate in the 1980s, back in Bristol after finishing his (tuition fee-free)
degree in astrophysics, having moved into his own council house in Hartcliffe, he rejected the opportunity to buy his home through the scheme.
He would have been a wealthier man if he had done so, but he objected
to the scheme on ideological grounds. He had a degree, he had a job, he
had 'succeeded', and it felt wrong to take into the private market a home
that might not be replaced with new social housing stock. So he didn't
buy. He moved out. New tenants moved in and, as soon as they could,
bought it through the scheme. He remembers that 'they put ornamental
stone lions on the gateposts'.

I asked him whether he regretted his decision. He smiled. 'My principles meant that my hands were clean, but they didn't stop the house
being sold,' he said. 'The moral of the story is not that I was right, it's
that we need a change in law rather than individual sacrifices. Who knew
what was going to happen? That everything would become so unaffordable. Would I do that again knowing that? Probably not.' Paul's personal
quandary cuts to the heart of the problem of gentrification: the more
people are impacted by unaffordable housing, the more likely they are
to think only of themselves, of how to protect their futures and shore up
their own finances. They may use Right to Buy, or become a landlord
through buy-to-let; they may move to a cheaper area to rent in the hope
of one day being able to buy, or to buy somewhere cheap in the hope of
making money on their home. In this economy, as the cost of living and
housing rises but wages do not, who could blame them? But although
such decisions make financial sense for the individual, they hurt the

fortunes (and wellbeing) of others. That's the push–pull of Britain's housing market.

To this day, urban renewal or regeneration is always premised on the idea of such progress, of socially balanced and mixed communities, but, just as Ruth Glass was sceptical that this was being achieved when slums were cleared in the 1960s to make way for municipal housing, there is reason to be sceptical now: the very blocks that were built on slum-cleared land, like the Aylesbury and Heygate estates in Elephant and Castle, have now been demolished and replaced with new builds that are not affordable to local people. What is most striking about these estates in particular – and why their destruction can be allegorical for that of so many communities – is that Tony Blair visited them on the morning of his election victory in 1997 to declare to TV crews 'there will be no forgotten people in the Britain I want to build'.

The unregulated private rented sector has played a huge role in undermining this, as it allows – no, *encourages* – people to 'invest' in up-and-coming areas, driving up prices and edging out those on low incomes. Without another huge drive to build social housing and introduce some sort of rent regulation, this will continue to occur in a feedback loop.

'It is a problem,' Paul conceded, 'when people buy a home in a "run-down area", only to make loads of money out of it, whether they intend to or not. This has been happening for a long time, though. It strikes me that it was only called a "housing crisis" when it started affecting what the middle classes could afford, too.'

Henry interjected. 'Exactly, and that's a reservation we all need to have about gentrification. Surely it's masochism! It's people hurting their own class, hurting other classes, all for profit. It's like capitalism canni-balising itself.'

There is a bigger context to consider, one which was already becoming apparent in the 1960s and which complicates our understanding of class, particularly as it relates to housing. Our economy has changed almost unrecognisably in the sixty years since Glass was writing. New jobs were created in IT, sales, admin, advertising, the media, which previously either did not exist or did not exist at scale, and which expanded what we once called the 'middle class'. At the same time, as Glass predicted, certain occupations were 'becoming extinct or likely to disappear' – we rarely hear talk now of miners, milkmen, lift and switchboard operators, typists and clockwinders.

By the year 2000, figures from the market research company Ipsos MORI show, the UK had become more 'middle class' than 'working class' and that households of manual and lower-paid workers had been in the minority since the turn of the millennium. It found that in 1968 two-thirds of all households were in the manual or lower-paid social grade bracket. By 2015, the proportion of people in this bracket was 45.8 per cent. This shift had led the soon-to-become Deputy Prime Minister John Prescott to declare as early as 1997 that 'we are all middle class now', and indeed it was a notion that underpinned New Labour's 'big tent' philosophy. It was a nice idea, but it just wasn't true.

As we can see now, we clearly still have a working class – construction workers, supermarket workers, cleaners, farm labourers, carers, hospital porters, Uber drivers, call centre workers, Amazon workers and Deliveroo riders – some of whom are economic migrants and the majority of whom are on zero-hours contracts. These low-income workers are, as a result, the people most likely to live in poor-quality, overcrowded, unstable and sometimes illegal housing. The Trade Union Congress (TUC) said that at the end of 2020 there were about a million workers on zero-hours contracts. Meanwhile, the middle classes have expanded, yes, in part due to a changing labour market and in part due to the rise in the number of people entering higher education, but they are, as Ruth Glass predicted, 'fragmented' and hardly wealthy. You can be deemed middle class now because you went to university and you have a professional job, but that doesn't necessarily mean that your job is secure, your income is mortgageable, your living conditions are good or your pension is substantial. 'There has been some re-shuffling of social groups,' Glass wrote, 'mainly among the middle classes. New minority groups have appeared. But none of this movement is matched by an increase in genuine social mobility.' She was right. Social mobility now goes into decline after university if you don't come from wealth. Consider Henry, who cannot afford to progress due to the exponential rise of housing costs beyond his wages. Social class, as ever, is related to who can afford to buy housing and who cannot, and who can afford to migrate in search of housing they can afford and who cannot. And, uncomfortable as it may be to consider, the perpetrators of one type of gentrification who move in search of affordable homes are as likely to be the victims of a similar process of pricing out elsewhere. Londoners who have moved to Brighton, pricing out locals like Anthony, continue the process of gentrification, driving up prices over the heads of locals as others have done to them.

In 2021, I spoke to Loretta Lees about her research. Through her work in London, she has developed a term to describe what happens when different forces of gentrification come together to make housing precarious: 'accumulative dispossession'. This can be caused by multiple dynamics – poverty, low pay, austerity, state-led gentrification, bureaucratic failures of the benefits system, evictions, the unregulated housing market at large – which result in the build-up of policies and practices which form what she calls 'attacks' on social housing and those who live in it, as well as renters, to create a gradual but brutal dismissal of those on low incomes over time and space.

While the proliferation of gentrification as a concept has given us a language for the visible and, indeed, less visible ways in which urban communities are transformed, she added that 'it's really important that we remember that gentrification is not a singular process'. Ruth Glass may have coined the term but, Lees told me, 'the process predates the term'. In British cities, in particular, because we have different types of housing tenure – freehold and leasehold, private rental and social rental – different kinds of gentrification occur simultaneously and have different impacts on different social groups. 'What you see in Bristol – where "regular" people move in, buy up homes and flip them – is a more organic process,' she said. 'What we are seeing in London and Manchester is that, too, but combined with the state-led gentrification of council estates as well as, sometimes, offshore companies coming in and buying up properties to rent out at scale.'

The consequences of all types of gentrification are equally serious. Consider Cornwall, where, for example, the local NHS trust cannot retain vital staff because there is nowhere affordable for key workers on low salaries to rent. Or London, where companies are seeing staff members leave because they can no longer afford to live in the capital and where they are at the same time struggling to recruit entry-level staff because of high housing costs.

## In Community Land We Trust

We finished our coffees and headed out for Henry's 'gentrification tour of Bristol'. In one area, Stokes Croft, which is to the north of the city centre, residents were taking action against what they saw as the spread of gentrification, coming together to buy buildings and bring them into community ownership – via the Stokes Croft Land Trust (SCLT) – in a bid to stop investors taking over as the area became more desirable. This part of town, dubbed Bristol's 'cultural quarter', is known for its creative community, vibrantly painted buildings, buzzing cafés and, of course, Banksy – Banksy is believed to be from Bristol.

Stokes Croft is, in effect, an outdoor art gallery – 'The Mild Mild West', a Banksy mural that depicts a teddy bear throwing a Molotov cocktail at three policemen, is sited right next to The Canteen bar in the middle of the area. Later, Henry connected me with local residents who feared that the area's status as a cultural hub was making it vulnerable to speculators and investment. A building that had been derelict for years, Westmoreland House, had been bought by developers who were going to demolish it and turn it into flats, but locals, like Henry, felt that something of their identity was being lost. Henry told me that the SCLT was fundraising to purchase one building – 17–25 Jamaica Street – but hoped to expand in the future, with their sights set firmly on several more properties. Change, they thought, might be inevitable, but gentrification was not. It was about giving residents a chance to shape their area, not just having developments imposed on them.

The fact is that in Bristol, as in many other places, the state is not doing enough to rebalance the housing market. In May 2016, the city's mayor, Marvin Rees, promised, as part of his election campaign, to build 2,000 new homes a year – 800 of them affordable – by 2020. Between

1,350 and 1,994 homes were completed each year in the city in the four years from 2016/17 to 2019/20; but of those only between 188 and 312 each year were affordable, according to figures provided by housing officers in September 2020. The think tank the Institute for Public Policy Research found that this was a pattern replicated across England with councils in the west, West Midlands and Greater Manchester also failing on affordable housing delivery. This was, in part, because of arbitrary caps imposed on how much local authorities could borrow to build and a lack of enforcement when it came to private developers meeting affordable home targets and planning regulations.

The overlapping narratives of relocation, regeneration and gentrification beg two important questions: Who are the communities most affected by displacement and unaffordable housing? And who is to blame? We might turn up obvious answers. To the first question: those on low incomes, women, Black people, Asian people, other minority ethnic groups and queer people. To the second: Tories, landlords, developers who hoard land, local councils which sell it off and the international plutocrats who buy it. But the obvious answers are not the right answers. Just as the story of the injustice imposed upon Generation Rent wages a commodious intergenerational warfare, resisting faceless villains risks becoming a convenient distraction from the political conditions that continue to engender a housing emergency. The right policies could help and there is an obvious and ready-made solution: social housing. Not just for those in dire straits, but for key workers, those on low to middle incomes and for the benefit of British society as a whole. Because, as Mindy Fullilove put it, 'the weakest people are most likely to be displaced but the displacement of any group of people has ripple effects through the global ecosystem. Those harms may be harder to see but should never be overlooked in assessing the true costs of displacement.'

# 6

# THE RENT TRAP

### Lancaster

*Council:* Lancaster City Council
*Average House Price:* In the year 2020/21 the majority of sales
in Lancaster were terraced homes, selling for an average of
£161,638. Semi-detached homes sold for an average of £192,911,
with detached houses fetching £332,454. Overall, sold prices in
Lancaster over that year were 10 per cent up on the previous year.
*Average Private Rent:* In 2021 the average rent for a one-bedroom
home was £686, for a two-bed it was £742, and for a three-bed it
was £774.

—

Samantha* turned thirty-four in 2019. She is what you might convention-
ally consider to be 'middle class'. Her parents owned the home she grew
up in, she went to university and she does what my nan would call 'a good
job', in the administration of the NHS. According to many metrics, this
does indeed make her middle class. She is not destitute or currently facing
homelessness but the housing emergency still affects every aspect of her
life. She feels alienated and estranged from the life she thought she would
have. The harm she is experiencing may be less obvious than that experienced by Anthony, Limarra, Tony, Kelly or Henry, but it is just as vital
in assessing the true nature of the dislocation caused by the housing crisis.

In 2019, Samantha earned £24,000 a year, well below the national
average, which, as of 2021, stands at £31,285, according to the ONS.

She is a vital key worker who does not qualify for social housing but cannot afford to buy a stable home of her own. She lives in Lancaster and has done so since she came here to go to university aged eighteen. She has no access to the family wealth that now supports nearly one in four home purchases. Samantha is the type of person we mean if we must talk about 'Generation Rent', someone for whom renting is not a stopgap between leaving their family home and buying a home of their own but a long-term housing solution. Someone who has looked on at the collapse of homeownership among young adults and seen that their chances of owning a home in the UK have more than halved in twenty years. Someone who, on paper, has 'made it' – university-educated and in a professional job – but who, in reality, is not earning enough to pay for the trappings of security supposedly associated with that.

Indeed, she is one Section 21 notice away from being left completely at sea. Having paid almost a third of her salary in rent (affordable housing should cost no more than 35 per cent of your post-tax income) to a landlord throughout her twenties and into her thirties and with no assets to show for it or to fall back on, her financial future is precarious. As we know from Tony's situation, as private renters age, that precarity places a burden on the state which, right now, it is not fit to bear. The situation in Lancaster is distinct from that experienced by Henry in Bristol because there has been less in-country migration to Lancaster and, since the EU referendum, fewer people are moving to Lancaster – indeed, more are moving away. But there are parallel forces at play: the inflation of rents and house prices beyond wages. As Loretta Lees has noted, just as it is assumed by some that the advantages of urban regeneration, or 'revi-talisation' as some policymakers see it, will trickle down and benefit the lower classes, there has long been an assumption that the same is true for rising house prices. Samantha is living proof that this is not the case.

The river Lune begins in Cumbria and runs down from the northern Pennines, forming a sort of city wall for Lancaster and gradually getting wider until it meets the sea at Sunderland Point. Samantha's rented house is outside of the city centre but just inside this natural boundary. She walks to work every day, rain or shine; the walk is pleasant but not short – about forty minutes each way. She could get a car, of course, but then she'd have to pay for insurance and petrol. The costs would defeat the current objective of all her efforts – to save enough money to buy a house. A few years back, she moved further out of town with her flatmates last year, partly because they were forced out of their previous property by their landlord and partly to save money. 'If I lived any further out, I'd actually be in the river,' she joked as we chatted. Breakfast is usually porridge, made at work. Hunger makes her walk faster and a box of oats goes a long way.

Every day, as she walks to the hospital, Samantha imagines her future home. She has to keep focusing on it, like meditation, she told me. Because that's why she is doing this – it is the end that justifies all of her means. She already knows that she'll paint the walls ochre, her favourite colour, and that it will have two bedrooms – so people can stay. This is something she misses: she doesn't want to invite her friends who have kids over – it's a reminder that she's still housesharing – and besides, having a 2-year-old running around when her flatmates are watching TV doesn't really feel appropriate. This means she doesn't see some of her closest friends as much as she'd like, especially the ones who live a long way away. She feels constantly displaced, socially – she is still renting, housesharing and not able to live her life fully due to the social and financial constraints that come with that.

Britain has always been a country where housing is a marker of social status. However, when secure tenancies were enshrined in law, it was possible for renters to decorate, to know how much their rent was going to be, to make their home their own. The instability of today's private rented sector is a consequence of the deregulation of the 1980s and not an essential characteristic of renting itself. Now, as a private renter, you are acutely aware that you are living in someone else's house. In every home you rent, you brush up against this fact. The sofa your landlord won't remove even though it takes up the entire living room, that mysterious mark on the wall, a mattress stained by someone else; together they make an uneasy and constant refrain, your life sung to the tune of the privilege of others, always in relation to your own comparative lack thereof. This means you exist in a state of what Karl Marx would call 'alienation' – the estrangement of a person from their humanity due to the inability to determine their own life and destiny because of external economic forces. For a private renter – any of the people who have shared their stories for this book – this exists in a legal sense, because you have a landlord to whom you have obligations. But it exists also in what the sociologist Dr David Madden and the late urban planner Professor Peter Marcuse called, in their definitive theoretical statement *In Defense of Housing* (2016), a 'psychosocial sense', because there can be nothing 'comfortable' about 'living under the control of another'. As things stand, ontological security is contingent on having enough money to buy your own housing. Homeownership is currently the most secure tenure, and this security is not available to people on low incomes and therefore the different groups that are locked out of homeownership: households headed up by single women, Black, Asian and minority ethnic groups, migrant workers, key workers. The freedom to set up a home as a space of psychological and economic stability, to live without fear, to exist without great difficulty, has become a privilege when it ought to be a right.

Samantha does feel alienated, from herself, from her peers who own homes and from a society that says, 'You are where you can afford to live.' All she wants in the world, all she has wanted for the best part of the last ten years, is a place of her own. If the time comes and she does manage to own her own home, and this, perhaps more than anything, spurs her on, she will be able to bring her 20-year-old cat to live with her – the cat has to stay with her parents because her current landlady doesn't allow pets. Studies show that having a pet can improve your mental health dramatically – even alleviating conditions like PTSD – but this is another basic right not afforded to many private renters. In 2018, Labour proposed making it a 'default right' for renters to have pets. And then, in 2020, the Conservative government declared that everyone 'should be able to enjoy the happiness that a pet can bring to their lives' – but it has not made any binding changes to compel landlords to accept private renters with animals. Samantha wells up thinking about her cat. This always happens. Why does it get to her so much? Not being able to have her cat living with her is a constant reminder of her situation, a signifier of the rights she lacks, of the fact that her house is not her home.

No pets. That's just one of the many ways in which renters' life choices are limited. There are the couples who are forced to move in together too soon because it makes financial sense; and those who put off having children because they can't afford a bigger place. That's not where it ends, though. A married lesbian couple recently got in touch with me to tell me that they had been evicted by their landlord who they believed was homophobic. I have also heard from trans and non-binary people who have encountered overt discrimination while viewing properties. The LGBTQ+ youth homelessness charity akt released a report in 2021 which showed that almost a quarter (24 per cent) of the homeless population in the UK are LGBTQ+-identifying.

Similarly, there are few safeguards against racial discrimination in the private rented sector. In 2020, a young Black woman, who chose to go by the name Aurore* for legal reasons, reached out to me because she had been evicted on the spot by her live-in 'friendlord' (someone you are friends with who happens to own property with a spare room that they would like to charge you to live in) and then removed by the police, even though no criminal activity had occurred.

Aurore had been sitting in the kitchen of the house in Bristol where she had rented a room for almost three months when her live-in flatmate/landlady and, formerly, friend evicted her there and then. At the time, she was on a research placement as part of her PhD and had had a friend to stay for the weekend. 'The landlady was really upset,' Aurore told me. 'She just flipped out and told me to pack my bags. I told her that she couldn't do that, I was a paying tenant, and she replied that me and my friend were being "loud and dominating" and told me to get out. When I challenged her she called the police.' So far, this sounds like a standard dispute in the murky arena where landlords are friends and flatmates of their tenants. What happened next shifted the dynamics: two white Avon and Somerset police officers, both carrying tasers, turned up and refused to go until Aurore left the property. 'The point is that a white person's blatant misrepresentation of events was taken as gospel over that of two Black women. We were not being loud or dominating,' Aurore told me. She believes that she was subjected to racial discrimination by both her landlady and Avon and Somerset Police – and filed a complaint. But because she was renting from a live-in landlady (making her what's known as an 'excluded occupier' and not a tenant), she had little to no recourse.

Troublingly, such agreements are becoming as commonplace as they are flimsy, with homeowners from younger generations renting out rooms to lodgers and friends to cover their mortgages. Aurore was in a precarious position – she was not protected by tenant law. However, her landlady should still have given her what's known as reasonable notice. Additionally, the police should, as a minimum, have checked Aurore's tenancy agreement and confirmed that her landlady was indeed the property owner. She told me they did not do this. When I approached the Avon and Somerset force, they denied racial profiling, but apologised and said they were 'addressing the training issues identified through the investigation into Aurore's complaint'.

One of the biggest problems with the 'unprofessional' private rented sector, where amateur landlords rent out part of their home or perhaps one or two properties, is that prejudices can flare up and infect what ought to be a professional transaction: the provision of housing in exchange for money. There is currently no overarching statutory regulation of private sector landlords, letting or managing agents, despite the fact that private rental is now the second-largest tenure behind home-ownership. This means that the exploitation of people in vulnerable or marginalised demographics is rife but, at the same time, difficult to guard against. And, as Aurore's story demonstrates, when the police are called, they often don't understand the complexities of private rented sector legislation.

All over the country, people's lives are being impacted by the perni-cious nature of private renting. 'There's so much you can't do as a renter and it does affect you …' Samantha told me. 'I suppose it's that feeling in the back of your mind that you're not a real adult, that you're sort of stuck in limbo and waiting for your life to properly start.' She shifted around. I knew she was uncomfortable. I was asking her to think about something that she had tried very hard to lock away. 'I can't even paint the walls in case it affects my deposit,' she said bluntly. 'It really, really upsets me. I hate it. I just hate it. I … it breaks my heart, you know? When you're paying to live somewhere, then it's your home, but the law doesn't see renters that way. It's a constant reminder that you're a sort of second-class citizen.'

Mass mortgaged homeownership is a relatively recent phenomenon in the UK, having emerged in the 1980s and 1990s. But, in that short time, buying a home has become a milestone, a marker of adulthood and a means of social progression. Sixty-three per cent of households in Britain own their own homes. Yet if we had secure and cost-effective homes for private rent and enough social housing, the 37 per cent of people who aren't currently accessing homeownership would feel less desperate. In Germany, a country where just 46 per cent of households own, there is less of a cultural drive towards homeownership. German renters are protected by a legal notice of contract termination of at least three months, and the longer a person rents their home, the longer that notice period becomes. Additionally, landlords can't evict people without a legally valid reason (*berechtigtes Interesse*, or 'legitimate interest'). In Britain, our cultural conflation of homeownership with success and renting with failure imbues an unshakeable and corrosive shame. Being caught in the rent trap is Sisyphean: each month you work to earn money to pay rent on a home you will never own and from which you could be evicted at any time. The 2018/19 English Housing Survey found that private renters spent about 33 per cent (as indeed Samantha does) of their household income (including Housing Benefit) on rent, while those who had bought with a mortgage spent an average of 18 per cent of their household income on it. So, is it any wonder that most people would rather own their own home?

North of Blackpool, south of Kendal and a stone's throw from the Forest of Bowland, the Yorkshire Dales and the Lake District, Lancaster has its perks – Samantha can get out easily into the countryside for hikes and to visit the beauty spots that people travel hours from all over the country for – but none of that quite cancels out the pressure of paying the rent each month. After tax and student loan repayments, Samantha's rent of £430 is almost a third of her monthly income; before Samantha has done anything at all – a food shop, a meal out, a cinema trip – there isn't much left. For Lancastrians who rely on state support but live in privately rented housing, there is another problem, too: in 2020 the average monthly rent for a two-bedroom property in Lancaster was, according to the ONS, £576; households assessed as requiring two bedrooms were entitled to about £525 per month in Housing Benefit via Universal Credit, even with the temporary emergency increase due to the pandemic, which left the average Lancaster renter £51 short. The policy of cutting Housing Benefit and introducing the Local Housing Allowance which had such a great impact on Kelly in Bromley meant that state support doesn't cover average rents not just in London but in less expensive areas, too.

In parallel, in the five years to 2018, house prices slowly but steadily rose by some 16 per cent in Lancaster. The market has, partly, been buoyed by a thriving buy-to-let market which revolves around the university and, while the increase might not be on the same scale as the rises seen in London, the south-east or Bristol, for someone like Samantha who, as an NHS employee, has only had minimal pay rises in recent years, it's still more than enough to mean that owning a home is receding further and further every year; her modest savings pot seems more and more pointless. Lancaster City Council acknowledges that the area faces a housing crisis with the availability of affordable 'intermediate housing' – homes for people like Samantha who don't qualify for social housing but who can't afford to buy outright with a deposit and so want to take advantage of a government-backed affordability scheme like Shared Ownership – the part-buy/part-rent scheme where people buy a percentage of their property with the intention of eventually 'staircasing' up to 100 per cent.

On the surface, government schemes intended to boost homeownership and get credit to less wealthy first-time buyers – such as Shared Ownership and the equity loan scheme Help to Buy – appear to help people like Samantha. These credit products are, as Boris Johnson told a virtual Conservative Party conference in 2020, intended to help turn 'Generation Rent' into 'Generation Buy'. But they haven't. In 2016 a report commissioned by the Ministry of Housing revealed that Help to Buy had helped to build 43 per cent of new homes over and above what would have been built without it because it had helped to fund developers as much as it had helped would-be buyers. That equated to 14 per cent of the total new build output between April 2013 and 2015. This may sound positive, but the problem is that many of the people who bought those homes were people who would probably have been able to buy a house without the scheme. The same 2016 report set out that the median income of working-age households in England was (adjusting for tax) under £30,000 a year. By contrast, official data from the same year released by the Ministry of Housing showed that the median income of those benefiting from the Help to Buy scheme was £42,000 – it wasn't helping people like Samantha. Shared Ownership is a little better, but still it is open to anyone with a household income of less than £80,000 (£90,000 in London).

'I definitely have pressure from family about "not being secure" because I'm renting,' Samantha told me, 'but that always comes without any appreciation of how much it actually takes to save for a deposit or get a mortgage on a single salary – there doesn't seem to be an acknowledgement of how long it takes to get the kind of deposit required when you're a single person. I've also had pushy comments from friends who've inherited property/money – there are two in particular, both on higher salaries than me – about how easy it is to buy property and how it saves so much money compared to renting, without acknowledging that they only got there because their circumstances were different.' In 2020, someone she worked with, on a similar salary, managed to buy somewhere, but it turned out that her deposit came from a family member. 'I know there is no money coming to me,' Samantha told me. 'I have to do this alone and it's hard: I'm not in a relationship and everyone I know who has bought a house has not only done it with their partner, but they've also had help or an inheritance.'

## The Good Tenant

Until recently, the emotional impact of private renting on low-income young people who wouldn't choose it and can't get family help has been an under-studied area. Few people have done qualitative research looking at the turmoil this causes for renters – like Samantha – who are unable to make their dream of homeownership a reality. Once again, it's important to distinguish between the essential characteristics of private renting full stop (not owning property) and its contingent features (for instance, the instability of tenancies post the Housing Act 1988 and the psychological toll of Britain's obsession with homeownership on those who can't access it – since, as previously mentioned, housing is a critical aspect of physical and mental health, social status and identity). Homeownership may not be the answer but, right now, it offers an escape from the precarity of the private rented sector.

This has been the key focus of Dr Kim McKee. McKee has done the fieldwork that fleshes out David Madden and Peter Marcuse's philosophy. She and her colleagues noted in their 2019 paper on the subject, '"Generation Rent" and the Emotions of Private Renting: Self-worth, Status and Insecurity amongst Low-income Renters', that 'shared properties in particular, which are on the rise, pose a much bigger threat to a tenant's mental health'.

Three days after Samantha and her housemates moved to the first house they shared together, they found out that their landlord had put the property up for sale. What followed was nearly twelve months of viewings, phone calls from letting agents at weekends, evenings and on bank holidays asking to be let in and, ultimately, an overwhelming feeling of anxiety and creeping uncertainty throughout the house. 'By the end I couldn't take it anymore,' Samantha recalled angrily. 'It made me realise how few rights tenants in England really have, because there was no way of us complaining. There was no regard for our mental wellbeing. I've started to think nobody cares about tenants in this country – it felt as if we were just little cash machines for the landlord to generate income while the house was up for sale but we had no right not to be harassed, not to have our home invaded or to be taken seriously.'

After that year, the three moved somewhere new together, which is where they spent the pandemic of 2020. They now have a conscientious landlord who treats them well, but Samantha hasn't forgotten that experience and knows how easily everything could change. 'This is why I am so determined now to own a place,' she said, 'but I have to make sacrifices. There's no way I would be able to save at all if I wasn't living with two other people, but, obviously, it's so much nicer to have your own space. I do worry about what all of this means for our services if key workers like me can't afford a secure home of their own.'

Private renters like Samantha often describe feeling like 'second-class citizens'. They have to be on their best behaviour, constantly aware that anything less could impact their ability to get a reference and live somewhere decent in the future. If you rent, you can't get into debt, you can't miss a direct debit or let your earnings dip. You can never truly relax. It is not just your relationship with money that's monitored. You're wary of doing anything to the space, of losing your key and needing to ask for a new one, of doing anything to suggest that you actually live in your home in case it is used against you. For Samantha, this is constantly in the back of her mind, an oppressive feeling that she must always be on her best behaviour. 'I definitely feel a sense of anxiety,' she told me during the second lockdown. 'I bought a lot of furniture in the first lockdown to try and control my environment more, but I wished I could properly decorate.' But she didn't dare because she had finally found 'a lovely landlady' and she felt even more pressure not to annoy her. 'I get stressed about making any changes,' she confided, sounding on edge as she spoke. Human beings are programmed to make their mark on the space they inhabit. Renters – who don't know when or where they will have to move next – are no less inclined to do this, and the popularity with younger people of Marie Kondo – a woman who promises to help us downsize and minimise our lives – and her minimal but stylish approach to interiors surely speaks to that desire to take back some control. As the geographer Professor Yi-Fu Tuan has written, humans exist in 'constant chaos', that's just life. And so, everything we do is an attempt to 'rest, at least temporarily, from the siege of inchoate experience'. But even gardening – which for those with the space to do so became a popular hobby as the pandemic confined us all to our homes – caused Samantha anxiety. She didn't want to plant trees, for example, 'because I don't know how the landlady would feel about it and I can't afford to upset her. I don't want to be evicted and I don't want her to put up the rent beyond what I can afford, so, in a way, I feel like I'm always on thin ice.' Life with a tricky landlord had been so awful that Samantha wanted to preserve her current arrangement for as long as she possibly could, but, as the stories in this book demonstrate, you can be a good tenant – you can be the perfect tenant – and it still doesn't mean you'll be secure.

Now that private renting extends well into adulthood for millions of people, the problems that come with it have taken on new significance. McKee argues that there needs to be more awareness of the impact that the 'lack of control and autonomy' private renters experience at home has on their wellbeing, because their 'living situation is dependent on the decisions taken by others – their flatmates and landlords'. Shared living comes up regularly in her research as a specific source of anxiety. 'It's very important,' she told me, 'to distinguish between the experiences of "forced sharing" with strangers for affordability reasons and "voluntary sharing" with friends or family. They are two fundamentally different experiences.'

Living in a house share might feel communal for some – strangers could become lifelong friends – but demeaning to others. It might help one person cut costs, but add to another's mental load in other ways. 'It might sound trivial,' Samantha told me, 'but having to organise everything you do around other people's schedules – from washing your pants to taking a bath – starts to ebb away at your sanity. You don't feel like an adult.' Of course, adulthood is never free from compromise; this is about the distinction between households formed by choice and households created out of necessity. When you live with a partner or have a family, you must work around others, too, but there is a particular burden that comes with negotiating with people who you are a) not in love with and b) not related to. We've all been there, or at least I have. Living in a house share can be brilliant and it's easy to romanticise the camaraderie, late-night DMCs and impromptu house parties once you're settled on the other side of it. We quickly gloss over the uncomfortable parts: the unidentifiable gunk in the sink; a hob left on overnight; not being able to get into the shower when you need to because your housemate's Tinder date is in there (which makes you miss their unlikeable boyfriend who seemed to stay six nights of the week but never contributed to bills); hearing your housemates having sex and never being able to unhear it; going to the fridge and finding that someone has eaten all of your food.

On Saturdays, Samantha tries to wake up early, so that she can have one or two precious hours in the house before her flatmates get up. She might make herself breakfast and watch TV alone in that time – it might not sound luxurious, but to her it's pure bliss. After a busy week at a busy hospital, this time alone, when she is not interacting with anyone, is priceless. You can download all the meditation apps you like, buy self-help books until you've exhausted Amazon and trawl Instagram for motivational quotes if that's your thing, but sometimes self-care – or being able to practise it – is as simple as having your own space and control over what happens in it. In a shared house, this is not something that can ever be guaranteed.

'When you come home, if you live in a shared house, you have to adjust what you want to do based on other people,' Samantha said to me. 'You don't have a total say over what your evenings look like, over what your life looks like. I might just be wanting to make a tea that involves more than one ring on the hob and not be able to.' On the rare occasion that both of her housemates are going to be away at the same time, Samantha will arrange to take some leave, have a day off work and enjoy having the house to herself. She is stressed, not in the grand 'I'm about to blow' sense, but she is, as she puts it, daily experiencing 'multiple constant little stresses. What I feel,' she added, 'is a constant, chronic stress of all the ways that I just don't want to be sharing a house but have to because I don't have a choice financially.' Housesharing, as anyone who has done it when they didn't really want to will know, can be death by a thousand cuts, and expensive ones at that. That was one of the reasons Henry didn't want to move out of his mother's house in Bristol into a shared house.

To make herself feel better, Samantha buys 'little meaningless things' like calligraphy pens and ink. She now has fifteen different pens and too much ink to count, fancy art supplies which are, she jokes, 'too fancy' for her art skills. It gives her a release. Yet, this expenditure weighs on her. 'I buy things and then I feel bad because I should have saved the money, so it's a constant cycle of negativity. I feel guilty all the time. I think back to going travelling for a year in my early twenties and wish I hadn't spent the money. I know, rationally, that it wouldn't have made much differ-ence, but I still feel guilty about it.'

The impact of millennial adultescence – the stunting of adult life by economic factors – should not be trivialised. It affects people's lives in profound ways, including, for example, when or whether to have children. These changes are so profound that some academics even consider it to be a new life stage. The term 'emerging adulthood' was coined by Professor Jeffrey Jensen Arnett, a psychologist at Clark University, Massachusetts. Arnett sees this as a distinct phase between adolescence and full adulthood, a time of identity exploration 'in love, work and world views' between the ages of eighteen and twenty-nine. His definition has attracted some criticism from developmental psychologists because it suggests that adultescence is an active choice rather than the result of a person's financial circumstances. As Dr Lorenza Antonucci, a sociologist and associate professor at the University of Birmingham, notes, this is why wealth is a more useful metric than class, particularly in the context of social mobility. Students from low-income backgrounds end up taking on more debt on top of their student loans to make higher education work and then face high housing costs in the private rented sector on top of that when they graduate, because they are less likely to be able to put down a huge deposit and buy. 'This is the scariest aspect of the higher education system in England now,' she says.

How can you plan a future for a family if you don't know where you'll be able to afford to live next year?

Social housing could provide a solution if we had enough of it, giving the sort of stability and security that my grandparents were able to use as a springboard. But as a single, working-age person, Samantha would be low priority for allocation of what remains. Yet she is the sort of person that municipal housing was originally intended for: a vital key worker. In London there is an acknowledgement of the need to do something to make sure that people who are key workers – NHS workers, police officers and teachers – do get priority access to buy or rent homes below market rates because, as things stand, they are being priced out of the city. Lancaster's housing market is not the same as London's but, none the less, Samantha's ability to stay where she is and remain in commuting distance of her job is precarious: reliant on her two housemates and her landlady.

Samantha is clear about her current situation. 'Luckily, we all get on well, but what will happen if one of us gets a job elsewhere, or if, for some reason, that changes,' she said. 'I never know if I'll have to move year to year, because affording the rent means three people's lives – three people who are not in relationships with or related to one another – having to stay the same rather than one. It's like a low-level background panic.'

Samantha needs stability. Some progress on this has been made in Scotland. New tenancy contracts introduced at the end of 2017 give tenants greater security, flexibility of tenure and more predictable rent increases as well as longer notice periods. The Scottish legislation also allows for the state to impose rent regulation by creating Rent Pressure Zones (RPZs). With these, local authorities can limit in-tenancy rent rises in areas where prices are out of control; this also allows tenants to appeal a rent rise, should they consider it excessive. Make no mistake, Scotland has a housing crisis. It is not a utopia, but the country has undoubtedly led the way in reforming the private rented sector in the United Kingdom. Positive as all this progress appears in a UK context, the protections for renters in Scotland still lag behind some other European countries.

In Germany, the Netherlands and Denmark, tenants can only be evicted for a specific reason. In those countries, even a landlord selling up does not necessarily result in tenants having to move; in some cases, children can even inherit tenancies from parents. Similarly, Italy, Belgium and Ireland have long-term tenancies which give tenants between three and ten years' protection. Only two European countries, Switzerland and Luxembourg, have a higher proportion of their populations living in the private rented sector than England while also having comparably poor protection from eviction. The causes and consequences of this align with England's: Switzerland lacks affordable housing; Luxembourg faces a crisis because low-income young people are fleeing the country due to high living costs.

Homeownership may be no panacea, but for as long as it remains the most secure form of housing, its appeal will endure. 'If you told me tomorrow, I could have a deposit, I would go and buy a house, I wouldn't go on holiday, I wouldn't buy a car – I would do whatever it took to buy a house,' Samantha concluded. 'Everyone needs a house. It should be a right. I don't understand why it isn't.'

PART TWO

# SQUALOR

*Before the coronavirus pandemic, the housing crisis was already seen by many sector experts as a public health crisis. By the end of 2020 it was clear that idea had become more mainstream. As the nation was locked down, ordered to stay at home, it became apparent that the people living in the 4.3 million homes that did not meet the minimum requirements defined by the government's Decent Homes Standard, and the nearly 800,000 people living in homes deemed over-crowded, were living through the pandemic with a very different perspective. More than that, overcrowded housing actually helped to spread Covid-19 in Britain and increased the number of deaths. People living in cramped condi-tions were, the Health Foundation's researchers found, more exposed to the virus and less able to reduce their risk of infection because they had nowhere to go and isolate. This was a key reason why poorer people and those from ethnic minority backgrounds were disproportionately affected by the virus during the pandemic. Other poor conditions, such as damp and insecure tenancies, have, the same researchers concluded, also led to a rise in other physical and mental health illnesses during the pandemic.*

# 7

# NO NAILS

### Wythenshawe, Manchester

*Council:* Manchester City Council
*Average House Price:* In the year 2020/21 the majority of sales in Wythenshawe were semi-detached homes, selling for an average of £220,527. Terraced houses sold for an average of £188,201, with flats fetching £127,640. Overall, sold prices in Wythenshawe in that year were 12 per cent up on the previous year and 20 per cent up on the 2018 peak of £169,712.
*Average Private Rent:* In 2021 the average rent for a two-bedroom home was £699. At the time of writing, there were no one-, three- or four-bedroom homes listed.

—

The house was halfway down a wide, quiet, tree-lined suburban street. Spaciously placed brown-brick semi-detached homes made up the carefully designed estate. It was October 2019, the sun was out but a chill hung in the air, the trees were turning. A pile of industrial debris – clumps of plaster, bits of wood – sat on the driveway, forcing a treacherous path to the front door.

'I'll put the kettle on,' I heard Amy's* partner Dan* shout in a welcoming way as she let me in. The couple's two dogs followed us as we made our way through the hall. 'Do you want sugar?' I sank into the large leather sofa in the living room that adjoined the kitchen, and they told me about what was going on. It hadn't been a good week. The rubble, it transpired, was left behind by workmen sent by their landlord; they wouldn't be back to move it. Inside, the living room walls were painted a cracked and peeling magnolia. Seeping brown water marks covered the once-white ceiling, while the plaster underneath peeked out like mottled flesh through translucent skin. There had been leaks. In the kitchen, which smelled of biscuits and damp, an empty light fitting hung above us, leaving the room dingy; something had leaked in here, too. A few months before my visit, after one of the kids had just got out of the bath, water had started steadily dripping into the kitchen below. Tiles were coming away from the wall, particularly around the plug socket which powered the kettle.

This wasn't what life in Wythenshawe – one of the oldest council estates in England – was meant to be like. Amy and Dan rented their property from a private landlord but, at one point, it had been a council house. It is one of hundreds of thousands – some 850,000, in fact – of social homes once owned by the state which have ended up in the private rented sector as a result of Right to Buy. The Wythenshawe estate was built in the 1930s and was intended to be a 'garden city' outside Manchester after the town planner Patrick Abercrombie identified the undeveloped land it now sits on as ideal for new suburban homes away from the city's industrialised centre. At the time, Manchester, the ninth most populous city in Europe, was one of the places that desperately needed new, quality housing to deal with overcrowding. Wythenshawe was favoured as a suitable location for building by the city's Public Health and Housing Committees. Construction started in earnest on an ambitious plan for a municipal garden suburb after 1931 when Wythenshawe was redesignated as part of Manchester, and by 1945 its Baguley, Royal Oak, Benchill and Sharston neighbourhoods had an estimated combined population of 21,000. As estates like Wythenshawe developed across the country, they significantly altered the landscape of British housing; they were part of the garden city movement that was started by the urban planner Ebenezer Howard, who founded the Garden City Association in 1899. Howard saw garden cities as 'the peaceful path to real reform', of which Letchworth, near Hitchin in Hertfordshire, was England's first example. Howard's work inspired the architect and MP Sir John Tudor Walters, who, with a committee of experts, set out on behalf of the state to create a blueprint for decent, desirable housing for working-class people after the First World War.

At some point, though, some of Wythenshawe's once-utopian social homes have ended up in the hands of private landlords. Dan and Amy's owned 'a few' in the area, all similarly modest family homes intended as municipal housing. Landlording wasn't his main job, Amy told me. He worked in construction by day – buy-to-lets were his pension, his lucrative side hustle. He was, Amy said, 'absolutely wadded'. This – one of the ugliest aspects of the housing crisis – is rarely addressed: that turning houses into assets and not homes has emboldened some ordinary people who are perfectly happy to screw their neighbours out of the right to decent shelter, because it makes them wealthier. If an eviction is, as Saskia Sassen sees it, the last link of a chain of decisions which ends with the renter but starts somewhere in a meeting room at a bank which relies on mortgages to make a profit, so is this. It's also why the private rented sector is so divisive – the majority of landlords are private individuals, and their buy-to-let properties are a key income source for them. What they are doing is entirely legal.

Historically, landlords have been defensive, loud and organised via groups such as the Residential Landlords Association and the National Landlords Association, which have had immense influence in Westminster. However, since the merger of these two organisations into the National Residential Landlords Association (NRLA) and the appointment of its first chief executive, Ben Beadle, in January 2020, there has been a palpable shift. Beadle has changed the organisation's tune and position significantly. 'The challenge is that we need good landlords onboard because they do provide a vital service, while dealing with the not insignificant number of bad ones,' he explained to me. 'We are absolutely against bad practice and we want to play our part in raising standards by training landlords and encouraging them to be accredited. We want to help landlords be better at what they do.'

This shift of perspective from the most respected landlord lobby group cannot be underestimated. Combined with legislative changes, it could raise standards in the private rented sector. In 2018, shortly before I met Amy and Dan, Parliament passed a landmark piece of legislation which was supposed to address poor conditions in the private rented sector, giving renters proper legal recourse for the first time. It was Labour MP Karen Buck's private member's bill Homes (Fitness for Human Habitation), and it would become the Homes Act 2019, requiring landlords to make sure their properties are in a fit state for people to live in, not only at the start of a tenancy but for its duration. Crucially, it gives tenants the right to take them to court if they do not. Under the act, tenants can take legal action over twenty-nine hazards, including inadequate ventilation and serious mould and damp caused by structural problems.

For the first time, legislation has left no room for doubt: conditions like the ones Amy and Dan were being forced to endure are the landlords' problem. If they don't sort them out, they are breaking the law. It was urgently needed: according to the 2017/18 English Housing Survey, the private rented sector has the highest proportion of 'non-decent homes', with 25 per cent (1.2 million) of privately rented homes considered in poor condition or 'non-decent', compared to 19 per cent of owner-occupied, 15 per cent of local authority and 11 per cent of housing association homes. A 'non-decent' home is one where, like Amy and Dan's, there is serious disrepair or damp.

Just as the instability of private renting is often rebranded as 'flexibility', the lack of control over conditions is often sold as a glorious 'lack of responsibility'. One of the benefits of being a renter is supposed to be that you're not responsible for forking out for repairs. If something breaks, leaks, cracks or starts growing mould, you can call your letting agent or landlord. After all, that is what you pay them for: to provide you with a home. The 2019/20 English Housing Survey revealed that while private renters were more likely (75 per cent) to be satisfied with repairs and maintenance than social renters (66 per cent), there were consistently three main reasons for dissatisfaction across both sectors: the landlord not bothering about repairs or maintenance (35 per cent); the landlord being slow to get things done (25 per cent); or the landlord doing the bare minimum (15 per cent).

How, then, did the tenant/landlord relationship become so warped? Why do so many landlords seem to think they are doing their tenants a favour and why do they not realise that they are providing a service?

Damp, like mould, sounds innocuous. It isn't. If you have either in your home, you are more likely to have or to develop respiratory problems, infections, allergies or asthma. Damp and mould can also impact the immune system. The premise of the Homes Act sounds pretty basic, right? You'd think that something as fundamental as landlords being accountable for keeping the houses they rent out habitable would already have been clearly enshrined in law. That ensuring tenants have proper legal avenues through which to complain when their homes are falling apart at the seams or unsafe would be a given.

Not so. As the number of private renters has grown, due to both the shortage of affordable homes to buy and the diminishing stock of social housing, legislation to protect renters and ensure decent conditions has failed to keep up. As Dave Cowan, a professor of law and policy at the University of Bristol Law School, put it after he finished a big piece of research into housing standards, it was 'piecemeal, out-dated, complex, dependent on tenure, and patchily enforced', and made 'obscure distinctions, which had very little relationship with everyday experiences of poor conditions'. Before Karen Buck's bill, there were provisions to ensure properties were 'fit for human habitation' – but these applied only to houses rented for below £80 per year in London and £52 elsewhere. If these numbers sound absurd, that is because these rent levels had not been updated since 1957.

In theory, there was also Section 11 of the Landlord and Tenant Act 1985, which required landlords of residential property to keep the structure and exterior in a decent state, as well as maintain the gas, electricity and water supplies. But under Section 11, if a property had deteriorated, the landlord was only required to repair it to the state it was in before. But how can it be determined if a home has deteriorated? And what if it was in poor condition to begin with? A huge problem with this piece of legislation was that it did not put the onus on the landlord to ensure that their property was in good repair, but, as the act had it, on the 'conscientious' tenant to flag disrepair. Landlords were not liable to carry out repairs until they had been put on notice that there was a need for them. On top of that, the legislation provided no clear definition as to what it called the 'reasonable time frame' within which the repair must be done.

This is how private renters like Amy and Dan ended up stuck in uninhabitable homes without real recourse for months, and even years, on end. Common problems such as mould and condensation were rarely caught by these provisions – even though they can damage furnishings and make tenants seriously unwell – because they were deemed to be symptoms, not 'examples' of disrepair. In one landmark case in 1985, the Court of Appeal decided that, even though a house was 'virtually unfit for human habitation' due to extreme condensation caused by old windows and poor insulation, the landlord (a local council) could not be held responsible because these problems were the result of a building design defect. The tenant could therefore not get any compensation for damage caused. There were similar cases and failed appeals throughout the 1990s and 2000s. Even when lawyers agreed that a house was uninhabitable, legally there was little they could do about it.

I once encountered this myself when I was living in a mouldy ex-local authority flat with serious condensation issues. I complained to my landlady, who wrote back telling me it was because I dried my clothes indoors after washing them, which she had noticed during a property inspection. This was an absurd accusation for a number of reasons: firstly, she had refused to install a tumble dryer; second, we didn't have a garden so there was nowhere outdoors to air laundry; and third, it turned out that there was chronic damp in the walls. I am, years later, still furious about this incident, though I realise that might seem petty. But these things stay with you. What, exactly, was I supposed to do?

That's why Buck's bill, with the introduction of legal recourse, was so vital. Its passage, however, was obstructed by the fact that the legislative lapse that preceded it was no accident. Conditions in the private rented sector have long been a political problem. Political in the sense that politicians knew how bad things were and took a laissez-faire approach because they didn't want to regulate landlords for fear of encroaching on what they saw as a 'free market'. Buck's Homes bill – which was drafted with two expert housing lawyers, Giles Peaker of Anthony Gold Solicitors and the barrister Justin Bates of Landmark Chambers – was initially voted down by 309 Conservative Party MPs in the House of Commons in 2017, just after the Grenfell Tower fire. It eventually passed in 2018 and came into force in March 2019. But legislation is not enough on its own: you need enforcement and, sadly, the legacy of the cuts made since George Osborne's austerity drive means that local authorities are struggling to find the resources to act against rogue landlords.

Today, estimates as to how widespread poor conditions are vary, but it's thought that, even with the Homes Act in place, somewhere between 1 million and 3 million privately rented homes pose a serious and sometimes potentially lethal risk to the safety and health of the tenants who live in them. Data from the 2020/21 English Housing Survey gives us information about how privately rented properties fare according to the Housing Health and Safety Rating System (HHSRS). It estimates that 4 million, or 16 per cent of homes failed to meet the Decent Homes Standard in 2020. Twenty-one per cent of these were in the private rented sector and 13 per cent were in the social sector. Those 4 million homes would have been home to people living with 'category 1' (i.e. the worst) hazards – dangerous boilers, exposed wiring, overloaded electricity sockets and vermin infestations. For a dwelling to be considered 'decent' it must conform to minimum standards, such as providing 'a reasonable degree of thermal comfort', being in 'a reasonable state of repair' and having 'reasonably modern facilities and services'.

Even before the Homes Act, residential private tenants could complain to the housing team at their local council about poor conditions. Under Section 9 of the Housing Act 2004, the council can carry out an HHSRS inspection, which rates hazards in the tenant's home according to how serious they are. But this, once again, puts the onus on the tenant to involve the council and on the council to carry out proper enforcement. Freedom of Information requests submitted by Generation Rent in early 2021 showed that this doesn't always happen. Requests were submitted to 110 councils, regarding their enforcement activity in 2019–20. Of the councils that responded, 76 recorded 11,570 category 1 hazards in private rented homes. But these councils only served 2,814 improvement notices, representing just 24 per cent of hazards found. Thousands of renters were still – in spite of the new laws brought in to protect them – left without the protections they are entitled to.

There's a wider context, too, one that has been ignored by politicians for too long. At the same time as facing down the crisis in housing, Britain is dealing with the global climate emergency. This crisis is also about home – our shared home. We are already seeing the effects of the global climate breakdown in Britain with flooding and unseasonal temperatures. That's why the ambitious target of setting the UK on the path to net zero by 2050 was announced by Prime Minister Boris Johnson at the end of 2020. The two emergencies are inherently linked. Poorly insulated homes are not energy efficient. They pollute our planet by contributing to carbon emissions. Yet, in 2021, the government scrapped the Green Homes Grant scheme in England just over six months after its launch as part of the 'build back better' coronavirus recovery package. The flagship scheme, which set out to enable homeowners to install energy retrofit measures such as low-carbon heating to decrease the amount of carbon dioxide a home produces or insulation up to the value of £10,000, promised to deliver 100,000 new jobs. Defending its decision to drop the scheme, the government said that take-up had been low. But according to Generation Rent, which analysed how energy efficient homes in the private rented sector were, only 12 per cent of landlords applied for a grant, even though two-thirds of private renters live in properties with a D energy efficiency rating and below.

The fact that a scheme to make homes environmentally friendly and, at the same time, improve the living conditions inside them for private renters was scrapped before it even got off the ground is a sad indictment of both our progress towards net zero and the government's commitment towards making privately rented homes fit for human habitation. Building new homes and retrofitting existing ones are two areas where we have the technology to take action to tackle the climate and housing emergencies right now. It requires investment, but it also requires encouragement and enforcement; the Green Homes Grant provided one – investment – but not the others.

We had a chance to take action to make people's homes warmer, less damp and more energy efficient and, in turn, improve the conditions we all share. We must connect the dots here, just as we must connect the dots between the impact of bad housing on the nation's physical, mental and economic health. Sophie Shnapp is a leading environmental consultant. In 2019, she co-wrote a paper for the European Commission which concluded that poor quality and inefficient housing is linked to ever-rising energy prices. Of course, the point here is that those living in the poorest-quality housing are also likely to be the least well off, so when energy bills go up, they will be hardest hit. The situation, she told me, is compounded by the relatively stagnant wages of renters who end up experiencing fuel poverty and, in some cases, poor health. This is where the housing and climate emergencies overlap with public health even when we are not in the crisis of a pandemic. In 2016, a report from the Building Research Establishment Trust – an independent charity dedicated to improving the built environment – analysed one year's worth of data and estimated that poor housing could be costing the NHS as much as £1.4 billion a year. Had it been properly implemented, and people actively urged to take it up, the Green Homes Grant could have been a joined-up approach to the crisis of conditions in the private rented sector, the public health risks that come with that, rising energy costs and the climate emergency.

'The stark reality is that poverty kills and this is not taken into account in political decision-making as much as it should be. Around 10 per cent of excess winter deaths are directly linked to fuel poverty,' Shnapp told me when we spoke about her research in this area. 'People are dying because they do not have enough money to pay their energy bills. Additionally, people living in the least efficient homes are 20 per cent more likely to die during winter than householders in the warmest properties.'

Shnapp also pointed out that similar schemes in Scotland and Wales have worked. The Welsh government's Warm Homes Nest scheme offers energy efficiency advice and improvements. She describes its outcome as 'protective'. Improving heating and ventilation in Welsh homes led to 17 per cent of children with severe asthma being reclassified as having moderate asthma, and reduced GP visits. Similarly, the Central Heating Evaluation programme in Scotland found that 40 per cent of people who received central heating improvements who had previously reported respiratory, circulatory or rheumatic health conditions said the condition had eased or improved since the intervention.

The failure of the Green Homes Grant in England provides a valuable lesson: we won't reach net zero emissions through poorly designed policy initiatives that display a lack of serious commitment from the government. We need long-term planning, investment and joined-up thinking that acknowledges the links between the crisis in conditions in people's homes and our shared environment outside of them. Improving the energy of buildings, particularly for low-income households, would have a great impact on the reduction of carbon emissions. This, Shnapp concluded, is 'key to supporting global climate agreements'. Improving everyone's health and standard of living fixes the housing crisis and benefits our planet.

As things stand, the lack of incentives for landlords to make their properties decent, combined with the lack of enforcement when it comes to the rights that renters do have, leaves people like Amy and Dan vulnerable to bad conditions and bad behaviour. It puts a strain on landlord/tenant relationships and, once again, leaves renters at risk of a revenge eviction if they deign to complain.

As Giles Peaker – not only one of the lawyers behind the Homes Act, but one of the best people to follow on Twitter if you want to learn about 'squalor in modern Britain', according to the *Guardian* – acknowledged when we discussed the legislation that, while it is 'a major step forward for renters, until Section 21 is actually abolished or retaliatory eviction provisions are reformed, for private renters, the threat of retaliatory eviction will remain'. In theory, renters are entitled to complain, to involve their council and to take legal action to get a Rent Repayment Order (RRO) put in place, but in practice, as long as Section 21 persists, renters have no real power. Think of how easily Tony was evicted by a so-called charitable organisation – private tenants who complain to landlords about issues in their home have a 46 per cent chance of being evicted within six months. And that doesn't account for those renters living in the shadow, illegal private rented sector of overcrowded HMOs, who wouldn't even be issued with an eviction notice.

On top of the enduring rule of Section 21, Peaker is constantly concerned about the limited availability of legal aid (due to ongoing government cuts, starting in 2012) and the lack of specialist housing solicitors, restricting a tenant's ability to take action. He's right to worry. The

Legal Action Group (LAG) has found that thousands of people are made homeless every year because they cannot find a lawyer to help them resist eviction. In 2016, it found that there had been an 18 per cent decline in the number of legal challenges brought, despite it being a time of record repossessions in the private rental market.

Similarly, Shelter, whose expert team in Manchester assisted Amy and Dan, told me that they were constantly overrun with cases. Since 2018, Shelter and the LAG have warned about the creation of 'advice deserts' – areas across England and Wales where there are few, if any, lawyers who can deal with legal aid housing cases. In the same year that they issued that warning, the Legal Aid Agency (LAA) effectively closed face-to-face advice for housing and debt cases in sixty-one local authorities across the country, from Cornwall to Wigan. We might now have the right legislation, but is there anyone left to enforce it and help private renters defend themselves if they can't pay for private solicitors? This was all compounded during the coronavirus pandemic as some people lost their jobs and struggled to pay rent. In September 2021, the Law Society warned that almost 40 per cent of the population of England and Wales did not have a housing legal aid provider in their local authority area. And, as support for renters was cut, the legislation promised to help them by Theresa May in 2019 did not materialise. On 20 May 2020 a parliamentary select committee said that the government needed to accelerate its plans 'to abolish "no fault evictions" under Section 21 within the next 12 months'. By early 2022, this still hadn't happened.

### Can't Complain

'Was there a large silver van on the street when you walked down?' Amy asked me suddenly. There was, I said. This, Amy replied, meant that her landlord was around. Having her landlord nearby had once seemed like a bonus, a selling point – he could easily check in and fix any problems. Now it had turned into a torment, a source of constant anxiety. He had, Amy confided, begun to threaten her and, when he couldn't be bothered to do it himself, he would have cowboy workmen in his employment do it. For months before Amy, on the advice of Shelter, got the council involved (which was shortly before we met), her landlord had ignored her messages. But soon after, she saw him on a nearby street. He called her over. 'He went a bit crazy,' she said, nervously rubbing the pad of one finger over the cuticle of another. 'He was like … "Why have you been getting the council involved, what business do you have doing that?!" It was pretty threatening, to be honest. He just kept saying, "You think you're f–ing clever, do you? You think you're clever?" So I replied, "I don't think I'm clever. I just think I'm a mum trying to protect my children from a house that's not safe," and walked off.'

Amy is tall, perhaps 5 feet 8 or 9 inches. She carried herself with the authority of a busy mum, but she seemed older than her thirty-six years; a glittering nose stud serves as a reminder of her youth. She had a lot on her plate. Dan had broken his back and, when we met, was out of work. At the time of our meeting, he was waiting for spine fusion surgery and looked visibly uncomfortable standing and sitting. His injury was preventing him from working as a labourer. Three of their four children have been diagnosed with autism, and so Amy, who is a former care worker, was more than occupied full-time looking after them. She would have liked to go back to work soon – to be earning her own money. When we met, though, the salary she could expect wouldn't offset childcare costs, even with the specialist support she received. As the campaign group Pregnant Then Screwed has repeatedly pointed out, recent figures from the Organisation for Economic Co-operation and Development (OECD) show that the UK has the second most expensive childcare system in the world – with the cost of childcare having increased by 27 per cent since 2009. As we know from Limarra, if Amy were to go back to work, her Housing Benefit entitlement would decrease. She was between a rock and a hard place.

Sitting on the sofa in Amy and Dan's living room I felt something vibrate. Instinctively, I reached to grab the thing making the sofa buzz, but it wasn't my phone, it was Amy's. 'It's him,' she said, sighing and suddenly seeming much smaller. Her fingers curled around her cardigan, drawing it across her. Dan sighed from across the room. Amy's phone and the message it carried from the couple's landlord, which had changed the energy in the room so quickly, was placed back between us, facing down.

She clearly didn't want to see the next message, and this was the best she could do to protect herself from it, even though everything around us was a reminder of her family's situation.

For too long landlords have operated with impunity – knowing they can more easily evict a complaining tenant than face repercussions for renting out substandard mouldy, damp, leaking, rat-infested homes. The impact of this has not been superficial. Research from NatCen (Britain's largest independent social research organisation) and Shelter in 2016 found that mothers were more likely to suffer clinical depression if they lived in bad housing – indeed, 10 per cent of mothers who lived in acutely bad housing were clinically depressed. Can it be any wonder when they are denied something as simple and necessary as being able to control whether their living environment is safe?

Manchester, like the rest of the country, has a social housing shortage. Amy was on a waiting list which, at the time of writing, had around 13,000 households on it. She was not deemed to be in urgent need. And so, unable to wait and not getting very far with their bidding for social housing, she and her family had moved into the privately rented semi-detached three-bed house, now causing so much pain, in 2014. The walls were covered in photos of them together, but one stood out. It was taken during a family trip to the Canary Islands before Dan damaged his back. Moving house now would have been difficult because of his injury and the kids, even if it hadn't been financially impossible.

When Amy had viewed this house, once the perfect home and now a living nightmare, taking it for £770 a month seemed a no-brainer. It appeared perfect, freshly painted with a garden for the kids and a driveway. There was nothing not to like. But, as we all know from *Changing Rooms*, a lick of paint can conceal a multitude of sins or, in this case, a catalogue of horrors. Landlords are masters of disguise. 'It looked so great when I first saw it,' Amy said as we sat watching her dog paw at the door to be let in from the garden; she decided he was too muddy. 'But now I realise what the landlord had done. He'd just had plasterboard put over mouldy walls, plastered and painted over it and made the place look decent without actually doing anything to address the damp.' This only made the property's underlying defects worse because concealing mould behind plasterboard means the wall cannot 'breathe', which traps the moisture and exacerbates the problem.

I remember a flat I once lived in where the shower curtain was stuck to the bathroom tiles with Scotch Tape adhesive pads instead of hanging from a rail. The economics of being a buy-to-let landlord are pretty simple: you want more money coming in than you're dishing out while you sit back and watch your 'nice little earner' climb steadily in value and eclipse the mortgage you've taken out on it. But keeping a property, particularly an older one like Amy and Dan's, in decent condition is expensive and requires diligence.

The private rented sector doesn't seem to work like other consumer markets. And yet, because of the financialisaton of housing, tenants have been turned into consumers: they pay landlords to provide a service – housing. But the truth is we have often more rights as consumers when we rent a car, buy a fridge-freezer or take out a loan than we do as private renters. Even free marketeer think tanks such as the Adam Smith Institute have begun to criticise this in recent years, calling for the consumer rights we're used to having in other markets, from utilities to financial services, to be applied to the private rented sector. 'It's so hopeless,' Amy said, sighing. 'It takes him weeks and weeks to do anything. And then, when he does call workmen and get them to come over, they always ask me for payment. I'm now out of pocket by more than a grand because of the problems with this house, the landlord never pays me back. He's now just pretty much ignoring my messages about it all.'

In 2018, the government introduced a 'rogue landlord database' in an attempt to appear as if it was doing something about this. A rogue landlord is one who knowingly flouts their obligations by renting out unsafe and substandard accommodation to tenants. However, only local authorities were able to make entries in the database after issuing a banning order against a landlord. As ever, the issue of enforcement came up. Six months after its launch, it was revealed that the database was completely empty. Not a single name had been entered. More than a year later, in 2019, a Freedom of Information investigation by the *Guardian* showed that only four entries had been made. There was outcry and the then Prime Minister, Theresa May, promised to give tenants access to the database, too, but this has yet to happen. By 2020, there were still only twenty-one names listed. A consultation had been opened in 2019 to look at how to reform the database and open it up. By early 2021, it still hadn't fed back. Back in 2018, it was estimated that there were about 10,500 rogue landlords operating in England, so how the database ended up with only twenty-one entries in two years is anyone's guess.

Amy showed me the straw, or rather sink, that broke the camel's back. The appliance in question was in the downstairs bathroom, and it was hanging off the wall, supported only by the copper pipes which fed its taps; they were perilously bent forward at a 90-degree angle, like candles reshaped by the glaring heat of direct sunlight. Where the sink was once attached, only a few glue marks remained. There were no holes, no broken plaster, just gummy marks where the No More Nails superglue had given way under the sink's weight. 'A plumber had just told me the shower was bust and we needed a new one and then this happened.' Amy heaved the words out, exhausted. 'Imagine if that sink had fallen on one of the kids. I can't. It was glued on! Glued!'

'I wish we were back there,' Amy said, pointing at the picture of the family in the Canary Islands once we had returned to the living room. The daily battle of trying to restore the conditions of her home had made her so anxious that she was taking diazepam – a powerful drug with an anxiolytic effect – in a bid to steady herself.

This story speaks to a long-established convention: rapacious rogue landlords renting out slum-like homes. The shadow of the notorious 1950s slum landlord Peter Rachman still hangs over the private rented sector. Rachman travelled around in a chauffeur-driven Rolls-Royce and bought up run-down houses in Paddington and North Kensington, west London, using loans from his building society. He gained notoriety for his exploitation and intimidation of tenants: letting homes out to people – particularly Black people – who struggled to rent elsewhere; he knew that he was their only hope, and paid little regard to whether his houses were habitable. The term 'Rachmanism' later entered the *Oxford English Dictionary*, to define 'extortion or exploitation by a landlord of tenants of dilapidated or slum property'. But, of course, notorious landlords do not only exist in the history books. Fergus Wilson is a former maths teacher who went on to become one of the UK's largest buy-to-let landlords in partnership with his wife, Judith, also a former maths teacher. In 2008, they were listed at number 453 on the *Sunday Times* Rich List, with a fortune of £180 million. By 2019, they had sold all their properties. Wilson gained infamy in 2014 when he sent eviction notices to every tenant of his who received Housing Benefit and told letting agents that he would no longer accept tenants receiving state support. This amounted to at least 200 evictions. Egregious as it sounds, the key thing to note about this story is that, as a private landlord, Wilson was completely within his legal right to issue eviction notices under the Housing Act. He, and many landlords like him, may do the job of the state – housing those in need – but, unlike the state, they have no legal duty to house their tenants. At the time, Wilson defended himself by arguing that cuts to Housing Benefit had damaged his business. 'Rents have gone north and benefit levels south,' he said. 'The gap is such that I have taken the decision to withdraw from taking tenants on Housing Benefit. From what I can gather just about all other landlords have done the same. Our situation is that not one of our working tenants is in arrears – all those in arrears are on Housing Benefit.'

Even after Section 21 is gone, without rent control or long-term protected tenancies (like the ones in Scotland), a landlord will be able to evict someone by proxy simply by putting the rent up. Surveys show that the vast majority of landlords have the financial resources to pay for repairs and maintenance. But the imbalance between demand for properties and supply, combined with the legislative imbalance in favour of landlords, means, exasperatingly, that there are few financial incentives for landlords to invest in their properties in order to attract renters. So, a landlord's decision about whether or not to invest in the maintenance and repair of their property is more likely to be driven by capital growth than rental incomes, further highlighting the warped relationship between the cost of rents and the conditions of rented accommodation: an expensive property won't necessarily be a decent one.

'The panic attacks have just got so bad as a result of the confrontations with our landlord,' Amy said to me, 'even taking the children to school, I'm having them, doing things that I have to do, that I don't have a choice about it. It's horrible, it is, it's horrendous. For the past week I've barely eaten. I even refused a McDonald's breakfast this morning as a treat and that's not me.'

As I got ready to leave, Dan spoke up. 'It's an epidemic, isn't it?' he said, referring to the housing crisis. 'Landlords snap up properties because they see these "How to do it yourselves" shows on TV in the morning and think, "Oh yeah, that's easy. I'll have a bit of that." But social housing's gone to pot, they sold it all with Right to Buy, all the council houses have gone. I grew up in one and now our kids live in one but it's a mess and owned by a guy who doesn't care.'

Clear-sighted, Dan had cut through the emotion of his family's situation. If the British dream is achieving homeownership, this is a nightmare. Once again, Right to Buy, a policy intended to help people achieve the holy grail of housing stability, owning a piece of the world for themselves, has backfired. 'Effectively, I'm a victim of a policy that helped my mum because she bought our house in Salford using Right to Buy,' Dan added. 'If all the council houses were still there, there wouldn't be this three-and-a-half-year wait, or whatever we're looking at, while we have to keep paying extortionate private rent.' Policies intended to generate support for a political party and help them to win elections become determining factors in people's lives beyond the Westminster bubble. Dan thinks about Right to Buy all the time. He can see how it is related to the crisis in housing because it is his lived reality.

About a week after my visit, Amy WhatsApped me. Finally, there was movement. In light of the fact that the council's inspection team had deemed their home a category 1 hazard and had also agreed that she was being 'harassed' by her landlord, she and her family had been given a more urgent housing allocation band. But they still faced a long wait for a socially rented home. The cycle continued: not enough social housing; new legislation with patchy enforcement; nowhere else affordable in the private rented sector to move to.

Months later, Amy WhatsApped me again with an update. Dan had finally had his back operation. The recovery was painful, as you would expect, but he was slowly going back to work. While he was in hospital, though, the shower at home had broken again, leaving Amy alone with the younger kids and no way to wash them or herself. The council took action against their landlord but, while he fixed the shower and, cosmetically at least, dealt with the damp, she told me that she'd never feel safe in her own home, knowing that, ultimately, her landlord still had all the power. He made it very clear that she had 'crossed' him. She was looking to move but, as ever, it was a question of what she and Dan could afford and how quickly they could move up the council's list. She was bidding for social homes but not winning. The priority was consistency for the kids and, unfortunately, that meant staying put until she had a viable solution.

'Dan's recovering, so we both sit and talk about what our future house is going to be like,' she wrote to me.

'Sounds great!' I replied.

Amy was typing …

'… the garden, the decking. Dan is thinking about the paddling pool he's going to build, maybe a barbecue. Hot tub, beautiful living room. Rose* will have a unicorn bedroom! We've already decorated our future house in our head. We just sit up for hours in bed talking about it.'

# 8

# MODERN SLUMS

### Weston-super-Mare, North Somerset

*Council:* North Somerset Council
*Average House Price:* In the year 2020/21 the majority of sales in
Weston-super-Mare were of semi-detached houses, selling for
an average of £242,851. Detached homes sold for an average of
£354,299, with terraced houses fetching £210,449. Overall, sold
prices that year were 13 per cent up on the previous year.
*Average Private Rent:* In 2021 the average rent for a one-bedroom
home was £630, for a two-bed it was £901, and for a three-bed it
was £1,298.

---

The place was damp. A dark spider's web of black mould spread across
the wall; spores bloomed in intricate clouds on top of white paint so
damp it looked as if it was sweating. A fresh coat of paint had clearly
been deployed to disguise years of dankness and leaks even worse
than those that Amy and Dan had been living with in Wythenshawe.
Twenty-seven-year-old Josephine* lived here with her three children,
all aged under ten. Her mother, Joy*, 61, who works as a courier,
was telling her story incredulously, because Josephine, who suffers
with severe anxiety and depression, was struggling to tell it herself. In
January 2019, Josephine's tenancy in Weston was up for renewal. Her
private landlord wanted to sell up and cash in, so he told Josephine
he would not be renewing her lease with a cursory but customary one

month's notice. Josephine and her family were left facing homelessness.

This was before the pandemic, and demand here – in this somewhat neglected former tourism hotspot – was less pressurised, and house prices and rents lower than in Peckham, on the Kent coast, in Essex or in nearby Bristol. So, unlike Limarra, Tony and Kelly, Josephine and her family were rehomed reasonably quickly, placed in another privately rented property. Housing options, like job options, are the ultimate postcode lottery. At first glance, the freshly painted ground-floor flat in a Victorian terrace seemed like a good solution: postcard pretty, its bay windows had views over the sea. The only downside was the rent, which was steep. Still, Josephine accepted it immediately: with three young children, she was not able to work and she didn't feel she was in a position to be picky. Her Housing Benefit covered the majority of the rent of £670, but she still had to top it up by about £70. This was a stretch. 'After she paid bills and bought food and clothes for the kids there was nothing left,' Joy told me. 'She was putting a brave face on it, but I know sometimes she was only having toast for tea so the kids could eat.'

From the outside, these terraces in Weston-super-Mare's centre appear grand. With their flint facades and turreted roofs, they hark back to a time in the town's history when it was a bustling seaside resort. Built during the prosperity of the Victorian tourist boom, when visitors flocked here in their thousands, they were once hotels and guesthouses. Now, according to Alan Rice, a 70-year-old former local councillor and renters' rights campaigner, many private renters like Josephine find themselves trapped inside their squalid, 'slum-like' conditions. These are the new slums of modern Britain – overpriced and unsafe – into which people who would once have been allotted good-quality, well-equipped council homes are placed by councils which have a social housing shortage. And, just as the ghetto landlords of the last century, like Rachman, knew they had a captive tenant market, allowing them to take advantage of Black families who couldn't rent from anyone else, slum landlords today know that they have nothing to gain by making improvements – if the current tenant doesn't like it, there will be someone else to fill their property. There will always be people on low incomes who can't afford to buy a home and not enough social housing to support them.

Weston-super-Mare embodies this problem. In 2016, just over 44 per cent of the homes in the town's two most deprived seafront neighbourhoods were privately rented. By 2017, the area had a concentration of 163 dangerous and poorly managed bedsits. More than 32 per cent of the rented housing in these wards was classed as non-decent, with more than 18 per cent of them containing the most harmful hazards, including extreme cold, unsafe electrics and fire risks (a figure which is just above the national average). Economically, Weston is one of the most deprived areas in North Somerset. In fact, North Somerset is a predominantly rural area but it has high income inequality due to the concentration of deprivation in Weston. Every month, about 300 people apply to North Somerset Council for social housing. Every month, they join a growing waiting list which, in 2021, was 3,300 families long. But, as the council's own guidance states, it is 'unlikely' that they will be offered social housing unless they are in 'severe circumstances', because only 600 properties become available each year. How does this connect to rising house prices? The average price of a home in North Somerset continued to rise by more than 5 per cent in 2018/19, according to Land Registry data, with local agents putting it down to rising numbers of Bristol residents moving out of the city to find an affordable bigger property. The cumulative effect is that the average property price in North Somerset is now higher than in the rest of the south-west, making it ever harder for first-time buyers and renters in the area. Indeed, as Bristol becomes more expensive, people are pushed out to places like Weston, which impacts prices in areas which are still just about affordable. This was particularly pronounced during the pandemic. The town was suddenly a hot ticket because of people wanting to move out of Bristol to be by the sea. *Somerset Live*, a local news website, reported in July 2021 that the town's property market was 'busier than ever'. One of the town's leading estate agents, David Plaister Ltd, told the publication that 'demand was outstripping supply with many properties selling in just a matter of days', adding that 'out of every ten properties we sell, between six and eight are to people from Bristol'. This is yet another example of how homeownership and private renting interact, and of how the housing market can shift quickly when an area suddenly becomes desirable and those on low incomes are priced out.

But before the coronavirus-induced demand for fresh seaside air, Weston's high numbers of private renters on low incomes, combined with a lack of social housing, created the perfect conditions for buy-to-let slum landlords to swoop in at the lower end of the market. They knew that they had a captive tenant base and a guaranteed income through Housing Benefit, but that little would be asked of them by their tenants, who had few rights anyway but were probably not aware of those that they did have.

For Joy, a line was crossed when the plaster fell off the wall in her grandsons' bedroom. 'It happened while they were sleeping,' she told me. 'The brickwork was left completely exposed. The wall was caving in because of the damp. The kitchen was damp. The heating didn't work properly, it was January. It was freezing.' Josephine's three children were then aged eight, five and two. The youngest had asthma and all the time they were living in this flat Joy had never seen him on his nebuliser so much. Children with asthma are put at risk when they are housed in cold, damp conditions. Epidemiological evidence shows that indoor dampness is associated with respiratory symptoms, aggravation of pre-existing asthma and development of new-onset asthma. This is because mould releases tiny spores into the air which can trigger asthma symptoms. Similarly, damp and cold tend to produce bronchitis-type symptoms and the presence of mould produces asthmatic-type reactions. But for parents like Josephine under pressure – financially, emotionally, from local council housing officers, from their landlords – it can be difficult to escape. In any case, why should it be down to her? Aren't we all involved if public money is being used to pay to house a family in a place that results in a child's health being at risk?

Not all parts of the UK are affected equally by the crisis of standards in the private rented sector. In England, the landlord register has been adopted more rigorously by some councils than by others; the same goes for enforcement, which is equally patchy. In 2019, a joint research project by the Chartered Institute of Housing (CIH) and the Chartered Institute of Environmental Health (CIEH) called for the government to get behind a compulsory national register and licensing scheme of landlords, with adequate resources for enforcements. At the time of writing, this still hadn't happened. In Scotland, all landlords must sign up to a landlord registration system and obtain a licence, which has to be renewed every three years. In Wales, landlord licensing has been mandatory since 2016 through a scheme called Rent Smart. This means that landlords must undergo training before being granted a licence and those who manage their properties poorly can lose their licence. It works. There have been prosecutions. One, in Saltney, on the England/Wales border, came about because the landlord had failed to address serious fire, excess cold, carbon monoxide and electrical hazards at the property. There were exposed live wires, no working fire alarms, no fire doors and no working heating system. The joint CIH and CIEH report found 'clear evidence that property standards have been improved' in areas where licensing schemes such as those in Wales and Scotland are implemented.

Weston-super-Mare is separated from Wales by the Bristol Channel. On a clear day, you can see Cardiff from the town's shores, but because Weston is in England the rental situation is very different. The same rules do not apply. As a result, as elsewhere in England, unscrupulous landlords know they can act with impunity. In England the only licensing scheme which is mandatory across the country is having to obtain a licence if you let out a large house in multiple occupation. But councils often struggle to enforce this because, put simply, they don't have the cash to send people round to check on every privately rented property. I have heard multiple reports of councils granting HMO licences without first inspecting the properties. Beyond that, we have selective landlord licensing for all rented homes; more than fifty councils now operate such a scheme for buy-to-let landlords, demanding that they sign up to a code of conduct. However, the government has not made them compulsory across the country and, even if a council wanted to license all of the private rented properties in its patch, it wouldn't be able to, because the scheme is limited to 20 per cent of the private rented housing in any local authority area unless there is Secretary of State approval. Because of decreased local government funding and the decimation of legal aid, such licences aren't always enforceable even where they do exist. Added to that, in 2020, during the pandemic, the government said that councils should 'adopt a pragmatic approach' on licensing enforcement and consider pausing the introduction of any non-mandatory licensing schemes to free up resources for more pressing concerns. Given that overcrowding and poor living conditions enabled the spread of the virus, this once again reveals housing to be a blind spot for our politicians.

For Joy, who had lived in the same social home for the last twenty years, watching her daughter's mental health deteriorate so rapidly as the result of her surroundings, with no proper policy to protect her, was painful. 'She was embarrassed, it ruined her confidence,' she said. 'She didn't want to go out because all of her clothes stank of mould. It reinforced her anxiety and her depression. I think she felt a bit worthless. She felt like a bad mother.'

Taking the situation into her own hands, Joy contacted everyone she could think of – the local MP, the council, local councillors, the letting agents, the landlord. Nothing changed. All she got, she recalls, were 'just platitudes, platitudes, platitudes. Nobody was taking it seriously.' Perhaps it's unsurprising that Joy, who experienced social housing security as a younger woman, was shocked by her daughter's experience. She was outraged at how much the system had diminished and deteriorated. She couldn't believe how little support or recourse there was for private renters. 'It just seemed like nobody really cared,' she told me disgustedly. 'You're not homeless so they just dump you and cross you off the list. Doesn't matter if where you're living is unsafe.' Joy's view was that the home her daughter's family was living in was 'unfit for a dog, let alone a human being'. She still had the mentality that social housing was a right, an entitlement, and carried zero shame about that. This, combined with the fact that she herself had a stable home, meant that she was able to take up her daughter's plight, to advocate for her.

We protest when the 'normal' political channels – voting, writing to your Member of Parliament, contacting your local authority – aren't working. Protest movements arise out of the traumas of daily life. They are the result of the realisation that social systems, whose fairness ought to be immutable, have become unfair and fluctuating, bent to the whim of those with wealth and power. In Weston-super-Mare, as in other parts of the country, a resistance to the injustice of Britain's housing crisis has been building, thanks to organisations such as ACORN, as well as to the work of dedicated individuals like Alan Rice. They are often doing the work of the state: social workers, councillors and legal advisors.

The UK has a long history of housing protest, mainly centring around rent strikes. The London Great Dock Strike in 1889 involved dock workers in the Port of London who withheld their rent to take a stand against dangerous working conditions, precarious employment and low pay. They won and, from their victory, came a strong trade union, the Dock, Wharf, Riverside and General Labourers' Union. In 1915, a Glasgow woman named Mary Barbour organised a rent stike in order to protest at the 25 per cent increases imposed upon renters by landlords looking to profit during the First World War. She and thousands of other renters physically resisted bailiffs and marched to demand the release of imprisoned strikers. When Lloyd George's wartime government heard about it, it implemented rent freezes. This was the first time rent control had been imposed on the private rented sector by government. In the 1930s, rent strikes were organised in Leeds by the Leeds Federation of Municipal Tenants Associations, and in London's East End by local Communist Party and Labour Party members, eventually resulting in the establishment of the Stepney Tenants' Defence League in 1937. In 1959, tenants in St Pancras, central London, set up the United Tenants' Association after the council approved rent increases above those recommended in the Rent Act 1957. It organised marches, meetings with councillors, rent strikes and a 16,000-signature petition. When all of these were ignored, it kept up the demonstrations until July 1960 when, following clashes with bailiffs and the police, the Public Order Act 1936 was evoked, banning its members from protesting. The years 1968 through to 1973 saw council tenants organise a number of rent strikes across east London in response to national rent increases which 9,500 tenants refused to pay. In January 1969, Horace Cutler, the Director of Housing of the (Conservative) Greater London Council (GLC) wrote to them warning that the council would take action if they did not pay the increase. The reaction of the organised tenants was to hold a series of demonstrations in early 1969, starting with 3,000 gathered outside the Hampstead home of Tony Greenwood, the (Labour) Minister of Housing and Local Government. They won. In November 1969 the government introduced a bill to ensure that the GLC kept to the norm of no more than a 7s 6d average increase in any one year. All other local authorities in the country had agreed to do this voluntarily.

Given the current state of private renting in England, you may wonder why more people don't protest more. In the past, conditions were just as dire but large workplaces where people saw one another every day, trade unions, churches and other mass working-class organisations made it easier to rally cooperation and action, even without social media. Today, social media does facilitate activism and organising, but it can also create the illusion of action. Who dares to complain, to strike or to protest when they fear it might make their situation worse – that it might get them evicted? I was struck by calls for a rent strike from wealthy left-leaning individuals at the start of the pandemic. I'm not sure any of the people interviewed in this book would or could take that risk, even if they wanted to. Having a County Court Judgment (CCJ) against their name for rent arrears could stop them from being able to find somewhere to live in the future. As Frances Fox Piven and Richard Cloward wrote back in 1977 in *Poor People's Movements: Why They Succeed, How They Fail*, 'protest is also not a matter of free choice; it is not freely available to all groups at all times, and much of the time it is not available to lower-class groups at all'.

Joy complained in 'every single way' she could possibly think of about her daughter's situation, because she just couldn't believe that 'a landlord was allowed to rent a place like that out'. However, it still didn't work. When she had exhausted all official channels, somebody suggested that she should get in touch with the renters' union ACORN and that's how she met Alan Rice. 'It's only because of him that the council agreed to find her somewhere else.'

### Resistance

Without the protections they need and with local authority enforcement lacking, some renters are turning to tenants' unions for help in plugging the gaps where the state is failing. ACORN tries to do that. Alan was ACORN's co-ordinator in Weston.

Now aged seventy, he had moved to the town in 2015, just before Banksy opened his pop-up Dismaland 'bemusement park' installation on the site of what was once known as Tropicana. In the 1960s and 1970s it had been a hive of activity. The building started life in 1937 as a lido known simply as 'The Pool' which, at the time, had the largest open-air swimming pool and highest diving board (an incredible Art Deco construction) in Europe. In 1983, the place was rebranded as Tropicana, complete with a fun pool, wave machines, beauty queen pageants and, of course, giant plastic pineapples and raspberries to fit the 'fun and fruity' theme.

In 2000, Tropicana closed and, despite several attempts to reopen it – one of which was thwarted by the 2008 economic crash – none had succeeded. Faded and boarded-up on the seafront, it became a symbol of the degradation and economic decline of coastal towns around the UK. Banksy might have attracted 150,000 visitors over five weeks, generating an estimated £20 million in revenue for the town, and brought the Russian feminist punk band Pussy Riot out to the Bristol Channel for their live UK debut, but none of this translated into long-lasting change for locals like Joy and Josephine.

Alan moved to Weston from Worthing in West Sussex to be closer to his daughter in Bristol and his son in Swansea. As a former councillor, he is someone who has always been involved with local politics but, he told me, it was Dismaland that really started him on his 'housing journey'. He first came to know about ACORN because they had a stall there. He got chatting to them about Weston's housing crisis and, four years later, he was not only a member of the union but pretty much working full time, unpaid, to support people – particularly renters – with their housing problems. He has helped many people get new homes, get deductions to their deposits back and complain about poor conditions. Alan is a homeowner, but he has enormous sympathy for the plight of renters. What has shocked him most – more than poor conditions – he explained, is 'the bureaucracy' people have to deal with if they want to move or complain. 'I was a councillor for years and, honestly, sometimes I do wonder if I'm making more of a difference like this,' he said. The work he was doing was, as he saw it, a symptom of, not a solution to, the housing crisis. Even back then, he was right. As we saw in the pandemic, ACORN and other local groups (including Tony's Colchester Renters) came into their own.

Concern about standards in Weston's private rented sector predated the pandemic, though. Locals were so concerned about the health of renters that in 2016 they established the Heart of Weston steering group – a community forum in which people could get together, discuss how to improve the community and produce reports – in an attempt to improve their health and wellbeing. In their conversations, they concluded that the private rented sector was a cause, not a symptom, of deprivation and poor health in Weston-super-Mare. Alan shared with me a report they put together which resembled something written by a benevolent Metropolitan Sanitary Association back in the 1800s: 'Five per cent of households don't have central heating, over one third of children who live in Central ward are in poverty, 500 adults and 119 children were helped by the foodbank.'

It was helping with the Heart of Weston steering group report that cemented Alan's commitment to housing activism. 'So many of the homes we're talking about here should really be described as "slums",' he said. 'If you're a private renter, your life is just worse than other people's – it's as simple as that. It causes lots of pain and anxiety and I'm just not sure people register that fact enough. They don't understand that vulnerable people get put in bad housing and they become more vulnerable.'

### Housing as a Public Health Crisis

Many people have a multitude of problems – money, mental health, unemployment, poor physical health – but unstable and unaffordable housing exacerbates all of them. On the flip side, stable and affordable housing can ease them. Alan started to contact local GP surgeries to try to discuss health and housing conditions after the steering group's report. 'When I found out that the life expectancy of people living in Central ward was at least ten years shorter than other parts of Weston, I just had to do something,' he said.

We know that bad housing makes people – like Anthony, Limarra, Tony, Kelly, Samantha, Amy and Dan and their children, Josephine and her young family – psychologically and physically sick. The work that has been done on the mental health side, by the likes of Dr Kim McKee, demonstrates in no uncertain terms that being forced to live in private rented accommodation long term, particularly in HMOs or houses in poor condition, has a detrimental impact on the mental health of many private renters. The threat to people's physical and to our society's public health more broadly, which we've known about since the late Victorian era, was not so widely discussed in the 2010s. We only remembered its potentially deadly impact when bad housing helped to spread coronavirus in 2020.

Until relatively recently, the explicit link between conditions, housing stress and the physical health of renters hadn't been properly explored, but as those directly impacted by the housing crisis enter positions of power where they can make a difference, that is changing. Dr Amy Clair, who herself is both a private renter and a millennial in her early thirties, was a research fellow in social policy at the University of Essex specialising in housing when we first met. She is now a researcher at the Australian Centre for Housing Research at the University of Adelaide but remains based in the UK. In recent years, her work has exposed the serious health implications of housing stress on private renters. In 2018, she produced a groundbreaking piece of research that showed a direct correlation between poor-quality housing and health problems. By taking blood samples from private renters and homeowners, Clair and her then colleague Dr Amanda Hughes were able to use data from biomarkers to examine what renting is actually doing to people's bodies.

Clair and I spoke at the start of 2019, shortly after her study came out. 'Biomarkers,' she explained to me over the phone from her office in Essex, 'are objective indications of medical states – they can predict certain diseases and tell us about the physiological processes going on in a person's body.' The biomarker that she focused on in her study is called C-reactive protein (CRP). It is associated with infection and stress. The liver produces CRP in response to inflammation. High CRP levels can, in some cases, indicate that there's inflammation in the arteries of the heart, which can mean a higher risk of heart attack, but they're also an indicator of autoimmune conditions such as arthritis and inflammatory bowel conditions and certain cancers. By taking blood samples from the people who participated in her study and cross-referencing their CRP levels with their housing situation – whether they were renting or owned their own homes – Clair hoped to establish whether private renters had higher CRP levels and, therefore, poorer health than homeowners. And they did. She also found that people living in detached houses – that is, which stand alone and usually have a garden – had lower CRP levels than people living in flats or semi-detached homes.

This isn't the first time that CRP has been found in people experiencing financial struggles or social stress. We already know that the presence of this marker is related to unemployment and having a low socio-economic position. So what this protein can also tell us about the impact of inadequate housing on those living in it is hugely significant. 'The fact that the effects of poor housing and housing instability are showing up in people's blood,' Clair said, 'proves that it is absolutely making a difference to their lives. I think this research really adds to the justification for improving the conditions in the private rented sector once and for all and if this doesn't nothing will.'

In 2020, Clair deepened her research in the context of coronavirus. She noted that, because private renters had higher levels of CRP and that those living in detached homes had better health than those living in other forms of accommodation, the increased time spent at home under lockdown could potentially exacerbate these effects. 'Larger, more spacious homes allow for a separate working space (if working from home), space for exercise, space for solitude and greater storage space for food and essential supplies,' she wrote. 'Private rented homes in England, however, are on average 28 per cent smaller than owner-occupied homes, and it is likely that the greater space and likelihood of having a garden afforded by detached homes in part explains the finding of lower CRP for people living in detached houses.'

The inequality was stark: for those in poor-quality housing, lockdown meant more time exposed to cold, damp and other hazardous conditions, with consequences for both their physical and mental health. 'The challenges brought on by Covid-19 are being faced by many people in addition to existing housing challenges,' Clair wrote in her report. She went on to say:

Disabled people face significant challenges finding suitable housing in the current housing market. Racism persists, limiting the housing options of people from ethnic minorities, and racist incidents associated with Covid-19 have also been reported. People in receipt of social security have increasingly found it difficult to find private and social landlords that will rent to them, as well as experiencing affordability, quality, and security issues. Covid-19 is exacerbating the challenges faced by many people navigating the housing market. The lockdown will also confine people to homes where they experience abuse, and there are concerns, with increasing supporting evidence, that domestic abuse will increase during the lockdown, particularly affecting women and children.

Pandemic aside, if we knew that the effect of living through Britain's housing crisis was stress – inflammation in the body – which can lead to disease, why aren't we doing anything about it? Just as mould exacerbates asthma, the stress of living in private rented accommodation inflames other health conditions. And yet this truth is rarely acknowledged when we talk about the housing crisis, which is often discussed as though it is an isolated structural problem, unrelated to public health.

The fact that Clair was herself a private renter – when she was doing her research she was living in a room costing £670 a month in Colchester – meant that, for her, these weren't theoretical questions or academic curiosities; her research was an extension of her own lived experience. Just as it matters which demographics enter journalism to tell our nation's stories, it matters who enters medical research. 'Younger researchers who rent,' Clair said when I asked her if she thought there would be more work like hers in years to come, 'don't need to be convinced that the stress of renting is "a thing" from the outset, we know that it is. We've seen it for ourselves. I know from my own experience that if I have a housing problem, it affects my health.'

In the early twentieth century, those in charge and with the power to facilitate change slowly accepted that housing was a public health matter. In 1901, the philanthropist Joseph Rowntree wrote about the 'inadequate and insanitary' housing of the 'struggling poor' and lamented the impact this was having on people's health. As the decades went on, politicians came to believe that poor housing impacted the health not only of its citizens but of the country as a whole, which is why municipal housing became a policy priority. But, through the social housing sell-off, the deregulation of the private rented sector and the privileging of the rentier class of landlords, this has been buried under arguments about free markets and the importance of mortgage finance to our economy. Even the Conservative-friendly argument, though it misses the point about the ethics and morality of this emergency – that bad housing is damaging the economy because it keeps people sick and economically inactive – seems to fall on deaf ears. And yet, this issue impacts our overstretched and underfunded NHS all the time.

Remember the Building Research Establishment Trust report which said poor housing could be costing the NHS as much as £1.4 billion a year? As a result, some Clinical Commissioning Groups (CCGs – the bits of the NHS which decide how funds are spent), such as Oldham and Sunderland, introduced 'social prescribing' schemes, where they funded the prescribing of home repairs and improved insulation with new boilers, double glazing and other insulation. They did this because they had found that hospitals were repeatedly discharging patients to recover at home who would actually become sicker because it was too cold or too damp. It was more cost-effective to invest in repairing their homes than it was to have them in hospital, bed-blocking or, worse, becoming more unwell. Robert Barr is the leader of the Liberal Democrat group on Warrington Borough Council and its spokesperson on housing. Prior to this he gained more than twenty years' experience on the boards of housing associations in the area. He told me that these decisions are made because prevention is better than cure. 'We found that CCGs would fund us to carry out housing improvements, because doctors recognised that poor housing conditions – the absence of a decent home – is a health risk,' he told me. 'Doctors would tell us that they were treating people with conditions that would keep recurring until their housing circumstances changed.'

This makes sense, but it shouldn't fall on the NHS to pay to make sure basic housing standards are maintained. That should fall on landlords, enforced by central government and local authorities. Josephine's situation is, sadly, typical of poor privately rented accommodation. I've visited local council temporary accommodation riddled with damp, the walls covered in black mould, where young children are suffering with asthma which their mothers believe is being exacerbated by living conditions. I've interviewed a family with two disabled children who were sleeping in one bed because they had been made homeless by their landlord. Both children had a rare life-limiting condition called Duchenne muscular dystrophy. The eldest needed a wheelchair, which was being kept in the car because there was no room for it in their temporary accommodation.

I've heard from Shelter advisors that they are regularly encountering people with severe health problems who cannot be discharged from hospital because their poor-quality housing might make their condition worse. 'Only recently, we worked with a family whose little girl wasn't allowed to leave the hospital where she was being treated for cancer, because the doctors couldn't risk letting her go back to the single room in the shared house that the family lived in,' one Shelter advisor told me in early 2020. 'Her treatment meant that she couldn't be around lots of different people, and the doctors said the child's health, and even her life, were being put at risk by her living conditions – an unimaginably frightening situation for any parent. So, the family turned to us for help in approaching the council to try and find a more suitable place to live.' The evidence is there, not only in the research but in the fact that NHS budgets are now being ploughed into bad housing. And yet nothing changes.

Back in the shadow of Dismaland, Alan Rice was frustrated. When we spoke, North Somerset Council hadn't prosecuted a single landlord for housing offences since 2015. He was not convinced that Karen Buck's Homes Act would be worth the paper it was printed on unless it had funding for proper enforcement. 'We have all these problems here,' he explained, sounding uncharacteristically defeatist, 'but two years ago, after a really long inquiry, the council decided not to introduce a licensing scheme for all landlords in the worst parts of the area.' And so, bad landlords in Weston continue not to be regulated in any meaningful way. I spoke to Alan on the phone again in 2021. There had been a change in the balance of power in the 2019 local elections, which saw the Conservatives lose overall control of the council and the Lib Dems make big gains along with Labour and the Greens, all of whom had a manifesto commitment to landlord licensing, though it had still not been implemented. 'I think what happened,' Alan said, 'is that a big landlord objected, and they dropped the idea. The landlord lobby effectively killed it.'

Like so many of the people I meet, Alan had lost faith in Westminster. 'They don't get this, because it's not their experience,' he said. 'We're talking about a broad range of people here: people who are on Housing Benefit and not in work; people who are in work and being topped up by benefits; and people who don't receive any benefits and work. I'm not sure politicians understand that. It doesn't make sense. If you look after other people's dogs, you need a licence. If you open a pub, you need a licence. But if you provide housing ...' There was silence. 'I'm just thinking,' he said finally. 'This is too urgent – it needs to be sorted out now, it's happening to people now. I just keep wondering ... is anyone listening?'

We know what the problems are, and we know how to tackle them. If the political will was there, people's health wouldn't be in jeopardy because of rogue landlords, unstable housing and homes that aren't fit to live in. Tenants' unions and grassroots activists are providing urgent help and advocacy to address the symptoms of the crisis in the private rented sector, but Westminster should act to address its causes.

# 9

# THE SHADOW PRIVATE RENTING SECTOR

### Bradford, West Yorkshire

*Council:* City of Bradford Metropolitan District Council
*Average House Price:* In the year 2020/21 the majority of sales
in Bradford were semi-detached houses, selling for an average
of £148,016. Terraced homes sold for an average of £108,420,
with detached houses fetching £266,240. Overall, sold prices in
Bradford were 4 per cent up on the previous year.
*Average Private Rent:* In 2021 the average rent for a one-bedroom
home in Bradford was £516, for a two-bed it was £648, and for a
three-bed it was £707.

—

A bright blue spring sky stretched out over West Yorkshire as I travelled
by train from Shipley to Bradford. The city is 227 miles north of Alan
Rice's one-man housing helpline in Weston-super-Mare and forty-five
miles north-east of Amy and Dan in Manchester. It lies between Leeds
to the east and Blackburn and Preston to the west. This is the centre
of a metropolitan district with a population of about 530,000 spilling
out into the surrounding rural areas. Once a booming textile capital,
Bradford, like much of the post-industrial north of England, has long
fallen on hard times. Over the past ten years, there have been various
attempts to revive the city, but the money available to do that has been

savagely hacked back. The council has seen £278 million cut from its budget, halving its spending power, and the area has the highest rate of child poverty in the Yorkshire and Humber region.

Too much of our understanding of the housing crisis is framed in a context which is not only characterised by the trope of 'Generation Rent' but a context which is only relevant to London and the south-east. This has flattened the regional nuances and complexities of the problems into one homogeneous story. In post-industrial cities like Bradford, with large migrant workforces and comparatively cheap rents, there is still a crisis. It just gets less mainstream press.

When Helen Syrop, 40, the mother of two children, picked me up from the station, she was fasting for religious reasons. She is a Christian who believes that it is her duty to work to end homelessness and rough sleeping in her home city. She has always volunteered at local churches and says her faith shapes her commitment to addressing inequality. It was for this reason that she founded Hope Housing ten years ago. The aim of the project, which runs on charitable donations, has always been to cover the many gaps in local authority housing provision. If hidden homelessness primarily affects women, and specifically mothers, then rough sleeping or street homelessness, as Helen encounters it, mainly impacts men. Over time, she has found herself (through circumstance rather than design) specialising in helping migrants from central and eastern Europe, who are known as A8 and A2 migrants. A8 migrants are people from eight of the countries that joined the EU in May 2004: the Czech Republic, Estonia, Hungary, Latvia, Lithuania, Poland, Slovakia and Slovenia; A2 refers to migrants from Bulgaria and Romania, countries that joined the EU in January 2007. According to the official statistics, in 2019 the majority of people who qualified for homelessness support in Bradford were of White British (69 per cent) or Pakistani (10 per cent) origin. The people Helen helps aren't generally eligible for state support, though she helps them argue otherwise. This is because of what's known as the No Recourse to Public Funds (NRPF) condition, usually applied to people who have come to the UK but do not have leave to remain, who have temporary immigration status or who have not paid tax because they are either not supposed to work or have been working cash in hand.

This exists because of Section 115 of the Immigration and Asylum Act 1999, which rules that such people have no right to access the majority of welfare benefits, including income support such as Universal Credit if they become jobless, other tax credits and housing support if they become homeless. The Combined Homelessness and Information Network (CHAIN) found that in 2021 just over one fifth (22 per cent) of rough sleepers in London were from central and eastern European countries.

When we met in 2019, in a pre-coronavirus world, Helen was unusual in her readiness to talk about helping people who had no access to state support. Grassroots organisations and charities generally didn't want to advertise that they were doing this. That all changed for the better because of the pandemic, when the government announced its 'Everyone In' strategy in March 2020, which meant trying to make sure everyone – regardless of their immigration status – was housed during the first lockdown. Through this scheme, councils across England accommodated 37,430 people who were rough sleeping or at risk of rough sleeping, including those who had NRPF. The total number of people helped is unknown, but the National Audit Office (NAO) reports that 2,000 of the people housed in London hotels alone in September 2020 were ineligible for benefits. This paved the way for more change in 2021, when the High Court ruled that there was a legal basis for councils to continue to help people who had NRPF, which set an important precedent. This ruling came out of an important legal case brought against Brighton & Hove City Council by Timon Ncube, a 61-year-old asylum seeker from Zimbabwe, after he was told by the council that it had no statutory duty to house him. As this chapter will discuss, this demonstrates that change is possible but, once again, highlights how toothless Britain's housing legislation is without proper funding to back it up.

Bradford has a long history of reliance on migrant workers. During the city's industrial expansion in the nineteenth century, Irish seasonal workers lived in some of its worst slum housing while enabling it to become a thriving textile town. Over time, German and German Jewish migrants joined them, helping to turn Bradford from an early industrial town into a Victorian city. In the twentieth century, after the Second World War, large numbers of displaced eastern European people

– particularly Poles and Ukrainians – arrived, taking jobs in the textile industry and significantly helping the post-war economic recovery. In the 1950s, 1960s and 1970s, various immigration schemes saw large numbers of workers and their families arrive from outside Europe – mainly from the Caribbean, India and Pakistan. Bradford's textile industry in the latter half of the twentieth century owed its survival largely to south Asian workers.

The comparatively cheap cost of property in Bradford, relative to Birmingham, Manchester or London, has meant that the city's private rented sector has fallen prey to predatory slum landlords, motivated by profit and with little regard for maintaining decent standards – or even the law. They buy up multiple buy-to-let properties and turn them into HMOs. Today, Helen told me as we drove down a road near the centre of town before stopping in front of a row of grand but dilapidated Yorkshire stone houses set back from the street by generous front gardens and stone stairways leading to large arched front doors, Bradford's migrant workforce is mainly from eastern Europe. The city has the fourth-highest number of manufacturing jobs of any city in the UK after London, Birmingham and Leeds. People come to fill those jobs from within the EU: mainly from Bulgaria, Latvia, Lithuania, Poland, Romania and Slovenia. And, when they do, they need somewhere cheap to live. The young men from this demographic whom Helen encounters work in nearby factories, food-processing plants and car washes, sometimes illegally and often cash in hand. 'They generally live in HMOs – some are more legal than others,' she said as we wound through the city. 'It's all fine until they get sick, lose their job and fall out with the landlord, and then they're evicted – just like that – with nowhere to go and no access to public help.'

This is where the crisis in housing interacts with Britain's deliberate creation of a 'hostile environment' for migrants, as Theresa May so notoriously said in a newspaper interview in May 2012 – even those our country relies on to do vital jobs. The living situations Helen described form what's known as a 'shadow' part of the UK's private renting sector. This is housing that operates in a legal grey area, where landlords refuse to provide tenancy agreements or even to confirm knowledge of their tenants' existence. The shadow rented sector largely consists of illegal sublets and operates under the radar of poorly resourced local authority enforcement teams. It is often home to vulnerable, low-income tenants who cannot afford to go elsewhere, are not familiar with the law or who fall back on unlawful arrangements in order to avoid the landlords' 'right to rent' immigration status checks which are mandated by the government. The full scale of the shadow private rented sector is difficult to gauge, but the most comprehensive investigation of it was done in 2020 by Cambridge House, a London-based organisation founded in 1889 to provide social services to the urban poor and campaign for social justice, in partnership with leading housing academics such as Dr Julie Rugg at the University of York. As Rugg notes, 'vulnerable tenants are targeted by landlords and letting agents deliberately undertaking multiple breaches of tenancy and housing law in order to maximise their rental profit'. Indeed, these landlords are choosing to rent property to people they know have few rights because it is lucrative and, when things go wrong, they can simply deny all knowledge of the arrangement. They achieve this by having a third party – often a lead tenant, known as the 'mesne' tenant, who collects rent on their behalf. This allows a landlord to claim that they have no knowledge of anyone who is subletting illegally from that tenant if anything goes wrong – which might include non-payment of rent leading to eviction or being caught in an immigration check.

In the past decade or so, Britain's private rented sector has been a breeding ground for the growth of such criminality in places where rents are high relative to property quality; market pressures create a tolerance for overcrowding among tenants; there is a growing population of economic migrants; there have been cutbacks in enforcement within an unwieldy legal framework; there is poor support for tenants seeking legal recourse and low penalties for convicted offenders; and a growing use of the internet has meant identities are harder to verify.

And yet, in the past twenty years, and particularly in the run-up to Brexit, it was not this story – the fact that vital but vulnerable migrant workers were experiencing the sharp end of the housing crisis – that received attention. Instead, what was tacitly accepted and normalised was the glibly racist and xenophobic narrative that immigration – the arrival of workers like the ones Helen helps when they fall on hard times – was contributing to housing shortages. It was spun into mainstream political discourse by members of the Conservative Party as they unthinkingly repeated Nigel Farage-isms in a bid to ward off the encroaching electoral threat of UKIP. In a speech in December 2012, Theresa May, then still Home Secretary, cited a London School of Economics report and claimed that more than a third of all new housing demand in Britain was caused by immigration, and that it was this that was pushing up house prices. 'And there is evidence that without the demand caused by mass immigration, house prices could be 10 per cent lower over a 20-year period,' she said. There was no shortage of *Daily Mail* headlines from the same period peddling the same ideas: 'Immigration "causing housing crisis"' (2003); 'Revealed: How HALF of all social housing in England goes to people born abroad' (2012); 'We don't have a housing crisis – we have a population crisis' (2017); 'Immigration has pushed house prices up by 20 per cent over a 25-year period, says Tory minister' (2018).

Given that we have seen record house price growth since leaving the EU and as a direct result of government policies such as the Stamp Duty cut, it is fair to say this last comment has proved deeply inaccurate. During the pandemic, figures from the ONS show that the average UK house price increased by 10.2 per cent, the highest annual growth rate seen since before the global financial crisis, in August 2007. Indeed, the idea that immigration is responsible for our affordable housing shortage can be easily debunked. Firstly, as the story of NRPF shows, there have been many migrant workers who have been unable to access support in recent years and, even if migration dips (as it did during the pandemic), the gap between supply and demand is now so big that it makes little difference to waiting lists. Second, let's be clear: according to a briefing note on the Houses of Parliament's own website, there is no evidence that social housing allocation favours migrants. On several metrics, the government's own data have shown for some time that immigration hasn't had any real material effect on the availability of affordable housing. It is not the reason that rents are unaffordable. It is not the reason that welfare has been stripped back. And it is not the reason that we don't have enough social housing.

None the less, this narrative – that the housing pinch points we are all experiencing, such as not being able to buy, unaffordable rents, a lack of social homes – are caused by mass immigration has been pervasive and persuasive. In 2018, the National Conversation on Immigration, run jointly by Hope Not Hate and British Future, produced the largest ever public survey on immigration, with more than 13,000 people surveyed. In the south-east, they found that a scarcity of affordable housing meant a common demand of those they surveyed was greater control over rates of immigration and over migrants' access to social housing. Whether these two things are connected in the south-east, where house prices are particularly high, is up for debate. Once again, like the tales of middle-class millennial Generation Renters and their feckless avocado consumption, it's easier to scapegoat unpopular demographics (young people) or groups who are already feared (foreign migrants) than it is to have a serious and nuanced conversation about the economic and political reasons for the housing crisis. Politicians genuflect to these views because it is politically expedient and they want to win elections.

So, let's keep debunking the notion that immigration is responsible for the housing crisis. It is an idea that has fundamentally reshaped Britain's politics in recent years. The impact of immigration on the housing market is complex and geographically specific but, broadly, the stats – the facts – tell a very different story to the one implied by those *Daily Mail* headlines. According to Oxford University's Migration Observatory, 74 per cent of recent immigrants (defined as those who have been in the UK for five years or less) were in the private rented sector in the first quarter of 2015: they were twice as likely to be renters as compared with the total immigrant population; and while 39 per cent of the total foreign-born population were in the private rented sector, this compared to just 14 per cent of the UK-born population. Added to that, far from driving up house prices, Dr Filipa Sà, a labour economist at King's College London, found that immigration actually lowers, rather than raises, house prices in some areas. In a 2014 *Economic Journal* article, she wrote that an increase of immigrants equal to 1 per cent of the initial local population leads to a 1.7 per cent reduction in house prices, based on immigration data from the ONS's Labour Force Survey. This, she explained, was because immigration often leads to an outflow of natives, which leads to a lower demand for housing.

Indeed, on top of that, the very London School of Economics report that May cited as the source for her 2012 claim also says: 'In the early years even better off migrants tend to form fewer households as compared to the indigenous population; to live disproportionately in private renting; and to live at higher densities. However, the longer they stay, the more their housing consumption resembles that of similar indigenous households.' This explodes the notion that immigration is the biggest strain on social, private rented and affordable owner-occupier housing – people who are recently arrived in this country live in worse-quality, more crowded housing. And so, migrant workers take up less space because they often end up in the privately rented housing that few other people would take up, and rogue landlords exploit that.

This is where HMOs like the one I stood outside with Helen that day come in. They, not social homes, are the housing of last resort for those on the lowest incomes. And they are often unlawful because no tenancy agreements have been signed. Their unwritten contracts are to housing what zero-hours contracts are to the gig economy – which is fitting because they are often home to those with the least stable employment. And, like the gig economy, they present a trap: those who live in them pay rent but exist on the margins and, when things go wrong, find themselves without a safety net. They speak to the increasing work and life precarity that is becoming an accepted feature of British society.

As Helen and I approached the building, we saw four young men sitting outside, joking, eating Haribos and drinking cans of Relentless. I told them I was a journalist and asked if I could record an interview with them. They agreed on condition of anonymity. Three of them told me they were 'cousins'. They were originally from Hungary. Their friend was also from Hungary. They all came here for work. The most talkative cousin called himself George,* but wouldn't tell me his real name because, as well as doing shifts in production in a nearby foam factory, he had a side hustle: selling phones and cars on Facebook but not paying tax on that work. The other two did ad hoc gardening and casual construction jobs. In practice, that's one area where immigration actually forms part of the solution to the housing crisis: in 2015 the Chartered Institute of Building noted that any caps on immigration would harm housebuilding rates, as not enough British-born workers were either trained or interested in careers in construction, and migrants had been filling the gap. All the fourth friend would tell me was that he 'worked with cars'. Whether this was work that was legal or not, he didn't say.

The three cousins were sharing one room, which they had found on Gumtree, in the HMO. They paid £80 each a week and each earned around £1,000 a month before bills. No letting agent was involved in this arrangement and none of the tenants could tell me what type of agreement, if any, they had signed with their landlord. The landlord knew the young men were all living in one room, but he 'doesn't care', George told me, because he's 'a good guy'. I looked at George directly and asked him if the landlord was collecting extra rent for the overcrowded room. He smiled at me, said nothing and sipped his drink.

The growth of shadowy shared renting has been analogous to the transformation of Britain's housing stock into HMOs. This has been a damaging trend for many years now. It is yet another side effect of the transition of many properties in this country's cities from homes into pension pots for small-time landlords who might seem accommodating to tenants, like the men I met in Bradford who were happy to cram into one room if it meant they could save on rent, but who, in reality, don't care about their legal or moral obligations as housing providers at all. When something goes wrong we might imagine that these landlords will suddenly become a lot less obliging. Data on this is patchy because it is notoriously difficult to collect. The English Housing Survey, which is published by the government department responsible for housing, is based on face-to-face interviews with resident households, but households in precarious situations are unlikely to make themselves available for such interviews. They are more likely to be considered vulnerable or to be economic migrants and may not speak English well. Ben Reeve-Lewis is a founder of Safer Renting and the co-author of the 2020 report *Safer Renting: Journeys in the Shadow Private Rented Sector.* He has been a tenancy relations officer for more than thirty years. He told me that 50 per cent of Safer Renting's clients do not have tenancy agreements.

The two houses Helen and I stood outside that day held between five and six households apiece, with each room home to more than one person, making them overcrowded according to two definitions, space and bedroom standards. The latter states that a home is legally overcrowded if two people, aged ten or over, who are not cohabiting or married have to sleep in the same room. Statutory overcrowding is a criminal offence, unless it falls within an exception, for example overcrowding due to natural family growth. The rooms, all the young men told me, were cold, before adding quickly that they couldn't really complain beyond that. They were, however, living in exactly the sort of overcrowded accommodation that would, just a year later, help spread Covid-19. The transmission of infectious diseases was a huge impetus for the slum clearances of the twentieth century, and living in overcrowded accommodation where disease was present meant that people like my own grandparents were given priority need for social housing. So, by allowing these conditions to exist once again, Britain's politicians had created a petri dish for the public health disaster that would unfold in 2020. When Covid-19 came, the severity of that situation was laid bare. If the virus got into one household in a shared rented or overcrowded property, it spread like wildfire.

In January 2021, the subcommittees of the Scientific Advisory Group for Emergencies (SAGE) said that the most effective way to reduce transmission of the virus inside one household and between others was for 'the [infected] person to self-isolate within a different room as far as possible' from other people. They listed ideas for preventing infection at home, including 'maintaining adequate physical distancing' and 'limiting the use of sharing surfaces or objects (e.g., towels)'. This, they estimated, would reduce infections by between 10 and 15 per cent. Meanwhile, Public Health England recommended that infected people 'use a separate bathroom from the rest of the household where possible'. But following this guidance was nigh on impossible for anyone living in a multi-generational household, temporary accommodation with shared bathrooms and toilets, or in a shared HMO. In the three years to 2019, an average of 787,000 (3 per cent) of the estimated 23 million households in England were overcrowded. That means that they had fewer bedrooms than they needed to avoid undesirable sharing, and they had no chance of observing the government's advice about isolating or shielding. On top of that, more than 100,000 families are known to live in one-bedroom homes. Anyone living under these circumstances who was required to self-isolate during the pandemic did so in punishingly claustrophobic conditions. Each trip to the shared bathroom or kitchen carried a risk of infection. And not only was there likely no garden to escape to, but there was also no living room. To explain this in simple terms: we did not have good enough quality housing to support the policies implemented to prevent the spread of the virus. Covid prevention standards were higher than the bedroom standard.

And so, the living conditions that George told me were fine and better than nothing in 2019 became potentially deadly in 2020, according to analysis from Professor Rebecca Tunstall at the University of York's Centre for Housing Policy. Very early on in the pandemic, she began looking into the impact of housing overcrowding. In early 2021, she told me that, after gathering her own data and analysing it, she found that all the available evidence suggested those living in overcrowded homes were at greater risk of infection and less likely to have a room to isolate in if they did get sick. Given that we know coronavirus is airborne, it makes sense that overcrowded housing, where it is difficult to isolate or ventilate properly, enabled it to spread. The official SAGE advice reflected and noted that hostels and hotel rooms had been provided for infected people who could not self-isolate safely at home in several countries, including Italy, Finland, Poland, Serbia and Lithuania. Tunstall concluded from her research that such a measure here would have prevented a number of deaths, given that an estimated 35,000 or 27 per cent of UK deaths prior to June 2021 were due to infection at home.

While we will never know exactly how many infections took place at home because the data hasn't been recorded at any time, we do know where Covid-related deaths have occurred. There can be no doubt that poorer people and those from minority ethnic backgrounds – who are statistically more likely to live in overcrowded housing or homes without spare rooms and bathrooms – were disproportionately impacted by the virus. Only 2 per cent of White British households are overcrowded, whereas for Bangladeshi it is 24 per cent; Pakistani, 18 per cent; Black African, 16 per cent; Arab, 15 per cent; and Mixed White and Black African, 14 per cent. Using data from the Ministry of Housing's household resilience study, Tunstall found that these groups were more likely to be shielding and isolating than other demographics; in 51 per cent of all households the isolator or shielder would have to share a room, and in 72 per cent they would have to share a bathroom. Such is the state of Britain's housing crisis that spare bedrooms, living rooms and homes with more than one bathroom are regarded as luxury commodities today. And we know from the English Housing Survey that more than two-thirds of homeowners aged sixty-five and over have at least two spare bedrooms, meaning that they are living in under-occupied homes.

So, once again, there is a huge disparity between the experience of private renters and homeowners which intersects with wealth and race-based inequity. Staying at home might have been safe for some during the pandemic, but home proved to be a major site of transmission for those living in cramped conditions. 'The exact location of infections is one of the big data gaps of the pandemic,' Tunstall told me over Zoom. 'But there can be no doubt that a substantial proportion of all Covid transmission in the UK would have occurred at home. A Chinese study found that during their lockdown, 69 per cent of infections were at home, for instance.'

Professor Tunstall also cited a UK study which found that, when the government's tier system was in operation during the pandemic, people in areas categorised as Tier 4 (that was, the most restricted) had an average of five contacts with other people per week, and 1.5 of these were at home. This study found that 78 per cent of 'close contacts' passed on to the NHS Test and Trace were household members. This research confirmed what we already knew: cramped housing fuelled the spread of coronavirus in Britain. As a 2020 report from the Health Foundation stressed, overcrowding was aiding transmission and might even have increased the number of deaths, particularly in poorer areas.

## Fine Until It's Not

Back on the doorstep of the Bradford HMOs, George told Helen and me that one of the things keeping him and his cousins in England was the 'very bad political situation' in Hungary. He said that life under the country's Prime Minister, Viktor Orbán, was difficult. Orbán is known for having introduced a public workfare system which aimed to get unemployed people back into the labour market in response to the 2008 economic crash. However, George says that, while it might have reduced unemployment on paper, what you can earn in Hungary often isn't enough to live on, let alone save – which he is able to do while working and living in the UK.

As morning turned into early afternoon, another resident joined us to sit out in the spring sun. Twenty-year-old Dominik* was originally from the Czech Republic. He moved to Britain in his early teens and did his GCSEs here. Until he was seventeen, he told me, he lived with his uncle and his cousins in their family home but, once he had completed those studies, he was asked to move out, get a job and find somewhere else to live because there wasn't enough space for him. He now shared a room with his girlfriend; he worked night shifts at a nearby factory where shampoo is bottled, she worked mornings. 'It's better here than in my country. Everything is so expensive at home. You cannot live a good, clean life there.' He meant make an honest living. George passed Dominik some Haribos. I asked Dominik what he thought of his landlord. Did he also think he was 'a good guy'? 'He's a good lad, yeah,' Dominik replied, nodding. 'I didn't have much money when I first moved in so I couldn't afford the deposit he wanted for the room, and he let me pay him slowly for that over time. I was proper struggling then, you know. He looks after me.' Stockholm syndrome, perhaps, because his landlord was charging through the nose and engaged in illegally renting out overfull rooms, but Dominik felt that his landlord was justified in his cut-throat outlook. If you can't pay, why should you be allowed to stay?

Before Helen and I left, I asked all of the young men – who were by this point crowded around George's phone watching something on YouTube and giggling – whether people often got evicted from this place. 'Oh yeah,' one of the cousins said, 'people come and go.' George looked up from his phone and added, 'Our landlord is all right as long as you're paying the rent, you know. That changes if you can't pay. It's fair enough, though, isn't it?' He looked intense for a moment. 'You've got to pay.' It dawned on me that, in some ways, this is fairer than Section 21, which means a landlord can evict you even if you do pay – and is testament to how low the bar is set in the private rented sector. I didn't know for sure that these young men were living in an illegal HMO, but the fact that rent was so much a matter of the landlord's largesse, and that there was such a high turnover of tenants, suggested that they were.

As we were leaving, Dominik and George told me another anecdote about their 'good guy' landlord. They remembered him joking around and bragging just a few weeks before my visit about how he had been 'forced' to evict fifteen people from another of his properties elsewhere in the city because they weren't paying. Did he actually do this? Who knows, but Helen would probably have heard about it if he had, and no reports had reached her ears. Perhaps he was using an implicit threat to maintain a power dynamic that reminded the young men who was in charge. What made him a 'good landlord' in their eyes was, after all, the lack of questions he asked and his lenient attitude towards housing legislation. And, because Britain's government is more interested in policing immigration than enforcing poor housing conditions, he was able to operate like that.

Under the Immigration Act 2014, the Right to Rent scheme requires all landlords in England to check a new tenant's right to be in the UK. A 2017 report by the Joint Council for the Welfare of Immigrants (JCWI) found that 42 per cent of landlords were, as a result, less likely to rent to anyone without a British passport. That leaves an unknown number who – like the Bradford men's landlord – are prepared to turn a blind eye to their tenants' immigration status.

As we got back into the car, Helen told me that she had helped two young men who had been evicted from these particular properties. At the point they came across her radar, they were already homeless and sleeping rough. 'One of them had lost his job and fell behind on his rent,' she explained. 'He owed about £140, but the landlord just kicked him out. It wasn't a legal eviction. The other one was also evicted illegally.' Illegal evictions generally involve someone being told or being physically forced to leave a property. Helen had stories of people she'd helped who went out and came home to find the locks changed and their possessions thrown in a heap outside – which is illegal. This is despite the existence of Section 21, which makes it easier than it should be to evict people legally, and in spite of the fact that, according to the law, all evictions must abide by a legal process whereby the landlord has to obtain a court order giving official notice of eviction to the tenant. This applies regardless of the existence or validity of the rent contract, or of a tenant's residence permit. Indeed, as Ben Reeve-Lewis told me, Section 54 (2) of the Law of Property Act 1925 says that you don't need a written contract to create a tenancy, unless the tenancy is to be for more than three years, in which case it must be signed, witnessed and lodged at the Land Registry. Even without a written contract a tenancy still exists by the common law doctrine of 'parol'. Renters in the shadow private rented sector have more rights than they may realise.

People are illegally evicted all the time. And yet we don't know exactly how often, because no official data is collected. Cambridge House does vital work in this area. Today, one of the frontline services it provides is Safer Renting, mentioned earlier, an independent tenants' rights advice and advocacy service working in partnership with the property licensing and enforcement teams from a number of London boroughs. A large portion of the work Safer Renting does is supporting tenants because HMO licensing, while mandatory, is so poorly enforced. The head of Safer Renting, Roz Spencer, once told me that she regularly hears of cases where tenants are illegally thrown out of HMOs in London but, when the police do become involved, they often side with the landlord, even though the landlord's actions have been unlawful, because they know so little about the complexities of housing law. Because of this, one of Safer Renting's key initiatives is to work with local authorities to train police officers in eviction law. Likewise, Helen and her team in Bradford are regularly alerted to landlords who flout the rules and illegally evict people who have a shaky economic or immigration status, leaving them without recourse to public support. Since Brexit, a Hungarian economic migrant needs to have requested settled status to claim benefits, should they lose their job or become unwell and unable to work.

'The problem,' Helen said, 'is that they think they're happy. They like the landlord. But as soon as there is a problem, they've got no protection because that landlord isn't going to do the right thing. You can tell by the way he operates that he only cares about the bottom line, which is why he doesn't care about piling people high.' Like so many predatory slum landlords, the one who owned those two houses in Bradford was aware of the harsh reality: his tenants were replaceable. Well, they were before the pandemic, but that has resulted in an exodus of EU workers from Britain, leaving the hospitality, construction and haulage sectors with severe labour shortages. None the less, we know that illegal evictions occurred throughout the pandemic because organisations such as Safer Renting kept reporting them. This is the tangible real-world result of the tenant disempowerment caused by the deregulation of and lack of enforcement in the private rented sector. It is inevitable that this affects society's most vulnerable. One of the most striking things about the young men I met in Bradford was not only that they didn't know they had any rights, but that, when I pressed them, they all said it was fair enough that a landlord could throw them out on the street if, for whatever reason, they stopped being able to make their rent. 'If you want something, you've got to pay,' George said.

In the car, Helen pointed out another two notorious HMOs, one a converted office block. When people are made homeless – often through no fault of their own – she and a team of translators act as a bridge to Bradford's homelessness and housing services as well as to the court system. 'We need a joined-up national approach to housing and home-lessness,' she said. As she talked, her phone rang relentlessly, the texts and calls coming in from clients (homeless people), other homelessness workers and colleagues at Hope Housing. Helen Syrop is a woman for whom the day always feels too short.

In the face of a housing crisis that we are so often told by journalists and politicians alike is now nigh on insurmountable, it's easy to be cynical. Easier, maybe, to give into it, sit back and do nothing because there feels no point in doing anything, or otherwise to lean in and become doggedly, Darwinianly self-interested. But, like Alan Rice in Weston-super-Mare, this work isn't so much a passion for Helen as a duty. She is just one of an unofficial network of individuals working in tenants' unions, inde-pendently or as part of small organisations, who are trying to plug the gaping holes left in the state's housing provision. She sees her work as a moral imperative. Admirable as it is, this – the goodwill of individuals, of charity – harks back to noblesse oblige, the notion that privilege entails responsibility and that those with it will help those without. But this notion hindered the inception of the welfare state in the first place because politicians could argue that social justice was the stuff of charity and not the role of the state. Helen Syrop and Alan Rice are not wealthy, nor are they members of the upper classes, and it is a sad indictment of how far we have fallen that individuals like them are doing the work of the state.

We arrived back at Helen's offices in the centre of town and sat down with cups of tea. She told me that she regularly meets people at night shelters who have just been evicted. She checks their tenancy agreements and finds that they are protected, they just had no idea that their eviction was unlawful. But by that point, they are already destitute. 'Sometimes it's the same address as a previous landlord. It's a landlord we've already taken to court and won against!' In 2018, new powers came into force under the Housing and Planning Act 2016 that empowered local authorities to remove England's worst rental property owners. Remember the under-used register of rogue landlords? That's the list of those guilty of unlawful eviction or harassment; using or threatening violence to gain entry into a premises; non-compliance with fire safety regulations and ignoring improvement notices for poor conditions. And yet, in 2021, poor conditions in the private rented sector remained commonplace: and only thirty-nine landlords and letting agents had received government banning orders since 2018.

To understand why it matters that so few rogue landlords and letting agents are caught and banned, beyond the obvious questions about mortality and the evident risk to public health you need to understand the link between illegal HMOs and other criminalised activities: tax fraud, the abuse of illegal immigrants and human trafficking. All of this, of course, once again speaks to Theresa May's infamous 'hostile environment' and those worst affected by it who are too afraid of what might happen if they report what they experience to public bodies. The young men we met might have been jovial and projected bravado, but there's no way of knowing whether there was some form of coercion at play in either their relationships with one another, their respective employers or their landlord. Modern slavery is believed to be the UK's largest organised crime activity after drug dealing. It is estimated that there are currently about 13,000 people impacted by it, most of them thought to have been trafficked here. You will find them working in nail bars, in farming and food processing, in car washes, doing sex work that isn't always consensual, as well as in domestic labour. It is a common misconception that a person can't be trafficked from within the EU. But that is not true. And while a person may technically be in the country legally, they may find themselves coerced into or dependent upon illegal work because they have no recourse to public funds and are vulnerable.

All low-cost, substandard accommodation – which includes illegal HMOs and what are known as 'beds in sheds', where there are sometimes, quite literally, people living in makeshift structures in gardens (sometimes barely concealed under tarpaulin, as I once saw in the east London borough of Newham) – is a huge enabler for this thriving market in human exploitation. Such accommodations act as red flags because, as the Chartered Institute of Environmental Health notes, without them 'the whole operation is jeopardised'. They allow for people to be kept cheaply – living 'freely' in return for their labour or cash in hand, without proper tenancy agreements – beholden to the landlord because they know their immigration status might be precarious and they fear repercussions.

As I got ready to leave Hope Housing and Bradford, Tomas Gallik and Martyn Hawley, two translators who work regularly with Helen, arrived. Translating, however, is not their main job. Both men work for a global non-profit organisation called Hope for Justice which works alongside the authorities to support the victims of human trafficking and get them out of modern slavery, including being coerced into prostitution or unpaid, off-the-books work in factories or car washes. Martyn had just been at a large illegal HMO in the city centre where young women – all from eastern Europe – were engaging in sex work arranged by their landlord. 'We're trying to get to the bottom of what's going on,' Martyn told me. 'Whether the women are consenting and whether their documents have been taken away from them.' Unravelling who is the victim and who is doing the exploiting in this kind of scenario is not always straightforward. 'We don't always know at first who is consenting and who is not,' Tomas explained, 'and it takes time for us to win people's trust before they will even speak to us, because they're afraid of what might happen if we involve the police.' Those affected by modern slavery rarely announce themselves, they said. Finding them requires special skills – languages (Tomas speaks four) and patience. 'People in modern slavery situations don't trust authority figures,' Martyn continued. 'They won't even necessarily identify as a victim. But the subtle signs are there. There's usually one more talkative and dominating person who says, "We are all fine" or "We are all related". They take over the discussion and don't really let anyone else talk.' I thought back to George and his cousins, whose situation was cause for concern even if there was no modern slavery at play.

In a country where cruel anti-immigrant rhetoric has become a mainstay of the media, politics and policy (see Windrush or the immigration removal centre Yarl's Wood for just two particularly high-profile examples of the state penalising and brutalising people who have moved to the UK from other places), you can hardly blame those trapped in modern slavery for being fearful of the authorities. Martyn and Tomas told me that demand for Hope for Justice's operation has grown significantly in recent years. This is mirrored by what charities like Hestia, which does similar work in London, say. The Home Office's referral system, the National Referral Mechanism (NRM), is supposed to have been streamlined and simplified but, in reality, those working in the sector say it is frustratingly slow. The official guidance is that victims should receive a decision on their trafficking case as soon as possible after a 45-day recovery period, but in 2020 the number of suspected modern slavery victims left waiting for more than two years for a Home Office decision surged by 52 per cent from 397 in 2019 to 605. And the average time taken from referral to conclusive grounds decisions made in the final quarter (October through December) of 2020 was 430 days.

As we talked, Helen nodded along, her brow furrowing as the discussion continued. For anyone waiting on a decision that will determine their future while living in unstable or temporary accommodation there is, she said, 'a constant anxiety'. She then recounted a case she had dealt with recently involving a Polish man in his fifties who had been living in an illegal HMO while working, she suspected, off the books in a meat-processing plant. He became unwell and unable to work and was thrown on to the streets, forcing him into homelessness. 'He had nothing,' she said, 'and because he hadn't been paying tax for years and was never officially here, he had no recourse to help at all.' That's how it goes. When a migrant worker who is being exploited is no longer required or able to work, they lose their home and any trappings of stability that came with it. This is something that George thought was 'fair enough' but which speaks to ideas of 'deserving' and 'undeserving' immigrants and has been internalised even by those at risk of losing everything if things go wrong.

A year after that conversation, because of coronavirus, local authorities across the country would voice concern about exploited people living in crowded accommodation catching the virus because it was even more difficult than usual for enforcement teams to carry out vital inspections. But these inspections, when they do happen, can be the first response to modern slavery and human trafficking. That is, of course, when they aren't being used as a proxy for immigration enforcement. As an investigation conducted by the *Independent* in March 2021 revealed, rough sleepers from EU countries were encouraged to return home during the pandemic despite having leave to remain. Once again, housing problems – whether that's illegality or homelessness – are a safeguarding issue. This is because they are often indicators of other issues – such as serious poverty, unemployment or domestic abuse. Without the joined-up approach to housing and homelessness that Helen so wishes for, the grave problems that intersect with the darker parts of the housing crisis will not be properly dealt with.

# 10

# NEARLY LEGAL

## Colchester

*Council:* Colchester Borough Council
*Average House Price:* In the year 2020/21 the majority of sales in Colchester were detached homes, selling for an average of £427,019. Semi-detached houses sold for an average of £300,555, with terraced homes fetching £244,387. Overall, sold prices that year were 10 per cent up on the previous year.
*Average Private Rent:* In 2021 the average rent for a one-bedroom home was £786, for a two-bed it was £1,014, and for a three-bed it was £1,346.

There was raw human waste pumping into the building through a toilet. It flooded the whole of the laundry room downstairs with an ominous brown liquid. This was just the latest in a litany of things that had gone wrong. Throughout the building, terrible mould had spread. Every day, something else would break. The nearest fire escape to her bedroom had been nailed shut. Yet, despite this catalogue of catastrophic errors which would have made any building unfit for human habitation, Nicola Gillin, aged thirty-six, a research fellow at Anglia Ruskin University, found that there was very little she could do to get anything fixed.

Nicola was a property guardian. Her home was the Old Rectory, an abandoned care home that had closed down after being condemned and told to stop operating by the Care Quality Commission (CQC). From the outside the large white building looked grand, but inside it was dangerous and falling apart.

Guardianship runs in parallel to the private rented sector. It is an emergent form of low-cost, unstable housing. A guardianship is an arrangement whereby a property owner – usually a developer, but often a local council – lets out rooms in abandoned, unoccupied or semi-derelict buildings which are due for demolition or redevelopment. Increasingly, guardianships provide homes for people who cannot afford private rents, because the rents are generally cheaper than market rents (though not by much these days). But, in exchange, guardians must give up something fundamental: their rights. Though housing lawyers are increasingly arguing and proving otherwise, guardians do not have the same rights as private tenants because they enter into licence agreements. The conditions stipulated by these agreements can include: not being able to have overnight visitors; not being able to have more than two friends on site at a time; no children; no candles; never speaking to the media; and, crucially, accepting the fact that, as a guardian, you could be asked to leave the building with, at best, one month's and at worst a couple of weeks' notice. If you do not leave, you face court proceedings. Your deposit does not have to be protected and it can be very difficult to get back.

Guardianships are nearly legal: they tread a fine line between the lawful and the unlawful. They operate in a deliberately grey area that falls outside most of the regulations, which, though often poorly enforced and not far-reaching enough, are applied to tenancies in an attempt to protect tenants. Remember that, legally, a private tenancy can only be ended on notice – two months' notice if there is no fault – followed by court proceedings. Any tenant's deposit has to be placed in an approved scheme, where it is protected. The tenant has a right to repairs being carried out, to privacy and to being able to exclude even the landlord from their home in certain circumstances. Guardian companies argue that property guardians do not have any of these rights (though, as this chapter will explore, expert housing lawyers dispute this). Guardians experience all the worst elements of the private rented sector with none of its paltry protections. Firstly, guardians have licence agreements (which are common in temporary accommodation, too), not tenancy agreements.

Licences generally offer renters even less protection from eviction than tenancies because they are intended to be flexible so the landlord can enter the premises at any time and the tenant has no right to renew the licence when it expires. Second, in an incredible capitalist brain twister, they often imply that people who become property guardians are doing a job of sorts. They are, as the name suggests, live-in security guarding empty properties against squatters. Yet they pay for the privilege. And so, property guardians are exploited on two fronts: by their alleged lack of tenants' rights and, if they are indeed doing a job, their total lack of employees' rights.

Living in abandoned buildings is not new. Even a decade ago, those now 'working' as guardians might have been the very people they are now hired to protect against: squatters. Squatting had its heyday in the early 1970s, when emerging ideas of communalism and anti-materialism coincided with a glut of empty and abandoned buildings. The population of inner London had declined dramatically as town planners condemned swathes of old housing stock for slum clearance and created new garden cities. Between 1941 and 1981, urban populations were cut almost in half as people moved out to the new suburbs. This enabled the creation of squats in many of Britain's cities, particularly in London. Even squatters, though, had more rights than guardians. But, in September 2012, under Section 144 of the newly introduced Legal Aid, Sentencing and Punishment of Offenders Act, squatting was criminalised by the Coalition government, punishable by up to six months in prison, a £5,000 fine or both. Property guardianships have since emerged as its capitalist reincarnation – it is a lucrative and largely unregulated business which returns hefty profits for building owners, but delivers little beyond temporary, cheapish shelter for guardians. It will come as no surprise that, until the end of 2020, guardian companies made themselves attractive to owners of empty commercial buildings by saying they could reduce their liability for business rates (a statutory tax collected by local authorities) by installing guardians and reclassifying a building as domestic via the Valuations Office Agency (VOA), which is part of Her Majesty's Revenue and Customs (HMRC).

Guardianships can, like squatting, have an inadvertent gentrifying effect because the presence of the radical and creative communities to whom they often appeal tends to make an area more desirable and, ultimately, attract developers. A long-term affordable housing or regeneration solution they are certainly not. Property guardianships are also a particularly egregious part of the housing market. In 2018, Tim Lowe, the founder of the property management company Lowe Guardians, wrote an op-ed for *City A.M.* in which he tried to make the case for guardianships as a 'solution' to homelessness. In it he connected the high number of applications from would-be guardians (more than 32,000 that year, according to him) to demand for this way of living. But guardianships cannot be the solution. As Lowe himself wrote, young people on low incomes are struggling to find affordable accommodation. The answer is not, then, to charge them to live under unstable contracts in abandoned buildings where the conditions are often poor, while building owners make hay from their misfortune.

Lowe wasn't the only one making these arguments. Below are quotes from two other guardianship providers which represent how they advertised their service:

Join the many professionals, key workers and mature/post graduate students across the UK who have chosen the new affordable alternative to renting.

(Ad Hoc, 2015)

'As a nurse, living for Camelot means I can afford to live in London. My colleagues really envy me; so much space for very little money.'

(Camelot, 2014)

Should a key worker not be able to afford to live in the city where they are employed? This is something that Sadiq Khan, the Mayor of London, has begun to address in the capital with what he calls 'intermediate housing' for NHS staff, police, firefighters, transport workers and teachers. It is commonly defined as affordable housing targeted at people who are unlikely to qualify for a social rent home, but who struggle to buy or rent a suitable home on the open market. This is an initiative needed at scale. The pricing out of key workers is not just a London problem; in late 2021, Royal Cornwall NHS Trust said that one of the biggest challenges it faced in recruiting staff from outside Cornwall was for them to find affordable housing to rent or buy.

Until those who fall between qualifying for social housing and the open market are looked after, it ought to be chilling that a private company, positioning itself as a responsible housing provider, is making these arguments when the nature of being a property guardian is that you need to be available and ready to move in and out of properties at short notice. One person's flexibility is another's instability. In their 2016 paper 'Living Precariously', the geographers Alexander Vasudevan, Gloria Dawson and Mara Ferreri argue that we ought to view property guardianships and the uncertainty they foster as a parallel development to the proliferation of zero-hours contracts in the world of work. They argue that the two are related because those in insecure work tend to live in insecure housing. They write that studying property guardianship 'sheds critical light on individual and collective practices of negotiation and adaptation' which are fundamentally related to the 'wider logics of urban dispossession and displacement' that are playing out in Britain's towns and cities. Many of the buildings being used for guardianships – former care homes, social housing, libraries, town halls and police stations – either belong to or once belonged to public institutions. And they are vacant largely because of the processes of privatisation and sale of public sector assets which were exacerbated by the public budget reduction measures introduced by the Coalition government. So we can see, once again, how these processes lead back to political policies which put profit above people and their basic human right to housing.

When they launched in the UK in the early 2000s, guardianships provided quirky living alternatives. Artists, designers and other creatives flocked to them, living in old schools, office blocks and disused council homes awaiting renovation for £200 or £300 a month. The market was small, it was niche and the rents were genuinely cheap. That is not the case for the guardianships I visited. Property guardianships are, like so many aspects of the housing crisis, often dismissed as a London problem.

That is also not the case. We don't know exactly how many people are resorting to this unstable way of life but, according to the Property Guardian Providers Association (PGPA), 60,000 people applied to be property guardians in 2019 – double the number who applied in 2018. Nobody has ever bothered to log how many people are living in guardianships nationally, so, beyond the figure the PGPA provides, the data doesn't exist. However, when I submitted Freedom of Information requests to local authorities across the UK as part of my ongoing investigation into this unregulated subsection of the housing market, I found that almost a quarter of councils – as many as ninety-three – had engaged guardianship companies to fill empty buildings that they owned within the last five years. That means that local government is profiting from a means of housing people which, in its own way, is just as exploitative as the shadow private rented sector. Some councils have had greater involvement with guardian companies than others. Five outside of London who have been particularly involved with guardian companies include Hampshire County Council, which has used the services of multiple guardian companies including Ad Hoc, South East Guardians and Camelot. Buckinghamshire County Council had contracts with Camelot from 2014 to 2018. Bristol has used both Camelot and Ad Hoc. Gloucestershire County Council had contracts with Ad Hoc in 2015 and 2016, Camelot in 2015, 2016 and 2017 and Guardian Property Protection from 2015 to 2019. Bradford Council's response to my request showed that it also had multiple agreements with Ad Hoc between 2014 and 2019.

It is important to note that not just private companies but local governments are profiting from guardianships where people who may not be able to afford living anywhere else are paying for often substandard and insecure accommodation. More than that, today the guardianship market has expanded and so the inherent injustice of guardianships cannot be ignored. The PGPA says that approximately a third of property guardians are key workers: teachers, nurses, doctors, police officers and emergency services workers. They say this as if it's a good thing. It isn't. These people do vital work, but they are so poorly paid in relation to private rents, which have risen beyond wage growth, that they cannot afford decent housing and are resorting to guardianships.

They are people like 37-year-old Jane,* an adult education teacher on the equivalent of a zero-hours contract in London. When I spoke to her at the end of 2018, she'd been a property guardian since 2012 and had watched the price of private rents rise steadily beyond her earnings. She was unable to afford private renting, did not qualify for social housing and had absolutely no chance of buying a property, so had become trapped in guardianships. 'I would never have thought in a million years that I'd be three years off being forty and I wouldn't have a secure job or a secure home as a teacher,' she told me. 'I wouldn't be a guardian if I had other options. It's difficult. My vulnerable housing situation and precarious employment go hand in hand. It's living in poverty, basically. The lack of security has affected me. It underpins everything I think, everything I do and every interaction I have.'

However, you'll rarely hear such guardians' stories. This is because there is usually a clause in their licences which forbids them from speaking to the press – if they do, they can be threatened with eviction and, in some cases I've witnessed, even harassed by guardian company representatives. But what happened at the Old Rectory remains one of the worst stories I have heard about a property guardianship. That doesn't mean it *is* the worst, it's just the worst one to make it into the mainstream press.

Nicola approached me about what was going on at the Old Rectory because she felt it needed to be recorded. Although she was earning £26,000 per annum when we spoke in 2019, her earnings in 2017 had been much lower (a £15,000 per annum tax-free PhD studentship stipend). It was this, coupled with three consecutive annual rent rises on her one-bedroom flat in Colchester, that had made her seek an alternative option outside of the private rented sector. Nicola was desperate. Paying £625 per month before bills for a one-bedroom flat on her own was not only bleeding her monthly income dry, it was draining her future resources. Nicola rarely buys clothes or goes on holiday. So, not only was seeing so much of her salary disappear into her landlord's bank account every month pushing back the possibility of her ever being able to buy a place of her own, she was acutely aware that it was stopping her saving for later in life. She, like Jane, was right to worry, although many younger people look the other way as a coping mechanism.

As the months passed, Nicola felt that she was watching her housing options dissolve. That's when she applied to live at the Old Rectory in Spring Lane, Lexden. It was a grand old house which had been developed to accommodate up to sixty residents, and had been operating as a care home until December 2016, when it had been closed after the CQC had deemed it 'inadequate' and 'unsafe'. The property guardianship company Camelot had taken it over and was now charging a licence fee of only £320 for a large, airy room in the property. Nicola jumped at the opportunity. But if, at first, it seemed too good to be true, that's because it was.

She moved in in March 2017, living alone in the sprawling building – though largely confined to her room, because Camelot, like so many guardian companies do, had padlocked off many of the empty rooms. By June, she had been joined by five other people. Despite the vast size of the building, there was only one kitchen and one working shower. She asked Camelot repeatedly not to move any more people in. But, within months, six residents grew to thirty. Nicola worked full time. She had to get up every day and find time to shower which, when you have thirty housemates and only one shower, is a logistical nightmare. This wasn't the only problem she faced, though. Part of the reason that the care home had been closed under a cloud of scandal was that the building was in desperate need of renovation; it was falling apart and, crucially, its twelve boilers were failing. When Nicola moved in, two were working, one of which later broke down. Wandering around the place, she found confidential paper waste that the care home staff had left behind, which included angry letters from relatives of residents, some of whom suffered with dementia, complaining about a lack of hot water. This, the worried sons, daughters and grandchildren of elderly people wrote, meant that their loved ones were not being properly bathed, their personal hygiene was being neglected and their dignity was in tatters. After reading the letters, Nicola realised that the building just wasn't fit for human habitation at all – even if she could get a shower slot, it wasn't always hot and, when winter came, the place – which was already damp and covered in sporing mould – was going to be freezing.

Another issue was that Nicola's privacy was repeatedly being breached. 'Camelot would attempt to gain access to our bedrooms without prior warning,' she recalled. Indeed, this is something I've heard from countless property guardians. 'As a lone female occupant, having two men from Camelot attempt to enter my bedroom at 8 p.m. while I was in bed alone was a frightening experience. Their behaviour in this respect was hugely upsetting for me and has had a lasting effect on me.'

During our correspondence, Nicola WhatsApped me regularly with updates. In one photo, she is seen wearing rolled-up denim dungarees and smiling in a large, empty bedroom with magnolia walls. This was taken just after she'd moved in, shortly before she discovered the true state of the building. In the next one, she's standing in a room full of junk where a leak has eroded the floor so badly that it looks as though it might fall through. Another photo comes through and it's of a fire exit door that has been nailed shut. Then she sends me some videos: a toilet leaking out brown water all over the floor; carpets soggy with the liquid.

Eventually, because of Nicola's persistent complaints, Camelot attempted to provide facilities for the growing number of residents. 'They put in two extra showers,' Nicola recalled, 'but they were flimsy plastic phone box-type things that weren't even fixed into the floor. You could just push them over and I didn't think they were safe to use. A few weeks later, workmen were sent to bolt them down.' By this point, the number of problems at the Old Rectory was fast becoming insurmountable. 'The pipes were all shot,' Nicola told me over the phone. 'There was raw human waste pumping into the building through the toilet near my bedroom. I reported it to Camelot, they did nothing.' That waste flooded the whole laundry room downstairs and, once again, nothing was done about it. Eventually Camelot sent a plumber, but he couldn't find out where the leak was coming from. In the end, two of Nicola's fellow guardians fixed it by shutting off the water supply with a screwdriver.

Unable to afford to go back to renting privately or move in with family, because her mother didn't have room for her, Nicola was beginning to feel that she was running out of options. Then, in mid-2017, something happened that would make her decision for her. A private company sent fire inspection officers round to carry out a fire alarm system check at the property, believing it was still functioning as a care home, because its contract had not been terminated when the place closed down. Immediately, the officers saw that there were people living there, despite its run-down state. Nicola showed me a video of them walking around the site as they systematically tested the fire alarms, finding to their obvious horror that they didn't work. This was just months after Grenfell. The fire inspectors called Essex County Fire and Rescue Service, who arrived very quickly and started asking lots of questions. One was whether Camelot came once a month to do any fire checks or drills. Of course they didn't. Nicola told them how the nearest fire escape to her bedroom had been nailed shut, but told me that she was so worried about being evicted that she asked them not to mention her name.

An investigation took place in which it was decided that Camelot were not only failing on fire safety, but that the company should have registered the Old Rectory as an HMO. On New Year's Day 2018, Nicola heard people outside the building knocking on doors. Her initial reaction was that it must be Camelot. She went downstairs and found two private housing officers from Colchester Borough Council. They told her and other guardians that they had been investigating the property and had decided that it was unsafe. Simultaneously, all resident guardians received an email from Camelot terminating their licences. Then, something unprecedented happened. Colchester Borough Council decided to prosecute Camelot for failing to license an HMO and various breaches of HMO regulations at the Old Rectory. It was the first time that a local authority had prosecuted a guardian company.

Until 30 January 2019, Nicola was pursuing Camelot Europe (the parent company) in court for what's known as a Rent Repayment Order (RRO), which is where a tribunal decides that a landlord has committed one of a number of offences, such as managing an unlicensed property, illegal eviction or failing to comply with a conditions improvement notice, to get back the £2,881.70 she had spent on living in an unsafe building. It was a first-tier property tribunal and Nicola says that throughout the process Camelot put pressure on her to settle out of court. Poor conditions and precarity aside, what Camelot did serves as a shocking reminder of the omertà hanging over property guardians. They had tried to organise collectively to make the place safe while living there, but it was difficult to get everyone on board because some residents feared what might happen if they made a fuss.

'Before my hearing, I got a phone call from a senior figure at Camelot asking if I would settle out of court,' Nicola recalled, still clearly stressed by the whole ordeal. 'I declined, because it would have required me to sign a non-disclosure agreement. It was a red line for me – they could not buy my silence.' And then, on 29 January, she received an unsolicited cheque in the post followed by an email from Camelot asking for the tribunal to be dismissed. She replied telling them that the cheque was for the wrong amount – just £2,000 – and that she would like to go ahead with the hearing. Camelot then agreed to send a second cheque for the remaining £881.70 she was owed plus £100 for her legal costs. She wanted to continue to pursue Camelot on public interest grounds, but was stopped because she received the money. Nicola was assisted by Flat Justice, an organisation formed to provide specialist help to tenants who want to make an RRO. Flat Justice offers free help with DIY applications, which it encourages, as well as a paid representation service. Nicola also used her experience with Flat Justice to help nine of her fellow guardians to do the same. Camelot settled each of their claims. Since their victory with Nicola, Flat Justice has successfully pursued another company, Live-In Guardians, for an RRO on behalf of another former guardian. A first-tier tribunal found that the guardian was due rent back, because Live-In Guardians had not licensed the building they lived in, a building formerly owned by the London Electricity Board, as an HMO. The company was also added to the Mayor of London's rogue landlord database.

When I caught up with Nicola in the summer of 2019, she was back at her mother's house. She didn't have space to study, which is a huge part of her job, and she was sleeping on a mattress on the floor, because there wasn't a bedroom for her. She was contributing to her mother's costs and managing to save a little, but, as with Tony, she was watching housing costs in Colchester become increasingly unrealistic. I asked her if she would consider going back to private renting. 'I've rented all my adult life one way or another,' she said. 'I am absolutely sick to the back teeth of being exploited and extorted by landlords of any kind, so ... no.'

Nicola told me that the experience she had at the Old Rectory had a negative and long-lasting impact on her mental wellbeing. 'When we were evicted, we had just twenty-eight days to find alternative accommodation and leave,' she said. 'This caused much distress and panic in the house. It was the council officers who gave us advice on protection from harassment and illegal eviction and reassured us that we couldn't be thrown out on to the street if we had nowhere else to go. Camelot did nothing.'

From her mother's, Nicola was able to look back on that period as a 'traumatic experience' which, as she put it, 'was compounded by the realisation that [she] never felt safe living in the building'. Even though she was living with family now and was safe, she told me that she still found herself instinctively going to check the door was locked before going to sleep because of how Camelot staff had repeatedly tried to enter her room. None the less, in spite of the stress and trauma, she had persevered in taking them to court because she felt it was her duty to do so. 'Many of the people who lived with me in the guardianship were there because they were already experiencing complex social problems and mental health issues. These were exacerbated by Camelot's behaviour and the trauma of it all,' she said. 'Many were also immigrants, some with limited English and almost zero knowledge of their housing rights in this country.'

Her dogged pursuit of Camelot was not the end of the story of their safety breaches in Colchester. In late 2019, Camelot Guardian Management Ltd became the first guardian company to be successfully prosecuted by a local authority and was found guilty of fifteen breaches of the Housing Act, including failure to register the Old Rectory as an HMO. Following the verdict, most of Camelot's property management subsidiary companies were liquidated and property guardians were issued new licence agreements by a new company, Watchtower Security Solutions Ltd. This practice is sometimes known as 'phoenixing' – when a company disappears itself, often in an attempt to avoid paying off debts or imminent legal action, and a new entity rises up in its place, sometimes even with the same personnel.

It is disingenuous of guardian companies to present themselves as providing an affordable housing alternative when their practices are so clearly unethical. Housing people in dangerous properties is unforgiveable full stop, but it is egregious that sometimes local councils – the very bodies who should be enforcing tenants' rights and seeking to drive up standards – are in on it, too.

### Elephant and Castle, London Borough
### of Southwark, December 2018

*Council:* Southwark Council

*Average House Price:* In the year 2020/21 the majority of sales in Elephant and Castle were flats, selling for an average of £481,601. Terraced properties sold for an average of £794,926, with semi-detached properties fetching £615,000. Overall, sold prices that year were 9 per cent down on the previous year and 10 per cent down on the 2018 peak of £604,359. This was a trend seen in many parts of London because of the number of people leaving the city during the pandemic, causing house prices to dip slightly in the capital but rise elsewhere.

*Average Private Rent:* In 2021 the average rent for a one-bedroom home was £1,886, for a two-bed it was £2,937, and for a three-bed it was £3,884.

—

So, how did international companies like Camelot manage to operate within a legal grey area not just in front of, but sometimes in direct collaboration with local councils?

One man who knows is Giles Peaker, who, when he is not drafting legislation like the Homes Act, is a solicitor specialising in housing and a partner at Anthony Gold, a law firm which sits on the Walworth Road near Elephant and Castle. Peaker will never bring it up if your paths should ever cross, but he was also named Housing Lawyer of the Year in 2018 for Legal Aid.

We first met in person on a cold and very wet day in the summer of 2018. I'd forgotten my umbrella, so I made my way towards his offices from Elephant and Castle tube station getting drenched in the pouring rain. It felt particularly poignant that the area I was walking through in Southwark had been the site of some of London's most contentious housing battles. This is a gentrification hotspot, where a blueprint for how not to 'regenerate' an area has been drawn in real time. When I visited before the pandemic, the Elephant and Castle shopping centre was still standing, its iconic pink elephant intact. But with every bit of regeneration around it – whether that's a freshly laid pavement or the gleaming Pret that will be visited by people who will never seek out the area's renowned Latin American food – the wrecking ball was swinging ever closer. On nearby Tiverton Street was some much-photographed graffiti in big yellow letters that read 'GENTRIFICATION: Please bear with us while we tear apart your community'.

As I passed what was once the Heygate Estate, it felt to me that the social cleansing of the area was deliberate. As Loretta Lees noted in 2018, 'More than 3,000 council tenants and leaseholders were displaced, the estate was demolished and its "mixed tenure" replacement, the newly built Elephant Park, was being marketed off-plan to investors in east Asia.' The shiny new development that was built on its ruins looked the same as every other new build project in London. Boarding enclosed the perimeter, promising a percentage of 'affordable' homes, but it was too late. A community had already been displaced here and, nearby, a similar conversation rumbled on over the Aylesbury Estate. Nobody, in this process, had bothered to address seriously the concerns of the area's Latin American community – one of the largest in the country. In 2016, Latin Elephant, a local charity made up of Ecuadorians, Brazilians, Colombians, Peruvians and others, had unsuccessfully lobbied to have the area turned into London's first official Latin Quarter. As Santiago Peluffo Soneyra, the co-director of Latin Elephant, said before the demolition, 'the clustering of businesses [here] is crucial to the dynamics of the community, if you disperse it, it loses its strength, its vibe, its heart and spirit'. The destruction was like losing 'Edgware Road, or Chinatown or Brixton'; 'the city is losing its multicultural identity', becoming 'more sterile' and turning into a place where 'you can no longer distinguish one place from another'.

I reached Peaker's offices. He had an umbrella. We sheltered underneath it and went out for a coffee. 'The new flats in the Elephant, which is what they've built where the Heygate was, are going for about half a million for a one-bedroom flat,' he told me as we sat down. 'They "regenerate", they introduce Shared Ownership, they say you can use Help to Buy and it just keeps property prices up,' he added. 'It's all related to the problems we're seeing with the private rented sector and subsections of it like property guardianships and HMOs – these ways of living were only ever meant to be a short-term interval for people who needed flexibility, but now it's a permanent way of living because people cannot afford stability.' Ironically, this process of accumulative displacement only breeds more of the same thing. Guardians move into a run-down building in a less desirable area. It becomes more desirable. Regeneration occurs. Prices go up. Repeat in a new place. Without enough social housing or some sort of guarantee as to how much rent can increase by, those who cannot afford their rent will always be forced to move in search of something cheaper and, when they do, they may, in turn, price other people out.

Peaker argues that property guardians have the same rights as private renters, whatever guardian companies may claim. He also argues that the properties they 'guard' are unlicensed HMOs. He believes that the decision Colchester Borough Council took to prosecute Camelot could be a game changer. 'It revealed that unlicensed HMOs are being managed by various guardian companies, sometimes with the complicity of local government,' he said. 'It might just give local authorities reason to question the stability and standards of guardian companies before contracting with them.'

Moving forward, the most pressing legal question is whether property guardian companies should be registering their properties as large HMOs. As far as Peaker is concerned, they should, under the terms of the Housing Act 2004. Large HMOs require a licence from the council to operate and the accommodation must meet a nationally prescribed standard. This licence is an important measure for ensuring the safety of tenants. 'For a licence to be granted, the local authority must be satisfied the property is safe, including fire safety measures, that rooms are of sufficient size, there are enough bathroom and kitchen facilities for the number of people, and the managers are "fit and proper" people to fill that role,' Peaker explained. 'The definition of HMO refers to "units of living accommodation" and payment being made for that occupation. Occupation under a licence certainly falls under those terms.' This – the recognition that guardianships qualify as HMOs – would force guardian companies to improve standards and give guardians better protections.

'It is a criminal offence to own or manage an unlicensed HMO,' he continued, 'which shows the seriousness of the issue. Guardian properties that would fall under a mandatory, additional or selective licensing scheme should have a licence application made before they are occupied, to ensure the safety of the guardians.'

Without proper regulation, the industry is leaving potentially vulnerable people who can't afford housing in the private rented sector unprotected and at the mercy of companies who do not have their best interests at heart. I have seen this first-hand. I once posed as a potential guardian in need of cheap digs at a disused building which was formerly Harrington Hill Primary School in Hackney, east London.

Aside from the young man wandering around in his dressing gown at 1 p.m., there was nothing to suggest I was not entering a working primary school as I was guided, along with three other prospective guardians, one of whom was a man in his late forties/early fifties, through a set of double doors with child-height handles. Cat,* a representative from Global Guardians, whizzed ahead of us through the school corridor towards the gym. 'I just need to make it clear that there is no heating in this building,' she told us glibly. 'No heating?' I repeated, shocked and forgetting for a moment that I was only posing as a potential guardian and not actually viewing the property. It was freezing inside the building, even though it was March. I thought instantly of how cold it would be in December or January. 'Obviously, we'll provide a plug-in heater for every unit,' she said, 'but there is no heating anywhere in the building.'

How much would I have been expected to pay to endure this? The smallest unit, Cat told me, was £475 a month including bills. The 'unit' in question was a small former office with a huge whirring IT server box overhead and desks nailed into three of its four walls. The bathroom was across the hallway and consisted of a flimsy temporary shower unit. There were two of these showers for every seven people. The communal kitchen contained two hotplates, microwave ovens, a sink and a fridge, but nothing resembling an actual oven. I asked Cat whether the desks in my hypothetical bedroom would be removed. 'I'm waiting for an answer on that from the client,' she replied brusquely. I noted that I would struggle to get a bed in the room if they weren't. 'Oh God, I know,' she said sympathetically. 'Look – you decide to take the room, I'll let you know what maintenance says.'

At £475, the price of the room seemed steep for what was on offer in Hackney, even though it included bills. I have friends who spend less than that on their mortgages. In any case, that was before I factored in Global Guardians' fees. Cat explained I'd need to pay my first month's licence fee up front, a deposit of one month's licence fee, £75 for a fire safety pack and £95 to be 'vetted' by Global Guardians. So that would have been a total of £1,120 – which is unlikely to be an amount many people on low incomes have to hand. I left the site acutely aware that being a guardian wasn't a lifestyle choice for anyone living there or visiting with the intention of moving in that day. As I made my way out through the school's battered double doors, the older man who had been at the viewing with me shot me a despairing look.

'Good luck with the rest of your search,' he said. As we walked along the tarmac driveway together, I asked him about himself. It turned out he was a freelance graphic designer.

'I'm renting but my landlord has put the rent up,' he explained. 'I've always lived in rented accommodation and never bought my own place, but now I can't make the rent in London, so I'm looking at guardianships because I don't know what else to do.'

How did he end up so compromised? I asked delicately.

'Well, I was actually living in a squat for most of my twenties and thirties. I lived very cheaply and then, when we couldn't squat anymore, I started renting, but by then it was already so expensive, and I haven't been able to save. I can't afford to buy; I can't afford to rent, so … here I am.'

In spring 2019, a government spokesperson told me that it was considering proposals to regulate the property guardianship industry. In an oral question in the House of Lords, Liberal Democrat peer Baroness Olly Grender asked Lord Bourne (then Parliamentary Under Secretary of State at the Ministry of Housing, Communities and Local Government) if he would 'reassure the growing number of property guardians that the full force of the current law will be applied and new regulations will be considered'. Lord Bourne replied that officials were planning to build on existing research in order to better understand the sector and 'planning work to look at the current position and to inform further possible action'. He added that the government was looking at a 'statutory definition' of a property guardian to ensure that they have a 'bedrock of rights'. By early 2022, that still had not happened.

# PART THREE

# UTOPIAN THINKING: THE PROBLEM OF CHANGE

*Historically, disasters – pandemics and world wars – have forced humans to break with the past and imagine the world anew. Will coronavirus do the same? We know that poor housing added to the hardship wrought by Covid-19. Policy responses to the pandemic have so far been necessarily short term. While short-term help was clearly needed, the pandemic provides an opportunity to rethink the direction of our social policies over the longer term. It has demonstrated that serious gaps in the social safety net can quickly become catastrophic when the system comes under pressure from the very sort of external forces it was meant to indemnify us against. The virus brought the entire world to a standstill. But in among the grief, the loss and the destruction, there is also opportunity. A chance to ask whether we want to return to normality at all. What if the pandemic was a gateway, in that it laid bare the severity of Britain's weakened social safety net and housing crisis and gave us a glimpse of what a new world might look like? If we want that world, we must keep asking what it should look like so that we can imagine it into existence and, above all, we must be ready to fight for it.*

# 11

# FALLOUT

**Norman Shaw South, House of Commons**

*Council:* Westminster City Council
*Average House Price:* In the year 2020/21 the majority of sales
in Westminster were flats, selling for an average of £1,137,816.
Terraced properties sold for an average of £1,258,333. Overall,
sold prices in Westminster in that year were 13 per cent down
on the previous year and 33 per cent down on the 2016 peak of
£1,713,556.
*Average Private Rent:* In 2021 the average rent for a one-bedroom
home was £3,199, for a two-bed it was £5,889, and for a three-bed it
was £9,057. At the time of searching, of 1,306 listings only forty-one
properties listed for private rent cost less than £1,000 a month.

—

It was 8.20 a.m. The sputtering Circle Line train I was on had ground to a
halt in Westminster tube station. As I made my way up through its cavern-
ous concrete hallways, my mind was fixated on the fact that, as MPs argued
over Britain's deal with the EU, only days earlier, on 19 December 2018,
an EU citizen – a 43-year-old Hungarian man named Gyula (pronounced
'jeweller') Remes, the 'gentle giant' as his friends knew him – had died in
one of the underpasses I was about to walk through. In recent years, these
tunnels had become refuge for a number of street homeless people. How
many politicians and Westminster staffers looked up from their phones
and really saw them as they made their way into work?

'There is something rotten in Westminster when MPs walk past dying homeless people on the way into work,' tweeted the Labour MP David Lammy, paraphrasing Shakespeare's *Hamlet*, shortly after Remes' death. Later in the day, the Liberal Democrat MP and former health minister Norman Lamb said in the leathery green chamber of the House of Commons, 'It is grotesque and obscene that we have a homelessness crisis visible outside the building.'

What does it take to bring about change in Britain's political system? A sum of £5,000 was raised in the days that followed Remes' death by an anonymous parliamentary staff member to ensure the homeless man would 'not be forgotten'. Flowers were brought and placed in plastic cups filled with water outside the tube station. A memorial candle burned alongside a row of Stella Artois cans – his favourite beer. In the weeks and months that followed, however, little changed. When Covid-19 arrived a little over a year later, rough sleeping was still at record levels. Like the private rented sector, our homelessness services were not ready for a public health crisis.

Street homelessness is linked to hidden homelessness and to the instability of the private rented sector, as it is to unaffordable house prices: rough sleeping is the most extreme end in a chain of reactions caused by housing precarity. At the time, Parliament's focus was elsewhere. In the shadow of Remes' death, Brexiteers stood outside the Houses of Parliament shouting 'Leave means leave!' and accosting MPs, particularly Remainer women, as they came and went from work, denouncing them as 'traitors' to democracy. The day after Remes' death and the Brexit debate, data was published by the ONS showing that in 2017 almost 600 street homeless people had died in England and Wales – a 24 per cent increase over five years. The late James Brokenshire, then Secretary of State for Housing, Communities and Local Government, told the Commons: 'Every death of someone sleeping rough on our streets is one too many. Each is a tragedy, each a life cut short. We have a moral duty to act.' He promised outraged MPs that the government was taking action by investing £1.2 billion to reduce and try to prevent homelessness. He reiterated its commitment to halving rough sleeping by 2022 and ending it by 2027. Things could change, couldn't they? Was this what it took, though? For a man to die right in front of our politicians?

Just as the housing crisis has been created in Westminster, it has shaped British politics. It is worth examining this relationship, for it has created a vicious circle that politicians in years to come, even if they have the will, might struggle to square: Britain is now addicted to and reliant upon rising house prices.

Politics is about telling stories. Politicians and the parties they represent exist because of the narratives they spin. We live through history; it is only in hindsight that we can separate fact from fiction. For a long time, nobody in power wanted to acknowledge the housing crisis – I am told that during the 2010s under David Cameron, the phrase 'housing crisis' was banned in the corridors of Whitehall. The dominant Conservative narrative was that there was no crisis, not because this was true but because it was easier (and more politically expedient) to manufacture a new truth than acknowledge reality. At the expense of private renters Cameron and his Chancellor George Osborne focused on increasing homeownership, mostly through the Help to Buy scheme. At the beginning of her premiership, Theresa May at least acknowledged the private rented sector with the Tenant Fees Act 2019 and wanted to make it easier for local authorities to build social housing, but she wasn't around long enough to bring about lasting change. Then, when Boris Johnson came to power, he stalled on the long-promised Renters' Reform Bill which is, among other things, expected to ban 'no-fault' Section 21 evictions, leaving it stuck in the parliamentary long grass throughout the pandemic even as MPs called for it to be expedited.

How did a schism between the accepted political stories about housing and the reality develop? How do Conservative politicians justify their reluctance to intervene in a meaningful way while underwriting rising house prices and rents?

Round the corner from the tube station, the revolving glass door of Portcullis House, where many MPs have their offices, took me into an antechamber where police officers cradle machine guns. I had come to meet Kevin Hollinrake. He was – and still is – the Conservative MP for Thirsk and Malton in North Yorkshire, but he was then also the chairman of a large national chain of estate agents, Hunters, which he co-founded in 1992. He stood down from this role in March 2021. Prior to that, according to the Members of Parliament register of interests he received a salary of £50,000 per year and a car allowance of £9,000 for around 192 hours of work a year at Hunters. It floated on the stock market in 2015 and now has more than 200 branches across the country. According to Companies House, its total revenue in 2018 – when I first met Hollinrake – was £4,985,604, with a total profit after tax of £1,191,094. In speaking to him, I hoped to understand how vested interests impact our politics from within.

Hollinrake, his researcher texted me apologetically, was running late. To make up for it, as he walked me through the wide carpeted corridors that led to Hollinrake's office in Norman Shaw South, I was offered tea, Yorkshire Tea. This meeting had come about because Hollinrake and I had had a disagreement on Twitter in 2018. Our dispute happened before the government's Tenant Fees Act was passed by Parliament, banning letting fees once and for all. I had criticised his stance on the issue. Because of his obvious vested interests in preventing the ban from coming into force, and potentially damaging his business, Hollinrake had sponsored a Westminster Hall Debate on the subject. These debates, unlike those which take place in the Commons, are open to the public and do not end in a vote on policy but, none the less, are a useful way of drawing attention to a particular issue and putting pressure on government. In the debate, Hollinrake was careful not to explicitly oppose a ban on letting fees – it was, after all, his own government's policy by that point – but he did raise reservations and argue that an 'outright ban' might have 'unintended consequences' such as pushing rents up. This was a thinly veiled and baseless threat regularly dangled by the lettings industry in the face of regulation.

On his website shortly after the debate, Hollinrake had written: 'Who, for example, should pay for such expenses as references, credit checks and income verification which do cost agents money? Currently, this is covered by the fee, but if this is banned, it would fall to the agent or landlord. They might take a cautious approach and favour better off tenants (following preliminary enquiries) over the less well off or those on housing benefit.' This is like arguing that a supermarket shopper should pay for the privilege of entering the shop and engaging with staff, in addition to the items they purchase. Landlords make money from their buy-to-lets and so the onus should be on them to foot these running costs.

I was not sure what to expect as I waited for Hollinrake. I sipped the tea and tried to understand his position. The time gave me the opportunity to re-read his biography on my phone. He was then – he is now – on the face of it, one of the 'few' who made up former Labour leader Jeremy Corbyn's 'many not the few'. And yet his own story is complex. The son of a milkman and a social worker, Hollinrake went to a state comprehensive school, Easingwold in North Yorkshire, which has since been turned into an academy. After that he went to Sheffield Hallam University (then a polytechnic), where he studied physics. Landed gentry he is not. This was striking to me. I rarely hear from people who consider homeownership a moral evil and want to abolish it altogether but, when I do, they are usually born into wealthy families that have always owned property and have never experienced serious housing instability. On the other hand, I often find those born with less aspire not only to homeownership but to making money through property speculation. This tracks: if all you know is the chaos of the private rented sector and bad landlords, or if you have ever faced homelessness, then homeownership becomes a nostrum for all the social and economic ills you have ever experienced. Who is right or wrong is beside the point: there are very good reasons that homeownership remains aspirational. Owning property appears to be a way out, a reliable remedy for uncertainty. In Britain, those from low-income backgrounds will try almost anything to make enough money to one day own a home. Or, in Hollinrake's case, several. From Sheffield, Hollinrake went to work for Prudential Property Services, at the time the largest estate agency in Britain, where he learned his trade.

'How are you? I'm so sorry for being late.' He breezed through the door. 'So ... on housing I'll tell you what I think, and we may agree to disagree on some things. There's a saying I use a lot in this place: "He or she who knows only their side of the argument knows little of that."' Was he also unsure of what to expect from me? It is an unfashionable thing to say, but too many people – on the left as well as the right – have become entrenched in their views on a variety of subjects and are reluctant to hear out those they disagree with. There has to be space for a conversation which is not composed of people holding embittered and embattled positions. Our society does not reward people or politicians who change their minds, let alone admit they were wrong. But it should. It is easy to dismiss the reverence towards 'fairness' that newsrooms like those at the BBC have. Done badly, as it too often is, it becomes an excuse for lazy reporting, conflating impartiality with passivity. But, done well, it fosters productive conversations, creating space for change, conciliation and coalition.

Hollinrake told me that his formative political experiences took place more than thirty years ago, when he was working as an estate agent in York. This was prior to Thatcher's deregulation of the private rented sector, which we first explored in chapter 2. 'Before those changes,' Hollinrake said, 'if you wanted to rent a house in York, it was a two-bedroom, dark, gloomy, damp terraced house – it wasn't very appealing at all. There was no broad availability of rented property because buy-to-let wasn't seen as something that was a safe investment.' The expansion of private renting brought about by Thatcher's government, as Hollinrake saw it, was proof that 'free markets work, as long as they're competitive'. I pushed him on this point – noting the number of privately rented properties which had been found to be unfit for human habitation, and that rents in many parts of the country are already unaffordable for most people on average salaries. Was that a functioning free market? 'The way to solve that ideally for me is to make the market more competitive, keep the market competitive,' he replied.

Hollinrake's reasoning – the idea that the laws of supply and demand should regulate prices instead of central government – is rooted in the notion that consumer forces play a role in keeping things affordable. Sometimes it works. If the exact same loaf of bread is 82p in Sainsbury's but £1.20 in Tesco, the average consumer will go to Sainsbury's. The bread they buy will be almost identical. This, a consumer's ability to 'vote with their feet', gives ordinary people power – in theory. But for it to work, supermarkets have to want to draw in new customers from their competitors. What if, instead, the demand for bread was so high everywhere that supermarkets knew they could charge any price they like, because people who wanted bread would still buy it and the supermarkets were not worried about losing customers to their competitors or, indeed, the fact that they might give up and make their own bread at home?

That's the position in which private landlords find themselves. In practice, leaning on the mysterious forces of competition has not resulted in the private rented market regulating itself. A home is not a loaf of bread. People can survive without eating bread (though, of course, grocery price rises make it harder for those on low incomes to feed themselves and their families); there are alternatives. But nobody can survive and function without a home. Like water, decent shelter is a basic requirement for survival. If an area is desirable and housing stock is limited, private rents will be driven up rather than down by market forces. If your landlord will not fix a rodent infestation, it is extremely unlikely that you can simply pack up your possessions and leave the next day. If your landlord puts up the rent, you either have to pay more or move further away from where you need to be. Private renters have many things to consider beyond the cost or quality of a property: does the house or flat have the right number of bedrooms for their family; is it in the catchment area for the right school; is it close to family and friends who provide support and childcare? Renters are consumers but, while market competition empowers landlords, it does not empower renters. And landlords and letting agents know this – that's why they so often charge a premium and push people to spend more than they can afford. Think of the reaction to the 2022 price hikes of another essential: energy. There was public outcry. There was government support (albeit paltry). And, even so, to give you some idea of how under-regulated rents are: energy companies are regulated by OfGem which monitors the costs being passed onto consumers and imposes price caps.

I pressed Hollinrake again. 'I can certainly see problems for people who want to live permanently in rented accommodation,' he conceded. 'Some people can feel they don't have secure tenure. And, especially in markets that are overheated, landlords can push rents up, which makes it unfair on some tenants.' But, I asked, does anyone *want* to live in a rented home? The data suggests otherwise. They're there because they cannot afford the British dream of owning. And, in any case, they don't just 'feel' that they are insecure. They *are* insecure.

Reframing reality. That is the power of political language and its thin veneer of respectability: it rationalises the irrational. In his 1946 essay 'Politics and the English Language', George Orwell wrote that 'political speech and writing are largely the defence of the indefensible', consisting of 'euphemism, question-begging and sheer cloudy vagueness'. Terms like 'free market' are deployed as if they are objective when, in fact, they are entirely subjective, born of one ideology which, when you hold it up to scrutiny, falls apart and flakes to the floor. Deceit is often disguised as logic because Britain's political system has been set up to be an adversarial, two-sided Punch and Judy show. In the Commons, the two sides of the chamber on which the main parties sit opposite each other are still designed to be two swords'-length apart. Of course, politicians no longer carry swords, but the symbolism remains: we have a political system which necessitates two different and opposing views. Disagreement can be a vital means of holding power to account but, on an issue such as the housing emergency, we now need expert-informed consensus to move forward irrespective of party politics.

At the time of my meeting with Hollinrake, I had heard from a reliable source that the then Prime Minister, Theresa May, was even warming up to the idea of rent control (but only if it was called rent regulation – semantics are everything in politics). When she took office, May gave what has been dubbed her 'burning injustices' speech. In it, she centred on the fact that housing was unfair and said 'the government I lead will be driven not by the interests of the privileged few'. Those enlisted by her from charities such as Shelter and tasked with fixing the housing crisis told me that she had those words printed out, framed and stuck on the wall outside her private office in Number 10. Toby Lloyd, who at the time was a special advisor to May on housing and local government (having left Shelter to join her team), said, 'That speech was a touchstone. It was referred to all the time.'

Everyone I spoke to in housing then was excited (and a little shocked) that a Conservative leader was seriously discussing ideas that had once been deemed radical. 'I was optimistic, possibly naively, because this was a government that was very hand-to-mouth and therefore not in a position to instigate slow, long-term change, but there was an opportunity and willingness from the Prime Minister and others in her team to enact small but significant changes which would make a difference quickly, like abolishing Section 21,' Lloyd told me.

'The challenge, for us,' he added, 'was that you can't think about the necessary ten-year reforms because you know you might not be there that long. I've always resisted the idea that change comes from having the right individuals involved in government, but it does. May hired social policy experts who were not the usual suspects climbing the greasy pole; she listened to them, and it made a difference.'

So, could Hollinrake be convinced of rent control's benefits? I asked. 'I don't believe in rent caps,' he said firmly, 'but I do believe in some regulation.'

'I suppose,' he added, sounding as if he could yet change his position, 'it depends on where you live. In London and the south-east particularly, you've got lots of tenants competing for few homes, so you see price rises. Whereas, in other regions, where you've got lots of properties and fewer tenants, you've got a more stable market. So I think, ideally, rents should increase at or below the level of inflation, according to the Retail Price Index.' That's a form of rent control in all but name.

Linking private rents to inflation is a good idea in theory but, given that they are already so high and, more to the point, that wages don't also rise in line with inflation, is this the best we can do?

'Yes, you're quite right,' he said. 'We need not only to deliver houses at market rent or at market sale levels but to deliver houses that are actually affordable.' The more we talked, the more Hollinrake seemed to accept the fact that housing was too expensive, that rents needed to be regulated and that the market could no longer provide a measure of what was reasonable because rent had become unhinged from what most people might deem affordable (i.e. less than a third of someone's income). 'Eighty per cent of market rent is unaffordable for many people in a lot of the parts of London,' he added. He was referring to Boris Johnson's increase in 2011, when he was Mayor of London, of the threshold for those eligible for 'affordable' rent in the capital to a level of up to 80 per cent of gross market rents. Hollinrake was correct, 80 per cent of an inflated rent which has risen beyond earnings cannot be affordable. Since then, under its Labour mayor Sadiq Khan, this has been thrown out and replaced with the 'London Living Rent', which is just less than half of market rent. Better, but what would be better still is if we linked rents to incomes.

Hollinrake surprised me that day. When pushed, he agreed that change is needed and yet he, like 308 other Conservative MPs, voted against Karen Buck's Homes (Fitness for Human Habitation) Bill when it first made its way through the House of Commons in 2016, because it was his party's policy. Before the vote, the government said that it would 'result in unnecessary regulation and cost to landlords, which will deter further investment and push up rents for tenants'. Buck's bill was eventually passed by both Houses and given royal assent in December 2018. It has not had the effect Hollinrake feared. And so he, like so many politicians I have met, was a jumble of contradictions. What we know to be true and what we choose to believe are not the same.

'I get it,' he said. 'There's something fundamentally wrong if you work hard and can't get on the property ladder. And I think one of the areas that we – the Conservatives – recognise that we've got wrong is that housing is just so unaffordable, so unfair. Communities are no longer mixed communities. I live in a little village in North Yorkshire. They're still quite expensive, some of these villages, nevertheless we live side by side with people, a wide community, big manor house in the village, council houses, former council houses. And we all get on great. And that's the wonderful mix of a village. Why can't the world be like that? To think Islington or Kensington or Pimlico end up just being all wealthy is wrong. People feeling locked out of homeownership if they want to buy a home is wrong. So, I think it's just a basic fairness, you want to make sure future generations have the same opportunities we did. And, as the saying goes, "Unless you engage young people in the village, they will burn it down just to feel the warmth." You've got to make sure people feel a part of this.'

Bucolic, perhaps, and certainly focused too much on homeownership as the solution, but Hollinrake's vision echoed those of Lloyd George, Addison and Beveridge. As I got ready to leave, he and I were dangerously close to finding common ground. I began to pack my things away. 'You know,' he said, as he stood up, 'I could talk to you about this all day.'

On the way out, I asked him whether he thinks party politics – the need to oppose an idea simply because it belongs to someone on the other side of the chamber – has blocked progress on housing. 'I'm not massively party political,' he told me. 'I do think that gets in the way rather than helps most of the time. What I believe, my deep-rooted philosophy on life, is that you should be able to work hard and get on and there should be no barriers to that. It should be a fair and level playing field.'

Perhaps, for Hollinrake, life has felt like a level playing field. He entered work during a buy-to-let boom and successfully made hay while the sun shone. And, in many ways, his own trajectory exemplifies the British desire to ascend the property ladder, transcend class and make it to the top table. So successful was he, in fact, that he, his wife and their four young children lived in the Grade 1 listed fifteenth-century Crayke Castle for a period. He put it on the market for £3.5 million in 2008, soon after he was selected as the Conservative candidate for Dewsbury at the next general election. 'The kids,' Hollinrake said, when asked by the *York Press* in 2008 about the sale of his slice of British history, 'have a wonderful Enid Blyton-type existence here.' The problems of this nostalgic and quintessentially British idealism are obvious. But we cannot ignore what a powerful force it is. Hollinrake reminds me of people in my own family. Born with little, they grew up in social housing and dreamed of becoming one of 'them' – the elite. That's the problem with social mobility: the implication is that those who work hard enough, are bright enough or get lucky enough ascend, not that things become fairer for everyone full stop.

Still, there he was: a Conservative politician and landlord whom I met because of a Twitter disagreement chatting to me over tea and openly acknowledging the need for rent regulation and more social housing. Two ideas which have featured heavily in various incarnations of Labour Party manifestos in recent years. Could they yet become Conservative policies?

## Playing Party Politics

Rent control has been creeping slowly back into the political mainstream since it became feared as a kind of red terror in the 1980s. As well as Sadiq Khan, it's something I've interviewed Siân Berry, the former leader of the

Green Party and a member of the London Assembly, about repeatedly since the mid-2010s. There is a tendency for mainstream political parties and their supporters in Britain to see a third party in our traditionally two-party political system as a spoiler. This mentality means that third-party candidates rarely get a fair hearing, but the Greens have done more than they are given credit for in terms of moving conversations on and introducing new ideas. They aren't the only ones. The Liberal Democrats have also done much to alleviate the housing crisis. The Tenant Fees Act 2019 began life as a suggestion from Baroness Grender. She was also the person who put forward the Renters' Rights Bill in the Lords, calling for a ban on letting fees for tenants, public access to a database of rogue landlords, compulsory electrical safety checks for renters and a ban on rogue landlords obtaining an HMO licence. The then Lib Dem MP Tom Brake supported her bill in the Commons and sponsored an Early Day Motion calling for fees to be banned. After Baroness Grender's bill passed its committee stage in November 2016, it was adopted as govern-ment policy and announced in the Chancellor's autumn statement as the Renters' Reform Bill, but by early 2022 it had still not become law.

Cross-party pressure from within Parliament – as Karen Buck's work also demonstrates – can move the needle and ultimately result in reform. Siân Berry rightly points out that in London rent controls were initially something she pushed when it was still deemed too radical by other poli-ticians; she did this before Khan made a manifesto pledge in 2019 to lobby central government for the mayor to have the power – as is common with mayors in other European cities – to introduce rent controls.

This can be in no small part because Berry is still a private renter. Her rented home is in Archway in north London, and renting continues to shape her politics. 'I've been a renter for the past twenty-five years,' she told me when we caught up in May 2021 to discuss the likelihood of rent control ever coming into effect, 'and I have tried really hard to bring a voice to renters in City Hall by highlighting the growing gap between people's rents and incomes; to bring the current mayor around to talking about rent controls. The first time I raised rent controls with Sadiq ... he was very down on it, he said we would never get the power to implement rent controls from the government. I suggested that he might want to put forward an amendment to the bill on rent control, but he didn't respond to that. It's been a long road but now he is a fan of the policy.' At the time of writing, the idea had been adopted as policy and featured in mainstream conversations, but London's mayor still didn't have the power to implement rent controls in the capital.

That could still change – in Paris, rent controls also made a comeback in 2019, and similarly in Berlin where, backed by Angela Merkel's government, a five-year rent freeze was approved in the same year. Let's hope it happens here soon. Both Khan and Berry make the point that rent controls in London could become a blueprint for the rest of the country, allowing us to see how a system like Scotland's locally implemented Rent Pressure Zones might also work across England and Wales.

If there is an obstacle standing in the way of solving the housing crisis it is not a shortage of progressive or tried and tested ideas that would work. It is this: the majority of people in Britain want to own a home of their own. According to the yearly British Social Attitudes Survey, homeownership remains the tenure of choice for the vast majority of people. Eighty-six per cent of Britons would buy their own home rather than rent. We are already a majority homeowning nation. In 2020, 63 per cent of households in Britain owned their own homes. Homeowners are, on the whole, likely to vote in their own interests. Politicians, on both the left and the right, know this. Manifesto policies are created behind the mirrored glass of focus group rooms all over the country. Polling data is scrutinised before they are put together, with one end goal in mind: winning. People have bought into the idea of housing both as a home and as an asset. They want a piece of the world to call their own. They also want to make more money than they can in work, retire on it and pass something valuable on to their children. So, since the 1980s, policies which promote homeownership and inflate house prices have proved popular and won elections.

Remember, Right to Buy was initially a Labour policy. Meanwhile, the Conservative Party, as David Cameron put it in 2015, 'have dreamed of building a property-owning democracy for generations'. In 1946, the deputy leader Anthony Eden gave a conference speech in Blackpool cementing this as the Tories' key objective. In 1975, Margaret Thatcher declared she was following in his footsteps in her ardent pursuit of this goal. Owning assets makes people more likely to vote Conservative, they reasoned, because they have something of their own to conserve.

Like Cameron before him, Boris Johnson has determinedly followed this well-trodden path with planning deregulation and inflationary monetary policies designed to create what he hoped would be a 'housing bonanza'. Why? Because it wins elections. Regardless of whether the means – his pandemic housing policies of Stamp Duty cuts and government-backed 95 per cent loan-to-value mortgages, which caused house prices across the country to rise at their highest rate in five years – justified the ends, Johnson knew that pushing homeownership made electoral sense and that, politically, it created a big problem for Labour.

How a person experiences the housing market has always influenced their voting preferences. Until the 1997 election, in which Tony Blair led New Labour to a landslide victory, the convention had always been that the Conservatives won more support from owner-occupiers. Indeed, as the Oxford geography Professor Danny Dorling has noted, the 1997 general election was the first (and only) one in which the Labour Party won more support than the Conservatives within the owner-occupier section of the British housing market. That is more than two decades ago.

Kevin Hollinrake was not the only politician I sat down with in Westminster. John Healey has been the Labour MP for Wentworth and Dearne in South Yorkshire since 1997. Once in Parliament, he rose quickly, and by 1999 he was a Parliamentary Private Secretary to the then Chancellor Gordon Brown. Most of his time, however, has been spent working on housing. Healey served as a junior minister at the Ministry of Housing, Communities and Local Government from 2007 to 2010 and then as Shadow Secretary of State for Housing from 2015 until 2020, when the new Labour leader, Keir Starmer, moved him over to Defence.

I met Healey in his office in early 2019 while he was still Shadow Housing Secretary. The previous year the Labour Party had published its housing green paper, 'Housing for the Many', which he thrust excitedly into my hand as we sat down to chat over (yet another) cup of Yorkshire Tea. Healey's patch is an area which borders the Peak District, from the north of Rotherham to the east of Barnsley. To the north, it is flanked by

Wakefield, to the east by Doncaster and to the south by Sheffield. It sits just to the south and west of Kevin Hollinrake's constituency of Thirsk and Malton.

That green paper contained crucial measures to end the housing crisis: £75 billion-worth of investment over five years allocated for building 100,000 new social homes a year – to be delivered by local councils – and at least another 50,000 'genuinely affordable' homes; a £1 billion fund to buy back social housing which had ended up in the hands of private landlords as a consequence of Right to Buy; and a national system of rent control. 'There is a basic argument for these measures,' Healey told me. 'In Germany, for instance, the rights and rules are stronger, and the private sector is twice the size of ours in Britain. When you've got a better functioning market – a fair market – it can work for the landlord just as it can for the renter.' It made sense, and housing experts endorsed it, but the British public didn't vote the Labour Party in. They didn't buy what was on offer, even though it would have helped to alleviate the pain of millions of people. Time and time again, studies have found that as homeownership has risen, it has become increasingly difficult for Labour to win, not just arguments about housing, but more broadly, because it is not seen as the party of homeownership or housing wealth. Labour's challenge is to figure out how to sell policies that will alleviate the crisis in housing to everyone, including homeowners.

Healey was clear-eyed about where British housing policy had gone wrong. 'The threads of it, I think, lie thirty to forty years ago, in that Thatcher period when the belief that government had a responsibility to ensure people were properly housed weakened; when more people began to think of housing essentially as an individual problem; and it accelerated also as something that became a financial vehicle, an investment, rather than something that people had as a necessity to live in – a home that was secure and decent.'

From speaking to him, I gained a sense of how flippant British party politics is. Good ideas don't always win votes. Vital policies aren't always popular. 'I was Labour's last housing minister in government, for the final eleven months before we lost the election in May 2010,' he told me. 'Getting better, fairer, stronger regulation and making the private renting market work better is unfinished business for me in many ways.' Before the 2010 election, Labour commissioned a large-scale review of the private rented sector – the Rugg Review – conducted by Dr Julie Rugg and David Rhodes, from the University of York's Centre for Housing Policy. A decade later, as I sat with Healey, almost all the problems Rugg and Rhodes identified were still raging on. It was clearly frustrating to Healey. 'In 2010, we were just confirming the legal and policy changes we would make as a result of that big independent analysis,' he told me. 'And, really, since then, the imperative to act, the arguments for acting, the failures in the market have all become much clearer, much stronger.' But, of course, the action has not been taken.

For now, the Labour Party knows that it has trouble on its hands. Far from being a bubble, the inflated house prices and record highs we saw during the pandemic may yet become the new normal in Britain because our economy is now so reliant on the housing market. Whether that's right or wrong, the majority of voters appear to be happy with it. Labour knows it has to do something to capture the imaginations of homeowners. That is why, in September 2021, the then Shadow Housing Secretary, Lucy Powell, stood before a packed hall of delegates at the party's annual conference in Brighton and made a big pitch for Labour as 'the party of homeowners and tenants', going on to say that the Tories were 'the party of speculators and developers'. This signalled a decisive shift for Labour, which had previously positioned itself as the party of social housing and renters' rights, while the Conservatives were the self-proclaimed party of homeownership. It was also a necessary shift.

As the cladding crisis, the building safety crisis and the emerging trend for longer and bigger mortgages all show us, homeowners are going to need support, too, in years to come. Housing will always be a central issue of both social and economic concern and this mirroring of left-wing views on the right is likely to continue because it is politically expedient to appeal to homeowners. What that might mean for the Conservatives remains to be seen, particularly if inflation, energy bills and interest rates keep rising.

But to end the housing crisis, we need all politicians to think beyond the electoral cycle, beyond winning and losing. Coalition is required on this issue. If the right to housing is accepted as a human right, it can become a central policy pillar and a consensus can be reached as to how to approach the instability of the private rented sector, restore social housing stock and tackle homelessness (both rough sleeping and hidden). If only there was a utopian blueprint, an exercise in future thinking or an off-the-shelf policy solution that we could implement to resolve the housing crisis. Or a radical housing initiative that could end homelessness of all kinds once and for all and reframe our relationship with and conception of housing.

There is one. It's called Housing First. It is a homelessness strategy first and foremost, but its ambition and success shows us what's possible as a guiding philosophy for ending the housing crisis.

# 12

# THE UTOPIAN REALISM
# OF HOUSING FIRST

### Hungerford, Berkshire

*Council:* Hungerford Town Council
*Average House Price:* In the year 2020/21 the majority of sales in
Hungerford were semi-detached homes, selling for an average of
£353,236. Terraced homes sold for an average of £305,517, with
detached properties fetching £495,260. Overall, sold prices in
Hungerford in that year were 11 per cent up on the previous year
and 5 per cent up on the 2018 peak of £348,238.
*Average Private Rent:* In 2021 the average rent for a one-bedroom
home was £650 and for a two-bed it was £863. At the time of
writing, there were no three- or four-bedroom homes listed for
private rent.

—

'Christ,' Barry said when I asked how he was feeling in the middle of
the first coronavirus lockdown. 'I was on the streets for years. My home
… this place, it's like a five-star hotel. I'm so lucky. Mandy – my support
worker – she's everything. I'd marry her if I could. I want the world
to know about what these guys have done for me.' Barry, 67, a former
rough sleeper, was wearing a burgundy polo neck tucked neatly into his
belted jeans underneath a grey jumper, his long grey hair curling where
he had swept it back.

'This place' was a one-bedroom maisonette in Hungerford at the end of a quiet, leafy residential street. Barry's neighbours were all outside enjoying the warm sun that signalled the shift from late spring to early summer – washing their cars and tending to their gardens. A balcony ran along the side of his house. Sometimes he smoked out there; he was thinking of putting up a trellis and planting something, like honeysuckle or passion flowers; he was enjoying working in the garden immensely. Formerly a borehole driller working on road maintenance, Barry was once married, and has a daughter, now in her twenties, with a child of her own.

Barry had just come in from his small but blooming garden. He had been repotting plants that he had saved from an uncertain fate in the discount aisle at Tesco. 'They were reduced from £12 to £2 each. Can you believe it?' he said, impressed with his bargain. Inside, stairs led up to his kitchen. Barry had decorated the hall window which looks out over the garden with stickers to give the effect of stained glass. 'I love my gardening,' he said. 'I want to plant a vegetable patch so I can grow my own food. I love my cooking, too. I'm great at making curries, you know! I do it all myself, I like doing it.'

The appliances in his kitchen gleamed, every surface was spotless. The living room had been thoughtfully filled with (mostly gifted) furniture. 'My friend gave me that lamp,' Barry said, pointing with pride. 'Mandy helped me get that sofa.' Sovereign – Barry's landlord, a housing association which describes itself as being driven by 'social purpose' – offered to decorate Barry's flat for him. But he wanted to do it himself. The only downside? He couldn't decide whether he wanted a blue or a yellow colour scheme. When we spoke, he was playing around with paint samples. On the windowsill in the living room, cards from Christmas were still up. 'I'm so grateful for everyone's support,' he said, his voice cracking with emotion.

If I hadn't known that he had, until very recently, been street homeless, I'd have thought Barry was just like any Baby Boomer born in the 1950s – a retired man enjoying the mortgage-free home he'd been able to buy when houses were still affordable, cashing in a final salary pension, pottering around and whiling away the hours, soundtracked by Steely Dan. But this stability was very, very new for him. Barry had been homeless for years.

When he was in his fifties, Barry's marriage fell apart. For more than a decade he has been estranged from his ex-wife. The financial fallout of his separation meant that Barry lost everything: his rented home, his family and, ultimately, his livelihood. He couldn't afford to rent anywhere and his mental health spiralled downwards. Drinking became a coping mechanism, a symptom and not a cause of his homelessness. 'Things happen, you know,' he told me. 'You're not working, you're drinking and one thing leads to another.' He drank to numb himself, moving around Berkshire, from Hungerford (where he slept outside the town hall) to Newbury, from Marlborough to Pewsey, making bus shelters and benches his home.

In British politics, when it comes to homelessness policy, there has been a pernicious and long-held misconception that homeless people can't be given homes until they are free of addiction and in employment. In part this is because there is insufficient funding for homelessness and in part because there is not enough affordable housing to go round. This means that women with children and families get priority (although even they, as we know from earlier chapters, struggle to get the help they are entitled to). It is also because of a toxic notion that not having a home is somehow the fault of the individual and not a side effect of economic forces which promote profit and precarity. As a prevailing ideology which locates the causes of inequality in individuals and not society, this has also been present in the policies that have allowed the deregulation of the private rented sector and the decimation of social housing. That thinking is slowly starting to shift, but the ideology still hangs over street homelessness and our attitude to housing as a whole – in Britain, you 'make your own luck'. As recently as 2018 we saw the late James Brokenshire, then the Secretary of State for Housing, Communities and Local Government, hauled over the coals for espousing such baseless dogma. Shortly before Christmas that year he was forced to backtrack after he suggested that the unprecedented rise in homelessness in Britain was being driven not by government policy but by 'family breakdowns' and 'the spread of psychoactive drugs'. But there is no doubt that the spike was indeed due to government policy. Britain is one of the richest countries in the world and, at that time, street homelessness had leapt up by a whopping 165 per cent in less than a decade. Under John Major and Tony Blair, government made huge strides in reducing street homelessness by putting energy, effort, money and focus behind that goal. Prior to the pandemic, I was visiting cardboard box encampments and interviewing people living in tents. These horrific sights had not been seen so prominently on Britain's streets since the 1980s and 1990s. As Rebecca Pritchard, then the Director of Services for Crisis, told me when we talked before the pandemic, this was a direct result of 'ten years of austerity and cuts to homelessness services'.

'Ten years ago – under Gordon Brown – when I was with central government, we discouraged local charities from giving people sleeping bags and tents because we saw it as enabling people to live in a dangerous way,' she said. 'A decade on, it's different. There just isn't the accommodation there was. There used to be something for everybody. It might not have been perfect but there was somewhere you could house everyone that was better than where they were. That just doesn't exist now because we have a housing shortage.'

It is worth reiterating that rough sleeping and hidden homelessness, while related, are not the same thing. Indeed, many people who become homeless do not show up in official figures at all. They include people who become homeless but find a temporary solution by staying with family members or friends or by living in squats or other insecure accommodation.

Barry had lived in his maisonette since December 2019 and it will be his for as long as he wants it and adheres to his tenancy agreement. For ever, if that's the case. It is his thanks to Housing First. The premise of Housing First is simple – you house homeless people immediately, regardless of their needs. There are no caveats, they are not told to stop drinking, preached at over drug use or told that they must get a job before they are eligible for housing; they are simply given a home and any treatment they need. The idea was dreamed up in the 1980s by a Greek Canadian psychologist named Sam Tsemberis. While working in New York he had a simple yet radical idea: maybe the best way to solve the problem of homelessness was to give people homes. The idea was viewed as outlandish and unworkable. Sceptics argued that complex issues like addiction and mental health had to be addressed first before someone was a suitable candidate for long-term housing. And furthermore, how would the cost be justified to hard-working taxpayers? Tsemberis proved them wrong. His scheme was found to be more effective than other approaches and was a huge success. Since then, the idea of giving homeless people homes has caught on around the world, perhaps most notably in Finland where, under Juha Kaakinen, the CEO of Y-Foundation, a Housing First-type organisation, street homelessness has now effectively been eradicated. Indeed, Finland is the only country in Europe where the number of homeless people is falling.

As Kaakinen wrote in a policy paper in 2017:

> This is not a coincidence. Since the 1980s, the state, volunteers, municipalities and NGOs have been working with determination to reduce homelessness. Of particular importance is that in the 2000s, the state has launched and funded programmes aimed at reducing homelessness, which have tackled the situation of the most vulnerable long-term homeless. With the help of the programmes, organisations and municipalities have, for example, provided new housing for the homeless and reformed the services aimed at them. All of these actors have wanted the same thing: to humanise the life of the homeless.

The Housing First scheme which helped Barry was operated by Sovereign, the largest housing association in the south of England, in partnership with Two Saints, a local homelessness support group, and West Berkshire Council. His rent was paid through Universal Credit to Sovereign. As he had only recently come off the streets, he had two support workers, Mandy Rigby from Two Saints and Janet Pye from Sovereign. They assisted him with repairs, the payment of his rent, admin and any physical or mental health issues he had. Prior to the pandemic, Sovereign was one of a handful of housing associations in England dipping its toe into Housing First, which has been particularly successful in Scotland, where it is now a central tenet of the Scottish government's Housing to 2040 policy and a major focus of political attention.

This approach – its Pathfinder programme has been operating for two years and is now implemented across five areas of the country – has seen 82 per cent of people helped to stay in the homes they have been given. This housing retention rate is up there with the best international comparisons. Scotland is now scaling up the programme and hoping, like Finland, to eradicate homelessness completely.

'It's just a miracle that I'm here,' Barry said when I asked him what Housing First had done for him. 'I want the world to know about this, I want everyone to know. I was born into an army family – strong in the arm, weak in the head. But this, this house is a gift. I'm drinking less and my life is on track. I just wish it had happened sooner because who knows what my life could have been.'

Housing First was conceived as a solution to rough sleeping and chronic street homelessness, but, with a bit of ambitious thinking, it could help us end homelessness while also ending the crisis in the private rented sector which is, as this book has established, also fuelling homelessness in a vicious circle. Barry's story is one of someone at the sharp end of homelessness, but if the extremes of his situation – addiction and long-term rough sleeping – can be overcome by something as simple as a stable and secure home, imagine what could be achieved if we made sure struggling families, single mothers and young professionals had the same stable base from which to move through the world. What else could they turn their energy to? What kind of society would we have if they did?

It is therefore possible to apply the Housing First principle – that nobody can be expected to do anything if they don't have a safe, secure and affordable home as a base, that nobody can live a stable and fulfilling life without housing security – to the crisis in the private rented sector. It could be used to underpin further regulation of that sector in a joined-up way to ensure that renters cannot be easily evicted, can stay in their homes for as long as they want, to shore up living conditions and to make sure that rents cannot be put up at short notice to beyond what a tenant can afford. The proposition of Housing First could also be expanded to include replenishing Britain's social housing stock and reconfiguring our relationship with property full stop. It could ensure that we never end up in a housing emergency again.

## The Right to Housing

The UK doesn't have a constitution. Nowhere is there an edict compelling our lawmakers to enshrine a 'right to housing', though there have long been calls to introduce a new law creating binding duties on government to guarantee to everyone a right to shelter and a right of access to adequate housing – particularly in the wake of the Grenfell Tower fire and the building safety scandal that has unfolded in its wake. Perhaps this also sounds idealistic. Well, it has already been agreed to by a growing number of countries less wealthy than the UK, which all see it as a social right that bolsters democracy. These include the Netherlands, which guarantees a right to adequate housing, and the Seychelles, which guarantees a right to shelter; also some Latin American countries, including Argentina, Colombia and Uruguay, which protect a right to housing. Several African states, including South Africa, also enshrine a right to housing in law, as do the fast-growing economies of Brazil and India. Their laws are different but they all share a rejection of the British commodification of housing in favour of a right to housing. In Germany, where rent controls have been introduced in recent years, Article 14 of the country's constitution states that owning property 'entails obligations. Its use should also serve the common good.' Similarly, Article 65 of Portugal's constitution forces the government to promote the construction of social housing where rents are compatible with people's incomes. And Costa Rica's constitution states that the government must construct low-cost housing.

Of course, it's one thing to enshrine the right to housing in law and quite another to make sure politicians are held accountable to that law. It was taken seriously in Costa Rica, where 80,000 new low-cost homes were built in the four years between 1986 and 1990 and the government created an entitlement for low-income families to be given affordable housing loans, with no more than 30 per cent of their income going on its repayment. Meanwhile, in Portugal, where high rents are increasingly locking younger people out of the private rented sector and homeownership, the picture looks very different, as it does in Germany, where, while rent controls and tenants' rights have done some good, the issue of international investors inflating the housing market persists.

Back in the UK, in recent years, balancing the property rights of landowners with human rights and, specifically, the socio-economic rights of communities and tenants has become a focal point in legal conversations about human rights, particularly in Scotland. It could shape conversations south of the border, too, particularly as the building safety and cladding scandals continue to raise questions about whether the leasehold system of property ownership has any place in modern society.

The right to housing ought not to be interpreted in a narrow or restrictive sense to mean merely shelter, having a roof over your head in times of crisis, or to continue to configure that shelter as a commodity. Instead, as defined by Article 11 of the International Covenant on Economic, Social and Cultural Rights (ICESCR), it is 'the right of everyone to an adequate standard of living for himself and his family, including adequate food, clothing and housing, and to the continuous improvement of living conditions'. The right to housing is the right to live somewhere in security, peace and dignity regardless of housing tenure, encompassing homeownership, privately rented and socially rented homes.

There are concrete and complex reasons why this hasn't already occurred in the UK. The incorporation of the ICESCR into UK domestic law was considered when the Human Rights Act was passed in 1988. However, it was ultimately dismissed by lawmakers and Parliament because it was felt that the inclusion of socio-economic rights was 'non-justiciable' – that is, incapable of being decided by legal principles or in a court. The incorporation of the right to housing would not be straightforward. That doesn't mean it shouldn't happen, it just needs to be defined properly.

Of course, a properly defined right to housing in Britain, underpinned by a commitment to the Housing First philosophy, would not necessarily be a silver bullet, but it would be a foundation on which legislation could be worked out; one that could bring the Housing First mindset to the forefront of our housing policy. It would only work if it was enforced and if we had enough affordable homes for everyone. But, as Scotland's homelessness laws and changes to private tenancies in recent years show, a Housing First approach which encapsulates the right to housing is completely doable.

## No Going Back

If this all sounds Pollyanna-ish, consider what happened in response to the coronavirus pandemic. The path from idealism to reality is neither as romantic nor as winding as we might have been led to believe.

In early 2020, as Covid-19 spread, it reminded us that our society – for all the technological advancements of the last few centuries – was only the sum of its fleshy parts. Far from being invincible, we were still as susceptible to natural disasters as we ever were and, like us, our free market, capitalist economy and the structures we had built on it were fallible. The welfare state that had been systematically eroded in the years leading up to the pandemic was going to become a fallback for those people who had previously never claimed benefits and who now found themselves in need of a safety net. Coronavirus served as a reminder that society is a delicate ecosystem. If something happens in one part, there are palpable ripples in other parts. If demand for a particular product ceases, the supplier goes out of business. If a supplier goes out of business, they cannot pay their debts and people lose their jobs. If a landlord starts to worry about their financial future, they decide to have a crack at charging their tenants more and, if the tenants can't pay, move to evict them.

On 11 March 2020, a new Chancellor, Rishi Sunak, talked the nation through his first budget less than a month into the job. Building affordable housing – which housing experts agreed was urgently needed – barely got a mention. Just one week later, the coronavirus crisis had become so serious that the government had started giving daily wartime-style televised press conferences. Radical measures were announced. Things we had previously been told could not be done, were done. Over the course of eleven days, between 17 and 27 March, as we all looked on in disbelief, the mood in Whitehall was, as a senior advisor at the Ministry of Housing, Communities and Local Government (MHCLG) told me over WhatsApp, 'careful and urgent'.

A furlough scheme was quickly implemented to stop people losing their jobs. It was Universal Basic Income in all but name, and a high one at that – up to £2,500 a month, which is more than all the main people I interviewed for this book earned when I met them. The Treasury also moved quickly to shore up the mortgage market by convincing banks to give homeowners mortgage holidays to avert mass repossessions if people could no longer make their monthly payments because their income was impacted by the pandemic. And, though private renters were largely neglected, the Local Housing Allowance was quickly increased from 1 April (although, as discussed earlier, it still did not cover market rents). None the less, things happened. And they happened fast.

At the same time, the MHCLG acted decisively on street homelessness. On 17 March it told local authorities to get homeless people off the streets through a scheme called 'Everyone In' – a de facto version of Housing First – a £3.2 million emergency fund to house the homeless in hotels and hostels where they could self-isolate, applying even to people with no recourse to public funds. Sadly, it has since been wound down. But the scale of this operation (though not perfect in its execution) and its significance in demonstrating that an end to homelessness is possible cannot be underestimated. Compared with the timescale of the Conservatives' previous promise to end (street, not hidden) homelessness by 2027, the equivalent of ten years of housing policy was rushed through in just ten days. And that promise became an actuality almost overnight; what had once been considered radical – politically 'impossible' – became possible. The progressive and socialist became Conservative. Charities, which had long been calling for these measures, were suddenly being listened to, their policy suggestions taken up wholesale.

If private renters were, shockingly, overlooked in the coronavirus response, perhaps it is because their plight, while no less or more important, is less emotive and inspires less political goodwill than rough sleeping, which is visible and visceral, particularly during a global pandemic. When it came to private renting, the response was, indeed, scandalous. The initial emergency coronavirus legislation didn't have a section on the eviction of private renters at all. One was added as an amendment at a second reading on 23 March. But even then, it was not the 'ban' that the Prime Minister had promised at Prime Minister's Questions, or that Robert Jenrick, then Secretary of State for Housing,

Communities and Local Government, had discussed on 18 March, but a delay on possession proceedings, which did nothing for existing possession claims. The government tried to defend the legislation, but behind the scenes Shelter, Crisis and expert housing lawyers such as Giles Peaker expressed grave concerns. On 27 March, the government announced that the court service would suspend all ongoing housing possession actions – meaning that no cases currently in or about to go in the system could progress to eviction. But why did the government not just bring forward the long-promised ban on Section 21?

What we did learn from the overall response – Everyone In, mortgage holidays, a stay on evictions – was summed up by Hannah Gousy, then the Policy and Public Affairs Manager at Crisis, when we spoke in May 2020: when the political desire (or, in this case, need) is there, the money can be found and anything is possible. 'We took proposals on Everyone In to them in the run-up to lockdown,' she said, 'and we saw changes really quickly. It shows just how much can be done when you have the political will. What this period has shown is that ending homelessness is possible. Thousands of homeless people have been moved off the streets in just weeks.'

Could the impetus from short-term coronavirus changes be converted into political momentum for long-term reform?

The answer to that question has yet to be determined, but, as the Local Government Association (LGA) noted in December 2020, what the success of Everyone In demonstrates is that we need a complete rethink, a political shift towards ensuring housing stability and preventing homelessness. This, it wrote, means 'maintaining increased support through the mainstream benefits system, increased protection for private renters, and a commitment across government to a programme of homelessness prevention'. The government announced additional funding through several different schemes (the Next Steps Accommodation Programme, the Cold Weather Fund and the Protect Programme), but it wasn't enough. Social housing waiting lists were set to potentially nearly double as a result of the pandemic.

A conception of Housing First which goes beyond rough sleeping is implicit in every one of the recommendations made by the LGA above. Applying the philosophy of Housing First to housing policy as a whole would mean seeing all of the housing market as part of a delicate economic system in which high rents are related to homelessness, among other ills, and acknowledging the role housing plays in people's wellbeing and life chances and making sure that there is enough affordable housing for everyone and putting policies in place to safeguard it. This entails thinking beyond the electoral cycle and accepting that housing needs a long-term big-picture approach.

What the pandemic did was make politics and policy more immediate. For the first time since the Second World War, what the government did directly impacted the lives of everybody – not just of select groups. This moved what is known as the Overton Window. This is an idea that was developed by the American lawyer Joseph Overton in the 1990s because he wanted to answer the question: why are so many good political policies – ones that make perfect sense, ones that could objectively improve people's lives – dismissed out of hand?

The answer is simple: politicians reflect public opinion rather than shape it. And it can take a while for new ideas to become accepted. Of course, there is an argument that they also shape it (for good and bad) when they want to by positing new ideas and bringing people with them. But the reason that they generally play safe is that they want to be elected.

The Overton Window is a model for understanding this, a framework for how ideas in society change over time and influence politics based on what is deemed acceptable to the electorate. Anything that lies outside of it is considered unthinkable or radical, and politicians risk losing popular support if they champion such ideas. If they want to hold on to power, politicians have to gauge what will be tolerated by the majority of people and propose policies accordingly. Which is why, as discussed previously, homeownership and house price inflation have been not only normalised but prioritised.

Yet coronavirus has proved that the Overton Window can shift rapidly. The pandemic was unexpected and beyond anyone's control. It moved the needle. We can see this in the fact that, since March 2020, receiving and accepting state support has become less shrouded in shame and stigma. State support is once again something for which not just high-profile people – such as the footballer Marcus Rashford, who campaigned for the government to extend free school meals outside of term time – are proudly prepared to advocate. This was confirmed by the British Social Attitudes Survey released in October 2020. It reported that public support for more generous welfare benefits – which includes housing support – is at its highest level for more than two decades. The survey also suggested that, post-Brexit, our views on social security and immigration were becoming significantly more liberal. There is a huge question mark hanging over what happens next, but we know this much: where the public go, politicians follow. In 2020, a YouGov poll found that, as well as a Universal Basic Income and the furlough scheme, there was public support for rent controls. The pollsters asked whether people supported a policy 'where the government sets caps on what landlords can charge, or freezing rents'. This policy was supported by 74 per cent of the public, with just 8 per cent unsupportive. Remember, also, how the Green Party moved the needle on rent control in London? Could now be the time to use the success of Everyone In to demonstrate that the Housing First principle works and that it can be extended? Because, if we have learned anything from the coronavirus, it is this: home is the centre of all life and our best frontline defence against external catastrophes.

## Helsinki, Finland, The World

Juha Kaakinen is a utopian dreamer: that is why he is the architect of Finland's large-scale successful national Housing First programme. He is tall, thoughtful and optimistic. He talks as though everything, anything, is possible. Over the years, I've had ongoing conversations with him about Housing First. One question I always return to is: how did he manage to convince politicians in his country that it could work? His answer is always the same: 'It required a complete reversal in how homelessness was thought about.'

In 1986, early in his career, Kaakinen went on a research trip. He wanted to see how bad homelessness could be, so, with a couple of colleagues, he went to a city in Europe which had a particularly large population of rough sleepers: London. 'I remember walking along the South Bank, behind the Royal Festival Hall, and seeing a lot of homeless people sleeping,' he told me in one of our chats. 'The thing is that, when the pandemic hit, the situation you had in your country was even worse than it was back then.' This, he said, was not inevitable. 'The problem you have – and this is something I hear from my colleagues in the UK – is that there's a lack of affordable housing that could be used for Housing First. Even if you wanted to, you can't do Housing First without having the housing first.'

He is right. To give some idea of why we can't make Housing First work in Britain as things stand, our social housing stock has plummeted to about the same level as Finland's, despite the UK population being twelve times that of Finland.

Kaakinen is a world leader in his field. He knows more about the merits and potential of Housing First than anyone, and he truly believes that this approach can be applied to more aspects of the crisis in housing than street homelessness. He thinks that it should be a blanket approach to housing, to living; not just for those, like Barry, with complex needs, but for society as a whole. The philosophy is simple. As he put it to me: 'Give someone a home and then support them in growing their life out from there. It strikes me that this is at once groundbreaking, but incredibly obvious.'

What's holding us back?

'I don't think this is solely an issue of money,' Kaakinen told me. Indeed, the pandemic response proved that not to be so. In any case, he also pointed out that the current system (if you can call it that) for dealing with homelessness (of all kinds, but particularly post-eviction from private rented accommodation) is hardly cost-effective. 'Providing temporary accommodation for homeless people costs more than providing permanent homes with the prospect that some people will start working again,' he said. Consider this: the total bill for temporary accommodation between April 2019 and March 2020 for local councils in England alone was £1.2 billion. This was an increase of 9 per cent on the previous year and 55 per cent over the previous five years. Of the total spent on this temporary accommodation, 87 per cent went to private accommodation providers. More than a third (38 per cent) of the money paid to them was spent on emergency B&Bs – £393 million – which are considered some of the least suitable places for families with children to live in. That figure had increased by a staggering 73 per cent in five years. And this is before we even factor in the cost of homelessness to the NHS because of how it impacts people's mental and physical health, or the cost to local homelessness services.

'So, it's not the money,' Kaakinen said firmly, 'that's so obvious to me. It's about ideology.' What is that ideology? The answer is complex. It is rooted in a lot of factors: that hidden homelessness is not deemed as serious as rough sleeping; the privatisation of social housing which occurred in the 1980s; the erosion of the welfare safety net; the belief in free market solutions; and an enduring stigma which implies that those who become homeless have done something wrong and that those who don't own housing are not working hard enough. These elements have converged to create a totally dysfunctional state-led approach which reinforces a costly cycle of displacement and disruption.

The evidence, not just from Finland but from parts of the US, Canada, Denmark, Spain and France, where Housing First has also been adopted, speaks for itself. In 2013, the Housing First Europe project reported that 97 per cent of the high-need homeless people using the Discus Housing First service in Amsterdam were still in their housing after twelve months. In Copenhagen, the rate was 94 per cent overall, with a similarly impressive level of 92 per cent reported by the Turning Point service in Glasgow. Indeed, as Professor David Halpern, director of the Behavioural Insights Team, writes in an urgent collection of essays published by the Centre for Homelessness Impact: 'Housing First is one of the few interventions to have rigorous evidence behind it.' It is tried and tested. As the statistics above show, it works.

As Kaakinen puts it, 'With a bit of creative thinking and political ambition there's no reason that the dots can't be joined and this approach applied to other kinds of homelessness. Instead of housing people for long periods in substandard and expensive temporary accommodation, we build more secure and affordable social housing, cut waiting lists and provide housing, first, so that they can get on with their lives.'

Mid-pandemic, I asked Kaakinen over Zoom if he ever just wanted to bang politicians' heads together. He laughed before saying, 'It is difficult for me to understand why we have such unequal societies, why we are not providing affordable housing in wealthy countries like the UK. It's because there is a very strong political motivation for encouraging people to see housing as a financial investment, not as the necessary social infrastructure it should be.

'Your government has been very slow in reacting to a worsening crisis in housing for years,' he added. 'You need to have somebody who is responsible for housing all of the time, who is always showing the way on housing policy but, right now, your politicians are sleeping at the wheel and they're in danger of waking up to reality too late.'

Instead of one person overseeing the trajectory of housing policy, what have we had? Since the Conservatives came to power in 2010, eleven housing ministers have churned through the revolving door of the department responsible for this policy area. Labour isn't much better. Since John Healey's departure in April 2020, there have been two shadow housing ministers. This, again, is why the issue of housing should be elevated above party politics, though, of course, kept accountable in the same way that our politicians are.

Consistency is key. That, Kaakinen told me, is why Housing First was able to succeed in tackling street homelessness in Finland. 'The state's firm guidance in Finland turned reducing homelessness into a shared goal,' he said. 'The process went on despite the economic recession that began in 2008, during which cuts were made to many other services provided by society.' Housing policy in Britain has not been so consistent. It has been subject to the whims of political parties.

### Housing as a Fundamental Right

At the time of writing, the long-awaited Renters' Reform Bill was being considered by Parliament. In April 2019, the Ministry of Housing, Communities and Local Government consulted on proposals to:

- end 'no-fault' evictions by repealing Section 21 of the Housing Act 1988;
- remove landlords' ability to grant new Assured Shorthold Tenancies, meaning that all tenancies would revert back to being Assured Tenancies. This would create open-ended tenancies (like the ones in Scotland), which would give tenants a greater peace of mind;
- introduce a lifetime deposit which would move with the tenant. This would mean that, once a tenant has paid a deposit for their first private rented property, the deposit could then be 'passported' with them (after monies had been deducted for any repairs or arrears) if they move and need to put down a deposit on another property. Tenants would not have to provide a whole deposit every time they move, just top up their existing one;
- improve standards in rented accommodation via: better enforcement of criminal landlords to give tenants and other landlords peace of mind; not just encouraging but obliging private landlords to use a redress scheme which the tenants would have the right to use; and creating a mandatory national register of landlords.

In November 2019, the Conservative Party manifesto included a commitment to introduce a Renters' Reform Bill that would repeal Section 21 and scrap new ASTs. Reviewing and passing the bill was put on hold due to the pandemic, but on 3 March 2021, Christopher Pincher, then the Minister of State for Housing, confirmed that the Renters' Reform Bill would be addressed once the urgencies of responding to the pandemic had passed. Of course, it was a vital piece of legislation in light of the urgency of responding to the pandemic, so this delay was short-sighted. In the Queen's Speech in May 2021, the intention to abolish Section 21 evictions and to introduce new lifetime deposits was reiterated. The other provisions in the bill were still to play for, with charities like Shelter lobbying hard to make sure it was properly drafted.

All of these measures could go a long way to ending the crisis in the private rented sector, but there is an argument that housing shouldn't be a party political issue at all. Can something as serious as housing safety and security be up for debate? Food safety standards are not, for instance. Nor is access to fresh, clean, drinkable water. If there was a unilateral commitment to a Housing First approach and the human right to housing, perhaps the political landscape would look very different.

It is important to note at this point that not all housing campaigners, advocates and stakeholders agree on these measures. That is not necessarily a bad thing, but it would be a mistake to assume that all centrist, right- or left-leaning housing experts agree among themselves, let alone with one another. Equally, sometimes there is a surprising amount of coalition among some unlikely allies, which is what happened with the Tenant Fees Act and Everyone In. Organisations such as Shelter and Crisis shy away from talking about rent control. This is for good reason – they are charities and if they want to maintain their charitable status they must remain (or appear to remain) apolitical. There is, however, a good case for including rent control here, too. As has been explored previously, locally administered Rent Pressure Zones have worked well in Scotland and in Northern Ireland, which introduced them at much the same time, in December 2016. There is no point scrapping evictions if a landlord can get rid of a tenant by putting their rent up to beyond what they can afford.

This brings us to the next piece of the puzzle: social housing. We don't have enough social housing. It doesn't have to be like this. In other parts of the UK, it isn't. In 2016, the devolved government of Wales joined Scotland and moved to scrap Right to Buy. Announcing the move in August, the then First Minister Carwyn Jones said: 'We must safeguard our social housing stock … this bill will seek to protect that stock from further reductions. The analogy I have used before is that it is like trying to fill the bath up with the plug out.' That same year, the Conservatives in England introduced a pilot programme to extend the scheme to include some housing association tenants. Shelter now estimates that the UK needs 3.1 million new social and genuinely affordable homes to help those trapped by the cost of high rents. This is not far off the number of homes lost through Right to Buy. Trying to fill up the bath with the plug out, indeed.

Building more social housing would restore municipal housing to the status of national asset. Indeed, one might argue that there were nascent notions of Housing First in the approach of twentieth-century politicians to housing. After the First World War Lloyd George called for a better standard of homes for British people because it was vital for the social and economic health of the nation. This idea underpinned the slum clearances and state-led municipal housing drive that followed. But, even if Britain builds at scale, there won't be enough social housing any time soon.

Ian Mulheirn is an economist who has seen the mistakes made by successive governments in recent years up close. He is the Executive Director for UK Policy and Chief Economist at the Tony Blair Institute for Global Change, and was previously a director of the Social Market Foundation, a Westminster public policy think tank specialising in economic research and policy design, and before that an economist at the Treasury. He thinks that supply – of both affordable housing to buy and social housing – is key, but told me that a more generous housing benefit system must be a priority if Britain is to tackle housing insecurity and poverty while the supply of affordable housing is sorted out. He applauds the government's decision to restore Housing Benefit to the lowest third of local market rents during the pandemic, but says that it 'wasn't enough' and 'shouldn't have taken a pandemic to trigger the policy change'.

If we apply the Housing First philosophy, then it forces an obvious question: why are we knowingly capping Housing Benefit below the cost of rent and pushing people into poverty? The Local Housing Allowance should never have been cut to the point that it stopped covering market rents. This connects back to the political neglect of the private rented sector. If there had been a joined-up approach, politicians would have realised that instability in the sector was linked to the rising cost of rents charged by private landlords and, therefore, the Housing Benefit bill. Instead, as Mulheirn says, the pernicious decision was made to cut Housing Benefit, which penalised private renters instead of limiting what landlords could ask them to pay.

Understanding how Housing First can be applied more broadly, but grasping its potential, 'demands politicians who have an understanding of human dignity', Kaakinen said before we ended our Zoom call. This is not a zero-sum game. Ending this emergency requires the joined-up approach that has been so missing. Putting housing first is an operating principle and a philosophy. It is an exercise in utopian thinking which centres on the importance of the home and the right to housing and, in doing so, shows us what's possible when there is a political commitment.

# 13

# OUT OF OPTIONS

### Sugar Hill Close and Wordsworth Drive, Oulton

*Council:* Leeds City Council
*Average House Price:* In the year 2020/21 the majority of sales in Oulton were detached properties, selling for an average of £410,261. Semi-detached properties sold for an average of £225,773, with terraced properties fetching £192,650.
*Average Private Rent:* In 2021 the average rent for a one-bedroom home in the Leeds area was £708, for a two-bed it was £887, and for a three-bed it was £1,227. At the time of searching, of 2,899 listings 1,404 properties listed for private rent cost less than £1,000 a month.

—

About a twenty-minute drive from central Leeds lies the Sugar Hill Close and Wordsworth Drive housing estate, in the village of Oulton. The driveways of seventy semi-detached homes peel off from these two winding, hedge-lined roads. They are prefabricated Airey houses. Designed by local man Sir Edwin Airey after the Second World War, they are functional two-storey concrete family homes with picturesque pitched roofs and spacious front and back gardens. Through his family building company, W. M. Airey & Sons, Airey was heavily involved in the construction of huts for American troops stationed in the UK during the Second World War. From these he pioneered the development of concrete slab units which could be quickly and easily assembled to make houses to replace those lost during the war. The first prototypes were built at Seacroft in Leeds by the Ministry of Works in 1945, and hundreds more were ordered to be built in Chingford in east London. In total, about 20,000 Airey houses were put up across the country to help solve the post-war housing crisis.

Sugar Hill Close and Wordsworth Drive, close to the Rothwell Colliery, were built by the National Coal Board (NCB) in the 1950s as affordable rented housing for miners and their families. The NCB sold off the estate in the late 1980s and, after passing through multiple owners, it was bought in 2001 by Pemberstone Group, a private investment fund with a large property portfolio. Corporate landlords, private equity firms like Pemberstone and pension and insurance funds invest in the private rented sector, too. One of the most notorious is Blackstone, the world's largest institutional landlord, which manages around $730 billion in funds globally, $230 billion of which was in real estate as of September 2021. Research carried out by two academics, Daniela Gabor, professor of economics and macrofinance at the University of the West of England, and Sebastian Kohl of Berlin's Free University, and published in January 2021, concluded that the rate at which institutional investors were buying homes was accelerating in major European cities and driving up house prices. Some pension funds, like Legal & General, were even focusing their energies on what is known as the 'build-to-rent' sector – purpose-built blocks owned by large investors – because, as they saw it, the growth of private renting made becoming a landlord a lucrative and stable investment.

The question is whether stable investments make stable homes. When I visited Oulton in late 2021, almost half of the homes were boarded up. Twenty-six remained occupied by private renters and ten were lived in by renters with protected tenancies. They were all being evicted by Pemberstone, which had been granted planning permission to demolish the historic houses and build homes for private sale in their place. The question of how we bring humanity to the housing crisis hung heavy in the air over the estate. I was there to meet the remaining residents who had come together to fight for what they believed was their right to housing. Pemberstone's original planning application proposed 49 market sale homes, 10 affordable homes in line with planning policy and 11 homes in which those on protected tenancies would eventually be rehoused after redevelopment. However, for the estate's private renters – households including key workers and pensioners – no alternative housing would be provided because they had standard Assured Shorthold Tenancies and Pemberstone had no obligation to them.

This wasn't the first time Pemberstone had been implicated in a housing dispute. In 2018, leasehold homeowners in two tower blocks in Manchester's Green Quarter were fighting Pemberstone, their freeholder, which had sent them bills for £10,000 plus each to remove dangerous and deadly Grenfell-style aluminium composite material (ACM) cladding from their homes. Eventually, a fund was set up by Pemberstone and the flats' original developer, and the leaseholders were spared the bill.

Back in Oulton, some people had already left their Airey homes – they didn't want to stay and try to battle their corporate landlord. But former miners, including 74-year-old Barry Abbey, who with his wife, Mavis, had lived on the estate since 1970 when Barry started working at Rothwell, were still there, fighting for their homes.

'What remains of the mining community is being torn apart,' Barry told me, as he sat beside Mavis in their garden, next to the shed-cum-workshop where he spent his retirement doing DIY. Barry was partially deaf, and Mavis would often repeat my questions to him. Their garden was full of plant pots that Barry had made in his shed from homemade moulds. 'The spirit of this place cannot be replaced. I won't be moved somewhere smaller where I don't have a garden,' Barry said, at once steely and mischievous. Although they faced losing their home and were living through the displacement of their community, Barry and Mavis were, perversely, the lucky ones. Their protected tenancy was from the NCB days, meaning that they were guaranteed a new home when the estate was redeveloped. Their private renter neighbours and friends weren't so lucky. In yet another example of how this piece of the Housing Act 1988 is directly contributing to displacement, anguish and homelessness, Pemberstone had begun serving Section 21 evictions in August 2021 to those renters.

Cindy Readman, 57, a teaching assistant, welcomed me into her home, just a few doors down from Barry and Mavis. It was autumn, there was a Halloween wreath on her front door and pumpkins lined her doorstep. Inside, a cat roamed around the warm home. One wall was painted bright turquoise and covered in framed family photos. Her garden, like Barry and Mavis's, brimmed with flowering plants. Cindy lived in her Airey home with her youngest son and her husband, John. In his sixties, John was also a former miner turned building facilities manager, now working at an office building in central Leeds. He and Cindy had moved to Sugar Hill in March 2006.

'I've lived here for sixteen years,' Cindy said. 'Now we're being evicted because our landlord is a private investment fund, and we don't know where we'll be able to afford to move to.' Cindy and John paid £580 a month in rent for their three-bedroom home. Their joint household income was about £37,000 and they would struggle to find anything comparable nearby. At the time, similarly sized privately rented homes in Oulton were going for between £795 and £995 per month, according to live online listings. Oulton was not immune to the house price and rent inflation that had swept the country during the pandemic. The village had become a desirable suburb of Leeds as people moved out of city centres in search of more space. In 2021, rents hit a ten-year high across the Yorkshire and Humber region. An NRLA survey found that nearly two-thirds (65 per cent) of private landlords in the region had reported that demand for their properties had increased in the second quarter of 2021. Indeed, demand in this area was higher than anywhere else in England and Wales, according to the survey. So, Pemberstone's proposed new houses on the site would be valuable, and easy to rent out or sell. In this context, the residents were citing 'gentrification' in their formal objections to the planned demolition of their homes – they were, they felt, being displaced because of an opportunity to profit from evicting them.

Pemberstone's argument was that the Airey homes on Wordsworth Drive and Sugar Hill Close were beyond repair and so could not be restored – according to a planning inspector's report, the concrete panels and pillars in the houses had deteriorated. Residents, however, believe that their homes had been 'deliberately' neglected and allowed to fall into disrepair by their landlord. At the time, a spokesman for Pemberstone said: 'These prefabricated homes are well beyond their expected lifespan and the remainder of the original estate was demolished and redeveloped years ago. It is becoming increasingly difficult to maintain them and to meet the ever-higher standards required, especially energy efficiency standards. Surveys have revealed structural damage and deterioration to all of the properties.' What is certainly true is that demolition would also be more profitable. Planning papers show that Pemberstone estimated that redevelopment would produce a profit of about £2.9 million, compared to an estimated £732,000 loss for refurbishing the homes. However, in the same planning report, the inspector 'agreed with both equality witnesses that the displacement could have a disproportionate effect on the young, old and disabled residents, and noted there were at least 16 households with these protected characteristics' who were on ASTs and, therefore, had few rights and 'would likely have to move from the site'.

All around the estate there were bright laminated yellow and red placards and banners that read 'Save Our Homes LS26'. For years, the residents had urged Leeds City Council to buy and refurbish their homes, but it had declined, deeming it too expensive. The story of Sugar Hill Close and Wordsworth Drive is a perfectly pressurised microcosm of the housing crisis: investment and speculation (this time on a corporate level); unprotected private renters with too few rights; rising house prices and rents; people on wages who could not meet those housing costs; a lack of social housing; and the ever-moving hand of gentrification.

Linda Elsworth, a 71-year-old pensioner with mobility problems, also lived on the estate, near Cindy and John. She had been in her three-bed house for six and a half years and was paying £485 per month for it – her benefits didn't cover the rent, so she topped it up each month from her pension. Standing in her front garden with a jumper wrapped around her shoulders, she told me that, in her view, 'gentrification' was 'exactly' what was happening to her. 'Our landlord [Pemberstone] has just done the bare minimum of maintenance here when they needed to do proper work. It's an excuse to make us homeless and build new homes so that they can sell for a profit,' she said, sounding tired and emotional. Linda would qualify for social housing but, at the time, as for so many authorities in the country, Leeds City Council's waiting list was protracted. When I spoke to a council spokesperson in December 2021, I was told that there were 26,000 live applications on the Leeds Homes Register. 'The number on our register has remained at a similar level for some years now, however the availability of council homes continues to reduce in the city,' the spokesperson told me. 'I have nowhere to go,' Linda added. 'My heart is broken. This is my sanctuary. It's my home. I can't imagine being homeless. It's social cleansing.'

Linda had moved to the estate to be close to her dear friend Hazell Field, a 58-year-old NHS worker who lived there with her husband and son. They had been close friends for years and spent Christmas together every year. 'I'm scared,' Hazell said. With a combined household income of £38,000, like Cindy and John, she and her family didn't know where they would end up and feared being torn from their community. 'We don't qualify for social housing because we do not have young children or claim benefits,' Hazell said, 'so the council expects us to find somewhere else to rent privately.' The council was doing all it could but its powers were limited. A Leeds City Council spokesperson said, 'The notices being served to residents of Sugar Hill Close and Wordsworth Drive in Oulton are from landlord Pemberstone, in accordance with national law. Our priority remains firmly on helping to minimise the stress and any hardship on the tenants concerned, providing all the help and guidance we can to ensure they have alternative accommodation and support.

'We are also committed to working with the developer of the site to ensure those tenants displaced will have priority for the new affordable homes, which the aim is now to have up to forty such properties available for rent. Moving forward, the council remains committed to lobbying government to change the law and end "no fault" evictions.'

This was a close-knit group of people. During the pandemic, younger residents did supermarket shops and picked up prescriptions for the more elderly; there was always someone knocking on a door to see if their neighbour needed support of any sort. No task was too big or too small. As our conversations drew to a close and the winter sun began to fall lower in the sky, a former resident, another ex-miner's wife, pulled up in her car to drop something off for Barry. Looking around at the boarded-up properties on the estate, she burst into tears. 'I'm sorry,' she said. 'I just can't bear to see it like this. Look what they've done.' Our current housing market accounts for the monetary value of property but not the social value of homes and community.

As Christmas 2021 approached, the eviction of the estate's private renters loomed. 'We are all desperately trying to find alternative accommodation,' John told me by text message. 'Physically and mentally, we are slowly sinking into a constant state of panic and despair.'

## Housing for the Long Term

Precarity, panic and anguish were all around in Oulton. For years, the housing crisis has been discussed as though it is intractable. It is not. Its side effects, the displacement and despair imposed upon ordinary people, have been dismissed as an inevitable consequence of an economy where some people win and others lose. They are not. There are solutions. The only way to meet people's housing needs is to give them a home. A housing-led approach which takes the principles of Housing First and extends them beyond those with complex needs would mean that Britain can have its cake and eat it, too: we can make the private rented sector functional and we can build more social housing.

There is an obvious point which still needs to be made: building expensive new homes in an inflated market doesn't lower the price of other housing if wealthy people can still overconsume by buying holiday lets and second homes. What Alastair Harper, Head of Public Affairs at Shelter, calls the 'trickle-down housing' approach of the 2010s and 2020s has failed, and new supply is not enough to fix the housing crisis. This is similar to the theory of trickle-down economics – the idea that a free market with minimal regulation will self-regulate and that wealth will somehow trickle down to everyone in an economy. 'The housing policy that dominated Westminster between 2010 and 2020 was underpinned by an erroneous belief that if enough homes of any sort were built this would magically somehow create housing for the most vulnerable people,' Harper told me in 2022. We already knew that wasn't working by 2015/16, because house prices were rising and so was homelessness. 'Plasters were stuck on, such as Help to Buy, in the hope it would fix the problem,' Harper continued. 'Again, it only made things worse, driving up profits for developers and house prices for all. The dominant approach of the last decade has failed – it's time to build the homes people need – social housing – in the places people are waiting for them.'

Now, house prices are bloated, the private rented sector is engorged and under-regulated, and too many people – including children living out their formative years – are stuck in limbo or stranded in temporary accommodation because we don't have enough social housing.

In September 2021, Boris Johnson moved Michael Gove over to the housing brief. Just as Theresa May had renamed the government department responsible for housing – changing its name from the Department for Communities and Local Government to the Ministry of Housing, Communities and Local Government, Johnson renamed it again. The Ministry of Housing became the Department for Levelling Up, Housing and Communities (DLUHC). 'Levelling up' was a nebulous concept which Boris Johnson had put front and centre of his administration, and one of the starkest examples of inequality in Britain is the urgent crisis in housing. Done right, a levelling-up agenda would help solve the seemingly intractable problem of housing, succeeding where other policies have failed in transforming this country's economic and social geography. Done wrong, it would be gentrification by another name, which would further entrench regional and social polarities.

Change is inevitable. There may be more pandemics, more natural disasters. Our economy will continue to evolve. The climate emergency will continue. Prime ministers and housing ministers will come and go. That's why Britain needs to think long term about the housing crisis. A Whitehall source told me that they felt hopeful about Gove's arrival. 'If we ever had a shot at fixing the housing crisis, this is it,' they said. Rumours of Gove's warm feelings towards social housing did the rounds as he played hardball on the building safety crisis, promising that leasehold home-owners would not have to pay to make their buildings safe. Meanwhile, the question of more renters' rights was still being addressed but, at least, not closed in favour of landlords. The same source told me that there was a bookshelf in Gove's office lined with progressive books including Guy Shrubsole's *Who Owns England?*, a 2019 study of land ownership and why it needs to be reformed. 'They're there because he wants us to know he's serious,' the source said. Whether he is around long enough to be serious remains to be seen.

Nothing holds society together or tears it apart like housing. Britain's housing inequality interacts with other structural inequalities – wealth, race, gender and sexuality. Black people are 70 per cent more likely to be impacted by the housing emergency than white people; Asian people are 50 per cent more likely; 54 per cent of people with a significant disability (1.8 million adults) do not have a safe or secure home, as compared with 30 per cent of those without. The same is true for 65 per cent of single mothers (1 million adults), as compared with 35 per cent of two-parent households. Forty per cent of gay or lesbian and 49 per cent of bisexual people are impacted by the emergency, compared with 32 per cent of heterosexual people. And households on less than £20,000 a year are 70 per cent more likely to be impacted than households with incomes of £40,000–£45,000 a year. We also know that one in four trans people have experienced homelessness at some point in their lives. These statistics tell us that we cannot tackle societal fairness until we resolve the housing emergency and, equally, that we cannot fix the housing crisis without acknowledging the prejudices, biases and inequities that underpin it.

So, what should that reform look like? When Michael Gove became Secretary of State for Levelling Up, Housing and Communities, experts who had studied the housing crisis told him how in no uncertain terms. They visited him with a shopping list of urgent policy changes, my Whitehall source said. These included:

- putting housing at the centre of the so-called 'levelling up' agenda and funding it accordingly;
- giving a longer time frame for solutions, such as the Affordable Homes Programme, which provides government grant funding to support the capital costs of developing affordable housing for rent or sale by local authorities – ten and not five years;
- making it easier for local councils to buy land on which to build social housing;

- a comprehensive and enforceable Renters' Reform Act should be passed without delay;
- reform of Right to Buy to stop it benefiting buy-to-let landlords;
- and developing a proper strategy to end homelessness.

These were hardly asking the earth. The real problem was not what needed to be done or whether the housing crisis was fixable, it was whether Gove would be around long enough to implement these changes.

It seemed as if Gove himself was aware of this. In early 2022, determined to make an impact during his time at the DLUHC, he pushed through several vital reforms. Firstly, in January, he opened a public consultation on the government's proposals for leasehold reform, which included making it cheaper and easier for larger numbers of leasehold homeowners to buy the freeholds of their homes and manage them themselves. This was a step towards finally undoing the feudal system of land ownership. Then, he announced that he would make sure that most leasehold homeowners impacted by the cladding crisis did not have to pay to make their homes safe. After years of uncertainty, the government was finally asking builders to pay to fix faulty homes. It was the right thing to do and long overdue.

Then, in February, he delivered his much-anticipated 'Levelling Up' plan, coincidentally on the same day that it was reported that house prices were increasing at their fastest rate for seventeen years (yet more evidence that, for some people, homeownership would never be a financially viable option). Gove's 400-page Levelling Up white paper read: 'There is significant unmet need for social housing, leaving people paying high rents in the private rented sector unable to save for a home of their own.' These words echo the diagnosis that the likes of the homelessness charities Shelter and Crisis, the lobby group Generation Rent and others had been offering for years. It felt, finally, as if the Conservatives understood the problem, but drawing the same conclusions as housing experts and committing to their proposed solutions are not one and the same.

The white paper also included a number of housing policy announcements (and in some cases, re-announcements). These included reforms to private renting such as: plans to make sure that all privately rented homes meet the Decent Homes Standard; abolishing Section 21 evictions; and plans to introduce a landlords register and crack down on rogue criminal landlords with fines and bans to stop repeat offenders.

Of course, an end to Section 21 was first promised by Theresa May in 2019, as was a landlords register. And the question of how cash-strapped local authorities would enforce the Decent Homes Standard went unanswered. There was no mention of rent regulation, a step too far even for Gove. There have been many attempts to reduce the gaps between the richer and poorer parts of the UK over the years and this one, at least, seemed to recognise that housing was central to doing that. But would any of the changes actually happen? In February 2022 unemployment was at historic lows and wage growth was running at 4.3 per cent – well above anything we saw between the financial crisis and the start of the pandemic – but that pay rise was being outpaced by the cost of living. So, even if those changes did happen, would they go far enough at a time when rents (which rose by 2 per cent in the twelve months to January 2022, up from 1.8 per cent in the twelve months to December 2021), house prices, inflation, interest rates and the cost of basics like food and energy were going up?

If the contradictory Conservative housing policies of 2010–2020 exacerbated the housing crisis, the next decade would need a laser-clear focus on fixing it. Ending homelessness and delivering truly affordable housing isn't complicated but it needs political consistency. It needs to be thought of as essential infrastructure, like the NHS or roads and railways, and prioritised accordingly. Michael Gove was making the right promises but the devil, as ever, was in the detail and, above all, in the delivery.

Our electoral system is meant to provide stability but, in recent years, it has achieved anything but. The private rented sector is damaging the lives of millions of people and causing taxpayers' money to be spent inefficiently. We have the foresight to know what to do – people will always need secure and affordable homes. A Housing First mentality can help to centre good-quality, publicly owned social housing, which would be an investment in people's futures, in Britain's future. This, combined with the reintroduction of robust renters' rights, could stem the human cost of the housing crisis.

Reform could be even more ambitious, though. The above would be a short-term emergency response to the housing crisis but there are ambitious, long-term solutions available to us. Britain has to acknowledge that the problem is not just that the housing market, unfettered as it is, has failed to provide decent, affordable housing. It is that it never can. Not least because of the way property development currently functions. So consider, for a moment, the way we tax landlords and property owners.

As things stand, landlords pay income tax on rent but they do not pay National Insurance – why not? After all, rental income is … an income. Everyone else's National Insurance payments are linked to their income. On top of that, when a landlord comes to sell their property, they don't pay income tax on the sale, only capital gains tax (CGT). But here's the thing: income tax – which people pay on what they earn – is a lot higher than capital gains tax – which people pay on assets and wealth. Higher and additional rate income taxpayers only pay 28 per cent tax on their gains from residential property and 20 per cent on gains from other chargeable assets. Income tax, meanwhile, is 40 per cent on incomes between £50,271 and £150,000 and 45 per cent on incomes over £150,000. Given that the sale of a rental property is as much a source of income as its rent, it's fair to say that buy-to-let landlords are not efficiently taxed. The need to reform taxes to make sure that housing wealth is taxed more efficiently is something that Labour leader Keir Starmer alluded to in 2022, saying that greater taxes on landlords could help to fund social care, and the left-leaning think tank Institute for Public Policy Research (IPPR) have also argued for tax reform in this area. The IPPR would like to see capital gains tax reformed so that income from wealth is taxed in the same way as income from work.

And we don't need to stop there. At the moment, it makes sense for landowners to hoard land. They can wait for it to go up in value as an area becomes desirable before they sell. Indeed, the land may be worth more sitting empty for a few years than if they built affordable homes on it. This is known as 'land banking' and you might think of it as a contemporary form of the enclosure that took place in Early Modern England when wealthy people took over common land so that they could charge other people to live or farm on it. You don't need to look far to see it happening. Consider Oulton, where an investment fund bought up land and waited for it to become more desirable before redeveloping it, displacing the people who call it home in the process.

A Land Value Tax could help solve this problem and curb this practice. It might not be popular, but taxes never are. Land Value Taxes are a way of taxing the unearned income that large landowners enjoy when they own prime real estate – for example, a disused carpark in the centre of London, or an empty townhouse in Manchester. Throughout history, economists have advocated such a tax. The eighteenth- and nineteenth-century economists David Ricardo, Adam Smith and John Stuart Mill all understood this issue and it's from their economic philosophies that we get the idea of taxing the value of land. For Ricardo, land was a natural and shared resource, of which there was only a finite amount. And so, to him, rent gained merely from owning land – 'paid to the landlord for the use of the original and indestructible powers of the soil' – was a form of surplus and unearned income which served to increase the wealth of individuals and not society as a whole. For Smith, 'nothing could be more reasonable' than taxing the value of land. Winston Churchill was also a fan. He said scornfully that a landlord 'contributes nothing to the process from which his own enrichment is derived'.

And, finally, house price growth – the sort that has priced people out of homeownership, kept them trapped in private renting and made buy-to-let a lucrative investment because homes appreciate so much in value – could be curbed. This inflation is spoken about as though it is inevitable – an irrevocable economic fact – but it is possible to do something about it. As John Healey suggested back in 2019 when he was still Labour's shadow housing secretary, the Bank of England could set a target for house price inflation to keep it low – much like the bank is tasked with keeping overall inflation at around 2 per cent. This would make sure that house prices don't run away, rising far beyond people's earnings.

These suggestions are all radical, yes. But not impossible. Stranger things have happened than imaginative change. In late February 2022, Michael Gove gave an interview that opened up a whole new conversation about housing at the heart of government. He told ITV's Daniel Hewitt that Britain needed to build more social housing and accept the fact that too many people were relying on unstable and unafford-able private renting. This was a shocking admission for a government minister to make. Gove then said that it was his full intention to build more social homes. 'We have a mission to increase the number of social homes and help people move out of the private rented sector,' he said. Finally, the person in charge of housing was publicly acknowledging that there needed to be serious, radical action taken to break the cycle of rent rises, evictions and homelessness. These were the sort of claims that would have been unthinkable for a Conservative housing secretary to make just a year before – perhaps there's hope that politicians in the not-so-distant future will be able to make even more radical suggestions on taxing landlords fairly, introducing a Land Value Tax, or even setting a target for house price inflation.

Whatever the solution politicians eventually settle on, private renting is no longer a stopgap for many, and it is not a tenure of choice – people rent from private landlords because they have no other options. The damage being done cannot be overstated and, for as long as the housing emergency continues, we will be poorer, less equal, less healthy, more unhappy and less environmentally friendly. But, far from viewing this with pessimism, I see an opportunity for change. There is so much to gain from fixing housing – more than we currently allow ourselves to imagine – but we need to allow revolutionary ideas to become reality once again. Bevan's notion of the mixed community was once radical: so was building social housing, so was clearing slums. We can see decent and affordable housing, once again, as the basis for a fair and functioning society and as a national investment which provides an economic return (rent if it is social housing) as well as a social one (because people would be happy and healthy) and not, as it is right now, as a way of segregating people according to how wealthy they or their families are.

You don't have to look far today for proof that housing wealth has still not trickled down: homes have become increasingly unafford-able and the number of families, including 121,680 children, living in temporary accommodation continues to increase while homeownership has not gone up. The number of young adults living in a home they own remains below 2003/2004 levels. There is a quote, often attributed to Albert Einstein, which goes something like: 'the definition of insanity is doing the same thing over and over again and expecting a different result'. Successive governments have tried to sort housing out by doing the same thing repeatedly: allowing house prices to inflate and weakly attempting to increase homeownership. It hasn't worked and to carry on down this track would, truly, be madness. The housing market continues to show us that it does not self-regulate. House prices and rents generally do one thing: get more expensive. We need social housing and we need intervention in the housing market to make it more stable.

For the residents being evicted in Oulton, yet more promises that something would, at some point, change offered little comfort as they were torn away from everything they knew. The housing crisis can't and won't be solved by building more housing, particularly if that housing is too expensive. We must recognise truly affordable housing as a fundamental right – as the bedrock of a healthy society – and take steps to make sure a larger number of people can access it via social housing. Until we do, renters will continue to live precarious lives while landlords see their homes as assets.

# DWELLING IN POSSIBILITY

'Here you come upon the important fact that every revolutionary opinion draws part of its strength from a secret conviction that nothing can be changed.'

George Orwell, *The Road to Wigan Pier* (1937)

Etymologists note that the form of the modern word 'house', old and ancient as it is, has changed very little over time. It comes from the Old English *hus* (a dwelling, shelter or building for living in). A house is the place where a person lives. It is an accommodating word, a word with rooms; the long u vowel sound that we still hear today sounds spacious. In human language, the need to house people has always been a constant. The word in other languages, such as French (*maison*), Italian (*casa*) and Russian (*dom*), once referred to covering or hiding someone or to something being fitted together. Today, to house somebody is to keep them safe; to give shelter, refuge, security. It is also to provide them with space where they are free to dream, to grieve and to hope: in other words, to live.

Like so many of the people in this book, like so many of the people in Britain today, I have experienced the housing crisis personally. Home – or rather, housing security – has always shaped my world view. I was seven years old when strange men came knocking on the door asking for my parents, trying to come in. I was seven years old when my father told me never to let them in. I was seven years old when I learned the word 'bailiff'. I was seven years old when my family lost our home (which my parents owned) and began renting. So, I know how quickly a change in housing tenure can impact your life. There was a recession then – the first of three that I have lived through – and my father lost his job. Listening at the kitchen door long after I was supposed to be in bed, I would try to decipher hushed fragments of conversations. Is somebody crying? I don't think it's Mum. No, it's Dad. Dad is crying. Dad doesn't cry. Why are they so worried? Should I be worried? The answer was yes. There was good reason to worry. We lost our house shortly after that and moved into a rented home.

And so, my own housing story involves the experience of housing stress at a young age. That was followed by years in the private rented sector as a student and young adult where I experienced all of its horrors: mould, damp, deposits lost to rogue landlords totalling thousands of pounds and, more recently, housing stress once again caused by the breakdown of a long-term relationship which made me unsure whether I'd be able to afford the home we had bought together using Help to Buy (with the help of money from this book plus a redundancy payout from my side and money from my ex-partner's grandparents on his).

For years I felt as if I had my bank balance (and my credit card limits) pinned to my forehead because I rented tiny box rooms, so what I could afford was obvious. But it was never as bad as when one of my close friends became my landlord (friendlord, if you will), not working and collecting rent from me every month while we lived in a flat that her parents had, effectively, gifted her. I got into debt to pay the rent that funded her lifestyle and then, after a year, her father told me he was putting the rent up. I was too embarrassed to admit I couldn't afford it, so I took out a loan. There's so much stigma about not having money that, ironically, you spend money you don't have to appear as though you do, and time you could spend on other things worrying about it.

From where I stand, no policy area has reinforced or rejuvenated Britain's wealth-based class system as much as housing. You can do everything right and it doesn't necessarily mean you will ever own your own home. House prices are now so high, whether you attain the social 'success' of becoming a homeowner has much less to do with traditional class markers (such as whether you went to university or do a 'skilled' job) and much more to do with what your parents have in terms of actual assets on which they can draw. Forget 'meritocracy' (if there can ever be such a thing), Britain is an inheritocracy. Just as wealth can be inherited, not having wealth is also hereditary. I got it from my parents, who got it from their parents, who got it from their parents. Like most inherited conditions, every now and then, you find yourself being asked about your housing status when you least expect it, in a way that makes you feel as if you've arrived at a themed party without receiving the fancy-dress memo. These days people don't even need to ask whether or not you have inherited wealth, it is easy to decipher – 'Oh, you *still* have housemates?' 'What do you mean, you have a Help to Buy loan *and* a mortgage? I didn't know that was a thing!' 'How come you don't have any savings?'

My experiences are far from unique and have featured lightly in this book. I am white and defined as a middle-class professional on an above-average income who now lives in a home that is, thankfully, secure in spite of what I have experienced, so my story is of limited use here because I am the exception to the rule. I might pay added tax in student loan repayments to the tune of thousands of pounds each year, but I also might not be in the position I am in had I not benefited from university tuition fees of £3,000 per year, rather than the £9,000 that students are expected to pay now, and publicly funded grants to study that no longer exist. Anyone who doesn't have financial assistance – people like me from low-income backgrounds – now graduates with upwards of £50,000-worth of debt. The fact that I have a platform from which I had the space and time to write this book owes much to the very real advantages afforded to me by my ethnicity, education and timing. I went to university when government grants still existed, I have a secure home which I can afford, I have a stable job. I fear that so many of the children I have met during my reporting will not be so lucky.

The possibilities of secure housing are endless. Tony is now settled in a rented bungalow in Witham, Essex. It is not ideal – he loves the countryside and the bungalow is on a housing estate. He lost Rebel in August 2019. He misses her deeply; she was his best friend, his companion. She was fourteen and had arthritis, but he thinks their last move together caused her health to deteriorate. However, he is grateful to have a roof over his head and has begun writing his life story. 'I've gone as far back as I can remember,' he told me in a chat via email in 2021. 'I keep coming back to when I divorced my first wife in 1984. The struggles of finding somewhere I could afford to live after that, somewhere I could have my children to stay, that's what has defined me. Over thirty-seven years I have had to move from home to home through no fault of my own, never managing to buy a home because it was too expensive.' We don't yet know what we could achieve as a society if everyone had a safe and secure home. What might Tony – what might all of us – have been freed up to focus on?

Kelly is still waiting for a stable and secure home. She believes this is because she has been tarred with the 'intentionally homeless' label. Is that fair? That she should be condemned to live in purgatory for years, never able to get on with her life after experiencing extreme trauma?

Limarra WhatsApped me as she was decorating her new home – a secure and affordable social housing flat owned by a housing association that will be hers for as long as she needs it. After two years living there, she will also have the right to buy it. She had repainted the walls fresh white and pale grey, had put up dark wooden blinds and even had space for a large corner sofa which is covered with throws and cushions where she can watch TV. Nevaeh is in secondary school. Her bedroom is painted a dusky rose pink. There is a sheepskin rug on the floor next to her bed and, in the corner, an electric keyboard where she can practise the piano. But that's not all Limarra's been doing.

'I work for Southwark Council in homelessness prevention,' Limarra told me when we caught up during the pandemic. 'I started as a case-worker, dealing with anyone who – like me – approached the council because they were homeless and doing their assessments. Now I'm in the reviews team – reviewing the decisions that have been made on where and how to house people. I do my best to bring humanity to these cases in a way I feel was never brought to mine. I can do it because I have stability now, my daughter has something stable and, what's more, I pay for everything myself – I'm no longer receiving any benefits because my rent, which I pay to the housing association, is affordable.' Limarra specialises in housing options for care leavers (any adult who has spent time in care) and she recently won an award for her work with children. 'A stable home is at the centre of everything – how can you expect a young person to go into employment or education without that?' she said.

Anthony is working again but still homeless and sofa-surfing. He almost has enough saved up for a deposit and to pay rent in advance on a new place. Samantha is still renting in Lancaster and worried she will never own. Nicola feels guilty. Her mother retired and was so alarmed by what she saw her daughter go through at the Old Rectory that she used her pension to help her buy a house in Colchester. 'I'm single, so there's not another person to pay for the other half, so Mum had to step in,' Nicola told me. 'I am painfully aware that if I didn't have my mum, I would still be living that horrendous life right now, either in a private rental being extorted or as a guardian. It doesn't feel great, it's not like my hard work paid off and bought me a house. Hard work doesn't make a difference in this country when it comes to housing.'

As Christmas 2021 approached, Amy and Dan were facing eviction. They had moved from Wythenshawe to a new privately rented home in another suburb of Manchester. 'It's actually worse than the last one,' Amy said over WhatsApp. 'There are leaks and electrical faults and the kitchen is falling apart. We kept complaining and we were served an eviction notice.' She expected that she and her family would be evicted around Christmas and placed in temporary accommodation. 'We're still waiting for a social home,' she said in her last text message. 'We're Band 2, so it's going to be a while. I'm deflated and stressed. Just want a secure home for my children. I hate it. X.'

Josephine has found somewhere more suitable to live in Weston-super-Mare. It is still in the private rented sector.

At the beginning of 2022, the battle for Sugar Hill Close and Wordsworth Drive in Oulton was continuing and evictions still loomed large for John and Cindy, Hazell, Linda and their private renter neighbours. 'We are both physically and mentally drained,' John said. 'The fear of being homeless is constantly in our thoughts. Cindy has not been very well in the last few weeks, and I believe it's because of all the worry and stress. I am finding it very hard to sleep and concentrate at work. We have a 7-month-old granddaughter, she helps to take our mind off it but life right now is constant emails and Zooms and meetings. I am trying to remain positive, but it feels like we are stuck in a dark tunnel, and we can't see the light yet.'

The toll on Hazell has been equally great. 'I'm currently signed off work with sinusitis,' she said in January 2022. 'The uncertainty has had a devastating impact on my health. I am not the woman I was when this started. I am much more tearful and depressed. I still don't know where we are going to end up,' she continued. 'The social houses we are bidding for are in Middleton and Hunslet, a way from Oulton because there is nothing affordable for us in that area. We haven't got anything yet and moving further away is going to add an extra bus to my commute which is another forty-five minutes each way to work. We need to solve the housing crisis. Private renting isn't sustainable, you can't guarantee when you move in that you won't be out in a year. It's a nightmare.'

Home shapes us more than we shape it; home is where a person becomes who they are. And, if that home is not stable or secure, their life chances diminish. This affects everything they do, every relationship they have – whether that's with family, colleagues, people in the pub or in their romantic life. What will we tell the hundreds of thousands of children who have lived in temporary accommodation? What about the ones who have been evicted? That they did not matter? That we didn't care enough? That they should have helped themselves? If we deprive people of basic stability on a large scale, what sort of instability will it embed in the fabric of our society in years to come? What sort of physical and mental damage is being done? These questions need to be asked. We need to put the damage that has already been done front and centre; forget about who is to blame for a moment, about which political party is right and which is wrong and focus on fixing this mess. We must consider what we are missing out on, what untold possibilities we have cut ourselves off from because we have allowed so many of our peers, colleagues and neighbours to suffer. Have we stopped to wonder how our shared home – Britain – and all the inequality and suffering it contains is shaping us all?

We are living in a country where poverty is entrenched, social mobility has gone into reverse, squalid living conditions like those seen in the early 1900s are normal for too many people, and a twinned sense of hopelessness and individualism prevails. This despondency and cynicism reinforces the systems that benefit from keeping so many people disenfranchised, caught in instability and precarity, living in a state of anxiety, unable to do much more than focus on getting through each day, week, month ahead of them.

The feminist writer and thinker Virginia Woolf understood this when she wrote in her 1929 essay *A Room of One's Own* that 'a woman must have money and a room of her own if she is to write', but Woolf's 'room' was always about more than just a space to write. Woolf herself was born into enormous privilege. She knew that was why she was able to expand and develop her creative genius. Her point was that women writers had historically not had the opportunity to express their genius because a lack of money and privacy prevented them from doing so. Her 'room' was a metaphor for the space and stability afforded to subjugated groups by economic independence at a time when very few women were able to afford spaces of their own. Almost a hundred years later, this is still the case. That's why the Women's Budget Group referenced Woolf in the title of its 2019 report, 'A Home of Her Own: Housing and Women', which concluded that there was nowhere – not a single place – in the United Kingdom where housing was affordable for a single woman on an average income. There are concrete reasons why we still live in a patriarchy. Just as there are concrete reasons why most decision-makers in our country are white. In her essay 'Homeplace (A Site of Resistance)', published in 1990, bell hooks observed that '[a]n effective means of white subjugation of black people globally has been the perpetual construction of economic and social structures that deprive many folks of the means to make homeplace'.

We know that the housing market shapes poverty. If a person is experiencing housing stress, what they can do with their life is limited; they are deprived of the space to dream, imagine and innovate a better world. And this prevents us all from progressing, and creates instead an environment in which xenophobia, self-serving protectionism, solipsism, racism, ableism, homophobia and transphobia and sexism can thrive. The fact that low-income people, women and Black, Asian and minority ethnic people are the most likely groups in Britain to experience housing stress reinforces patriarchal systems, class and racist structures.

But there are things that we can do, both within our communities and individually. We can donate to charities. We can join tenants' unions. We can do charity work ourselves. In this book, we have heard about individuals who do all of this. But we must also remember that, in doing so, they are filling in the gaping holes of the welfare safety net, doing work that ought to be done by the state. Such charitable work is a cosmetic fix for the problems caused by capitalism in its current form; it enables the logic that underpins that system: that injustice is inevitable, necessary even, for some to succeed. We should be alarmed that it is housing charities like Shelter and Crisis, tenants' unions like ACORN, and individuals like Alan Rice that are propping up the state. Their philanthropy is noble, but in doing that work, they let the state off the hook and, without meaning to, justify the cuts that have been made to welfare. It is the 'Big Society' David Cameron conceived of when he signed off on austerity and the noblesse oblige that, for so long, prevented social reform after the Industrial Revolution. Charity is the tacit acceptance that wealthy people will step in where the state fails. It does nothing to make society more equal.

In 2021, in Weston-super-Mare, Alan Rice – who now carries out his volunteering under the name Weston Housing Action – was still fighting to license privately rented homes. 'I will persevere,' he told me.

Helen Syrop was still spending countless hours running her charity, Hope Housing, in Bradford. She told me when we talked during the pandemic, when we still didn't know what Brexit really meant for homeless people with NRPF, 'I love helping people to get homes but I get very frustrated at the inequality and injustice in the system, and sometimes get tired trying to help people when there are so many barriers to making things work.' She was, she said, 'especially angry with the way that migrants are treated and the fact that people have to keep fighting so that those who become homeless can have something as basic as a home'.

As she saw it, the pandemic had been a huge catalyst for positive change but it shouldn't have taken such a disaster to change things. 'Systems across government – welfare benefits, the asylum process and housing – all need to be working together with a compassionate approach if we want to end homelessness and fix the crisis in housing,' she said to me. The pandemic, then, showed us what was possible, but it also showed us that we have a long way to go. It showed us that any solution for this mess will come down to two things: firstly, political will; and, second, the government accepting that it has to care for people that it currently doesn't want to care for.

We all need to recognise, once and for all, that we are all connected, that we live in a social, economic and environmental ecosystem. Yet not a month goes by in which someone I know who presents as outwardly liberal confides in me that, while they accept the need to sort out the crisis in housing, they are worried because 'their home is their pension', their investment. And they worry that reform may damage their future. That is not a reason to do nothing, to quietly vote for politicians whose policies actively worsen this situation. When your house goes up in value, someone else is priced out of homeownership. Once these recognitions are not only made but internalised, you can lobby politicians and vote for those who genuinely want to challenge and change the status quo. That might mean not always voting in your own interests.

We know that change occurs when there is political will. Coronavirus has shown us that. The Overton Window shifts, the needle moves. We may yet find the 'radical' ideas of the former leader of the Labour Party Jeremy Corbyn – a four-day working week, nationalised universal broadband – adopted by the centre right. Stranger things have happened. We have already seen an iteration of Universal Basic Income – it was called the furlough scheme. Under crisis, the politically impossible can very quickly become possible. The progressive can be conservative when it is necessary and politically expedient.

## A More Compassionate Politics

Is a loving and compassionate approach to housing policy anything other than common sense? Neoliberalism has reframed love as apolitical and unrealistic. It has become consigned to the remit of romantic relationships and, let's be honest, we aren't even doing a great job of understanding it there. This has led to a cynical politics of individualism, a disbelief in even the possibility of change. But love of another – a loving approach to being in the world – is not impossible or abstract. It is a practice which can be applied to social and political communities to great effect. What we have right now is the exact opposite of love. Let's not forget that, in 2018, Philip Alston, then the UN's Special Rapporteur on extreme poverty and human rights, ended a two-week fact-finding mission to the UK with a stinging declaration that levels of child poverty here were 'not just a disgrace, but a social calamity and an economic disaster'. The UK, he said, had inflicted 'great misery' on its people with 'punitive, mean-spirited and often callous' austerity policies driven by a political desire to undertake social re-engineering rather than economic necessity. Inequality causes people to suffer emotionally and psychologically. That, in the end, harms us all.

The established ways of thinking about the housing emergency have not solved it, they have not liberated our society. Neither has the radical activism happening at a grassroots level. And nor has our party political electoral system. History is repeating itself. The system is rigged. Britain's economy relies on house price inflation, and it is not designed to be equal or fair. An implicit logic that some people are acceptable collateral damage in servicing that system is coded into our politics and our society. All of the signs suggest that we need new methods, attitudes and approaches to something as fundamental as the right to housing. Britain needs to take stock of the quality of the lives most people are living and consider how we should aspire to live. A shift in our consciousness to a more holistic approach to existence and to actively look to see how the fabric of all of life is connected needs to take place. The philosophy of Housing First is a good place to start.

The politics of love are re-entering conversations about how we move forward. Max Harris, Fellow of All Souls College, Oxford, and Philip McKibbin, a writer from New Zealand, have explored this. In April 2019, before the pandemic, they organised a conference on the subject in Oxford. They asked what love means, how love might bring about stronger societies, how it fits with anger and conflict and how it relates to various forms of oppression. In the context of all that has happened since – the coronavirus crisis, the groundswell of support for Black Lives Matter, the horror of watching as India, the world's largest manufacturer of coronavirus vaccines, became overwhelmed by new strains of Covid-19, Russia's invasion of Ukraine – positing love as a political concept is more important than ever. By which I mean civic love, love as a political emotion.

This idea has a long historical, political and philosophical tradition. Great democratic leaders and thinkers, including Auguste Comte (who had the idea of a secular religion of humanity), Jean-Jacques Rousseau, John Stuart Mill, Abraham Lincoln, Mohandas Gandhi, Martin Luther King Jr, Rabindranath Tagore and bell hooks all understood the importance of cultivating emotions, for they are the resources inherent in human psychology. As the philosopher Martha Nussbaum writes, 'Love is what gives respect for humanity its life, making it more than a shell.'

This is not a question of sentimentality but an exercise in thinking about our own needs, in thinking beyond the system we currently inhabit and asking, really asking, whether we can live with ourselves under the status quo. This is not an exercise in retribution but in trying to conjure a prophetic vision of the future through reconciliation and compassion. All humans are vulnerable, all humans need shelter. There is no shame in that but there is shame in denying it to the most exposed. It is possible to be angry about where we are now and to realise that this anger will, ultimately, not bring about change. It is possible to be afraid for your own future and fortunes and extend compassion to others when you decide which politicians to vote for. It is possible to benefit from house price inflation personally and recognise that it is harming the society you live in. If we want to change the world, to step into the unknown and embrace what's possible, then we must abandon cynicism. We must embrace idealism. In an inverted way, that's what the bankers who invented the complex financial instruments for selling dodgy mortgages on the global market which caused the financial crash in 2008 did. They created the reality that they themselves wanted to inhabit, and in which they made money from other people's debts. That was some serious blue-sky thinking.

If that doesn't convince you of what's possible, consider this: just over fifty years ago it was illegal to be gay in Britain. It is only a little over a hundred years ago that women got the right to the vote. Those who fought for women's enfranchisement were branded 'crazy', arrested, imprisoned and force-fed while incarcerated. Less than two hundred years ago, slavery was still legal. Britain's economy depended on the enslavement of human beings and huge numbers of influential people had vested interests in protecting that. And exactly eighty years ago William Beveridge had a vision. He wanted to end poverty. The report he produced in 1942 captured the imaginations of the public and politicians; its message was clear – tinkering around the edges wouldn't be enough. Britain, Beveridge said, needed to build institutions like the NHS; it needed a welfare state. What he envisioned was a society where not only was there state support for anyone who fell on hard times but where fewer people experienced hardship full stop. I'm not suggesting we ought to be nostalgic for what happened in the twentieth century or that it was perfect. But, rather, that we should embrace a similar sense of radical ambition for social change and push things forward.

His work might not be complete, but he proved that change is possible. Why can't everyone have a safe, secure and affordable home? Why can't we imagine an economy that is less dependent on house price inflation? Why can't we live in a more caring and equal world? Whatever your politics, it is hard to justify the hardship and instability caused by the current status quo in British housing. There is no way back. Only forward. We don't know what's possible until we try.

Investing in more social housing would benefit everyone, not just those who live in it. It would, as Shelter have noted, reduce competition and pressure in the private rented sector. This would give private renters more power because landlords would be competing for their attention against decent and secure social homes. If we had enough good-quality social housing, it could also generate competition for better-quality privately rented properties by setting a higher standard for homes across the board.

Home is where everything begins. It is where our personal relationships stem from. It is the base from which we engage with society, with our community. If we start to treat housing as what it is – essential infrastructure – and fix the housing crisis, we will find that other social and economic issues shift, too. But, until we do, let's be clear: there is no economic or political reason, no philosophical or ideological justification for how people are being forced to live in Britain right now.

# GLOSSARY OF THE HOUSING CRISIS

**Affordable Housing**
The government definition of affordable housing is 'social rented, afford-able rented and intermediate housing provided to specified eligible households whose needs are not met by the market'. However, as this book explains, some affordable rents are not as affordable as they could or, indeed, should be.

**Assured Shorthold Tenancy (AST)**
Introduced in 1997, this is the most common type of tenancy for private renters. ASTs can be fixed term, usually 6 or 12 months, or they can be rolling weekly or monthly periods.

**Bedroom Tax**
This policy was one of the most controversial to be brought in during austerity. The Bedroom Tax is shorthand for the government's decision to remove what was known as the spare room subsidy in the Welfare Reform Act 2012. The change came into force on 1 April 2013. In practice, it meant that any social housing tenant who had a spare room had their housing benefit (now Universal Credit) reduced by 14 per cent. Those who had two or more spare rooms were subject to a 25 per cent reduction. Under the rules, children under sixteen of the same gender are expected to share a bedroom and children under ten are expected to share regardless of their gender.

**Fair Rents**

These are now incredibly rare. Fair rents are the regulated rents which renters who took out tenancy agreements before 15 January 1989 were able to get. Renters were able to register their rents to make sure they didn't increase too much. To give you an example of how they work in practice, I once spoke to a woman who lived in Soho and who had been paying more or less the same rent for forty years. Fair rents are effectively controlled and can only be reduced by so much each year based on something called the Maximum Fair Rent calculation.

**Help to Buy**

Introduced by David Cameron and George Osborne in 2013, Help to Buy is an equity loan scheme intended to help first-time buyers. However, there were actually two iterations of the scheme initially: one was available to everyone, not just those buying a home for the first time. As it exists now, Help to Buy means you can buy a property with a 5 per cent deposit as well as a government loan for 20 per cent of the purchase price (40 per cent in London), which is interest-free for five years. As this book went to press, the intention was that the scheme would cease to be available to new buyers after 31 March 2023.

**Homes (Fitness for Human Habitation) Act 2018**

This was the legislation proposed by Labour MP Karen Buck to ensure rented homes meet basic health and safety standards, but which was voted down in 2016. It finally became law in the wake of the Grenfell Tower fire. Though the act did not bring in any new legal obligations for private landlords, it does require them to meet their obligations when it comes to property standards and safety. However, as discussed in this book, cash-strapped local authorities don't always find it easy to enforce.

**Housing First**

This is an approach to street homelessness or rough sleeping. The premise is simple: you house homeless people immediately, regardless of their needs. There are no caveats: no moralising about drinking or drug use, they are not told that they must get a job before they are eligible for support – they are simply given a home, as well as any treatment or support they need. In this book I discuss how Housing First could become an operating philosophy for housing policy beyond street homelessness.

**Intermediate Rent**

This is a rent, usually lower than market rent in any given area, that is offered by a social housing provider. The idea is that they are available to those on lower incomes. Intermediate rents can vary between 65 and 80 percent of market rent which, when you consider how high market rents are in some areas, doesn't necessarily mean that intermediate rent is affordable. Indeed, it's worth noting that intermediate rent isn't necessarily the same as 'affordable rent'. Affordable rent was introduced by the Coalition government in 2011. Unlike intermediate or key worker housing it was meant to be rented out in the same way as social housing. It was decided that affordable rent would be set at 80 per cent of market rents.

In London, when Sadiq Khan became mayor in 2016, he scrapped affordable rent and introduced the London affordable rent, which is less than half of market rent.

**Key Workers**

For a long time this has meant vital public sector workers such as nurses, ambulance drivers, police officers, teachers and those involved in food production. However, as the coronavirus pandemic showed, we ought to broaden our definition to include supermarket workers and gig-economy delivery services.

**Land Value Tax**

Put simply, this is a tax on the value of the land itself and not the structures built on it. That value may be dictated, for instance, by its location or any granted planning permission to build on the site.

**Leasehold**

This is a controversial system of property ownership which has its roots in Britain's feudal system. Under a leasehold structure, you buy a home for a certain number of years, meaning you technically lease it from a landlord or freeholder. Until recently, this often involved paying them extortionate ground rents on top of your mortgage.

**Property Guardianship**
Property guardians are private renters who usually occupy disused buildings. They have limited rights and can be thrown out at short notice. As discussed in this book, property experts argue that they are, in fact, entitled to the same rights as other private renters.

**Rent Pressure Zones**
Scotland's system of rent regulation. If a local council is concerned about rent increases in a certain area, they can ask the Scottish government to have that area designated as a 'rent pressure zone', which allows them to limit how much landlords can put up rents by.

**Right to Buy**
This scheme, introduced under Margaret Thatcher, allows most people living in council and housing association homes to buy that home at a discount.

**Shared Ownership**
This is a part-buy, part-own system of homeownership which allows people to buy a share of their property. The idea is that they will buy more over time. This gradual increase of equity is known as 'staircasing'.

**Statutory Homelessness**
This is a legal state of homelessness which a person must be deemed to fulfil before they can access support. According to the government's own definition you are considered to be statutorily homeless if a local authority decides that you do not have accommodation in which you can legally stay (because you have been evicted) or in which you cannot reasonably stay (because it is unsafe).

# NOTES

**Epigraph**

Helen Charman, 'The Tenancy', *support, support* (London: Offord Road Books, 2018).

**Author's Note**

*60 per cent of people in Britain*: Patrick Butler, 'Most Britons regard themselves as working class, survey finds', *Guardian*, 29 June 2016, www.theguardian.com/society/2016/jun/29/most-brits-regard-themselves-as-working-class-survey-finds

*a quarter of people in such jobs*: NatCen Social Research, 'Social Class', in *British Social Attitudes 33* (2016), p. 9, www.bsa.natcen.ac.uk/latest-report/british-social-attitudes-33/social-class.aspx

*'people find stories of the past'*: 'Why do so many middle class professionals insist they are working class?', LSE, 19 January 2021, www.lse.ac.uk/News/Latest-news-from-LSE/2021/a-Jan-21/Why-do-so-many-middle-class-professionals-insist-they-are-working-class

*social class is subjective*: Kate Pickett and Richard Wilkinson, *The Spirit Level: Why Equality is Better for Everyone* (2009; London: Penguin, 2010).

**Prologue**

*the average rent for a one-bedroom home was £1,265*: The house price statistics at the start of each chapter are taken from the online property website rightmove.co.uk. Please note these will therefore be asking prices and not sale prices. The rent statistics are taken from the property search engine home.co.uk and were live at the time of writing.

*Each monthly payment is an investment*: Although there are certain circumstances where banks do evict homeowners. And, of course, if your home turns out to be covered in dangerous cladding, or to have serious safety defects which make it go down in value for another reason, negative equity is like having a financial albatross fastened around your neck. Not all homeowners have it easy. Not all homeowners are cash rich. Homeownership is no panacea and it, too, is underscored by outdated legislation which can be seen most clearly in the leasehold scandal wherein homeowners are still tenants beholden to a freeholder. The Leasehold Knowledge Partnership is an excellent resource if you are impacted by this.

*Brighton was ranked as the worst UK city*: www.thomas-sanderson.co.uk/resources/best-cities-for-single-renters/

*there is a cap*: www.gov.uk/benefit-cap

*the amount adults who are over sixteen*: Brighton & Hove City Council, 'Private Sector Rent and Local Housing Allowance Comparison Report, 31 January 2020', www.brighton-hove.gov.uk/sites/default/files/2020-09/Rent%20and%20%20local%20housing%20allowance%20comparison%2031%20January%202020.pdf

*until he was officially kicked out of his home*: You have to apply to the council to have your homelessness case assessed. UK homelessness legislation applies to those at risk (i.e. within eight weeks) of eviction. But resources are stretched, waiting lists are long and single people without children are disadvantaged even though they should receive help, if not a home, under the Homelessness Reduction Act 2017.

*as the Association of Community Organizations for Reform Now*: In the United States, ACORN formally disbanded after facing intense criticism over voter-registration fraud allegations after conservative activists, posing as a pimp and a sex worker, secretly videotaped organisation employees allegedly giving advice on evading taxes and setting up a brothel. There is no suggestion that anything similar has happened in the UK. Read more about this here: www.theweek.com/articles/496396/fall-acorn-timeline

*rents in England rose by 16 per cent*: Thomas Weekes, 'Rents rises vs. wage rises in England 2011–2017', Shelter (August 2018), england.shelter.org.uk/professional_resources/policy_and_research/policy_library/rents_rises_vs_wage_rises_in_england_2011-2017

*private renters spend a third of their pre-tax earnings on rent*: www.statista.com/statistics/752217/household-rent-to-income-ratio-by-region-uk/

*there are currently 17.5 million adults*: Shelter, '17.5 million people now impacted by the housing emergency', 26 May 2021, england.shelter.org.uk/media/press_release/17_5million_people_now_impacted_by_the_housing_emergency_. Estimates as to the scale of the crisis in housing in Britain vary. This figure from the housing charity Shelter encompasses people who rent privately as well as the street homeless and those in temporary accommodation. Shelter used data from the Office for National Statistics to make its calculations. The English Housing Survey (EHS) is another good source of data, but it can be patchy. This is because of how the data is collected. Each year a sample is drawn at random from a list of private addresses held by the Royal Mail. Householders at those addresses are invited to take part in the survey by letter. Those in the most precarious housing or for whom English is not a first language are less likely to participate.

*Women and people who are not White British*: Race Disparity Unit, 'Renting from a private landlord' (2020, 2021). Available at www.ethnicity-facts-figures.service.gov.uk/housing/owning-and-renting/renting-from-a-private-landlord/latest

*The number of families who became homeless*: Shelter, 'Over half of homeless families in England are in work, shock new figures show', 23 July 2018, england.shelter.org.uk/media/press_release/over_half_of_homeless_families_in_england_are_in_work,_shock_new_figures_show

*most of which are privately owned*: Vicky Spratt, 'Welcome to Eros House, where desperate families are forced to live in "inhumane" flats that cost up to £380 per week', *i Paper*, 14 December 2018, inews.co.uk/opinion/the-mould-is-in-my-childs-bed-the-families-temporarily-housed-in-dilapidated-former-office-block-are-still-there-one-year-later-235452

*a 430 per cent increase*: 'LGA – 430% increase in B&B spend for people who are homeless reveals urgency for more social housing', Local Government Association, 3 July 2021, www.local.gov.uk/about/news/lga-430-increase-bb-spend-people-who-are-homeless-reveals-urgency-more-social-housing

*the right to adequate housing*: *The Right to Adequate Housing: Fact Sheet No. 21/Rev.1*, UN-Habitat (2014), www.ohchr.org/documents/publications/fs21_rev_1_housing_en.pdf

*One third of all households in poverty*: Alison Wallace, David Rhodes and Firona Roth, 'Home owners and poverty', Joseph Rowntree Foundation, 15 February 2018, www.jrf.org.uk/report/home-owners-and-poverty

*'and demand a rent even for its natural produce.'*: Adam Smith, *An Inquiry into the Nature and Causes of the Wealth of Nations* (1776), Book 1, Chapter 6. Available online at geolib.com/smith.adam/won1-06.html

*the unconditional and unqualified ownership of property*: Jean-Jacques Rousseau, *The Social Contract* (1762; London: Penguin, 2004).

*1,187,641 households*: 'Shelter: 1.15 million households stuck on social housing waiting lists, while there was a net loss of over 17,000 social homes in the last year', PolicyMogul, 28 January 2020, policymogul.com/monitor/key-updates/6587/shelter-1-15-million-households-stuck-on-social-housing-waiting-lists-while-there-was-a-net-loss-of-over-17-000-social-homes-in-the-last-year

*6,850 social homes were sold off*: You'll notice a slight decline in the number of Right to Buy sales here between 2020 and 2021. This is because there was a seven-week freeze on the housing market introduced in March 2020 to stop the spread of coronavirus, effectively preventing most purchases and sales. This also stopped valuations, which make up a key part of the Right to Buy sales process. This data is measured by financial year, e.g. 2019–2020 and 2020–2021. Live tables of Right to Buy sales here: www.gov.uk/government/statistical-data-sets/live-tables-on-social-housing-sales#right-to-buy-sales

*It found that over the past thirty years*: Vicky Spratt, 'Housing wealth rocketed in 2021 and it should change how we think about class', *i Paper*, 23 December 2021, inews.co.uk/opinion/housing-wealth-2021-change-how-think-about-class-1363935

*Banks became more risk averse*: Basel II is an international set of banking standards. See www.bis.org/basel_framework/

*interest rates were high*: Peter Miller, '30-Year mortgage rates chart: Historical and current rates', The Mortgage Reports, 21 January 2022, www.themortgagereports.com/61853/30-year-mortgage-rates-chart

*launched the 'buy-to-let' mortgage*: Rob Thomas, 'Reshaping housing tenure in the UK: the role of buy-to-let', Intermediary Mortgage Lenders Association (May 2014), www.imla.org.uk/perch/resources/imla-reshaping-housing-tenure-in-the-uk-the-role-of-buy-to-let-may-2014.pdf

*the number of loans granted to landlords*: Patrick Collinson, 'UK mortgage lending to landlords soared in last quarter of 2014', *Guardian*, 17 February 2015, www.theguardian.com/money/2015/feb/17/uk-mortgage-lending-landlords-first-time-buyers

*council homes sold through the Right to Buy scheme*: This could be a conservative estimate as the data was last obtained by *Inside Housing* using Freedom of Information requests in 2017. See Nathaniel Barker, 'Exclusive: 7% rise in former Right to Buy homes now rented privately', *Inside Housing*, 7 December 2017, www.insidehousing.co.uk/news/news/exclusive-7-rise-in-former-right-to-buy-homes-now-rented-privately-53507; and Patrick Collinson, 'Four in 10 right-to-buy homes are now owned by private landlords', *Guardian*, 8 December 2017, www.theguardian.com/society/2017/dec/08/right-to-buy-homes-owned-private-landlords

*£22 billion a year on Housing Benefit*: Paul Johnson, 'Doubling of the housing benefit

bill is sign of something deeply wrong', Institute for Fiscal Studies, 4 March 2019, ifs. org.uk/publications/13940

*About half of that*: Damien Gayle, 'Private landlords get £9.3bn in housing benefit from taxpayer, says report', *Guardian*, 20 August 2016, www.theguardian.com/society/2016/ aug/20/private-landlords-9bn-housing-benefit-taxpayers-national-housing-federation-report

*the private rented sector in the UK grew*: 'UK private rented sector: 2018', Office for National Statistics (18 January 2019), www.ons.gov.uk/economy/ inflationandpriceindices/articles/ukprivaterentedsector/2018.

*In the twenty-five years since*: Hilary Osborne, 'Home ownership in England at lowest level in 30 years as housing crisis grows', *Guardian*, 2 August 2016, www.theguardian. com/society/2016/aug/02/home-ownership-in-england-at-lowest-level-in-30-years-as-housing-crisis-grows

## 1 Sheltered Dreamers

*developers built affordable homes*: A great starting place if you want to dig into the history of the welfare state more broadly is Derek Fraser, *The Evolution of the British Welfare State: A History of Social Policy since the Industrial Revolution*, 5th edition (London: Palgrave Macmillan, 2017).

*about half of all homes built*: *Municipal Dreams: The Rise and Fall of Council Housing* (London: Verso, 2018) by the historian John Boughton is a wonderful book based on his brilliant blog. It is a landmark reappraisal of council housing which looks in depth at the competing ideologies that have promoted state housing and condemned it, as well as the economics that have always constrained our housing ideals.

*ought not to be brushed over*: For further reading on this, see Rebecca Tunstall, *The Fall and Rise of Social Housing: 100 Years on 20 Estates* (Bristol: Policy Press, 2020), p. 268.

*homelessness charity of the same name*: en.wikipedia.org/wiki/Centrepoint_(charity)

*more than £7 million*: www.knightfrank.co.uk/properties/residential/for-sale/ centre-point-residences-103-new-oxford-street-london-wc1a/KRD161007

*an ongoing social housing conditions scandal*: Tara O'Connor, 'Croydon Council housing boss leaves just months after starting in wake of Regina Road scandal', *MyLondon*, 9 November 2021, www.mylondon.news/news/south-london-news/ croydon-council-housing-boss-leaves-22116477

*one of the first people to establish a link*: J. R. Ashton, 'Back to back housing, courts, and privies: the slums of 19th century England', *Journal of Epidemiology & Community Health* 60 (2006), 654, jech.bmj.com/content/60/8/654

*the middle classes became convinced*: Edwin Chadwick, *Report on the Sanitary Condition of the Labouring Population of Great Britain* (1842; Edinburgh: Edinburgh University Press, 1965).

*the same could happen here*: Again, I'd recommend Derek Fraser's *Evolution of the British Welfare State* for further reading on this.

*'What family life is possible under such conditions?'*: Friedrich Engels, *The Condition of the Working Class in England* (1845; London: Penguin Classics, 2009).

*tenants can never be evicted during winter*: 'Trêve hivernale: Why you can't be evicted in winter in France', *The Local*, 5 December 2019, www.thelocal.fr/20191205/france-facts-you-cant-be-evicted-in-winter

*perhaps things would look different*: Asa Briggs, 'Reforming Acts', BBC History, 17 February 2011, www.bbc.co.uk/history/british/victorians/reforming_acts_01.shtml

*the fear of a Bolshevik-style revolution*: John Boughton's blog, 'Municipal Dreams', at municipaldreams.wordpress.com, and related book.

*short of their recommended space guidelines*: Julian Joyce, '"Shoebox homes" become the UK norm', BBC News, 14 September 2011, www.bbc.co.uk/news/uk-14916580

*set out the blueprint*: www.nationalarchives.gov.uk/pathways/citizenship/brave_new_world/welfare.htm

*thousands of copies were sold each day*: hansard.millbanksystems.com/commons/1943/may/18/house-of-commons-official-report-sales#S5CV0389P0_19430518_HOC_177

*Council rent in Croydon*: 'Final Internal Audit Report: Housing Rents (Reduced Scope), June 2020', Mazars LLP/Croydon Council, www.croydon.gov.uk/sites/default/files/articles/downloads/2019-20%20Housing%20Rents.pdf

*that rent had risen*: api.parliament.uk/historic-hansard/commons/1981/dec/16/council-house-rents

*dilapidated and run-down social housing*: There is also a crisis in conditions in social housing today. This book's focus is on the private rented sector and so there is not space to dig deeper into that. However, Croydon presents a particularly egregious example. In 2021 the council became effectively bankrupt, having lent £200 million to a housebuilding firm that delivered just three purpose-built council homes in five years. However, there have been reports of serious neglect in their existing stock, with tenants saying they are being forced to live in dangerous squalor with black mould and severe damp because the council won't carry out repairs. See 'Croydon shamed over "dangerous squalor" in council flats', *Inside Croydon*, 22 March 2021, insidecroydon. com/2021/03/22/croydon-shamed-over-dangerous-squalor-in-council-flats/

*At the start of the twentieth century*: Martin Pugh, *We Danced All Night: A Social History of Britain Between the Wars* (London: Bodley Head, 2008), p. 60.

*By 1981, 5.5 million homes*: Department for Communities and Local Government, *Housing in England: Overview*, National Audit Office (19 January 2017). Available at www.nao.org.uk/wp-content/uploads/2017/01/Housing-in-England-overview.pdf

*This housebuilding drive meant*: Kath Woodward, *Social Sciences: The Big Issues*, 3rd edition (Abingdon: Routledge, 2014), p. 10.

*just 17 per cent of households*: Race Disparity Unit, 'Renting social housing' (2020, 2021). Available at www.ethnicity-facts-figures.service.gov.uk/housing/social-housing/ renting-from-a-local-authority-or-housing-association-social-housing/latest

*400 households became homeless every day*: Graine Cuffe, 'Nearly 400 households made homeless every day after eviction ban lifted', Inside Housing, 27 January 2022, www. insidehousing.co.uk/news/news/nearly-400-households-made-homeless-every-day-after-eviction-ban-lifted-74071

*New Labour's leadership bopped*: www.gettyimages.co.uk/detail/video/ interior-shots-of-labour-party-members-dancing-to-d-ream-news-footage/499894932

*The song had soundtracked*: Great British Politics, 'Labour's 1997 Party Political Broadcast – Things Can Only Get Better', YouTube, 5 June 2015, www.youtube.com/ watch?v=gi5j7jjhm4M&ab_channel=GreatBritishPolitics

*But during their thirteen-year stint*: There is not enough space in this book to adequately assess New Labour's legacy on housing. It's fair to say it was a mixed bag. Both Blair and Brown failed to build enough new social homes but they did work to drive up standards in social housing successfully. They also led a huge drive to get new homes for private sale built, reaching record highs not seen since the 1980s. For a thorough but accessible long-read on this subject I'd recommend an article from *Inside Housing* which was published as David Cameron took office: Gene Robertson, 'Labour's legacy', 7 May 2010, www.insidehousing.co.uk/insight/insight/labours-legacy-19459

*New Labour actually managed to build*: 'Labour "should apologise for social housing failure"', *Evening Standard*, 11 November 2013, www.standard.co.uk/news/politics/ labour-should-apologise-for-social-housing-failure-8932797.html

*more homes were lost through Right to Buy*: Grainne Cuffe, 'Right to Buy sales drop by a

third in past 12 months', *Inside Housing*, 2 November 2011, www.insidehousing.co.uk/
news/news/right-to-buy-sales-drop-by-a-third-in-past-12-months-73138

*the Labour Party's manifesto in 1959*: Labour Party, *1959 Labour Party Election
Manifesto: Britain Belongs to You: The Labour Party's Policy for Consideration by the
British People*, labour-party.org.uk (1959, 2001). Available at www.labour-party.org.uk/
manifestos/1959/1959-labour-manifesto.shtml

*'Every tenant … will have a chance first to buy'*: Right to Buy is one of the most
impactful and enduring privatisations of the Thatcher era. If you want to know more,
Colin Jones and Alan Murie's *The Right to Buy: Analysis and Evaluation of a Housing
Policy (Real Estate Issues Book 9)* (Oxford: Wiley-Blackwell, 2006) is an accessible book
which analyses it rigorously. They point out that the notion that municipal housing
should be sold on was even older than the 1959 Labour manifesto: 'Nineteenth-century
housing legislation required that council-built dwellings in redevelopment areas
should be sold within 10 years of completion.' They write that voluntary (not as a right
and unsubsidised) sales grew in the 1950s: 5,825 in May 1956 alone. Labour's manifesto,
then, merely crystallised the idea. By 1972 the Conservative environment secretary,
Peter Walker, declared at his party's conference that the ability of council tenants to
buy their homes was a 'very basic right', and that they should be offered a 20 per cent
discount on the market price.

*'for most people, owning one's house …'*: Aled Davies, '"Right to Buy": The
Development of a Conservative Housing Policy, 1945–1980', *Contemporary British
History* 27:4 (2013), 421–44.

*'We shall also ensure that 100 per cent …'*: Conservative Party, *Conservative General
Election Manifesto 1979*. Available at www.margaretthatcher.org/document/110858

*his thinking informed the policymaking*: How they interpreted it, though, differed. See
David Torrance, *Noel Skelton and the Property-owning Democracy* (London: Biteback,
2010).

*which has remained broadly steady*: www.statista.com/statistics/804446/property-tenure-
distribution-in-the-united-kingdom/

*'the biggest act of economic and social self-harm'*: Jim Strang, 'Right to Buy is the biggest
act of economic and social self-harm ever inflicted on this nation', *Inside Housing*, 6
June 2019, www.insidehousing.co.uk/comment/comment/right-to-buy-is-the-biggest-
act-of-economic-and-social-self-harm-ever-inflicted-on-this-nation-61697

*'the most significant and lucrative act of privatisation'*: Jones and Murie, *The Right to Buy*.

*more than half of council properties sold through the scheme*: Liane Wimhurst, '40% of right-to-buy properties end up in hands of private landlords', *i Paper*, 8 December 2017, inews.co.uk/news/uk/40-right-buy-properties-end-hands-private-landlords-109297

*Hundreds of private landlords*: Michael Savage, 'Ministers urged to halt right-to-buy scheme', *Guardian*, 19 January 2019, www.theguardian.com/society/2019/jan/19/ministers-urged-halt-right-buy-council-homes-rented

*In his 2010 austerity budget*: HM Treasury, *Budget 2010*, June 2010. Available at assets.publishing.service.gov.uk/government/uploads/system/uploads/attachment_data/file/248096/0061.pdf

*Osborne's thinking was back to front*: Mike Brewer et al., 'The curious incidence of rent subsidies: evidence of heterogeneity from administrative data', Institute for Fiscal Studies, 19 October 2019, ifs.org.uk/publications/14517

*Boris Johnson's government unfroze LHA*: It is worth noting that the position of social renters was different to that of private renters. As Rebecca Tunstall notes in *The Fall and Rise of Social Housing*, we know that although, on average, they had lower incomes, those incomes were more virus-proof. They also had lower rents which fell below the LHA. Their landlords – local authorities and housing associations, as opposed to private individuals – generally stuck to the government's guidance not to evict people.

*The extent to which successive governments*: At the time, I reported on this for the *i Paper*. You can read more here: 'When it comes to housing during coronavirus, Rishi Sunak's claim that "we are all in this together" isn't true', 16 April 2020, inews.co.uk/opinion/housing-coronavirus-renting-rishi-sunak-418924

*The Chancellor's support package*: Vicky Spratt, 'Coronavirus help for renters: The assistance available if you are renting in the UK', *i Paper*, 27 March 2020, inews.co.uk/opinion/coronavirus-rent-help-government-uk-home-pay-assistance-how-claim-explained-412072

*you can buy a flat in Dorrington Court*: www.rightmove.co.uk/properties/71201970#/

*or rent one privately*: www.rightmove.co.uk/properties/70771572#/

*Macintosh's work, her vision*: Pre-war, most council housing was for those on middle incomes. This continued afterwards on some estates. If you'd like to know more about this, there is very good analysis in Chapter 10 of Rebecca Tunstall's *The Fall and Rise of Social Housing*. The aspirational nature of council housing is also discussed by John Boughton in *Municipal Dreams*.

*'It is a portal, a gateway'*: Arundhati Roy, 'The Pandemic is a Portal', *Financial Times*, 3 April 2020.

## 2 Life for Rent

*average house sale prices in Peckham increased*: Melissa Lawford, '"Posh" Peckham's house prices fuelled by bank of mum and dad', *Financial Times*, 15 August 2018, www.ft.com/content/39b91420-9c84-11e8-88de-49c908b1f264

*'from Mum and Dad'*: Ibid.

*'year zero'*: See Gavriel Hollander, 'Thirty years on: how the Housing Act changed everything', *Inside Housing*, 24 January 2019, www.insidehousing.co.uk/insight/insight/thirty-years-on-how-the-housing-act-changed-everything-59821

*banks tend to give mortgages more readily*: This is evidenced in the fact that in the boom years of 1996–2006 first-time buyers were entering the market in large numbers, putting homeownership close to an all-time high. But when the financial crisis hit, lending to them was cut in half and landlords were seen as a less risky bet by lenders.

*20.3 per cent of households*: www.statista.com/statistics/286444/england-number-of-private-rented-households

*the return of rentier capitalism*: Thomas Piketty, *Capital in the Twenty-First Century*, tr. Arthur Goldhammer (2013; Cambridge, MA: Harvard University Press, 2014) is an important work though, of course, not everyone agrees with its contents. A key claim made by Piketty is that income inequality has increased sharply since the late 1970s, with a particularly dramatic rise in the share of total income going to the very highest earners in the US and Europe. He believes this trend towards greater wealth inequality is very likely to continue, because the returns from capital are likely to grow faster than the economy itself, and faster than the owners of that wealth are likely to be able to spend it. This is, he argues, is the 'central contradiction of capitalism'.

*'there's no such thing as society'*: Margaret Thatcher in *Women's Own* magazine (3 October 1987).

*average house prices have risen*: Donna Ferguson, 'Twenty years on – the winners and losers of Britain's property boom', *Guardian*, 23 January 2016, www.theguardian.com/money/2016/jan/23/britain-property-boom-losers-winners-housing-market-renting

*earning returns of almost 1,400 per cent*: This was more than four times the equivalent investment in commercial property, UK government bonds or shares, and seven times the return on cash. See Hilary Osborne, 'Buy-to-let landlords earn returns of up to 1,400% since 1996', *Guardian*, 11 April 2015, www.theguardian.com/money/2015/apr/11/buy-to-let-landlords-earn-returns-of-up-to-1400-since-1996

*private renters didn't benefit*: Tom Weekes, 'Flatlining wages, surging rents and a national affordability crisis', Shelter, 3 August 2018, blog.shelter.org.uk/2018/08/flatlining-wages-surging-rents-and-a-national-affordability-crisis/

*private rents were unaffordable*: 'How affordable is renting privately in the UK?', 18 July 2019, www.pwc.blogs.com/economics_in_business/2019/07/how-affordable-is-renting-privately-in-the-uk.html

*29 per cent of people were finding it difficult*: Ministry of Housing, Communities and Local Government, *English Housing Survey 2017 to 2018: Private rented sector*, National Statistics (2019). Available at assets.publishing.service.gov.uk/government/uploads/system/uploads/attachment_data/file/817630/EHS_2017-18_PRS_Report.pdf

*He believed that social justice was a 'mirage'*: Andrew Lister, 'The "Mirage" of Social Justice: Hayek Against (and For) Rawls', CSSJ Working Papers Series, June 2011, www.politics.ox.ac.uk/sites/default/files/inline-files/SJ017_Lister_MirageofSocialJustice.pdf

*'personal freedom and economic freedom are indivisible'*: Margaret Thatcher, 'Speech to Conservative Central Council ("The Historic Choice")' (20 March 1976), www.margaretthatcher.org/document/102990

*Capitalism is defined*: dictionary.cambridge.org/dictionary/english/capitalism

*democratic socialism*: dictionary.cambridge.org/dictionary/english/democratic-socialism

*the expense of the personal freedom*: We must acknowledge that not all private landlords are wealthy people who own multiple properties. Almost half of landlords own just one property, but half of all private rented sector tenancies are let by the 17 per cent of landlords who have five or more properties. See Ministry of Housing, Communities and Local Government, *English Private Landlord Survey 2018: Main report* (2019). Available at assets.publishing.service.gov.uk/government/uploads/system/uploads/attachment_data/file/775002/EPLS_main_report.pdf

*she should have been offered more help*: england.shelter.org.uk/housing_advice/homelessness/get_help_from_the_council

*'intentionally homeless'*: england.shelter.org.uk/housing_advice/homelessness/rules/intentionally_homeless

*'women and mothers'*: For further reading, see a report co-written by Reeve for the Centre for Homelessness Impact: Emma Bimpson, Hannah Green and Kesia Reeve, *Women, homelessness and violence: what works?*, Centre for Homelessness Impact (July 2021). Available at assets-global.website-files.com/59f07e67422cdf0001904c14/61017dbd205aeb5f3bdd366b_CFHI_WOMEN_REPORT_V03.pdf

Newsnight *was forced to issue an apology*: Interestingly, *Newsnight* has since deleted the video and it is no longer accessible online.

*'judged and victimised'*: Shanene Thorpe, 'I felt judged and victimised by Newsnight', *Guardian*, 31 May 2012, www.theguardian.com/commentisfree/2012/may/31/shanene-thorpe-judged-victimised-newsnight

*the average annual poverty premium*: Sara Davies, Andrea Finney and Yvette Hartfree, 'The Poverty Premium: When low-income households pay more for essential goods and services' (University of Bristol, 2016). Available at www.bristol.ac.uk/geography/research/pfrc/themes/finexc/poverty-premium/

*according to the JRF*: p. 11 of their 2022 state of poverty report, www.jrf.org.uk/report/uk-poverty-2022

*according to the Department for Work and Pensions' own data*: Vicky Spratt, 'DWP Universal Credit crackdown could force renters to repay thousands', *i Paper*, 7 July 2021, inews.co.uk/news/dwp-universal-credit-crackdown-renters-repay-thousands-1078689

*unlawful to discriminate against renters*: Jasmine Andersson, '"No DSS" bans on housing benefit ruled unlawful: what the court ruling means for tenants', *i Paper*, 14 July 2020, inews.co.uk/news/no-dss-bans-on-housing-benefit-ruled-unlawful-537243

*lone women or women with dependent children*: Agenda, 'Briefing: Homeless Women' (January 2019), weareagenda.org/wp-content/uploads/2019/02/Agenda-Briefing-homeless-women-Jan-2019.pdf

*women's incomes fall more than 50 per cent short*: Vicky Spratt, 'No Room Of Her Own: The Truth About The Gender Housing Gap', *Refinery29*, 18 July 2019, www.refinery29.com/en-gb/2019/07/237953/womens-budget-group-housing-report#slide-4

*insidious racism*: Sarah Neal, '*Race, Community and Conflict* fifty years on', *Ethnic and Racial Studies* 38:3 (2015), 379–85.

*'housing stress' is much higher*: Kevin Gulliver, *Forty Years of Struggle: A Window on Race and Housing, Disadvantage and Exclusion* (Birmingham: Human City Institute, 2016). Available at humancityinstitute.files.wordpress.com/2017/01/forty-years-of-struggle.pdf

*high levels of anxiety and depression*: Humbelina Robles Ortega et al., 'Post-Traumatic Stress Disorder Symptomatology in People Affected by Home Eviction in Spain', *Spanish Journal of Psychology* 20 (2017); see also www.ugr.es/en/about/news/ugr-study-warns-enormous-impact-evictions-mental-health

*more likely to attempt suicide*: Yerko Rojas and Sten-Åke Stenberg, 'Evictions and

Suicide: A Follow-up Study of Almost 22,000 Swedish Households in the Wake of the Global Financial Crisis', *Journal of Epidemiology and Community Health* 70:4 (2016), 409–13.

*You are supposed to be given help*: england.shelter.org.uk/housing_advice/homelessness/get_help_from_the_council/

*£10,000 of public money for each booking*: Tom Wall, 'Revealed: the private landlords profiting from England's housing crisis', *Guardian*, 13 October 2019, www.theguardian.com/society/2019/oct/13/private-landlords-profits-housing-crisis-homelessness-councils-england

*'I was told it could be years'*: It's worth noting that London is in the eye of the storm in this respect. However, waiting times for social housing have increased in most places around the country. According to the National Housing Federation, in 2020 the true number of people in need of social housing in England alone was 3.8 million. See the National Housing Federation, *People in housing need: A comprehensive analysis of the scale and shape of housing need in England today* (15 September 2020). Available at www.housing.org.uk/resources/people-in-housing-need/

## 3 The Problem with Generation Rent

*social housing shortage in Essex*: For ONS statistics on the Essex housing shortage, see Paige Ingram, 'The Essex towns where there "won't be enough houses" for everyone by 2041', *Essex Live*, 12 November 2019, www.essexlive.news/news/essex-news/essex-towns-wont-enough-houses-3527226

*average rental cost of a two-bedroom home increased*: 'Rent prices in Colchester outpace income growth', *Essex County Standard*, 13 August 2018, www.gazette-news.co.uk/news/16411459.rent-prices-colchester-outpace-income-growth/

*living costs for poorer households*: Richard Partington, 'Living costs rising faster for UK's poorest families than richest', *Guardian*, 25 April 2019, www.theguardian.com/uk-news/2019/apr/25/living-costs-rising-faster-for-uks-poorest-families-than-richest

*The length of time a person has to wait*: See england.shelter.org.uk/housing_advice/council_housing_association/how_councils_allocate_housing

*'increasing the overall supply'*: Emma Lunn, 'Demand on PRS "greater than ever before"', *Landlord Today*, 21 March 2016, www.landlordtoday.co.uk/breaking-news/2016/3/demand-on-prs-greater-than-ever-before

*tried to extol the 'benefits' of renting*: 'Explained: the advantages of renting over buying',

HomeLet, 9 June 2017, homelet.co.uk/tenants/blog/article/explained-the-advantages-of-renting-over-buying

*more households with children*: 'UK private rented sector: 2018', Office for National Statistics (18 January 2019), www.ons.gov.uk/economy/inflationandpriceindices/articles/ukprivaterentedsector/2018

*badly impacted by the 2008 financial crash*: Sarah O'Connor, 'Millennials poorer than previous generations, data show', *Financial Times*, 23 February 2018, www.ft.com/content/81343d9e-187b-11e8-9e9c-25c814761640

*'scarring' effect on our wages*: Stephen Clarke, 'Coming of age during a downturn can cause scarring – and it takes up to a decade to heal', Resolution Foundation, 13 May 2019, www.resolutionfoundation.org/comment/coming-of-age-during-a-downturn-can-cause-scarring-and-it-takes-up-to-a-decade-to-heal/

*growing number of older renters*: 'Number of pensioners living in poverty tops two million, with Black and Asian older people most at risk', Age UK, 16 June 2021, www.ageuk.org.uk/latest-press/articles/2021/number-of-pensioners-living-in-poverty-tops-two-million/

*surge in 55- to 64-year-olds renting*: Sarah Davidson, 'Number of retired renters DOUBLES in a decade: Landlords plan to invest in homes for elderly as social care crisis fails to keep pace with demand', This is Money, 5 November 2020, www.thisismoney.co.uk/money/buytolet/article-8884541/Number-retired-renters-doubles-decade.html

*the highest numbers of older renters*: Ibid.

*'if you want a house, stop buying avocado toast'*: Sam Levin, 'Millionaire tells millennials: if you want a house, stop buying avocado toast', *Guardian*, 15 May 2017, www.theguardian.com/lifeandstyle/2017/may/15/australian-millionaire-millennials-avocado-toast-house

*'the young have never had it so good'*: James Delingpole, 'The gilded generation – why the young have never had it so good', *Spectator*, 10 May 2014, www.spectator.co.uk/article/the-gilded-generation---why-the-young-have-never-had-it-so-good

*'QE-fuelled asset bubble'*: Quantitative easing is a monetary policy which the Bank of England leaned into after the financial crisis. It involves buying bonds to lower the interest rates on savings and loans with a view to stimulating spending in the economy. See the Bank of England, 'What is quantitative easing?', www.bankofengland.co.uk/monetary-policy/quantitative-easing

*only 7 per cent of the British population go to private school*: *Elitist Britain 2019: The educational backgrounds of Britain's leading people*, Sutton Trust/Social Mobility Commission (2019). Available at www.suttontrust.com/our-research/elitist-britain-2019/

*no fewer than 45 per cent went to private schools*: Lewis Goodall, 'The BBC gender pay gap is bad – but its class gap is worse', Sky News, 23 July 2017, news.sky.com/story/the-bbc-pay-gap-is-bad-its-class-gap-is-worse-10957166

*'You can only break out of the circle'*: Pierre Bourdieu, *On Television*, tr. Priscilla Parkhurst Ferguson (1996; New York: The New Press, 1998).

*'stealing their children's future'*: In 2010, David Willetts wrote *The Pinch: How the Baby Boomers Took Their Children's Future – And Why They Should Give It Back* (London: Atlantic Books, 2010).

*'hoarding homes'*: Alex Wellman, 'Older people "hoard" family homes', *Inside Housing*, 19 October 2011, www.insidehousing.co.uk/news/news/older-people-hoard-family-homes-29115

*increasingly concentrated in low-paid occupations*: Richard Blundell et al., 'Young people increasingly concentrated in low-paid occupations, and young men increasingly struggling to progress – even before COVID-19', Institute for Fiscal Studies, 31 July 2020, ifs.org.uk/publications/14968

*policies which promise to protect people's housing wealth*: Vicky Spratt, 'The fairest way to pay for social care is to tax landlords properly on their housing wealth', *i Paper*, 14 September 2021, inews.co.uk/opinion/social-care-levy-fairest-way-pay-tax-landlords-housing-wealth-1198068

*income increase of almost 70 per cent*: Branko Milanović, *Global Inequality: A New Approach for the Age of Globalization* (Cambridge, MA: Harvard University Press, 2016).

*more right-leaning than you might think*: Vicky Spratt, 'Gen Z are more right-leaning than you might think – in this economy who can blame them?', *i Paper*, 11 January 2022, inews.co.uk/opinion/gen-z-are-more-right-leaning-than-you-might-think-in-this-economy-who-can-blame-them-1394488

*lack of appropriate homes*: Robert Booth, 'Lack of homes suitable for older people fuels housing crisis – report', *Guardian*, 14 July 2019, www.theguardian.com/society/2019/jul/14/lack-of-homes-suitable-for-older-people-fuels-housing-crisis-report

*relocate to less urban areas*: 'Why are so many buyers escaping to the country?', Rightmove, 10 August 2020, www.rightmove.co.uk/news/articles/property-news/escape-to-the-country

*we have an ageing population*: Richard Best and Anya Martin, *Rental Housing For An Ageing Population*, APPG for Housing and Care for Older People (2019). Available at www.housinglin.org.uk/_assets/Resources/Housing/Support_materials/Other_reports_and_guidance/HAPPI-5-Rental-Housing.pdf

*'ageing in distress and squalor'*: Age UK, 'Ageing in squalor and distress: older people in the private rented sector' (2016). Available at www.ageuk.org.uk/globalassets/age-uk/documents/reports-and-publications/reports-and-briefings/safe-at-home/rb_oct16_ageing_in_squalor_and_distress_report.pdf

*'inevitable catastrophe' of homelessness*: Amelia Hill, 'UK's renting millennials face homelessness crisis when they retire', *Guardian*, 17 July 2019, www.theguardian.com/society/2019/jul/17/renting-millennials-homelessness-crisis-retire

*mental health of older homeowners*: Philippa L. Howden-Chapman et al., 'The Effect of Housing on the Mental Health of Older People: The Impact of Lifetime Housing History in Whitehall II', *BMC Public Health* 11 (2011), article 682.

*deprived of the basic ontological security*: Though, of course, we must not idealise the past too much. As a Black single parent, it's likely that Limarra would have been discriminated against in the private rented sector in the 1950s, 1960s and 1970s and, as Rebecca Tunstall notes, she wouldn't necessarily have fared better when it came to local council social housing allocations. Tunstall's book *The Fall and Rise of Social Housing* is comprehensive and rigorous if you want to read up on this further.

*'logics of expulsion'*: Saskia Sassen, *Expulsions: Brutality and Complexity in the Global Economy* (Cambridge, MA: Harvard University Press, 2014), p. 212.

*out of their dignity*: Paul Watt, '"This Pain of Moving, Moving, Moving": Evictions, Displacement and Logics of Expulsion in London', *L'Année sociologique* 68 (2018), 67–100, www.cairn-int.info/revue-l-annee-sociologique-2018-1-page-67.htm

*Banning Section 21 evictions*: In 2017, a new type of tenancy came into force in Scotland. It is called the Private Residential Tenancy and replaced the Assured and Short Assured Tenancy agreements for all new tenancies. Crucially, it is open-ended, which means a landlord can no longer ask a tenant to leave simply because a fixed term has ended.

## 4 Root Shock

*house prices rose steadily between 2011 and 2017*: 'Bromley house prices and property data', Kinleigh Folkard & Hayward, www.kfh.co.uk/south-east-london-and-north-kent/bromley/sold-data

*One hundred and eighty-one were sent to the West Midlands*: Neil Elkes, 'London boroughs have moved 181 families to the West Midlands', *Birmingham Mail*, 25 April 2018, www.birminghammail.co.uk/news/midlands-news/london-boroughs-moved-181-families-14571414

*574 to Essex and 750 were relocated to Kent*: Robert Booth, 'Number of homeless households moved out of London soars', *Guardian*, 29 October 2018, www.theguardian.com/society/2018/oct/29/number-of-homeless-households-moved-out-of-london-soars

*almost 200 homeless households were relocated*: Dean Kilpatrick, 'Nearly 200 homeless households moved to Medway from Bromley', *Kent Online*, 5 June 2018, www.kentonline.co.uk/medway/news/nearly-200-households-moved-from-london-to-medway-184083/

*The 98,300 households in temporary accommodation*: Vicky Spratt, '"Exporting" single mothers to places hundreds of miles from their homes is causing long-lasting trauma', *i Paper*, 25 August 2021, inews.co.uk/opinion/exporting-single-mothers-to-places-hundreds-of-miles-from-their-homes-is-causing-long-lasting-trauma-1164973

*reduce public expenditure by £225 million by 2015*: '"Thousands" hit by government benefit cap now in work', BBC News, 6 February 2014, www.bbc.com/news/business-26065080

*serious implications for at least 100,000 households*: Centre for Regional Economic and Social Research, Sheffield Hallam University, *The impact of recent reforms to Local Housing Allowances: Differences by place*, Department for Work & Pensions (July 2014). Available at assets.publishing.service.gov.uk/government/uploads/system/uploads/attachment_data/file/329794/rr873-lha-impact-of-recent-reforms-differences-by-place.pdf

*average gap between private rent and Housing Benefit*: Michael Savage, 'Benefit cap leaves poor families with mounting debt, study shows', *Guardian*, 3 November 2018, www.theguardian.com/society/2018/nov/03/benefit-cap-leaves-poor-families-with-mounting-debt-study-shows

*two-thirds more likely to find themselves in rent arrears*: Giovanni Tonutti, 'Benefit Cap: Policy in Practice's evidence to the Work and Pensions Select Committee', Policy in Practice, 10 October 2018, policyinpractice.co.uk/benefit-cap-policy-in-practices-evidence-to-the-work-and-pensions-select-committee/

*'root shock'*: Mindy Thompson Fullilove, *Root Shock: How Tearing Up City Neighborhoods Hurts America, and What We Can Do About It* (New York: One World/Ballantine Books, 2004).

*'some handle for the problem …'*: Ibid.

*'housing dynamics are deeply implicated …'*: Matthew Desmond and Rachel Tolbert Kimbro, 'Eviction's Fallout: Housing, Hardship, and Health', *Social Forces* 94:1 (2015), 295–324, scholar.harvard.edu/files/mdesmond/files/desmondkimbro.evictions.fallout.sf2015_2.pdf

*They cite several studies*: These are: Sarah Burgard, Kristin Seefeldt and Sarah Johnson, 'Housing Instability and Health: Findings from the Michigan Recession and Recovery Study', *Social Science and Medicine* 12 (2012), 2215–24; and Janet Currie and Erdal Tekin, 'Is There a Link Between Foreclosure and Health?', NBER Working Paper 17310 (Cambridge, MA: National Bureau of Economic Research, 2011).

*qualitative studies that show that people*: These are: Marc Fried, 'Grieving for a Lost Home', in *The Urban Condition: People and Policy in the Metropolis*, edited by Leonard Duhl (New York: Basic Books, 1963), pp. 151–71; and Lynne Manzo, Rachel Kleit and Dawn Couch, '"Moving Three Times Is Like Having Your House on Fire Once": The Experience of Place and Impending Displacement among Public Housing Residents', *Urban Studies* 45:9 (2008), 1855–78.

*research has confirmed a link between evictions*: National Low Income Housing Coalition, 'Evictions Associated with Depression, Higher Stress, and Worse Health', 1 March 2021, nlihc.org/resource/evictions-associated-depression-higher-stress-and-worse-health

*according to figures released by the ONS in 2018*: 'UK private rented sector: 2018', Office for National Statistics (18 January 2019), www.ons.gov.uk/economy/inflationandpriceindices/articles/ukprivaterentedsector/2018

*Research conducted by Shelter*: Sarah Credland and Helen Lewis, *Sick and Tired: The Impact of Temporary Accommodation on the Health of Homeless Families*, Shelter (December 2004). Available at england.shelter.org.uk/professional_resources/policy_and_research/policy_library/sick_and_tired_-_the_impact_of_temporary_accommodation_on_the_health_of_homeless_families

*psychological stress and low quality of life*: See, for instance, Thomas Ritz et al., 'Asthma Trigger Reports Are Associated with Low Quality of Life, Exacerbations, and Emergency Treatments', *Annals of the American Thoracic Society* 13:2 (2016), 204–11.

*moving is associated with poorer mental health*: Tim Morris et al., 'How Do Moving and Other Major Life Events Impact Mental Health? A Longitudinal Analysis of UK Children', *Health & Place* 46 (2017), 257–66, www.sciencedirect.com/science/article/pii/S1353829217300503

*Almost a quarter (24 per cent) of people*: Shelter, 'Black people are more than three times as likely to experience homelessness', 1 October 2020, england.shelter.org.uk/media/

press_release/black_people_are_more_than_three_times_as_likely_to_
experience_homelessness

*'spoiled identity' of being labelled homeless*: See Jenny Preece, Elisabeth Garratt and Jan
Flaherty, 'Living through Continuous Displacement: Resisting Homeless Identities
and Remaking Precarious Lives', *Geoforum* 116 (2020), 140–48, www.sciencedirect.
com/science/article/pii/S0016718520302189

*'belonging' … '… wider family networks'*: Jenny Preece, 'Belonging in Working-class
Neighbourhoods: Dis-identification, Territorialisation and Biographies of People and
Place', *Urban Studies* 57:4 (2020), 827–43.

*460 homes in the area but for private sale*: Amy Nickalls, 'Hundreds of homes being
built in Medway', *Kent Online*, 13 April 2018, www.kentonline.co.uk/kent/news/
plan-to-create-world-class-destination-181307/?cmpredirect

*'moving three times …'*: See Manzo et al., '"Moving Three Times Is Like Having Your
House on Fire Once"'.


## 5 Priced Out

*'the most desirable place to live in Britain'*: 'Bristol named best place to live in Britain in
2017', BBC News, 19 March 2017, www.bbc.co.uk/news/uk-england-39320118

*most expensive places to set up home in Northern Ireland*: Mark Bain, 'Hooray for
Holywood as seaside town is rated the best place to live in Northern Ireland', *Belfast
Telegraph*, 12 April 2019, www.belfasttelegraph.co.uk/news/northern-ireland/
hooray-for-holywood-as-seaside-town-is-rated-the-best-place-to-live-in-northern-
ireland-38007541.html

Voices of Bristol: Gentrification and Us: Henry's book is a lively and local account of
what it feels like to grow up in a city that changes around you. Henry Palmer, *Voices of
Bristol: Gentrification and Us* (Bristol: Arkbound, 2019).

*you may have to wait*: www.gov.uk/council-housing

*By 2019, the average house cost £304,900*: Hannah Baker, 'House prices in Bristol now 11
times average salary', *Bristol Post*, 5 April 2019, www.bristolpost.co.uk/news/business/
house-prices-bristol-now-11-2722092

*only place in the country where rents fell*: Vicky Spratt, 'As rents fall in London, three
renters explain why they left amid the Covid-19 pandemic', *i Paper*, 14 October 2020,
inews.co.uk/opinion/london-rent-prices-falling-uk-regions-rents-leaving-715304

*rising at the fastest rate on record*: Rupert Jones, 'Rents outside London soaring at fastest

rate on record, agencies say', *Guardian*, 8 September 2021, www.theguardian.com/
business/2021/sep/08/rents-outside-london-soaring-at-fastest-rate-on-record-
agencies-say

*faster than the average UK wage growth*: Vicky Spratt, 'The scale of the housing crisis
outside of London can no longer be ignored', *i Paper*, 17 October 2019, inews.co.uk/
opinion/comment/housing-crisis-uk-outside-london-property-market-prices-351642;
and 'Contributions to earnings growth in the UK: 2018', Office for National Statistics
(29 April 2019), www.ons.gov.uk/economy/nationalaccounts/uksectoraccounts/
compendium/economicreview/april2019/contributionstoearningsgrowthintheuk2018

*one of the least affordable cities in which to rent*: Data from the ONS analysed by Open
Property Group. See Elise Britten, 'Bath is the second least affordable city for renting
in the country', *Somerset Live*, 6 October 2019, www.somersetlive.co.uk/news/property/
bath-second-least-affordable-city-3393565

*UK's fastest rental growth*: 'UK rents "rising at fastest pace in 13 years"', *Guardian*, 16
November 2021, www.theguardian.com/money/2021/nov/16/uk-rents-rising-zoopla

*'One by one … district is changed'*: Ruth Glass, 'Introduction', *London: Aspects of Change*
(London: MacGibbon & Kee, 1964), pp. xiii–xlii.

*Wealthy people move into less wealthy areas*: The work of Professor Loretta Lees is the
best place to start if you want to know more about contemporary gentrification. She
is an internationally renowned urban geographer. Put simply, she is the expert on this
issue. Sadly, much of Ruth Glass's work is out of print but you can access it in libraries
and you'll find analysis of it in *The Gentrification Reader* (London: Routledge, 2010),
which was co-edited by Lees.

*forcibly removed*: Mira Bar-Hillel, 'Residents of the Heygate estate forced to move out
of London', *Evening Standard*, 2 August 2013, www.standard.co.uk/news/london/
residents-of-the-heygate-estate-forced-to-move-out-of-london-8743216.html

*only 116 of which will be socially rented housing*: elephantandcastle.org.uk/
overview-of-the-plans/

*communities are disrupted*: Further reading on this can be found in Loretta Lees
and Hannah White, 'The Social Cleansing of London Council Estates: Everyday
Experiences of "Accumulative Dispossession"', *Housing Studies* 35:10 (2020), 1701–22.

*gentrifying nature of regeneration schemes*: Helen Pidd, 'Manchester's new Factory aims
high but fails to build in social housing', *Guardian*, 24 July 2015, www.theguardian.
com/uk-news/the-northerner/2015/jul/24/manchesters-new-factory-aims-high-but-fails-to-
build-in-social-housing

*less about lack of homes (supply)*: Neal Hudson of Residential Analysts conducted this research for Sky News. See Ed Conway, 'Line 18: How the UK is facing five housing crises at once', Sky News, 10 April 2019, news.sky.com/story/line-18-uks-housing-crisis-wont-be-solved-by-building-more-homes-11503447

*'adjacent places to any gentrified area become'*: Glass, *London: Aspects of Change*, p. xx.

*more people left London than moved to the city*: Paul Swinney and Andrew Carter, 'London population: Why so many people leave the UK's capital', BBC News, 18 March 2019, www.bbc.com/news/uk-47529562

*Londoners bought homes outside the capital in 2021*: Rupert Neate, 'Tired of life? No, just tired of London: record £55bn spent buying homes outside the capital', *Guardian*, 26 December 2021, www.theguardian.com/society/2021/dec/26/tired-of-life-no-just-tired-of-london-record-55bn-spent-buying-homes-outside-the-capital

*and Cornwall*: Laura Whateley, 'Meet the Cornwall commuters', *The Times*, 20 July 2018, www.thetimes.co.uk/article/meet-the-cornwall-commuters-mwctkjjcd

*'a Cheshire life is closer to London than you think'*: 'Cheshire commute to London. Cheshire life is closer to London than you think', Jackson-Stops, 10 April 2019, www.jackson-stops.co.uk/articles/cheshire-commute-to-london-cheshire-life-is-closer-to-london-than-you-think

*'people at the end … new migrant workers'*: Glass, *London: Aspects of Change*, p. xvii.

*ACORN was founded in Bristol in 2014*: www.acorntheunion.org.uk

*heavily criticised by the* Bristol Cable: Alex Turner and Lucas Batt, 'Interactive Map: Bristol council's homes under the hammer', *Bristol Cable*, 8 April 2016, thebristolcable.org/2016/04/interactive-bristol-councils-homes-under-the-hammer/

*'becoming extinct or likely to disappear'*: Glass, *London: Aspects of Change*, p. xx.

*proportion of people in this bracket was 45.8 per cent*: George Arnett, 'UK became more middle class than working class in 2000, data shows', *Guardian*, 26 February 2016, www.theguardian.com/news/datablog/2016/feb/26/uk-more-middle-class-than-working-class-2000-data

*'we are all middle class now'*: 'Profile: John Prescott', BBC News, 27 August 2007, news.bbc.co.uk/1/hi/uk_politics/6636565.stm

*about a million workers on zero-hours contracts*: Brian Stuart Finlay, 'One million Britons will be on zero-hour contracts by end of 2020', *The Conversation*, 27 February 2020, theconversation.com/one-million-britons-will-be-on-zero-hour-contracts-by-end-of-2020-132338

'*There has been some re-shuffling of social groups*': Glass, *London: Aspects of Change*.

*Social mobility now goes into decline*: Social Mobility Commission, *Social Mobility Barometer: Public Attitudes to Social Mobility in the UK, 2019–20* (2020). Available at assets.publishing.service.gov.uk/government/uploads/system/uploads/attachment_data/file/858908/Social_Mobility_Barometer_2019-2020.pdf

'*accumulative dispossession*': See Loretta Lees and Hannah White, 'The Social Cleansing of London Council Estates'.

*nowhere affordable for key workers*: 'Camborne NHS nurse "may have to leave job" over housing crisis', BBC News, 25 November 2021, www.bbc.co.uk/news/uk-england-cornwall-59409301

*companies are seeing staff members leave*: Ben Chu, 'London housing crisis forcing workers to quit their jobs, says CBI survey', *Independent*, 26 April 2018, www.independent.co.uk/news/business/news/london-housing-crisis-cbi-survey-workers-quit-capital-house-prices-rent-a8321551.html

*figures provided by housing officers in September 2020*: Amanda Cameron, 'New figures reveal exactly how many affordable homes have been built in Bristol', *Bristol Post*, 18 September 2020, www.bristolpost.co.uk/news/bristol-news/new-figures-reveal-exactly-how-4530278

*This was, in part, because of arbitrary caps*: Darren Baxter and Luke Murphy, *Priced Out? Affordable Housing in England*, Institute for Public Policy Research (2017). Available at www.ippr.org/research/publications/priced-out-england

## 6 The Rent Trap

*supports nearly one in four home purchases*: Legal & General and Cebr, *The Bank of Mum and Dad* (2020). Available at www.legalandgeneral.com/landg-assets/personal/retirement/_resources/documents/bomad-2021.pdf

*their chances of owning a home in the UK*: Jonathan Cribb, Andrew Hood and Jack Hoyle, 'Just 1 in 4 middle-income young adults own their own home – down from 2 in 3 twenty years ago', Institute for Fiscal Studies, 16 February 2018, ifs.org.uk/publications/10506

*there has long been an assumption*: Loretta Lees, 'Gentrification and Social Mixing: Towards an Inclusive Urban Renaissance?', *Urban Studies*, special issue 'Gentrification and Public Policy' 45:12 (2008), 2449–70.

*the estrangement of a person from their humanity*: See Karl Marx and Frederick Engels,

*Economic and Philosophic Manuscripts of 1844* (Blacksburg, VA: Wilder Publications, 2011).

*'psychosocial sense' … 'living under the control of another'*: David Madden and Peter Marcuse, *In Defense of Housing: The Politics of Crisis* (London and New York: Verso Books, 2016), p. 16.

*Studies show that having a pet*: Nick Keppler, 'This Is What Your Brain and Body Do When You Hang Out With Animals', *Vice*, 17 August 2018, www.vice.com/en/article/ywkeqv/pet-health-benefits-brain

*almost a quarter (24 per cent) of the homeless population*: Jo Bhandal and Matt Horwood, *The LGBTQ+ Youth Homelessness Report*, akt/YouGov (2021), www.akt.org.uk/report

*what's known as reasonable notice*: This story was originally reported in the *i Paper*, where you will find a statement and, ultimately, an apology from Avon and Somerset Police: Vicky Spratt, 'Racism in housing: "I was evicted on the spot, and then removed by police"', 7 July 2020, inews.co.uk/opinion/racism-in-housing-i-was-evicted-on-the-spot-and-then-removed-by-police-492484

*Sixty-three per cent of households in Britain*: www.ethnicity-facts-figures.service.gov.uk/housing/owning-and-renting/home-ownership/latest

*landlords can't evict people*: Marle, 'You guide to German rental laws and tenant rights', Housing Anywhere, 4 September 2021, housinganywhere.com/Germany/tenant-rights-in-germany

*about 33 per cent … those who had bought with a mortgage*: Ministry of Housing, Communities and Local Government, *English Housing Survey: Housing Costs and Affordability, 2018–2019*, National Statistics (2020). Available at assets.publishing.service.gov.uk/government/uploads/system/uploads/attachment_data/file/898397/2018-19_EHS_Housing_costs_and_affordability.pdf

*in 2020 the average monthly rent*: Nick Lakin, 'People in Lancaster "pushed into deep poverty and hardship" due to gap between Universal Credit and rent costs', *Lancaster Guardian*, 8 January 2021, www.lancasterguardian.co.uk/news/uk-news/people-lancaster-pushed-deep-poverty-and-hardship-due-gap-between-universal-credit-and-rent-costs-3089460

*house prices slowly but steadily rose*: 'What really happened in the Lancaster Housing Market in January 2019?', JDG, 5 February 2019, www.jdg.co.uk/blog/property-selling-tips/what-really-happened-in-the-lancaster-housing-market-in-january-2019.html

*the area faces a housing crisis*: Lancaster City Council, 'Developing affordable

housing' (2016). Available at www.lancaster.gov.uk/planning/housing-strategy/
developing-affordable-housing

*helped to build 43 per cent new homes*: Bert Provan, 'How "Help to Buy" helps mainly
the privileged', LSE BPP blog, 23 October 2017, blogs.lse.ac.uk/politicsandpolicy/
how-help-to-buy-helps-the-privileged/

*the median income of those benefiting*: Ministry of Housing, Communities and Local
Government, *Housing: Statistical Release* (2018). Available at assets.publishing.service.
gov.uk/government/uploads/system/uploads/attachment_data/file/760258/HTB_
Equity_Loan_statistical_release_Q2_2018.pdf

*a household income of less than £80,000*: Emma Lunn and Patrick Collinson, 'Is shared
ownership a vital first step on the property ladder, or a slippery slope?', *Guardian*, 26
March 2016, www.theguardian.com/money/2016/mar/26/shared-ownership-first-step-
property-ladder-slippery-slope-affordable-pitfalls

*it's important to distinguish between the essential characteristic*: It's also worth noting that
social renting has too many of the same disadvantages of renting. This book doesn't
address conditions in social housing, but tenants may experience no-pets rules, poor
conditions, wait a long time for repairs and be told that there are limits to home
improvements that they can make, too. Once again, I would direct you to Rebecca
Tunstall's work on this.

*'shared properties in particular … a tenant's mental health'*: Kim McKee, Adriana Mihaela
Soaita and Jennifer Hoolachan, '"Generation Rent" and the Emotions of Private
Renting: Self-worth, Status and Insecurity amongst Low-income Renters', *Housing
Studies* 35:8 (2019), 1468–87.

*'constant chaos' … '… the siege of inchoate experience'*: Yi-Fu Tuan, *Landscapes of Fear*
(1979; Minneapolis: University of Minnesota Press, 2013).

*'emerging adulthood'*: Jeffrey Jensen Arnett, 'Emerging Adulthood: A Theory of
Development From the Late Teens Through the Twenties', *American Psychologist* 55:5
(2000), 469–80, www.jeffreyarnett.com/ARNETT_Emerging_Adulthood_theory.pdf

*'This is the scariest aspect'*: Dr Lorenza Antonucci originally spoke to me for *Refinery29*.
See 'A Decade On, I Am Still Repaying My Student Loan', 3 May 2021, www.
refinery29.com/en-gb/student-loan-inequality

*In London there is an acknowledgement*: Mayor of London, 'Mayor proposes
priority housing for London's Covid heroes', 4 August 2020, www.london.gov.uk/
press-releases/mayoral/mayor-proposes-priority-housing-for-key-workers

*Switzerland lacks affordable housing*: Marie Glaser, 'The Situation of Social Housing in Switzerland', *Critical Housing Analysis* 4 (2017), 72–80.

*Luxembourg faces a crisis*: Thomas Klein and Yannick Lambert, 'Luxembourgers flock across borders for cheaper housing', *Luxembourg Times*, 31 May 2021, www.luxtimes. lu/en/luxembourg/luxembourgers-flock-across-borders-for-cheaper-housing-60b3859dde135b92368cf04e

## Part Two: Squalor

*with a very different perspective from the rest of us*: Clair Thorstensen-Woll, 'Poor housing can no longer be swept under the carpet', The King's Fund, 22 September 2020, www.kingsfund.org.uk/blog/2020/09/poor-housing-covid-19

*overcrowded housing actually helped to spread Covid-19*: Adam Tinson and Amy Clair, *Better Housing Is Crucial for Our Health and the COVID-19 Recovery*, The Health Foundation (2020). Available at www.health.org.uk/publications/long-reads/better-housing-is-crucial-for-our-health-and-the-covid-19-recovery

## 7 No Nails

*It is one of hundreds of thousands*: Lord Richard Best, 'Conversion of private rented homes to social housing could help turn the tide of this crisis', *Inside Housing*, 8 April 2021, www.insidehousing.co.uk/comment/comment/conversion-of-private-rented-homes-to-social-housing-could-help-turn-the-tide-of-this-crisis-70325

*it gives tenants the right to take them to court*: Karen Buck, 'My Homes (Fitness for Human Habitation) Bill becomes law', 30 January 2019, www.karenbuck.org.uk/campaigns/2019/01/30/my-homes-fitness-for-human-habitation-bill-becomes-law/

*A 'non-decent' home*: Ministry of Housing, Communities and Local Government, *English Housing Survey 2017 to 2018: Private rented sector*, National Statistics (2019). Available at assets.publishing.service.gov.uk/government/uploads/system/uploads/attachment_data/file/817630/EHS_2017-18_PRS_Report.pdf

*The 2019/20 English Housing Survey*: 'The English Housing Survey 2019–20 – what did we learn?', HomeLet, 28 July 2018, homelet.co.uk/landlord-insurance/landlord-lowdown-blog/article/the-english-housing-survey-2019-20-what-did-we-lea

*'piecemeal …' '… everyday experiences of poor conditions'*: Dave Cowan, 'Closing the Gaps: Health and Safety in the Home', University of Bristol Law School blog, 14 November 2017, legalresearch.blogs.bris.ac.uk/2017/11/closing-the-gaps-health-and-safety-in-the-home/

*'fit for human habitation'*: Wendy Wilson, *Homes (Fitness for Human Habitation) Bill 2017–19*, House of Commons Library (14 December 2018). Available at researchbriefings.files.parliament.uk/documents/CBP-8185/CBP-8185.pdf

*Section 11 of the Landlord and Tenant Act 1985*: www.legislation.gov.uk/ukpga/1985/70

*the legislation provided no clear definition*: Sayeeda Choudhury, 'How soon should a landlord address disrepair? How long is too long?', Hodge Jones & Allen blog, 13 October 2020, www.hja.net/expert-comments/blog/housing-help/how-soon-should-a-landlord-address-disrepair-how-long-is-too-long/

*The tenant could therefore not get any compensation*: www.bacommercial.com/case-law/quick-v-taff-ely-borough-council-1985/

*There were similar cases and failed appeals*: Andrew Dymond, 'Housing law', *Law Society Gazette*, 8 March 2002, www.lawgazette.co.uk/news/housing-law/36422.article

*voted down by 309 Conservative Party MPs*: fullfact.org/economy/did-mps-vote-against-homes-having-be-made-fit-live-in/

*somewhere between 1 million and 3 million privately rented homes*: Benjamin Kentish, 'Third of private rented homes fail basic health and safety standards, new analysis finds', *Independent*, 11 August 2017, www.independent.co.uk/news/uk/home-news/private-rental-homes-health-safety-standards-fail-third-landlords-lease-flats-houses-a7883016.html

*Data from the 2020/21 English Housing Survey*: Department for Levelling Up, Housing and Communities, *English Housing Survey: Headline Report, 2020–21*, National Statistics (2021), p. 45. Available at assets.publishing.service.gov.uk/government/uploads/system/uploads/attachment_data/file/1039214/2020-21_EHS_Headline_Report.pdf

*an 18 per cent decline in the number of legal challenges brought*: Owen Bowcott, 'Thousands left homeless by shortage of legal aid lawyers, say charities', *Guardian*, 18 December 2016, www.theguardian.com/society/2016/dec/18/thousands-homeless-shortage-legal-aid-lawyers-charities

*the Legal Aid Agency (LAA) effectively closed face-to-face advice*: 'Advice deserts set to grow as LAA tenders fail to attract bids', Legal Action Group, April 2018, www.lag.org.uk/article/204777/advice-deserts-set-to-grow-as-laa-tenders-fail-to-attract-bids

*'abolish "no fault evictions" under section 21'*: *Protecting rough sleepers and renters: Interim Report – First Report of Session 2019–21*, House of Commons/Housing, Communities and Local Government Committee (22 May 2020). Available at committees.parliament.uk/publications/1216/documents/10264/default/

*the second most expensive childcare system in the world*: Vivien Pailas, 'The high cost of childcare in the UK and why it matters', Pregnant Then Screwed, 7 June 2019, pregnantthenscrewed.com/2019/06/07/the-high-cost-of-childcare-in-the-uk-and-why-it-matters/

*Freedom of Information requests submitted by Generation Rent*: Vicky Spratt, 'Thousands living in mould-ridden, dangerous homes received no help from councils against landlords, data shows', *i Paper*, 28 April 2021, inews.co.uk/opinion/mould-dangerous-homes-no-help-councils-landlords-data-974080

*'squalor in modern Britain'*: Tamsin Rutter, 'Tackling squalor in Britain's homes: five to follow on Twitter', *Guardian*, 4 August 2014, www.theguardian.com/society-professionals/2014/aug/04/tackling-squalor-britains-homes-five-follow-twitter

*'poor quality and inefficient housing …'*: Yamina Saheb, Sophie Shnapp and Daniele Paci, *From nearly-Zero Energy Buildings to net-Zero Energy Districts*, Joint Research Centre, European Commission (2019), e3p.jrc.ec.europa.eu/sites/default/files/documents/publications/2018-12-18_from_nearly_zero_energy_buildings_to_net_zero_energy_districts_final_for_pubsy_upload2.pdf

*as much as £1.4 billion a year*: Mike Roys et al., *The Full Cost of Poor Housing*, BRE Trust/IHS (2016). Available at www.brebookshop.com/samples/327671.pdf

*17 per cent of children with severe asthma*: Ian Watson et al., *Making a Difference: Housing and Health: A Case for Investment Executive Summary, 2019*, BRE Trust/Public Health Wales NHS Trust. Available at phw.nhs.wales/files/housing-and-health-reports/a-case-for-investment-executive-summary/

*40 per cent of people who received central heating improvements*: www.gov.scot/binaries/content/documents/govscot/publications/strategy-plan/2016/10/action-plan-deliver-affordable-warmth-rural-scotland-proposed-scottish-rural/documents/00508138-pdf/00508138-pdf/govscot%3Adocument/00508138.pdf

*mothers were more likely to suffer clinical depression*: Dawn Foster, 'Poor housing is bad for your mental health', *Guardian*, 4 February 2016, www.theguardian.com/housing-network/2016/feb/04/poor-housing-bad-mental-health; www.nhsconfed.org/publications/innovation-housing-care-and-support

*calling for the consumer rights*: Lewis Shand Smith, *Consumer Rights in the Private Rented Sector*, The Smith Institute (2020). Available at www.smith-institute.org.uk/book/consumer-rights-in-the-private-rented-sector/

*the database was completely empty*: Simon Goodley, 'Tenants will get access to rogue landlord database, says PM', *Guardian*, 24 October 2018, www.theguardian.com/business/2018/oct/24/government-policing-of-rogue-landlords-labelled-pathetic *only four entries had been made*: Simon Goodley, 'No rogue landlords issued with banning orders in 12 months', *Guardian*, 15 April 2019, www.theguardian.com/ business/2019/apr/15/no-rogue-landlords-issued-with-banning-orders-in-12-months

*there were still only twenty-one names listed*: Will Kirkman, 'Flagship Government register to track thousands of rogue landlords has just TWENTY ONE names on it in almost two years since its launch', This is Money, 6 February 2020, www.thisismoney. co.uk/money/buytolet/article-7960979/Government-rogue-landlords-register-just-21-names-in.html

*A consultation had been opened in 2019*: www.gov.uk/government/consultations/ rogue-landlord-database-reform

*10,500 rogue landlords operating in England*: Simon Goodley, 'Banned but still in business: law fails to stop rogue landlords', *Guardian*, 23 October 2018, www. theguardian.com/business/2018/oct/23/rogue-landlords-rental-law-guardian-itv-news

*This amounted to at least 200 evictions*: Laurna Robertson, 'PRS landlord to evict tenants on housing benefit', *Inside Housing*, 6 January 2014, archive.ph/20140112125256/ http:/www.insidehousing.co.uk/tenancies/prs-landlord-to-evict-tenants-on-housing-benefit/7001479.article#selection-421.0-433.16

*'Rents have gone north …' '… are on Housing Benefit.'*: Emma Lunn, 'Buy-to-let property supremo shuts door on housing benefit tenants', *Guardian*, 4 January 2014, www.theguardian.com/money/2014/jan/04/buy-to-let-landlord-evicts-housing-benefit-tenants

*46 per cent chance of being evicted*: Citizens Advice, 'Complain and you're out: Research confirms link between tenant complaints and revenge eviction', 24 August 2018, www. citizensadvice.org.uk/about-us/about-us1/media/press-releases/complain-and-youre-out-research-confirms-link-between-tenant-complaints-and-revenge-eviction/

*the vast majority of landlords have the financial resources*: Hannah Gousy, *Can't Complain: Why Poor Conditions Prevail in Private Rented Homes*, Shelter (March 2014). Available at assets.ctfassets.net/6sxvmndnpnos/xndVNspFXTIoldOF3JQRC/ e90236b995fa69eb5cc2bf87f7794fff/6430_04_9_Million_Renters_Policy_Report_ Proof_10_opt.pdf

## 8 Modern Slums

*In 2016 just over 44 per cent of the homes*: North Somerset Council, *Proposal for a Selective Licensing Scheme of the Private Rented Sector in Weston-Super-Mare (Part)* (2016). Available at n-somerset.inconsult.uk/gf2.ti/-/658722/19978309.1/PDF/-/

Proposal_for_selective_licensing_scheme_in_part_of_WsM_D.pdf. All statistics cited are North Somerset Council's own.

*by 2017 … just above the national average*: North Somerset Council, *Review of Housing Conditions* (2017). Available at n-somerset.inconsult.uk/gf2.ti/-/870786/32422693.1/PDF/-/Review_of_Housing_Conditions_consultation.pdf

*concentration of deprivation in Weston*: 'Exploring local income deprivation', Office for National Statistics (24 May 2021), www.ons.gov.uk/visualisations/dvc1371/#/E07000223

*3,300 families long*: North Somerset Council, 'Applying for Social Housing' [n.d.], n-somerset.gov.uk/my-services/housing/applying-social-housing

*The average price of a home in North Somerset*: Gareth Newnham, 'House prices in North Somerset continue to rise despite Brexit looming', *Weston Mercury*, 28 February 2019, www.thewestonmercury.co.uk/news/house-prices-in-north-somerset-increase-five-percent-in-a-year-1-5909280

*the average property price in North Somerset*: See, for instance, Eleanor Young, 'House prices soar as first-time buyers struggle to purchase homes', *Weston Mercury*, 2 August 2018, www.thewestonmercury.co.uk/news/people-turn-to-renting-over-buying-in-north-somerset-1-5633352

*'out of every ten properties we sell'*: Heather Pickstock, 'Why Weston-super-Mare is the town everyone wants to move to', *Somerset Live*, 29 June 2021, www.somersetlive.co.uk/news/somerset-news/weston-super-mare-town-everyone-5512686

*Children with asthma are put at risk*: A. M. Tod et al., 'Understanding Influences and Decisions of Households with Children with Asthma Regarding Temperature and Humidity in the Home in Winter: A Qualitative Study', *BMJ Open* 6:1 (2016).

*Damp and cold tend to produce*: Andrew Brookes, 'Leaving Me Breathless – Damp, Mould and Asthma', Anthony Gold blog, 18 August 2011, anthonygold.co.uk/latest/blog/leaving-me-breathless-damp-mould-and-asthma/

*a compulsory national register*: CIH and CIEH, *A licence to rent: A joint research project between Chartered Institute of Environmental Health and Chartered Institute of Housing* (January 2019), www.cieh.org/media/2552/a-licence-to-rent.pdf

*this still hasn't happened*: David Cox, '"No plans" to introduce national landlord register', Propertymark, 7 November 2019, www.propertymark.co.uk/resource/no-plans-to-introduce-national-landlord-register.html

*'clear evidence that property standards have been improved'*: CIH and CIEH, *A licence to rent*, p. 10.

*the scheme is limited to 20 per cent*: www.gov.uk/government/publications/selective-licensing-in-the-private-rented-sector-a-guide-for-local-authorities

*'adopt a pragmatic approach'*: Stephen Maunder, 'Mapped: the areas where buy-to-let landlords need licences in 2020', *Which?*, 20 April 2020, www.which.co.uk/news/2020/04/mapped-the-areas-where-buy-to-let-landlords-need-licences-in-2020/

*in London's East End*: Steven, 'East London rent strikes, 1938–9', libcom.org, 26 June 2017, libcom.org/history/east-london-rent-strikes-1938-9

*which 9,500 tenants refused to pay*: Bert Moorhouse, Mary Wilson and Chris Chamberlain, 'Rent Strikes – Direct Action and the Working Class', in Ralph Miliband and John Saville (eds), *The Socialist Register* (London: Merlin Press, 1972), pp. 133–56.

*a series of demonstrations in early 1969*: Ibid.

*'protest is also not a matter … lower-class groups at all'*: Frances Fox Piven and Richard Cloward, *Poor People's Movements: Why They Succeed, How They Fail*, 2nd edition (1977; New York: Vintage Books, 1979)

*the Heart of Weston Steering Group*: Donna Davies and Helen Yeo, *Weston-super-Mare Central ward: Health Needs Assessment*, Public Health, North Somerset Council (May 2016). Available at n-somerset.gov.uk/sites/default/files/2020-05/Central%20Ward%20health%20needs%20assessment_0.pdf

*a detrimental impact*: Kim McKee and Adriana Mihaela Soaita, 'The "frustrated" housing aspirations of generation rent', UK Collaborative Centre for Housing Evidence (2018). Available at housingevidence.ac.uk/wp-content/uploads/2018/08/R2018_06_01_Frustrated_Housing_Aspirations_of_Gen_Rent.pdf

*what renting is actually doing*: Amy Clair and Amanda Hughes, 'Housing and Health: New Evidence Using Biomarker Data', *Journal of Epidemiology and Community Health* 73:3 (2019), 256–62.

*what this protein can tell us*: Amanda Hughes et al., 'Unemployment and Inflammatory Markers in England, Wales and Scotland, 1998–2012: Meta-analysis of Results from 12 Studies', *Brain, Behavior, and Immunity* 64 (2017), 91–102.

*'Larger, more spacious homes … people living in detached houses'*: Amy Clair, 'Homes, health, and COVID-19: how poor housing adds to the hardship of the coronavirus crisis', Social Market Foundation, 2 April 2020, www.smf.co.uk/commentary_podcasts/homes-health-and-covid-19-how-poor-housing-adds-to-the-hardship-of-the-coronavirus-crisis/

*'The challenges brought on by Covid-19 … particularly affecting women and children'*: Ibid.

*as much as £1.4 billion a year*: Mike Roys et al., *The Full Cost of Poor Housing*, BRE Trust/IHS (2016). Available at www.brebookshop.com/samples/327671.pdf

*'We found that CCGs … their housing circumstances changed'*: This interview originally appeared in my column in the *i Paper*. See 'The housing crisis is a public health crisis – renting is making people sick', 23 January 2020, inews.co.uk/opinion/ the-housing-crisis-is-a-public-health-crisis-renting-is-making-people-sick-389231

*'the council decided not to introduce a licensing scheme for all landlords'*: For more information, see n-somerset.gov.uk/sites/default/files/2020-04/17-18%20PC%2068%20 signed.pdf

*'The landlord lobby effectively killed it.'*: Ibid.

## 9 The Shadow Private Renting Sector

*£278 million cut from its budget*: 'Mayor calls austerity an "act of national self-harm"', BBC News, 22 June 2020, www.bbc.com/news/uk-england-53109087

*the highest rate of child poverty*: Jo Winrow, 'Child poverty across Bradford is highest in Yorkshire', *Telegraph & Argus*, 5 April 2021, www.thetelegraphandargus.co.uk/ news/19204325.child-poverty-across-bradford-highest-yorkshire/

*According to the official statistics*: City of Bradford Metropolitan District Council, *A Review of Homelessness in Bradford* (2019). Available at bradford.gov.uk/media/5756/ bradford-homelessness-evidence-base-2020-to-2025.pdf

*just over one fifth (22 per cent) of rough sleepers*: Combined Homelessness and Information Network, *CHAIN Annual Report: Greater London, April 2020–March 2021*, Greater London Authority (2021).

*2,000 of the people housed*: Ministry of Housing, Communities and Local Government, *Investigation into the housing of rough sleepers during the COVID-19 pandemic*, National Audit Office (11 January 2021). Available at www.nao.org.uk/wp-content/ uploads/2021/01/Investigation-into-the-housing-of-rough-sleepers-during-the-COVID-19-pandemic.pdf

*the High Court ruled that there was a legal basis*: NRPF Network, 'High Court rules councils can accommodate rough sleepers with no recourse to public funds during the Covid-19 pandemic', 22 March 2021, www.nrpfnetwork.org.uk/news/ accommodating-rough-sleepers

*This ruling came out of an important legal case*: 'The Queen (on the application of Timon Ncube) v. Brighton and Hove City Council and The Secretary of State for Housing, Communities and Local Government', Royal Courts of Justice, EWHC 578 (Admin), (2021). Available at www.bailii.org/ew/cases/EWHC/Admin/2021/578.html

*Bradford's textile industry … owed its survival*: www.saltairecollection.org/wp-content/uploads/Migrations-to-work-in-Bradford-1820-1970s.pdf

*fourth-highest number of manufacturing jobs*: www.bradford.gov.uk/business/bradford-economy/about-bradfords-economy/

*'10 per cent lower over a 20-year period'*: Theresa May, 'Home Secretary speech on "An immigration system that works in the national interest"', transcript of speech delivered on 12 December 2012. Available at www.gov.uk/government/speeches/home-secretary-speech-on-an-immigration-system-that-works-in-the-national-interest

*'Immigration "causing housing crisis"' (2003)*: *Daily Mail*, 20 July 2003, www.dailymail.co.uk/news/article-189224/Immigration-causing-housing-crisis.html

*'Revealed: How HALF of all social housing in England goes to people born abroad' (2012)*: Gerri Peev, *Daily Mail*, 15 April 2012, www.dailymail.co.uk/news/article-2130095/Calls-British-people-given-priority-social-housing-queue-revealed-foreigners-HALF-properties.html

*'We don't have a housing crisis – we have a population crisis' (2017)*: Richard Littlejohn, *Daily Mail*, 17 November 2017, www.dailymail.co.uk/debate/article-5091383/We-don-t-housing-crisis-population-crisis.html

*'Immigration has pushed house prices up by 20 per cent over a 25-year period, says Tory minister' (2018)*: John Stevens, *Daily Mail*, 8 April 2018, www.dailymail.co.uk/news/article-5592189/Immigration-pushed-UK-house-prices-20-cent.html

*no evidence that social housing allocation favours migrants*: 'Migrants and Housing', *Postnote* 560 (August 2017), Parliamentary Office of Science and Technology. Available at researchbriefings.files.parliament.uk/documents/POST-PN-0560/POST-PN-0560.pdf

*a Hungarian economic migrant needs to have requested settled status*: for more information see brexit.kormany.hu/residency-and-visas

*largest ever public survey on immigration*: Jill Rutter and Rosie Carter, British Future and HOPE not hate, *National Conversation on Immigration: Final Report*, National Conversation (September 2018). Available at nationalconversation.uk/wp-content/uploads/2018/09/FINAL-2-national-conversation-september-report-2018-09-final.pdf

*According to Oxford University's Migration Observatory*: Dr Carlos Vargas-Silva and

Mariña Fernández-Reino, *Briefing: Migrants and Housing in the UK: Experiences and Impacts*, The Migration Observatory (22 October 2019), migrationobservatory.ox.ac.uk/resources/briefings/migrants-and-housing-in-the-uk-experiences-and-impacts/

*an increase of immigrants equal to 1 per cent*: Filipa Sà, 'Immigration and House Prices in the UK', *Economic Journal* 125:587 (2015), 1393–424.

*'In the early years … similar indigenous households.'*: Christine Whitehead et al., *The Impact of Migration on Access to Housing and the Housing Market: A Project for the Migration Advisory Committee: Final Report*, LSE (16 December 2011). Available at assets.publishing.service.gov.uk/government/uploads/system/uploads/attachment_data/file/257238/lse-housing.pdf

*any caps on immigration would harm housebuilding rates*: Katie Allen, 'Construction industry in plea to retain migrant workers', *Guardian*, 3 March 2015, www.theguardian.com/business/economics-blog/2015/mar/03/construction-industry-plea-retain-migrant-workers

*Statutory overcrowding is a criminal offence*: for more information see england.shelter.org.uk/professional_resources/legal/housing_conditions/overcrowding

*'the [infected] person to self-isolate …' '… surfaces or objects (e.g., towels)'*: Environmental Modelling Group, the Scientific Pandemic Insights Group on Behaviours and the Scientific Pandemic Influenza Group on Modelling, 'Reducing within- and between-household transmission in light of new variant SARS-CoV-2', Scientific Advisory Group for Emergencies (15 January 2021). Available at assets.publishing.service.gov.uk/government/uploads/system/uploads/attachment_data/file/952799/s1020-Reducing-within-between-household-transmission.pdf

*'use a separate bathroom'*: Vicky Spratt, 'People in overcrowded housing should have been given Covid isolation hotel rooms – lives could have been saved', *i Paper*, 18 March 2021, inews.co.uk/opinion/overcrowded-housing-people-covid-isolation-hotel-rooms-saved-lives-917766

*according to analysis from Professor Rebecca Tunstall*: Ibid.

*we know coronavirus is airborne*: Julian W. Tang et al., 'Covid-19 has redefined airborne transmission', *BMJ* 373 (2021).

*such a measure here would have prevented*: The Ethnicity Sub-group of the Scientific Advisory Group for Emergencies (SAGE), 'Housing, Household Transmission and Ethnicity' (26 November 2020). Available at assets.publishing.service.gov.uk/government/uploads/system/uploads/attachment_data/file/943178/S0923_housing_household_transmission_and_ethnicity.pdf

*Only 2 per cent … Black African, 14 per cent*: www.ethnicity-facts-figures.service.gov.uk/ housing/housing-conditions/overcrowded-households/latest

*'69 per cent of infections were at home'*: Mingwang Shen et al., 'Assessing the Effects of Metropolitan-wide Quarantine on the Spread of COVID-19 in Public Space and Households', *International Journal of Infectious Diseases* 96 (2020), 503–5, www.sciencedirect.com/science/article/pii/S120197122030326X

*Professor Tunstall also cited a UK study*: Christopher Jarvis et al. on behalf of CMMID COVID-19 Working Group, 'Report for SPI-M-O and SAGE: Comparison of mean contacts for Tier 4 and non-Tier 4 areas in England from CoMix social contact survey: Report for survey week 38', London School of Hygiene and Tropical Medicine, 21 December 2020. Available at assets.publishing.service.gov.uk/government/uploads/ system/uploads/attachment_data/file/955026/s1000-comix-report-survey-week-38.pdf

*overcrowding was aiding transmission*: Adam Tinson and Amy Clair, *Better Housing Is Crucial for Our Health and the COVID-19 Recovery*, The Health Foundation (2020). Available at www.health.org.uk/publications/long-reads/better-housing-is-crucial-for-our-health-and-the-covid-19-recovery

*42 per cent of landlords*: 'Migrants and Housing', *Postnote*.

*an exodus of EU workers from Britain*: Léonie Chao-Fong, 'EU workers departing "will leave UK industries in total crisis"', *Big Issue*, 23 June 2021, www.bigissue.com/latest/ employment/eu-workers-leaving-will-leave-uk-industries-in-total-crisis/

*poor conditions in the private rented sector remained commonplace*: Daniel Lavelle, 'Only 39 rogue landlords and agents hit with banning orders', *Guardian*, 5 April 2021, www.theguardian.com/society/2021/apr/05/only-39-rogue-landlords-and-agents-hit-with-banning-orders

*those guilty of unlawful eviction or harassment*: Daniel Lavelle, 'Only 39 rogue landlords and agents hit with banning orders', *Guardian*, 5 April 2021, www.theguardian.com/ society/2021/apr/05/only-39-rogue-landlords-and-agents-hit-with-banning-orders

*there are currently about 13,000 people*: Anti-Slavery International, 'Slavery in the UK', www.antislavery.org/slavery-today/slavery-uk/

*surged by 52 per cent*: May Bulman, 'Surge in suspected modern slavery victims waiting years for Home Office decisions, figures show', *Independent*, 2 January 2020, www.independent.co.uk/news/uk/home-news/modern-slavery-victims-home-office-decisions-delays-nrm-a9261331.html

*the average time taken from referral*: Home Office, *Modern Slavery: National Referral Mechanism and Duty to Notify Statistics: UK, Quarter 4 2020 – October to December*

(2021). Available at assets.publishing.service.gov.uk/government/uploads/system/uploads/attachment_data/file/970945/national-referral-mechanism-statistics-uk-quarter-4-2020-october-to-december-hosb0721.pdf

*rough sleepers from EU countries*: May Bulman, 'Surge in rough sleepers sent back to EU countries at height of lockdown', *Independent*, 11 March 2021, www.independent.co.uk/news/uk/home-news/surge-in-eu-nationals-reconnected-to-home-countries-at-height-of-lockdown-b1814590.html

## 10 Nearly Legal

*Her home was the Old Rectory*: This report originally appeared in the *i Paper*: Heather Saul and Vicky Spratt, 'Property guardian company prosecuted over former care home where more than 30 guardians lived with one kitchen', 29 March 2019, inews.co.uk/opinion/comment/property-guardian-company-prosecuted-over-former-care-home-where-more-than-30-guardians-lived-with-one-kitchen-274724

*Licences generally offer renters*: See england.shelter.org.uk/housing_advice/private_renting/types_of_renting_agreement

*by installing guardians and reclassifying a building as domestic*: This practice was effectively ended by the Court of Appeal in December 2020. See 'London Borough of Southwark v. Ludgate House Ltd & Anor', The Court of Appeal (Civil Division), EWCA Civ 1637 (2020). Available at www.bailii.org/ew/cases/EWCA/Civ/2020/1637.html. See also nearlylegal.co.uk/2020/12/property-guardians-exclusive-occupation-and-non-domestic-rates/

*young people on low incomes*: Tim Lowe, 'Opinion: Why we should follow the French by considering guardianship as a way to fill empty homes with those in housing need', *City A.M.*,17 December 2018, www.cityam.com/opinion-why-we-should-follow-french-considering/

*'Join the many professionals…' '… for very little money.'*: Taken from Alexander Vasudevan, Gloria Dawson and Mara Ferreri, 'Living Precariously: Property Guardianship and the Flexible City', *Transactions of the Institute of British Geographers* 42:2 (2016), 246–59.

*'intermediate housing'*: Sadiq Khan posited the idea of intermediary housing in March 2021 to address the fact that key workers were being pushed into unstable housing and, ultimately, further and further out of the capital. See Nathaniel Barker, 'Khan confirms plans to prioritise key workers for intermediate affordable housing', *Inside Housing*, 12 March 2021, www.insidehousing.co.uk/news/news/khan-confirms-plans-to-prioritise-key-workers-for-intermediate-affordable-housing-69960

*one of the biggest challenges it faced*: 'NHS staff unable to find rental homes in Cornwall', BBC News, 4 November 2021, www.bbc.co.uk/news/uk-england-cornwall-59154103

*'sheds critical light …' '… urban dispossession and displacement'*: Vasudevan, Dawson and Ferreri, 'Living Precariously'.

*'inadequate' and 'unsafe'*: 'Care home to close after inspectors branded it "inadequate" – leaving residents needing new home for Christmas', *Essex County Standard*, 13 December 2016, www.gazette-news.co.uk/news/14961635.care-home-to-close-after-inspectors-branded-it-inadequate-leaving-residents-needing-new-home-for-christmas/

*The company was also added*: My investigation into the links between local government and property guardian companies originally appeared in the *i Paper*. See Vicky Spratt, 'The UK councils who have used private companies to house low-income workers in empty buildings', 20 December 2019, inews.co.uk/opinion/the-uk-councils-who-have-used-private-companies-to-house-low-income-workers-in-empty-buildings-376283

*being marketed off-plan to investors in east Asia*: Loretta Lees, 'Challenging the Gentrification of Council Estates in London', Urban Transformations blog, 16 March 2018, www.urbantransformations.ox.ac.uk/blog/2018/challenging-the-gentrification-of-council-estates-in-london/

*'the clustering of businesses …' '… one place from another'*: Jessica Perera, '"You need to look closely, because Elephant and Castle is a model for other dispossession projects"', Institute of Race Relations, 28 November 2019, irr.org.uk/article/you-need-to-look-closely-because-elephant-and-castle-is-a-model-for-other-dispossession-projects/

*'reassure the growing number …' … 'bedrock of rights'*: Vicky Spratt, 'Property guardians: Government considering proposals to regulate the industry', *i Paper*, 26 March 2019, inews.co.uk/news/property-guardians-government-considering-proposals-to-regulate-the-industry-273452

## 11 Fallout

*to ensure the homeless man would 'not be forgotten'*: Jacob Phillips, 'Parliament staff help raise £5,000 after death of homeless man', Sky News, 21 December 2018, news.sky.com/story/parliament-staff-help-raise-5-000-after-death-of-homeless-man-11587957

*'Every death of someone … a moral duty to act.'*: 'Deaths of Homeless People', House of Commons Debate, vol. 651, col. 988 (20 December 2018). Available at hansard.parliament.uk/Commons/2018-12-20/debates/D15752D5-62E1-4A39-8EBB-63D770785E30/DeathsOfHomelessPeople

*according to the Members of Parliament register of interests*: Jim Scott, 'Did Thirsk and Malton MP Kevin Hollinrake earn anything from second jobs and donors?', *Northern Echo*, 12 November 2021, www.thenorthernecho.co.uk/news/19711041. much-thirsk-mp-kevin-hollinrake-paid-donors-jobs/

*with a total profit after tax of £1,191,094*: Companies House, 'Hunters Property Group Limited, Annual Report and Financial Statements for the year ended 31 December 2018'.

*'Who, for example … those on housing benefit.'*: Kevin Hollinrake, 'Tenant Fee Ban? Yes, but how will we enforce it?', 7 September 2017, www.kevinhollinrake.org.uk/news/ tenant-fee-ban-yes-how-will-we-enforce-it

*Hollinrake went to work for Prudential*: 'About Kevin Hollinrake', www. kevinhollinrake.org.uk/about-kevin-hollinrake

*unfit for human habitation … unaffordable for most people*: Hannah Gousy, *Safe and Decent Homes: Solutions for a Better Private Rented Sector*, Shelter (2014). Available at england.shelter.org.uk/__data/assets/pdf_file/0003/1039530/FINAL_SAFE_AND_ DECENT_HOMES_REPORT-_USE_FOR_LAUNCH.pdf

*'burning injustices' … 'the government I lead …'*: Theresa May, 'Statement from the new Prime Minister Theresa May', transcript of speech delivered on 13 July 2016. Available at www.gov.uk/government/speeches/statement-from-the-new-prime-minister- theresa-may

*Boris Johnson's increase in 2011*: Jenny Jones, 'Who can afford Boris Johnson's new affordable housing?', *Guardian*, 26 July 2011, www.theguardian.com/housing- network/2011/jul/26/boris-johnson-jenny-jones-housing

*'result in unnecessary … rents for tenants'*: 'Housing and Planning Bill', House of Commons Debate, vol. 604, col. 706 (12 January 2016). Available at hansard.parliament. uk/commons/2016-01-12/debates/16011271000002/HousingAndPlanningBill

*on the market for £3.5 million*: Mike Laycock, 'Historic home on market for £3.5 million', *York Press*, 16 July 2008, www.yorkpress.co.uk/news/3209854. historic-home-on-market-for-35-million/

*it was adopted as government policy*: Oxfordshire Liberal Democrats, 'Lib Dem campaigners win campaign to abolish rental fees', 27 November 2016, www. oxonlibdems.uk/2016_renterreforms; see also commonslibrary.parliament.uk/ research-briefings/cbp-8756/

*Eighty-six per cent of Britons would buy their own home*: Glen Bramley, 'Housing:

Homes, Planning and Changing Policies', in *British Social Attitudes 28*, NatCen Social Research (2012), p. 123, www.bsa.natcen.ac.uk/media/38952/bsa28_8housing.pdf

*63 per cent of households in Britain*: Race Disparity Unit, 'Home ownership', Ministry of Housing, Communities and Local Government (2020). Available at www.ethnicity-facts-figures.service.gov.uk/housing/owning-and-renting/home-ownership/latest

*the convention had always been*: D. Dorling, C. J. Pattie and R. J. Johnston, *Voting and the Housing Market: The Impact of New Labour* (London: Council of Mortgage Lenders, 1999). Available at www.geog.ox.ac.uk/research/transformations/gis/papers/dannydorling_publication_id4095.pdf

*the Labour Party won more support than the Conservatives*: Ibid.

*'Housing for the Many'*: Labour Party, *Housing for the Many: A Labour Party Green Paper* (2018). Available at labour.org.uk/wp-content/uploads/2018/04/Housing-for-the-Many-final.pdf

*studies have found that as homeownership has risen*: Some very interesting research has emerged about how house prices impact politics. As Ben Ansell of Nuffield College, Oxford, and his co-researcher David Adler argue in their 2019 paper 'Housing and Populism', people who had benefited from rising house prices in the 2010s were more likely to vote Remain in the EU referendum than those who had not. In Bristol, for instance, they found that wards with inexpensive housing, such as Hartcliffe and Withywood and Filwood, showed more than 60 per cent support for Leave. By contrast, wards with expensive housing, such as Clifton and Redland, had very low support for Leave – under 25 per cent. Overall, they found a very strong positive relationship between house prices and support for Remain. Areas with low median house prices of around £100,000 in 2015 averaged a 30 per cent Remain–70 per cent Leave split, whereas those with high median prices above £500,000 averaged the reverse: 70 per cent Remain–30 per cent Leave. In short, those who had profited from house price increases were happy with the status quo (i.e. being in the EU) and those who had not were prepared to take a risk (i.e. vote to leave). In subsequent papers, Ansell has explored this further. To read more, I'd recommend the following: www.tandfonline.com/doi/full/10.1080/01402382.2019.1615322

*Labour commissioned a large-scale review*: Julie Rugg and David Rhodes, *The Evolving Private Rented Sector: Its Contribution and Potential* (York: Centre for Housing Policy, University of York, 2018). Available at www.york.ac.uk/media/news-and-events/pressreleases/2018/the-evolving-private-rented-sector.pdf

*a decisive shift for Labour*: Vicky Spratt, 'Labour has decided to challenge the Tories as a party of homeowners', *i Paper*, 29 September 2021, inews.co.uk/news/analysis/labour-challenge-tories-party-home-ownership-1220698

## 12 The Utopian Realism of Housing First

*'family breakdowns'* … *'the spread of psychoactive drugs'*: Jasmine Andersson, 'Rise in homelessness is not our fault, Conservative housing secretary says', *i Paper*, 20 December 2018, inews.co.uk/news/homelessness-uk-figures-housing-secretary-james-brtokenshire-182740

*165 per cent in less than a decade*: 'Number of rough sleepers in England soars by 165% since 2010', Crisis, 31 January 2019, www.crisis.org.uk/about-us/media-centre/number-of-rough-sleepers-in-england-soars-by-165-since-2010/

*'This is not a coincidence …'*: Y-Foundation, *A Home of Your Own: Housing First and Ending Homelessness in Finland* (2017). Available at ysaatio.fi/assets/files/2018/01/A_Home_of_Your_Own_lowres_spreads.pdf

*the Scottish government's Housing to 2040 policy*: Shelter, *Housing First in Scotland: Topic Briefing* (April 2019). Available at assets.ctfassets.net/6sqqfrl11sfj/3UloXNIhEszhRHP8z8osti/77a8033ff46bef8ee9c0c49b4f0dca65/Housing_First_in_Scotland_FINAL.pdf

*82 per cent of people helped to stay*: 'Housing First Pathfinder interim evaluation report published', 22 November 2021, homelessnetwork.scot/2021/09/22/housing-first-pathfinder-interim-evaluation-report-published/

*enshrine a right to housing*: If you'd like to read more about this, Geraldine Van Bueren QC, a professor of international human rights law at Queen Mary University of London, and a former Equality and Human Rights Commissioner, has written well on it for the *Guardian*: 'A right to housing should be part of UK law', 1 March 2016, www.theguardian.com/society/2016/mar/01/right-to-housing-uk-law-homelessness

*'entails obligations …'*: Harald Siebler, 'Article 14: Property and the right of inheritance shall be guaranteed', deutschland.de, 21 May 2019, www.deutschland.de/en/topic/politics/the-german-basic-law-article-14-property-and-the-right-of-inheritance-shall-be

*Article 65 of Portugal's constitution*: Sandra Pereira, 'A fundamental right', *Parliament Magazine*, 31 March 2020, www.theparliamentmagazine.eu/news/article/a-fundamental-right

*Costa Rica's constitution states*: Constitute Project, 'Costa Rica's Constitution of 1949 with Amendments through 2011', tr. Maria del Carmen Gress. Available at constituteproject.org/constitution/Costa_Rica_2011.pdf

*80,000 new low-cost homes were built*: 'The right to shelter', *New Internationalist* 229 (5 March 1992), newint.org/features/1992/03/05/medals4

*high rents are increasingly locking younger people*: Pereira, 'A fundamental right'.

*the issue of international investors*: Reality Check Team, 'Rent control: Does it work?', BBC News, 3 February 2019, www.bbc.co.uk/news/business-47028342

*particularly in Scotland*: Douglas Maxwell, a researcher at the University of Oxford's law faculty, examines this here: 'Socio-Economic Rights and Land Reform in Scotland: Learning from South Africa', Oxford Human Rights Hub, 3 December 2018, ohrh. law.ox.ac.uk/socio-economic-rights-and-land-reform-in-scotland-learning-from-south-africa/

*right to live somewhere in security*: www.ohchr.org/en/issues/housing/pages/internationalstandards.aspx

*The incorporation of the right to housing*: For further reading on this, including the potential pitfalls and difficulties of such an idea, try Jessie Hohmann, *The Right to Housing: Law, Concepts, Possibilities* (Oxford: Hart Publishing, 2013).

*'Everyone In'*: In 2021 the government faced a legal challenge over its flagship Everyone In homelessness scheme amid confusion over whether it'd been scrapped and how local authorities are meant to approach rough sleeping in its wake. For more information, you can read my report for the *i Paper*, 'Government faces legal challenge over flagship homelessness scheme amid claims it's been quietly scrapped', 22 December 2021, inews. co.uk/news/government-homelessness-scheme-everyone-in-judicial-review-1364107

*The government announced additional funding*: Local Government Association, 'Homelessness and temporary accommodation, House of Commons, 2 December 2020' (30 November 2020). Available at www.local.gov.uk/parliament/briefings-and-responses/homelessness-and-temporary-accommodation-house-commons-2

*Social housing waiting lists*: Local Government Association, 'Housing waiting lists could double next year with one in 10 stuck in queue for more than 5 years – new research' (13 October 2021). Available at www.local.gov.uk/about/news/housing-waiting-lists-could-double-next-year-one-10-stuck-queue-more-5-years-new

*our views on social security and immigration*: Patrick Butler, 'Britons' support for welfare benefits at highest level for 20 years – study', *Guardian*, 29 October 2020, www. theguardian.com/society/2020/oct/29/britons-support-for-welfare-benefits-at-highest-level-for-20-years-study

*our social housing stock has plummeted*: Vicky Spratt, 'Jeremy Hunt's Housing First plan is surprisingly radical – but it shows he doesn't understand Britain's housing crisis', *i Paper*, 17 July 2019, inews.co.uk/opinion/columnists/jeremy-hunt-shows-he-doesnt-understand-britains-housing-crisis-31493

*a staggering 73 per cent in five years*: The amount spent on temporary accommodation (TA) by councils in England is published by the Ministry of Housing,

Communities and Local Government (MHCLG). See Shelter, 'Bill for homeless accommodation soars to £1.2 billion', 22 October 2020, england.shelter.org.uk/media/press_release/bill_for_homeless_accommodation_soars_to_1_2_billion

*eleven housing ministers have churned*: Vicky Spratt, 'We've had nine housing ministers in nine years. No wonder we're in such a mess', *i Paper*, 21 November 2019, inews.co.uk/opinion/comment/uk-housing-general-election-party-manifestos-policies-prices-365604

*locally administered Rent Pressure Zones*: www.legislation.gov.uk/asp/2016/19/part/4/chapter/3/crossheading/designation-and-effect-of-rent-pressure-zone

*'We must safeguard … with the plug out.'*: Judith Evans, 'Wales joins Scotland to end sales of Right to Buy council homes', *Financial Times*, 7 August 2016, www.ft.com/content/d4861ee2-5b15-11e6-9f70-badea1b336d4

*a pilot programme to extend the scheme*: Brian Milligan, 'How will the extension of Right to Buy actually work?', BBC News, 28 April 2016, www.bbc.com/news/business-32884747

*the UK needs 3.1 million*: Shelter, 'Three million new social homes key to solving housing crisis', 14 January 2019, england.shelter.org.uk/media/press_release/three_million_new_social_homes_key_to_solving_housing_crisis2

## 13 Out of Options

*the Sugar Hill Close and Wordsworth Drive housing estate*: This story was originally reported in the *i Paper*, where you will find a full statement from Pemberstone and Leeds City Council: Vicky Spratt, '"I'm heartbroken and scared": How gentrification is breaking up a former mining community in Leeds', 21 December 2021, inews.co.uk/news/long-reads/leeds-gentrification-breaking-up-former-mining-community-1361018

*at Seacroft in Leeds*: historicengland.org.uk/images-books/photos/item/P/H00080/001

*ordered to be built in in Chingford*: historicengland.org.uk/images-books/photos/volume/PSA01/04/H00265

*about 20,000 Airey houses were put up'*: 'Airey Homes', Leeds Civic Trust, 10 August 2018, leedscivictrust.org.uk/airey-homes/

*it was bought in 2001 by Pemberstone Group*: Corporate Watch, 'Pemberstone group: We profile the company trying to demolish 70 homes in a Leeds estate', 24 September 2020, corporatewatch.org/pemberstone-group-leeds-estate/

*Pemberstone's original planning application*: 'Council report reiterates commitment to Sugar Hill Close and Wordsworth Drive residents', leeds.gov.uk, 12 October 2021, news.leeds.gov.uk/news/council-report-reiterates-commitment-to-sugar-hill-close-and-wordsworth-drive-residents

*two tower blocks in Manchester's Green Quarter*: Vicky Spratt, 'Our flats have Grenfell-style cladding and we're being forced to pay £10k each to get rid of it', *i Paper*, 8 October 2018, inews.co.uk/opinion/comment/our-flats-have-grenfell-style-cladding-and-were-being-forced-to-pay-10k-each-to-get-rid-of-it-205585

*between £795 and £995 per month*: housesforsaletorent.co.uk/houses/to-rent/west-yorkshire/oulton.html

*rents hit a ten-year high*: Rebecca Marano, 'Leeds rent prices up as Yorkshire and Humber sees 10-year rental growth high', *Yorkshire Evening Post*, 23 September 2021, www.yorkshireeveningpost.co.uk/lifestyle/homes-and-gardens/leeds-rent-prices-up-as-yorkshire-and-humber-sees-10-year-rental-growth-high-3375282

*two-thirds (65 per cent) of private landlords*: Rhianna Abrey, 'Demand for rental housing in Yorkshire and The Humber highest in England and Wales', NRLA, 3 September 2021, www.nrla.org.uk/news/demand-for-rental-housing-in-yorkshire-and-the-humber-highest-in-the-country

*the residents were citing 'gentrification'*: democracy.leeds.gov.uk/documents/s188179/1%2017-0633-FU.pdf

*were beyond repair*: www.kingschambers.com/assets/PDF/news/cases/LEEDS%20 15%20JANUARY%202021.pdf

*produce a profit of about £2.9 million*: democracy.leeds.gov.uk/documents/s216344/1%20 17-06933-FU%20Appeal%20Decision.pdf

*'agreed with both …' '… move from the site'*: Ibid.

*the residents had urged Leeds City Council*: Richard Beecham, '"Can we buy these homes next?" Asks councillor as Leeds council given approval to buy up poor flats', *Leeds Live*, 11 February 2021, www.leeds-live.co.uk/news/leeds-news/can-buy-homes-next-asks-19815402

*26,000 live applications*: Vicky Spratt, '"I'm heartbroken and scared"'.

*The Ministry of Housing became*: Alannah Francis, 'Michael Gove re-brands ministry as Department for Levelling Up, Housing and Communities', *i Paper*, 19 September 2021, inews.co.uk/news/michael-gove-re-brands-ministry-department-for-levelling-up-housing-communities-1206745

*Black people are … of £40,000–£45,000 a year*: These statistics are taken from Shelter's 2021 report *Denied the Right to a Safe Home* (see Shelter, '17.5 million people now impacted by the housing emergency', 26 May 2021, england.shelter.org.uk/media/ press_release/17_5million_people_now_impacted_by_the_housing_emergency_). All calculations were made using ONS, national census or Family Resource Survey data. Trans people were not specifically referred to in the Shelter report, so the statistic on housing stress faced by this demographic is taken from Stonewall. For more information about trans people and housing inequality, I'd suggest diving into Shon Faye's book *The Transgender Issue: An Argument for Justice* (London: Allen Lane, 2021).

*the Affordable Homes Programme*: www.gov.uk/guidance/apply-for-affordable-housing-funding

*the government was finally asking builders*: Vicky Spratt, 'Leasehold homeowners are struggling with extortionate service charge costs, but change may be on the horizon', *i Paper*, 19 January 2022, inews.co.uk/opinion/columnists/leasehold-homeowners-service-charge-costs-extortionate-change-horizon-1410222

*in the twelve months to December 2021*: 'Index of Private Housing Rental Prices, UK: January 2022', Office for National Statistics (16 February 2022), www.ons.gov.uk/economy/inflationandpriceindices/bulletins/indexofprivatehousingrentalprices/january2022

*a contemporary form of the enclosure*: For more reading on this try Brett Christophers' *The New Enclosure: The Appropriation of Public Land in Neoliberal Britain* (London: Verso, 2019).

*A Land Value Tax could help*: If you are interested in the idea of a Land Value Tax, I'd recommend Josh Ryan-Collins' 2017 book *Rethinking the Economics of Land and Housing* (London: Zed Books), which he co-authored with Laurie Macfarlane and Toby Lloyd.


## Epilogue

*'Here you come upon …'*: George Orwell, *The Road to Wigan Pier* (1937; London: Penguin Modern Classics, 2001).

*The word in other languages*: Anatoly Liberman, 'Our habitat: house', OUP blog, 21 January 2015, blog.oup.com/2015/01/house-word-origin-etymology/

*the Women's Budget Group referenced Woolf*: Vicky Spratt, 'No Room Of Her Own: The Truth About The Gender Housing Gap', *Refinery29*, 18 July 2019, www.refinery29.com/en-gb/2019/07/237953/womens-budget-group-housing-report#slide-4

*'[a]n effective means …'*: bell hooks, 'Homeplace (A Site of Resistance)', in *Undoing Place?: A Geographical Reader*, edited by Linda McDowell (London: Routledge, 1997).

*'great misery' … '… and often callous'*: Robert Booth and Patrick Butler, 'UK austerity has inflicted "great misery" on citizens, UN says', *Guardian*, 16 November 2018, www.theguardian.com/society/2018/nov/16/uk-austerity-has-inflicted-great-misery-on-citizens-un-says

*Max Harris, Fellow of All Souls College*: www.torch.ox.ac.uk/event/the-politics-of-love

*'Love is what gives respect …'*: I am referring to Martha Nussbaum's book *Political Emotions: Why Love Matters for Justice* (Cambridge, MA: Belknap Press, 2013), but, of course, bell hooks wrote about this at length through the lenses of womanhood and race. She did this most notably in *All About Love: New Visions* (New York: William Morrow, 2000) but also in *The Will to Change: Men, Masculinity, and Love* (New York: Simon and Schuster, 2004).

# FURTHER READING

These are all books that have informed my writing and shaped my thinking about housing over the years. This list does not include every book that I consulted for *Tenants*, nor is it a complete reading list for the subject of housing – it also includes books which are not direct references in the text, but which I think might be interesting if you want to take your reading further. Including a book here does not necessarily mean I agree with its arguments but that it has challenged me on my own ideas. They are all worth taking a look at if you are interested in housing, wealth, class, compassion as a political resource and the origins of Britain's welfare state.

John Boughton, *Municipal Dreams: The Rise and Fall of Council Housing* (London: Verso, 2018)

Pierre Bourdieu, *On Television*, tr. Priscilla Parkhurst Ferguson (1996; New York: The New Press, 1998)

Rutger Bregman, *Utopia for Realists: And How We Can Get There* (London: Bloomsbury, 2017)

Emma Dabiri, *What White People Can Do Next: From Allyship to Coalition* (Penguin, 2021)

Matthew Desmond, *Evicted: Poverty and Profit in the American City* (London: Penguin, 2016)

Friedrich Engels, *The Condition of the Working Class in England* (1845; London: Penguin Classics, 2009)

Derek Fraser, *The Evolution of the British Welfare State* (London: Macmillan, 1973)

Ruth Glass, *London: Aspects of Change* (London: MacGibbon & Kee, 1964)

Lynsey Hanley, *Estates: An Intimate History* (London: Granta, 2007; revised edition, 2012)

bell hooks, 'Homeplace: A Site of Resistance' in *Undoing Place?: A Geographical Reader*, edited by Linda McDowell (London: Routledge, 1997)

bell hooks, *All About Love: New Visions (Love Song to the Nation #1)* (2000; New York: William Morrow, 2016)

Amelia Horgan, *Lost in Work: Escaping Capitalism* (London: Pluto Press, 2021)

Jane Jacobs, *The Death and Life of Great American Cities* (1961; London: Bodley Head, 2020)

Colin Jones and Alan Murie, *The Right to Buy: Analysis and Evaluation of a Housing Policy (Real Estate Issues Book 9)* (Oxford: Wiley-Blackwell, 2006)

Leslie Kern, *Feminist City: Claiming Space in a Man-made World* (London: Verso, 2020)

Loretta Lees, Tom Slater and Elvin Wyly, eds, *The Gentrification Reader* (London: Routledge, 2010)

Anna Minton, *Big Capital: Who is London For?* (London: Penguin, 2017)

Martha Nussbaum, *Political Emotions: Why Love Matters for Justice* (Cambridge, MA: Belknap Press, 2013)

Nathalie Olah, *Steal as Much as You Can: How to Win the Culture Wars in an Age of Austerity* (London: Repeater, 2019)

George Orwell, *The Road to Wigan Pier* (1937; London: Penguin Modern Classics, 2001)

Kate Pickett and Richard Wilkinson, *The Spirit Level: Why Equality is Better for Everyone* (2009; London: Penguin, 2010)

Martin Pugh, *We Danced All Night: A Social History of Britain Between the Wars* (London: Bodley Head, 2008)

Chris Renwick, *Bread for All: The Origins of the Welfare State* (London: Allen Lane, 2017)

Josh Ryan-Collins, *Why Can't You Afford a Home?* (London: Polity, 2018)

Michael J. Sandel, *The Tyranny of Merit: What's Become of the Common Good?* (London: Allen Lane, 2020)

James C. Scott, *Seeing Like a State: How Certain Schemes to Improve the Human Condition Have Failed* (1998; New Haven: Yale University Press, 2020)

E. P. Thompson, *The Making of the English Working Class* (1963; London: Penguin Modern Classics, 2013)

David Torrance, *Noel Skelton and the Property-owning Democracy* (London: Biteback, 2010)

Rebecca Tunstall, *The Fall and Rise of Social Housing*: *100 Years on 20 Estates* (Bristol: Policy Press, 2020)

David Willetts, *The Pinch: How the Baby Boomers Took Their Children's Future – And Why They Should Give It Back* (London: Atlantic Books, 2010)

Raymond Williams, *Culture and Politics: Class, Writing, Socialism* (London: Verso, 2022)

# ACKNOWLEDGEMENTS

Coming to the end of a story is a familiar sensation for a journalist. Writing this book was, unlike telling most stories, a marathon and not a sprint. Thank you, first and foremost, to the people who shared their lives with me. They are the lifeblood of this book. Their stories are not over, they are still unfolding. It has been a privilege to join them on their journeys.

Thank you to my agent Emma Paterson, who met me for coffee and shaped this book when I didn't even know it could be possible. I am grateful to be represented by her. She is not only an agent but an intuitive editor and reader. Without her guidance, this book wouldn't have made it into the world. Thank you also to Monica MacSwan at Aitken Alexander Associates.

Thank you to Louisa Dunnigan, who ran this marathon for more than four years and faced every challenge along the way with me. This book would not exist without the stamina of an editor so devoted to this subject. Many thanks too to Rebecca Gray.

Thank you to Kathryn Holliday. Big brain, eagle eyes, optimist and incisive editor. Thank you to Sally Holloway for her rigorous edits and for taking on this project, to Patrick Taylor for proofreading and to Chris Bell for indexing.

Thank you to the whole team at Profile, including Graeme Hall, Valentina Zanca, Samantha Johnson, Rosie Parnham and Flora Willis.

I was very fortunate to receive additional funding for this book from the Society of Authors via the K. Blundell Trust award in 2018. Without that money, this book would never have made it into the world. Thank you to them for all that they do to support writers.

*Tenants* has benefited from the time, energy, expertise and generosity from expert early readers, all of whom are the fiercest minds in their field.

Thank you first to Professor Becky Tunstall. She is the most rigorous and devoted reader and her own work, I have no doubt, will continue to challenge the status quo in housing.

Thank you to Ian Mulheirn for feeding in on what he calls the 'dry economics side' but I call the most vital piece of the puzzle in understanding the crisis in housing.

Thank you to Professor Loretta Lees for her support and encouragement.

Thank you to Alastair Harper, who knows more about what has really gone on in housing policy over the last few years than anyone!

Thank you to Bob Barr for his perspective and wisdom on this subject, so kindly given.

Journalists do not exist without their editors. The vital and collaborative relationship between the writer and editor is too often ignored. Our names might end up on book covers and bylines but we do no work alone.

Thank you to Heather Saul. Nothing that I have done at the *i Paper* since 2018 would have happened without Heather. I couldn't ask for a better editor, thank you for always being so thoughtful and thorough, for pushing me to do better and, above all, for believing in the importance of this subject when not all editors and publications did. She has taught me so much. Thank you also to Barbara Speed, an incisive editor, thinker and getter of things done.

Thank you, also, to everyone else over at the *i*. Olly, Amy, Rich, Albert and many more. You make it all happen.

Thank you also to Gillian Orr for always championing my work and encouraging me to think in new ways.

Thank you to Rebecca Holman who gave me a job that changed my life, the first I had as a print journalist after I left TV and radio. You always looked for solutions and not problems and backed the most rogue ideas like … campaigning to get letting fees banned in England and Wales which … we did!!! Thank you also to Lauren Holley-oake, *The Debrief*'s publisher, who also believed in the importance of taking risks and backed us when we did.

Thank you to Martin Rosenbaum and Giles Edwards, who took me in when I was starting out as a journalist at the BBC, teaching me how to be a journalist, to make Freedom of Information requests and tell complex stories.

Thank you to Helen Small, Lynda Mugglestone, Sally Bayley and Madeleine Forey for teaching me how to think critically and how to write. Thank you also to all of my teachers but, in particular, Stephanie Ironside, Deryn Kenton and Neil Strowger, who never questioned whether any of this was possible, even though I certainly did.

I learn so much from the experts – economists, academics, grassroots homelessness workers – I have access to as a journalist. I see my job as interrogating their ideas and bringing their work to a wider audience. Thank you in particular to Giles Peaker, Neal Hudson, Darren Baxter, Josh Ryan-Collins, Jonny Webb, Amy Clair, Kim McKee, Jenny Preece, everyone at ACORN, the team at Shelter, the team at Crisis, Amina at the London Renters' Union, Caitlin, Alicia, Dan, Tilly and previously Georgie at Generation Rent, Henry in Bristol and Jane Carmichael at Magpie. Thank you to Anna Minton for advice along the way.

Thank you to the people in my own life who have held my hand through times of housing stress, particularly in recent years, and then continued to hold it on the other side. Mum, Kelly, Dad, Nanny Doreen, Grandad John, Nanny Edith, Grandad George, Chris M, Calum, Kristina, Jess, Rebekah and Manny, Alice Q, Marion, Elsa, Charlotte M, Kim W, Ros, Sarah B, Fi, Elizabeth FB, Sirin, Zing, Kate L, Debs, Lucia, Otegha, Megha, Janey, Lucia, Nathalie O, Rose P, Emma H. You are lifeboats. Emily B, I couldn't have done this without your support. Sophie W, you're a true mate and an amazing reader. Kole, thank you for the pep talks. And, finally, eternal gratitude to Elizabeth Wilson – even Oprah needs a life coach.

# INDEX

**A**

Abbey, Barry and Mavis 240, 243

Abercrombie, Patrick 128

'accumulative dispossession' 93, 102–8

ACORN (community union) 4–6, 16, 102, 150, 152–3, 260

Ad Hoc (guardian company) 184, 186

Adam Smith Institute 140

Addison Act (1919) 28

Addison, Christopher 28, 210

affordable homes 21, 67, 70–71, 109, 166–7, 184–5, 209–10, 215, 226, 231, 235, 251–2, 265

Affordable Homes Programme 246

Age UK (charity) 76

ageing population 75–7

    mental health and 76–7

Airey, Edwin 238

Airey houses 238–9, 241

All-Party Parliamentary Group for Housing and Care for Older People 76

Alston, Philip 261–2

aluminium composite material (ACM) cladding 240

Amsterdam, Netherlands 232

Anthony Gold Solicitors 132, 193

Antonucci, Lorenza 123

Argentina 224

Arnett, Jeffrey Jensen 123

Artisans' and Labourers' Dwellings Improvement Act (1875) 26

Association of Residential Letting Agents (ARLA) 15

Assured Shorthold Tenancy (AST) 43, 234, 240, 265

Assured Tenancies 234

Attlee, Clement 28–9

Avon and Somerset Police 114–15

**B**

Bachelard, Gaston 21, 38

Ballycastle, Co. Antrim 95

banking regulations 14

Banksy 108, 152

Barbour, Mary 151

Barr, Robert 158

Bates, Justin 132

Bath, Somerset 97

BBC (British Broadcasting Corporation) 69, 206

Beadle, Ben 129

'beds in sheds' 178

Belgium 124

bell hooks 259, 263

'belonging', *see* location/place

benefit cap 82, 92–3

*Benefits Street* (TV documentary series)
   49
Berlin, Germany 213
Berry, Siân 211–13
Best, Richard 76
Bevan, Aneurin 'Nye' 28–9, 104, 251
Beveridge, William 19, 29, 210, 264
Beveridge Report (1942) 29
Bexhill, East Sussex 75
'Big Bang' (financial markets) 14–15
biomarkers, 155–6
Blackpool 101
Blackstone (corporate landlord) 239–40
Blair, Tony xiii, 32, 105, 214, 221
Bolsover, Derbyshire 34
Boughton, John 27
Bourdieu, Pierre 69
Bourne, Nick, Baron Bourne of
   Aberystwyth 197–8
Bradford, West Yorkshire 161–4, 168–70,
   175–6, 178
Bradford Council 186
Brake, Tom 212
Brazil 224
Brexit xiii, 165–6, 175, 202, 260
Brighton, Sussex 1–7, 97, 163
Brighton and Hove, 34
Bristol 94–7, 102–4, 107–9, 147, 186
*Bristol Cable* 103
Bristol Community Land Trust 102
British Future (think tank) 167
British Social Attitudes Survey (BSAS)
   xiv, 213, 229
Brixton, London 100
Brokenshire, James 202, 220
Bromley, south London 81–2, 86
Brown, Gordon 32, 214, 221
Bryant, John 44
Buck, Karen 130–32, 159, 210, 212
Buckinghamshire County Council 186

'build-to-rent' sector 239
Building Research Establishment Trust
   135, 158

## C

C-reactive protein (CRP) 155–6
Callaghan, James 33
Cambridge House centre 165, 175
Camelot Guardian Management Ltd
   184, 186, 188–93, 195
Cameron, David ix, 14, 32, 82, 203, 213,
   260
Canterbury, Kent 34
capital gains tax (CGT) 249
*Capital in the Twenty-First Century*
   (Piketty) 45
capitalism 43, 45–7, 77, 260
   rentier capitalism 45
Care Quality Commission (CQC) 181, 188
*Cathy Come Home* (TV drama) 55
Central Heating Evaluation programme
   (Scotland) 135
Centre For Towns think tank 75
Centre Point, London 22
Ceredigion, Wales 101
Chadwick, Duncan and Edwin 25
Chartered Institute of Building 168
Chartered Institute of Environmental
   Health (CIEH) 148–9
Chartered Institute of Housing (CIH)
   34, 148–9
Chartist movement 25–7
Chatham, Kent 79–80
Cheshire West and Chester, 34
children 66, 113–14
   childcare 138
   health 24, 85, 90, 135, 148, 159
   homelessness 8, 81
   housing displacement and 59, 85, 90,
      232, 251

poverty 37, 50, 154, 162, 262

Churchill, Winston 250

*City A.M.* 184

cladding crisis 10, 216, 225, 240, 247

Clair, Amy 155–7

class, *see* social class

Clegg, Nick 82

climate change 134, 136

Cloward, Richard 152

Coggeshall, Essex 61–3, 65

Colchester, Essex 63, 181, 187, 190–92, 195

Colchester Renters campaign group 65, 75, 153

Cold Weather Fund 228

Colombia 224

Combined Homelessness and Information Network (CHAIN) 163

*Communist Manifesto, The* (Marx & Engels) 26

Communist Party 151

community land trusts 102

Comte, Auguste 263

*Condition of the Working Class in England, The* (Engels) 26

Conservative Party ix, 32–3, 46, 72, 82, 132, 160, 166, 203, 210–16, 227, 233–5, 247–8, 251

*Constitution of Liberty* (Hayek), 46

Copenhagen, Denmark 232

Corby, Northamptonshire 75

Corbyn, Jeremy ix, 205, 261

Cornwall 107–8, 185

coronavirus pandemic 3, 6, 27, 39, 75–6, 98, 125, 199, 226–9, 260–61
   eviction ban 32
   homelessness and 163, 180, 227–9
   impact on housing 36–7, 51, 96, 147–8
   overcrowding and 170–72, 180
   poor housing and 125, 155–7

private renters and 227–8

corporate landlords 239–43

Costa Rica 224

council housing, *see* social housing

Covid-19, *see* coronavirus

Cowan, Dave 131

Craw, Dan Wilson 70

Crisis (homeless charity) 221, 228, 235, 247, 260

Croydon 21–4, 30, 37–8

Cutler, Horace 151

**D**

*Daily Mail* 166, 167

*Daily Telegraph* 43

David Plaister Ltd 147

Dawson, Gloria 185

Dawson's Heights estate, East Dulwich 38

Decent Homes Standard 125, 133, 248

Delingpole, James 68

Denmark 124, 232

Denton, Greater Manchester 75

Department for Levelling Up, Housing and Communities (DLUHC) 245–7

Department for Work and Pensions (DWP) 51

Department of Social Security (DSS) 51

Derry, Northern Ireland 101

Desmond, Matthew 84–5

Dickens, Charles 92–3

disability 157, 159, 246

Discus Housing First, Amsterdam 232

Dismaland (Banksy) 153

DnR Vinyl, 23

domestic abuse 52, 157

Dorling, Danny 214

Douglas-Home, Alec 33

Duffy, Bobby 73

Duncan, William 25

**E**

East Ayrshire, Scotland 101
*Economic Journal* 167
Eden, Anthony 33, 213
education 69, 123, 255
Education Act (1870) 26
Einstein, Albert 252
Elephant and Castle, London 100, 105, 193–4
Elsworth, Linda 242–3, 257
emergency B&Bs 57, 232
'emerging adulthood', 123
energy efficient homes 134–6
energy price caps 207
Engels, Friedrich 26, 70
English Housing Survey 46, 169, 172
　2017/18: 130
　2018/19: 116
　2019/20: 130
　2020/21: 133
Equality Act (2010) 51
*Escape to the Country* (TV series) 95
estate agents 11–12, 41
*Evening Standard* 41
'Everyone In' scheme 227–8, 235
*Evicted* (Desmond) 84
evictions 5–6, 36, 77, 83–4
　children and 59, 85, 90
　guardianship and 182
　illegal evictions 174–5
　legal aid 136–7
　mental health and 53–5, 57, 65, 83–5
　physical health and 85
　Section 8 271
　Section 21 2–4, 32, 42–3, 55–6, 64, 136–7, 175, 202, 209, 228, 234
'Eviction's Fallout: Housing, Hardship, and Health' (Desmond) 84
'excluded occupiers' 114

**F**

Farage, Nigel 166
Ferreri, Mara 185
Field, Hazell 243, 257–8
*Financial Times* 41
Finland 222–3, 230–31, 233
Flat Justice 191
free market forces 12–13, 206–8
Friedman, Sam xiv
'friendlords' 114–15
Frome, Somerset 94
Fullilove, Mindy 83–4, 90, 98, 109

**G**

Gabor, Daniela 239
Gallik, Tomas 178–9
Gandhi, Mohandas 263
garden cities 128–9, 183
Garden City Association 128
gardening 120
gender housing gap 52
Generation Rent (lobby group) xvi–xvii, 70, 74–5, 134, 247
Generation Rent (term) 65–71, 75–6, 111
generations 66–76
　Baby Boomers 67, 71
　Generation X 67
　Generation Z 73
　intergenerational inequality 66–74
　millennials 66–8, 73, 76
*Generations: Does When You're Born Shape Who You Are?* (Duffy) 73
gentrification 94–5, 98–109, 193–5, 241
Germany 116, 124, 213, 215, 225
Gillin, Nicola 181, 187–92, 257
Glasgow, Scotland 150
Glass, Ruth 98–9, 101–2, 105–7
Global Guardians (property management company) 196–7

Gloucestershire County Council
186

Gousy, Hannah 228

Gove, Michael 245–8, 250–51

Greater London Council (GLC) 151

Green Homes Grant 134–6

Green Party 160, 212, 230

Greenwood, Tony 151

Grender, Olly, Baroness Grender 197,
212

Grenfell Tower fire 10, 132, 224

*Guardian* 50, 68, 136, 140

Guardian Property Protection 186

guardianship 182–92, 195–8, 270
local authorities and 186

Guinness Partnership 24

# H

Haldane, John Scott 36

Hampshire County Council 186

Harris, Max 262

Harvey, David 93

Hawley, Martyn 178–9

Hayek, Friedrich 46

Healey, John 214–16, 233, 250

health, *see* public health

Health Foundation 125

Heart of Weston steering group 154

Help to Buy scheme 14, 32, 117–18, 203,
244, 266

Hestia charity 179

Hewitt, Daniel 250

HMOs, *see* house sharing

Hollinrake, Kevin 203–11, 214

'Home of Her Own: Housing and
Women, A' (report) 259

homelessness 8, 9, 47, 162–3, 201–2,
220–23, 230–33
coronavirus pandemic and 163, 180,
227–8

'hidden homelessness' xv, 59, 162, 202,
221
ideology and 232
'intentionally homeless' 48–9, 56–7
LGBTQ+ and 114
politics and 220–33
race and 52, 114
rough sleeping xv, 52, 162–3, 202–3,
221
statutory homelessness 52, 56–7, 268
street homelessness, *see* rough sleeping
*see also* Housing First

HomeLet (insurance company) 66

homeownership 9–10, 14–15, 34, 111,
113, 116, 118–19, 124, 213
politics and 203, 205, 213–14
*see also* house prices; mortgages; Right
to Buy scheme

'Homeplace (A Site of Resistance)'
(hooks) 259

Homes (Fitness for Human Habitation)
Act (2019) 130–33, 136, 159, 210, 266

Hope for Justice 178–9

Hope Housing 162, 178, 260

Hope Not Hate 167

house prices 8, 13–15, 46, 67–8, 94–8,
117, 166, 202, 250
gentrification and 94–5, 98–109
immigration and 167
Stamp Duty 14, 98, 166
unaffordable homes 11–12, 36–9, 104,
209–10, 251
*see also* mortgages

house sharing 2, 110–12, 121–4, 136,
149
'forced sharing' 121
HMOs (house in multiple occupation)
2, 149, 155, 164–5, 168–70, 172–8,
195–6
'shadow rented sector' 164–5, 168–75

'voluntary sharing' 121

Housing Acts 267
   1949: 29, 104
   1980: 31
   1988: 16, 31–2, 42–4, 119, 240
   2004: 133, 195
   *see also* evictions: Section 21

Housing and Planning Act (2016) 103,
   177

Housing Benefit 3, 16, 19, 34–6, 50–51,
   117, 236
   benefit cap 82
   cuts 35–6, 117
   discrimination 51, 142

housing charities 259–60

'housing crisis' 12–13, 36–7, 50, 88–9,
   105, 143, 150, 242
   climate change and 134–5
   politics and 203–37, 248–9, 260–61
   public health and 125, 135–6,
     157–8
   reforms 248–52, 260–62

Housing First 217, 218, 221–3, 225,
   228–37, 244–5, 248, 262, 266

Housing First Europe 232

'Housing for the Many' (green paper)
   214–15

Housing Health and Safety Rating
   System (HHSRS) 133

housing market 12–13, 15, 36, 39, 45–6,
   73, 99, 147, 240, 252
   gentrification and 94–5, 98–109, 241
   immigration and 167
   lack of demand, 101
   new homes 28, 32, 100, 108–9, 117–18
   politics and 214
   racism and 52, 157
   *see also* Generation Rent;
     guardianship; house prices; Housing
     First

housing policy 9, 45, 93, 233, 247–52,
   261–2

housing standards, 129–36, 139–44,
   149–50, 152
   damp and mould 131–2, 139–40, 148,
     150
   energy efficient homes 134–6, 242
   hazards 133, 146–7, 149–50
   health and 131–6, 139, 148, 154–9
   overcrowding 170–72
   slum housing 26, 28, 105, 141, 146–9,
     152–4, 170

housing stress xv–xvi, 10, 52, 67, 73, 155,
   253–4, 259

Housing, Town Planning &c. Act, *see*
   Addison Act

Howard, Ebenezer 128

Howell, Anthony 1–7, 257

Hudson, Neal 101

Hughes, Amanda 155

Human City Institute 52

Human Rights Act (1988) 225

Hungary 172–3

Hungerford, Berkshire 218–19

Hunters estate agents 203–4

I

immigration 162–9, 172–80, 230
   HMOs and 164–5, 168–70, 172–8
   'hostile environment' 164, 177
   housing market and 167–8
   migrant workers 52, 102, 162–9, 176,
     180
   'shadow rented sector' and 164–5, 168,
     172–7

Immigration Act (2014) 174

Immigration and Asylum Act (1999) 163

*In Defense of Housing* (Madden &
   Marcuse) 113

income 73

*Independent* 180
India 224
Industrial Revolution 24–5
*Inside Housing* magazine 34, 44
Institute for Fiscal Studies 35, 71
Institute for Public Policy Research
    (IPPR) 109, 249
Intergenerational Foundation 71
intergenerational inequality, *see*
    generations
'intermediate housing' 184
International Covenant on Economic,
    Social and Cultural Rights (IcESR)
    225
investment funds 239–42
*i Paper* (newspaper) xvi
Ipsos MORI 106
Ireland, *see* Northern Ireland; Republic
    of Ireland
Italy 124

**J**

Jackson-Stops estate agency 102
Jenrick, Robert 36, 227
Johnson, Boris ix, 36, 72, 117, 134, 209,
    213–14, 227, 245
Johnson, Paul 35
Joint Council for the Welfare of
    Immigrants (JCWI) 174
Jones, Carwyn 235
Jones, Colin 34
Joseph Rowntree Foundation (JRF) 37,
    50
journalism 69–70, 157

**K**

Kaakinen, Juha 222, 230–33, 236
key workers 107–9, 123, 185–6, 267
Khan, Sadiq 184, 209, 211–13
Kimbro, Rachel Tolbert, 84–5

King Jr, Martin Luther 263
Kinleigh Folkard & Hayward 80
Kohl, Sebastian 239
Kondo, Marie 120

**L**

Labour Party ix, 29, 32–3, 113, 151, 160,
    211, 213–16, 233
    New Labour, 32, 106, 214
Labouring Classes Dwelling Houses Act
    (1866) 26
Laing, R. D. 54
Lamb, Norman 202
Lammy, David 202
Lancaster 110–12, 116–17, 123
'land banking' 249–50
Land Value Tax 250–51, 267
Landbay (mortgage lender) 46
Landlord and Tenant Act (1985) 131
landlord licensing 148–50
Landmark Chambers 132
landowners 225, 249–50
Latin Elephant (charity) 194
Law of Property Act (1925) 175
Law Society 137
leasehold reform 247
Leeds 97, 242–3
Leeds Federation of Municipal Tenants
    Associations 151
Lees, Loretta 93, 98, 107, 111
Leese, Richard 100
Legal & General 239
Legal Action Group (LAG) 137
legal aid 136–7
Legal Aid Agency (LAA) 137
Legal Aid, Sentencing and Punishment
    of Offenders Act (2012) 183
Lendlease (real estate investment group)
    100
Letchworth, Hertfordshire 128

letting agents 11–12, 177
letting fees xvi, 12, 204, 212
'levelling up' 245, 247–8
LGBTQ+ 246, 263
    discrimination 114
Liberal Democrat Party, 160, 212
Lincoln, Abraham 263
Live-In Guardians (property
    management company) 191
Liverpool 101
Lloyd George, David 21, 151, 210, 236
Lloyd, Toby 208–9
Loach, Ken 55
local authorities 26, 28, 31, 109, 133, 177,
    186, 203, 248
Local Government Association (LGA)
    8, 228
Local Housing Allowance (LHA) 35–7,
    81, 117, 227, 236
Localism Act (2011) 81
*Location, Location, Location* (TV series)
    95
location/place 85–6, 90–92
London, 34, 37, 46, 96–7, 101–2, 123, 131
    gentrification and 98–102, 107–8,
        193–5
    Great Dock Strike (1889) 151
    guardianship 183, 185
    London Housing Panel 93
    'London Living Rent', 210
    rent control 212–13, 230
    rent strikes 151
*London: Aspects of Change* (Glass) 99
love, politics of 262–3
'low-price low-income market' 101
Lowe Guardians (property management
    company) 184
Lowe, Tim 184
Luxembourg 124

**M**
Macintosh, Kate 38
Macmillan, Harold 33
Madden, David 113, 119
Magpie Project 81
Major, John 221
Manchester 100, 107, 128, 139, 240
Marcuse, Peter 113, 119
Marx, Karl 26, 112
May, Theresa ix, 32, 137, 140, 164, 166,
    168, 177, 203, 208–9, 245, 248
McKee, Kim 59, 119, 121, 155
McKibbin, Philip 262
mental health 53–5, 57, 65, 76–7
Merkel, Angela 213
Milanović, Branko 73
Mill, John Stuart 250, 263
Milton Keynes 16, 34
Ministry of Housing, Communities and
    Local Government (MHCLG) 226–7,
    269
mortgages 2–3, 14–15, 23, 33, 44, 68, 214,
    216, 227, 266
    'buy-to-let' 15, 17, 44, 266
    interest rates 14–15, 51, 68
    mortgage interest relief 44
Mulheirn, Ian 236
Munday, Becky 41
Murie, Alan 34

**N**
NatCen Social Research 139
National Audit Office (NAO) 163
National Coal Board (NCB) 239
National Conversation on Immigration
    167
National Housing Federation 44
National Insurance 29, 249
National Landlords Association
    129

National Referral Mechanism (NRM) 179

National Residential Landlords Association (NRLA) 66, 129

Nationwide house price index 46

Ncube, Timon 163

Neate, Polly 75

Netherlands 124, 224, 232

*Newsnight* (TV programme) 49–50, 69

Next Steps Accommodation Programme 228

NHS (National Health Service) 107, 135, 158–9, 184–5
   Clinical Commissioning Groups (CCGs) 158

*Nightmare Neighbour Next Door, The* (TV documentary series) 49

No Recourse to Public Funds (NRPF) 162–3, 166

'non-decent' homes 130

Norman Shaw South Building, Westminster 201, 204

North Somerset 147, 159

Northern Ireland xv, 95, 235

Nottingham 97

Nuneaton and Bedworth, 34

Nussbaum, Martha 263

**O**

*Observer* 57

Office for National Statistics (ONS) 14, 16

OfGem 207

Old Rectory, Colchester 181–2, 187–92

'ontological security' 54

Orbán, Viktor 173

Organisation for Economic Co-operation and Development (OECD) 138

Orwell, George 39, 208, 253

Osborne, George 14, 32, 35–6, 133, 203

Oulton, West Yorkshire 238–43, 250, 252, 257–8

out-of-borough housing placements 80–81

Overton Window 229

Overton, Joseph 229

**P**

Palmer, Henry 94–8, 102–8

Paragon (mortgage lender) 67

Paris, France 213

Pathfinder programme (Scotland) 223

Peaker, Giles 132, 136, 193–6, 228

Peckham, London 40–42, 48, 82–3, 86, 95

Peluffo Soneyra, Santiago 194

Pemberstone Group 239–43

Pendle, Lancashire 101

People's Charter (1838) 25

pets 64, 113

phenomenology 91

'phoenixing' 192

Pickett, Kate xiv

Piketty, Thomas 44–5

Pincher, Christopher 234

Piven, Frances Fox 152

*Poetics of Space, The* (Bachelard) 21

Policy in Practice (software company) 82

*Poor People's Movements: Why They Succeed, How They Fail* (Piven & Cloward) 152

Portugal 224

poverty 10, 37, 49–51, 67, 84, 135, 154, 236, 258–9, 261–2
   child poverty 37, 50, 154, 162, 262
   poverty premium 50
   'relative poverty', 50

Powell, Lucy 216

Preece, Jenny 90–91

Pregnant Then Screwed campaign group 138

Prescott, John 106
PricewaterhouseCoopers 46
Pritchard, Rebecca 221
private developers 108–9, 117, 184, 245
private landlords 10–12, 15–17, 33–6,
    43–6, 115, 129, 206
    bad practice 129–30
    'buy-to-let' 15, 17, 44–6, 129, 149
    complaints 64–5, 136
    energy efficient homes 134–6
    free market and 206–8
    'friendlords' 114–15
    homophobia 114
    Housing Benefit discrimination 51
    intimidation 65, 137–8
    landlord licensing 115, 148–50, 160
    pets 64, 113
    racial discrimination 114–15
    repairs and maintenance 130–33,
        139–42
    rogue landlords 140–42, 146–8, 164,
        167–9, 173–7, 212, 234
    'shadow rented sector' 164–5, 168–9,
        172–5
    *see also* guardianship; Housing Act
        (1988); housing standards
Property Guardian Providers
    Association (PGPA) 186
*Property Ladder* (TV series) 95
property values, *see* house prices
Protect Programme 228
protected tenancies 142
'psychosocial sense' 113
public health 24–5, 125, 135, 154–9, 171
    mental health 53–5, 57, 65, 83–5, 139,
        155, 157
    physical health 85, 131–2, 148, 159
    *see also* coronavirus pandemic
Public Health Act (1875) 26
Public Health England 170

Pussy Riot (musical group) 153
Pye, Janet 222

**R**
race and ethnicity xiv–xv, 114, 246, 259
    discrimination 114–15, 157
    homelessness and 8, 52, 90
    *see also* immigration
Rachman, Peter 141, 146
'Rachmanism' 141
Rashford, Marcus 230
Readman, Cindy and John 240–41, 244,
    257
Redcar, North Yorkshire 101
Rees, Marvin 108
Reeve, Kesia 48, 57
Reeve-Lewis, Ben 169, 175
Reform Act
    1832: 25, 26
    1867: 26
    1884: 26
Remes, Gyula 201–2
rent 7, 19, 34–5, 37
    cost to household income ratio 7, 76
    Local Housing Allowance (LHA)
        35–7
    low-income renters, 13, 35, 71, 101–3,
        106, 118–23
    rent control 43, 124, 142, 151, 208–9,
        211–13, 230, 224, 235
    rent rises 98
    rent strikes 151–2
    rent trap 116–19
    unaffordable private rents 15–17
Rent Act (1957) 151
Rent Pressure Zones (Scotland) 124, 213,
    235, 268
Rent Repayment Order (RRO) 136,
    190–91
Rent Smart 149

Renters' Reform Bill 203, 212, 233–4, 247

rentier capitalism 45

Republic of Ireland xv, 124

Residential Landlords Association 66, 129

Resolution Foundation 14, 67

Rhodes, David 216

Ricardo, David 250

Rice, Alan 146, 150, 152–4, 159–60, 177, 260

Ridley, Nicholas 43

Rigby, Mandy 222

Right to Buy scheme, *see* social housing

'right to housing' 224–5

Right to Rent scheme 174

*Road to Wigan Pier, The* (Orwell) 39, 253

Rogers, Will 2

rogue landlords, *see* private landlords

*Room of One's Own, A* (Woolf) 259

'root shock' 83–4

Rousseau, Jean-Jacques 11, 263

Rowntree, Joseph 157

Roy, Arundhati 39

Royal Institute of British Architects (RIBA) 29, 75

Rugg, Julie 165, 216

**S**

Sà, Filipa 167

Safer Renting 64, 169, 175

*Safer Renting: Journeys in the Shadow Private Rented Sector* (Reeve-Lewis) 169

Saltney, Wales 149

Sassen, Saskia 77, 129

Scientific Advisory Group for Emergencies (SAGE) 170–71

Scotland xv, 124, 135, 148–9, 213, 222–3, 225, 235

Section 21 evictions, *see* evictions

secure tenancies 112

Seifert, Richard 22

Seychelles 224

'shadow rented sector' 164–5, 168–75

Shared Ownership scheme 117–18, 268

Sheen, Kelly 79–92

Sheen, Morgan 80, 86–90

Shelter (homeless charity) xvi, 7, 32, 51, 75, 137, 138, 139, 159, 208, 228, 234–5, 244, 247, 260, 264

Shnapp, Sophie 134–5

Shrubsole, Guy 245

single mothers 51–2

Skelton, Noel 33

slavery 26, 178–80, 263

Slavery Abolition Act (1833) 26

slum housing 26, 28, 105, 141, 146–9, 152–4, 170

Smith, Adam 10, 250

Smith, David 66

Smith, Paul 102–5

social care cap (2021) 72

social class xiv, 26, 105–7, 254–5

social inequality xiv, 68–73

middle-classes xiv, 11, 33, 70, 36, 72–3, 105–6, 245–6, 262

social mobility 106–7, 211

class divide 95–6

working classes xiv, 25–6, 106

social housing 9, 13, 16, 21–2, 24–5, 28–38, 64, 88, 96, 123, 202, 211, 235–6, 250–51, 268

housing standards, 133

in the 1950s 24

'priority need' 64

public health and 24

Right to Buy scheme 13, 16, 31–5, 103–4, 143, 213, 235, 247, 268

state-subsidised housing 28–31
social media 151
social status 112
*Somerset Live* 147
South Africa 224
South East Guardians (property
   management company) 186
South Norwood Hill, Croydon 22–4,
   30–31, 37–8
Southwark Council 193
Sovereign housing association 219, 222
Spanish Flu pandemic (1918–19) 27–8
*Spectator* 68
Spencer, Roz 175
*Spirit Level, The* (Pickett & Wilkinson) xiv
squatters 183
Stamp Duty 14, 98, 214
Starmer, Keir ix, 214, 249
Stepney Tenants' Defence League 151
Stevenage, Hertfordshire 34
Stokes Croft, Bristol 108
Stokes Croft Land Trust (SCLT) 108
Strang, Jim 34
Stratton, Allegra 49–50
Sugar Hill Close and Wordsworth Drive
   housing estate, Oulton 238–43,
   257–8
Sunak, Rishi 226
*Sunday Times*
   Best Places to Live in the UK guide
      94–5
   Rich List 142
Sutton Trust, 69
Switzerland 124
Syrop, Helen 162–5, 168–70, 172–3,
   175–80, 260

**T**
Tagore, Rabindranath 263
taxation 249–50

temporary accommodation 57–8, 81,
   89–90, 159, 231–2, 258
Tenant Fees Act (2019) xvi, 11–12,
   203–4, 212, 235
tenants 7–10, 118–24
   deposits xvi, 64, 153, 182, 234
   letting fees xvi, 12, 204, 212
   protected tenancies 142
   rent strikes 151–2
   repairs and maintenance 130–33,
      139–42
   rights 112–13, 119, 130, 140, 182
   stress and 155–8
   tenancy contracts 124
   tenants' unions 152–3
   *see also* evictions; guardianship; private
      landlords; public health
Thanet, Kent 101
Thatcher, Margaret ix, 13, 31–3, 42–3,
   45–6, 206,213–14
Thorpe, Shanene 50
Trade Union Congress (TUC) 106
trade unions 26
trafficking 178–80
'trickle-down housing' 244
Tropicana, Weston-super-Mare 153
Tsemberis, Sam 221–2
Tuan, Yi-Fu 120
tuberculosis (TB) 24
Tudor Walters Report (1918) 28
Tunstall, Rebecca 171–2
Turning Point service, Glasgow 232
Twain, Mark 2
Two Saints (homelessness support group)
   222

**U**
UKIP (UK Independence Party) 166
United Nations (UN) 9
United Tenants' Association 151

Universal Basic Income 261, 272
Universal Credit 36, 51
University of Granada, Spain 54
urban regeneration 105, 111
*Urban Studies* journal 93
Uruguay 224

**V**

Valuations Office Agency (VOA) 183
Vasudevan, Alexander 185
'Vent Your Rent' campaign 65, 74
*Voices of Bristol: Gentrification and Us* (Palmer) 95

**W**

Wales xv, 135, 149, 235
Walters, John Tudor 28, 128
Warm Homes Nest scheme (Wales) 135
Watchtower Security Solutions Ltd 192
wealth xiv, 71, 123
*Wealth of Nations, The* (Smith), 10
welfare benefits 230
welfare state 27–9, 31, 77
Westminster, London 201–2
Weston Housing Action 260

Weston-super-Mare, North Somerset, 145–50, 152–4
*Who Owns England?* (Shrubsole) 245–6
Wilkinson, Richard xiv
Willetts, David 70
Williams, Jane 81
Wilson, Fergus 141–2
Wilson, Judith 142
women 8, 51–2, 259, 263
    domestic abuse 52, 157
    gender housing gap 52
    single mothers 51–2, 246
Women's Budget Group 8, 52, 259
Woolf, Virginia 259
World War I (1914–18) 27, 151
World War II (1939–45) 238–9
Wythenshawe, Manchester 127–9

**Y**

Y-Foundation (Finland) 222, 230
*York Press* 211

**Z**

Zaman, Nadia 81
Zoopla 97, 98